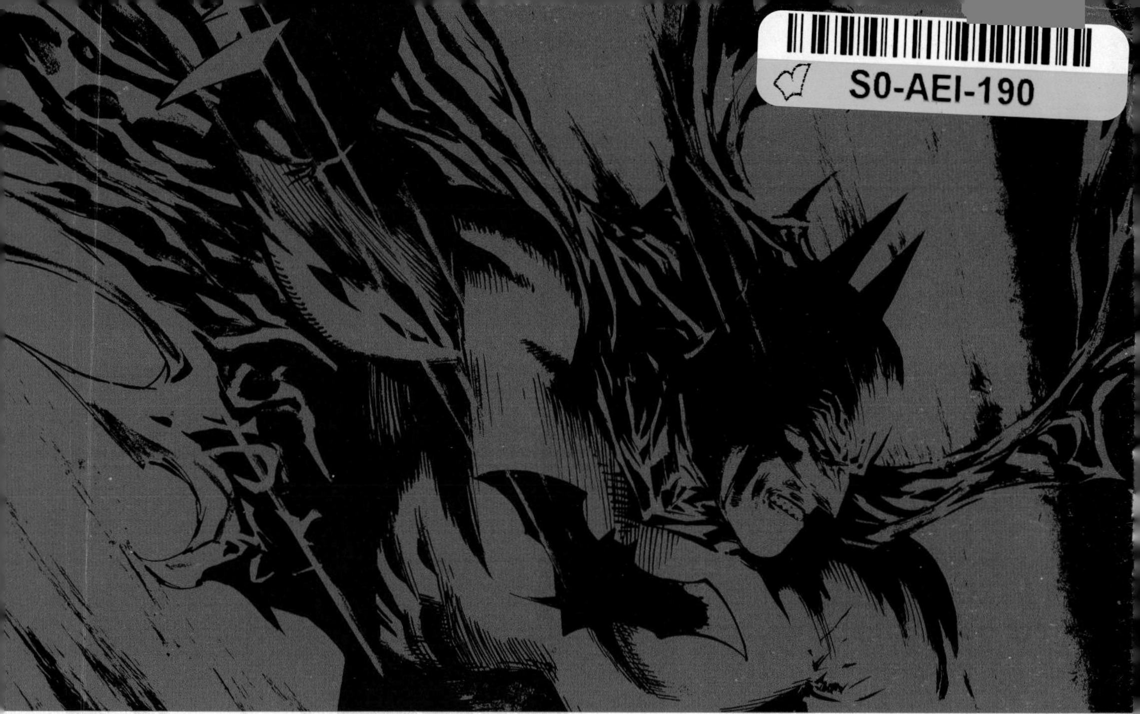

BATMAN
THE BLACK GLOVE

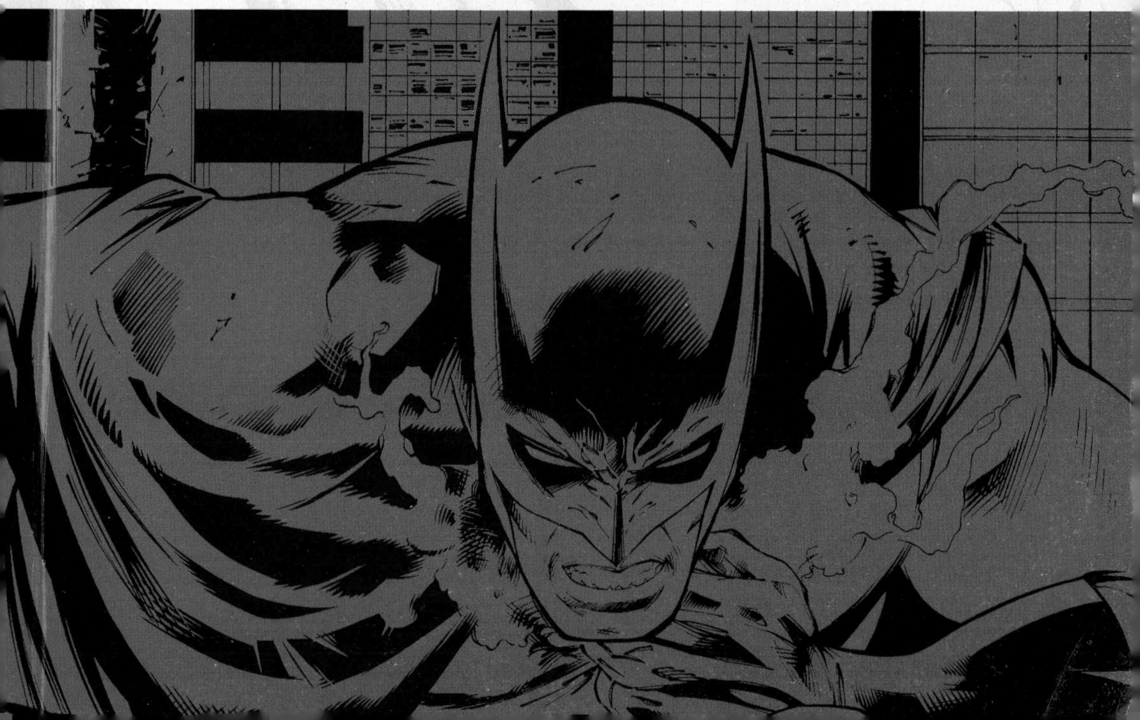

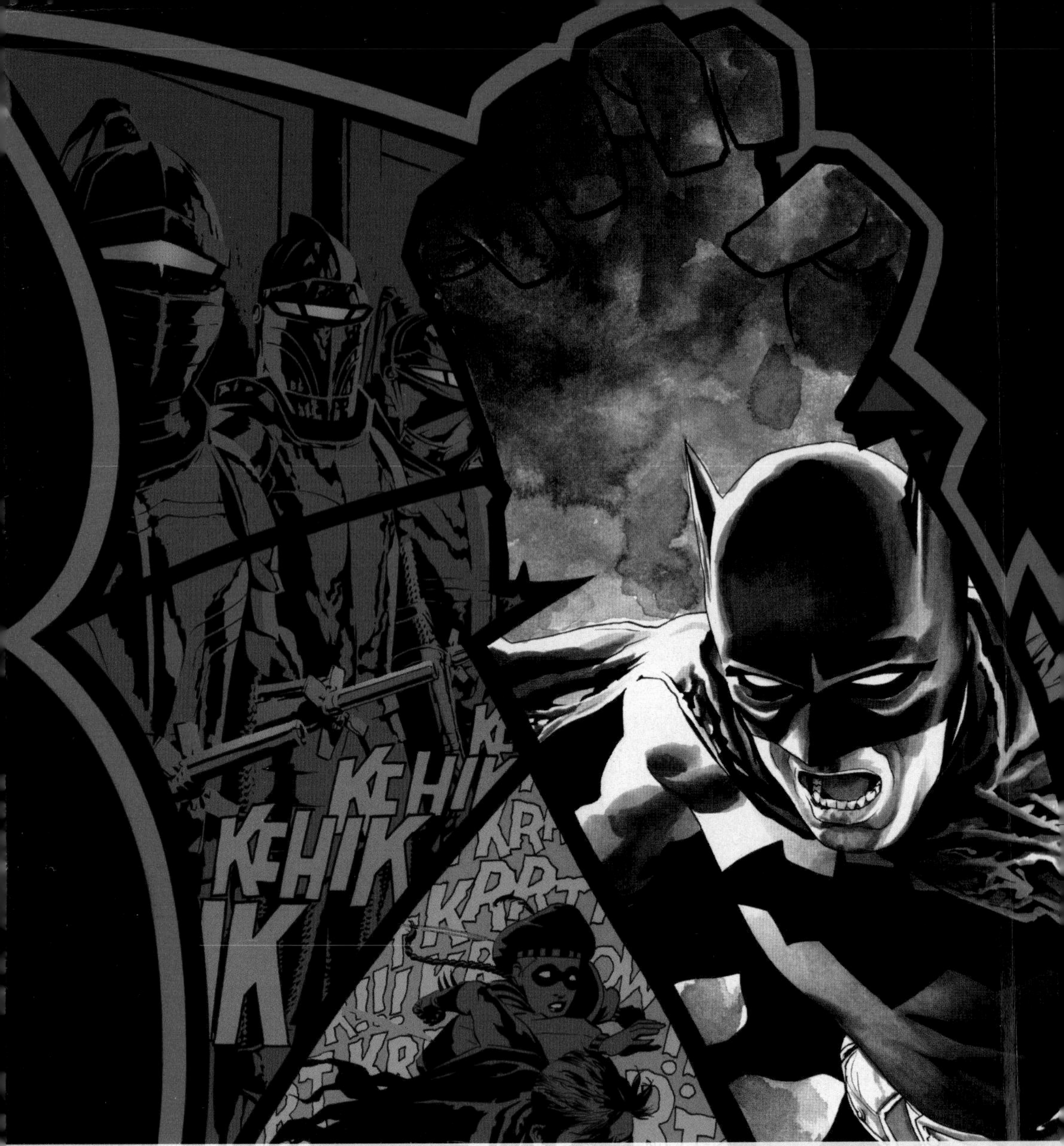

Dan DiDio Senior VP-Executive Editor **Mike Marts** Editor-original series **Jeanine Schaefer** Associate editor-original series **Bob Harras** Editor-collected edition
Robbin Brosterman Senior Art Director **Paul Levitz** President & Publisher **Georg Brewer** VP-Design & DC Direct Creative
Richard Bruning Senior VP-Creative Director **Patrick Caldon** Executive VP-Finance & Operations **Chris Caramalis** VP-Finance **John Cunningham** VP-Marketing
Terri Cunningham VP-Managing Editor **Alison Gill** VP-Manufacturing **David Hyde** VP-Publicity **Hank Kanalz** VP-General Manager, WildStorm **Jim Lee** Editorial Director-WildStorm
Paula Lowitt Senior VP-Business & Legal Affairs **MaryEllen McLaughlin** VP-Advertising & Custom Publishing **John Nee** Senior VP-Business Development
Gregory Noveck Senior VP-Creative Affairs **Sue Pohja** VP-Book Trade Sales **Steve Rotterdam** Senior VP-Sales & Marketing **Cheryl Rubin** Senior VP-Brand Management
Jeff Trojan VP-Business Development, DC Direct **Bob Wayne** VP-Sales

Cover by J.H. Williams III Publication design by Amelia Grohman

BATMAN: THE BLACK GLOVE

DC Comics, 1700 Broadway, New York, NY 10019 | A Warner Bros. Entertainment Company
Printed in USA. First Printing. HC ISBN: 978-1-4012-1909-3 SC ISBN: 978-1-4012-1945-1

BATMAN
THE BLACK GLOVE

GRANT MORRISON WRITER

J.H. WILLIAMS III   TONY S. DANIEL   RYAN BENJAMIN PENCILLERS

**J.H. WILLIAMS III   TONY S. DANIEL   JONATHAN GLAPION   MARK IRWIN
SANDU FLOREA   SALEEM CRAWFORD** INKERS

DAVE STEWART   GUY MAJOR COLORISTS

KEN LOPEZ   JOHN J. HILL   ROB LEIGH   RANDY GENTILE   STEVE WANDS   TRAVIS LANHAM   SAL CIPRIANO LETTERERS

BATMAN created by **Bob Kane**

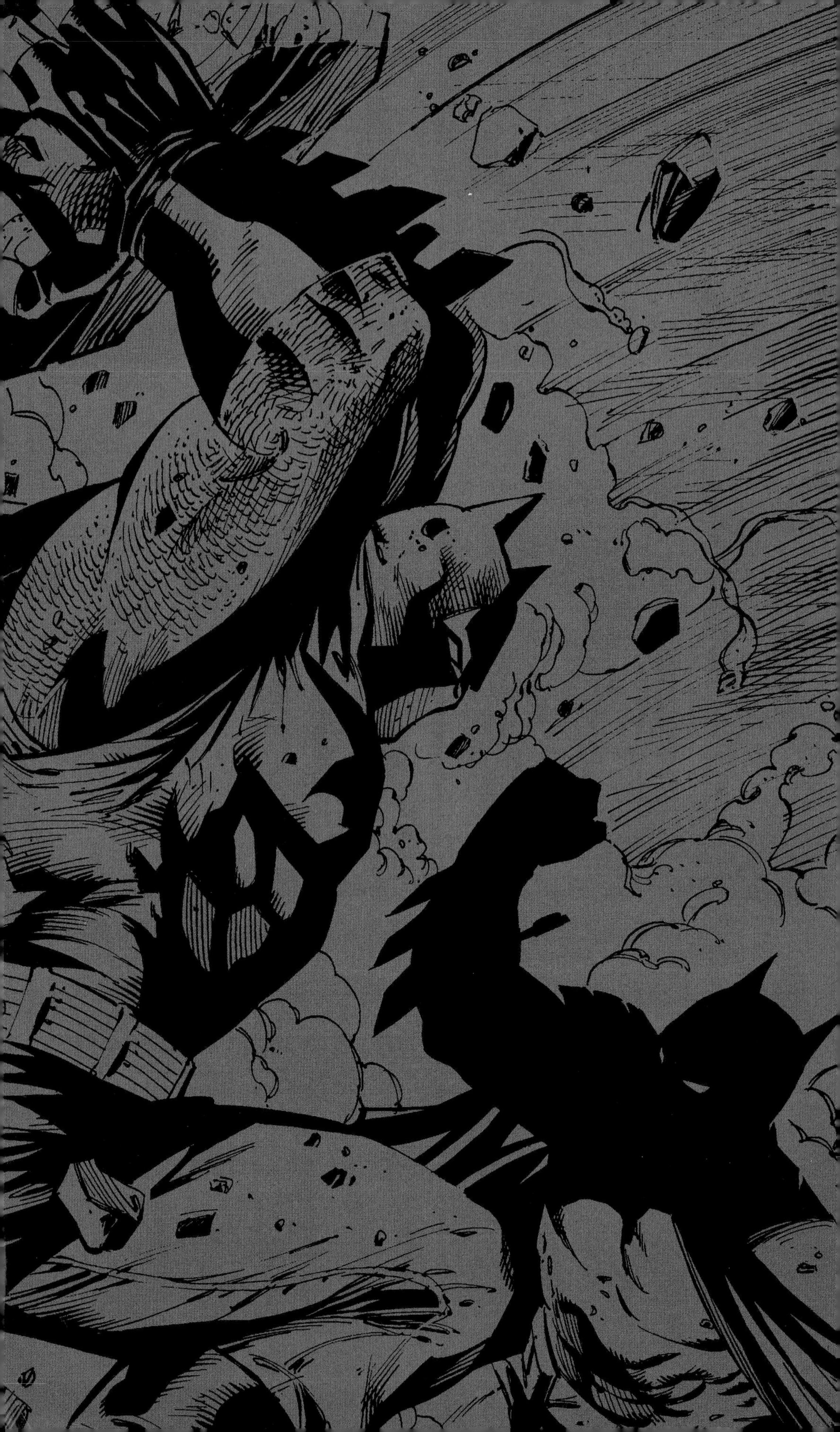

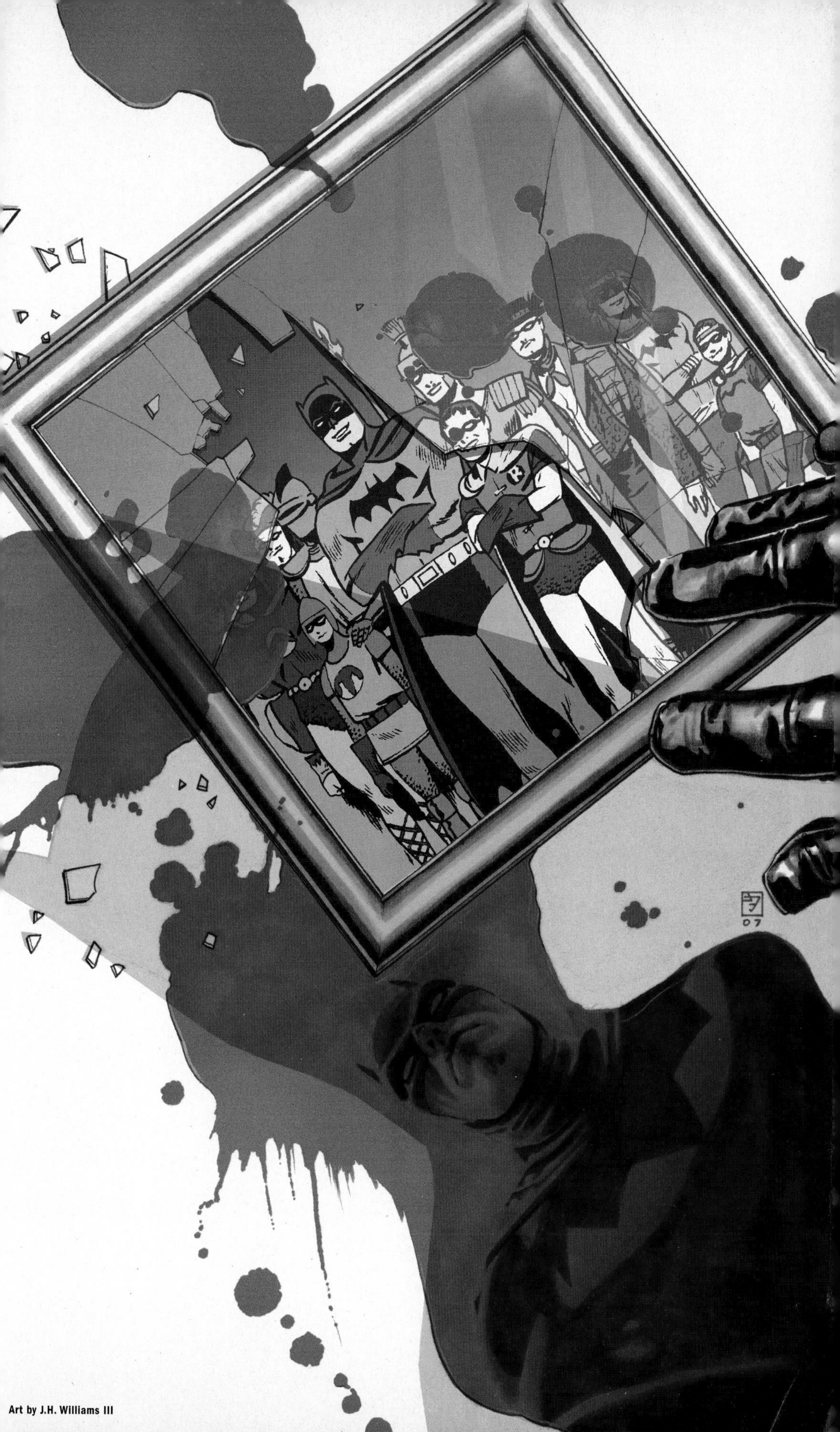

Art by J.H. Williams III

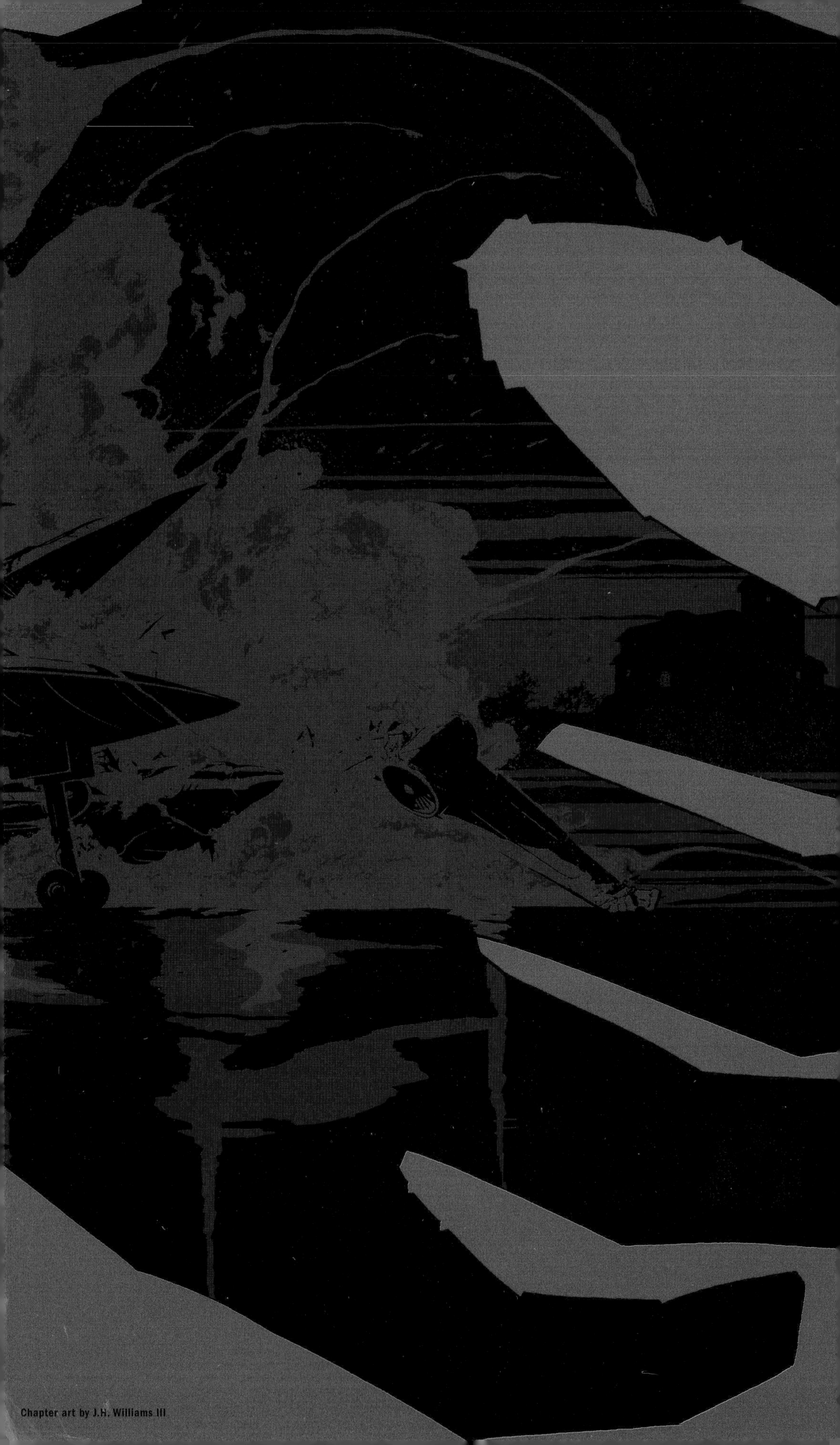

Chapter art by J.H. Williams III

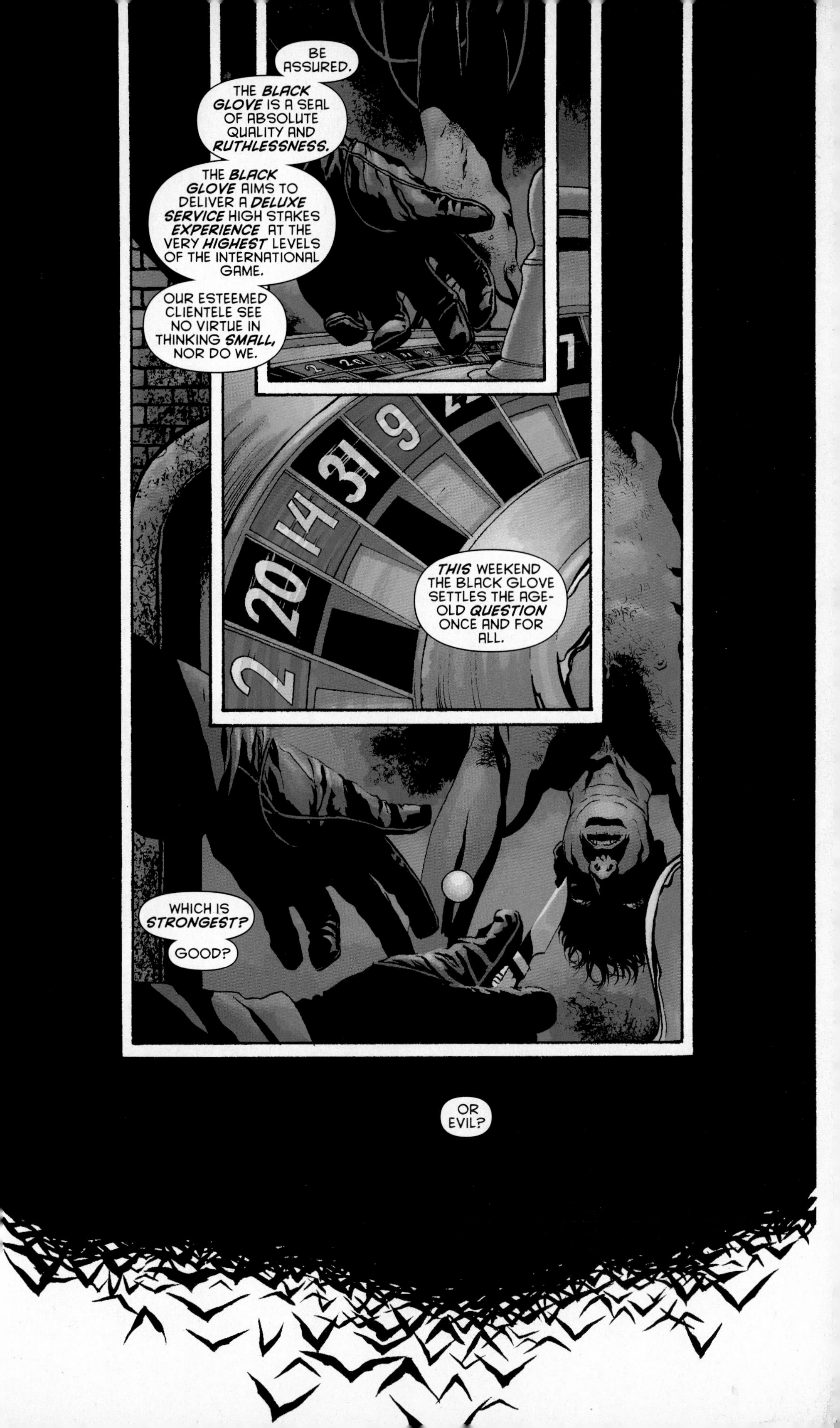
BE ASSURED.
THE BLACK GLOVE IS A SEAL OF ABSOLUTE QUALITY AND RUTHLESSNESS.
THE BLACK GLOVE AIMS TO DELIVER A DELUXE SERVICE HIGH STAKES EXPERIENCE AT THE VERY HIGHEST LEVELS OF THE INTERNATIONAL GAME.
OUR ESTEEMED CLIENTELE SEE NO VIRTUE IN THINKING SMALL, NOR DO WE.
THIS WEEKEND THE BLACK GLOVE SETTLES THE AGE-OLD QUESTION ONCE AND FOR ALL.
WHICH IS STRONGEST?
GOOD?
OR EVIL?

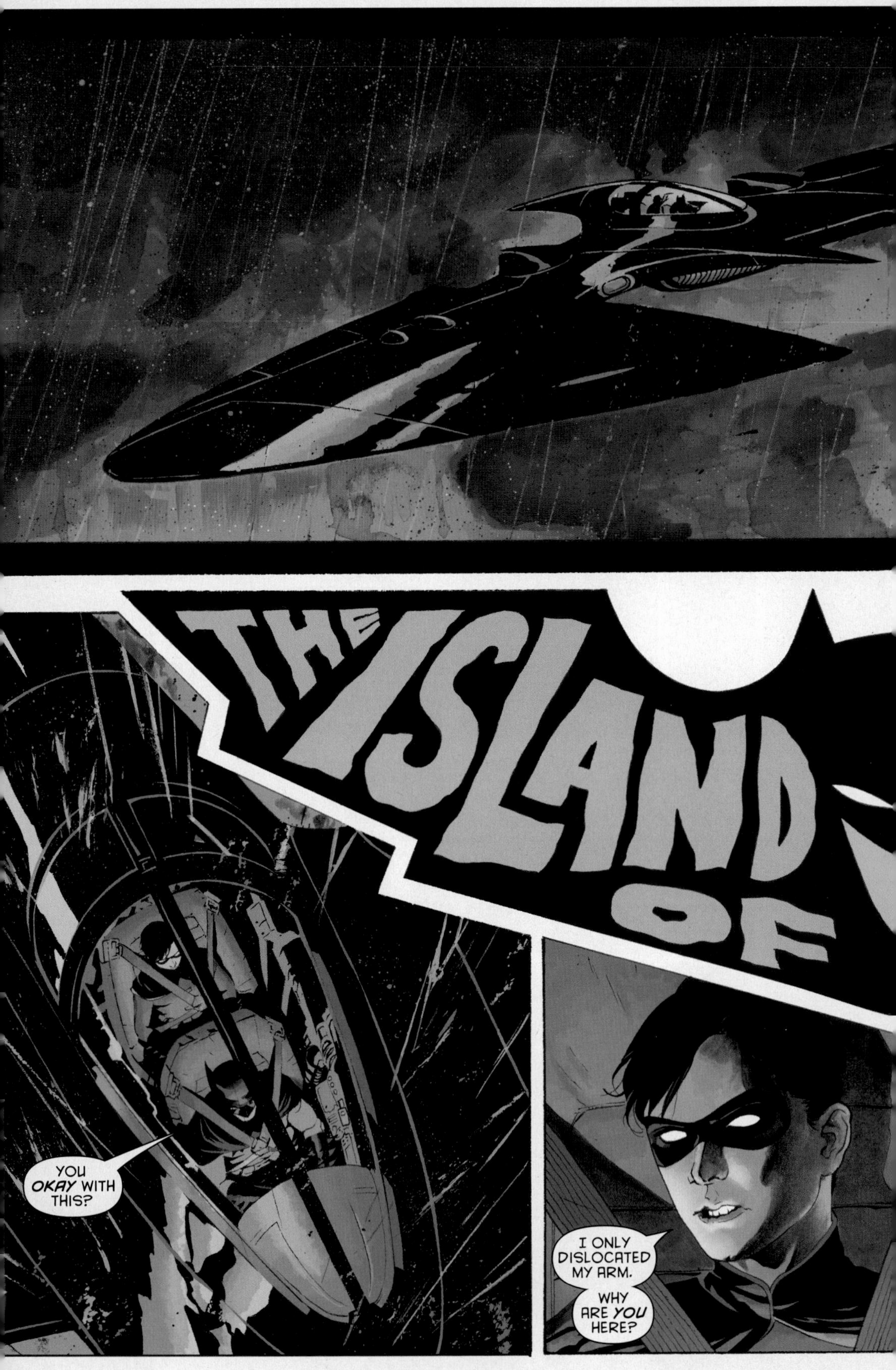
THE ISLAND OF
YOU *OKAY* WITH THIS?
I ONLY DISLOCATED MY ARM.
WHY ARE *YOU* HERE?

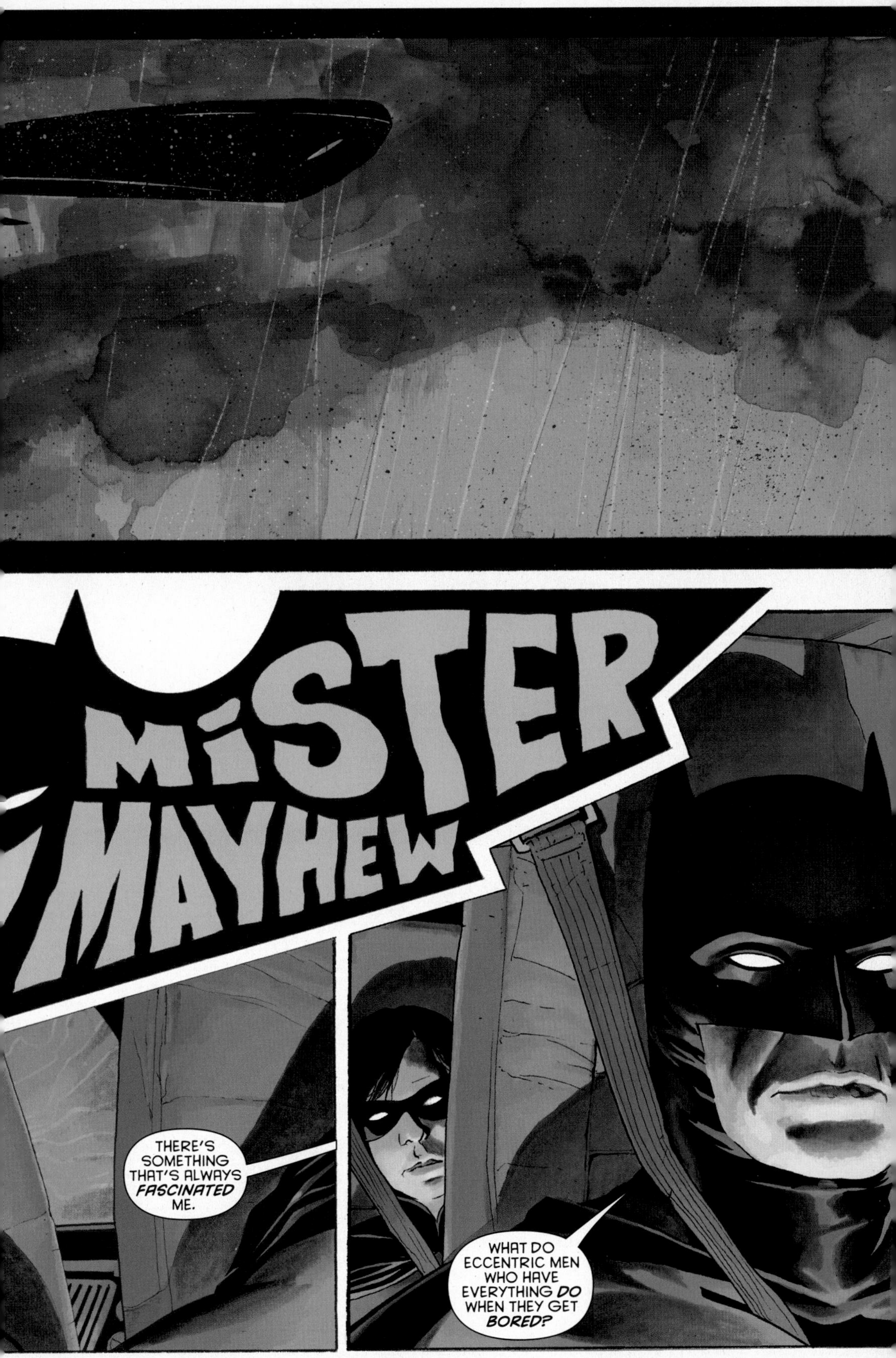
MISTER MAYHEW
THERE'S SOMETHING THAT'S ALWAYS *FASCINATED* ME.
WHAT DO ECCENTRIC MEN WHO HAVE EVERYTHING *DO* WHEN THEY GET *BORED?*

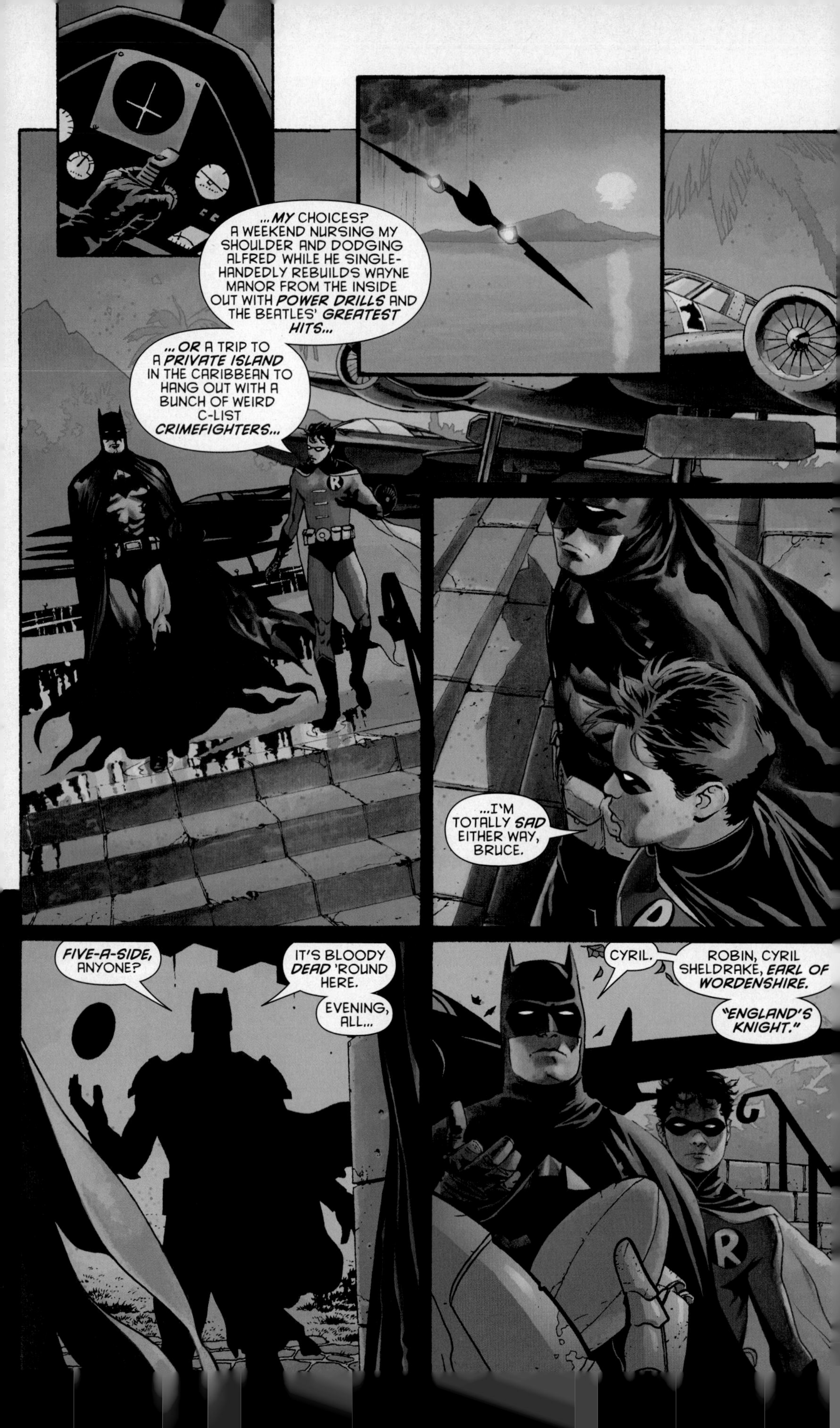
...MY CHOICES? A WEEKEND NURSING MY SHOULDER AND DODGING ALFRED WHILE HE SINGLE-HANDEDLY REBUILDS WAYNE MANOR FROM THE INSIDE OUT WITH POWER DRILLS AND THE BEATLES' GREATEST HITS...
...OR A TRIP TO A PRIVATE ISLAND IN THE CARIBBEAN TO HANG OUT WITH A BUNCH OF WEIRD C-LIST CRIMEFIGHTERS...
...I'M TOTALLY SAD EITHER WAY, BRUCE.
FIVE-A-SIDE, ANYONE?
IT'S BLOODY DEAD 'ROUND HERE.
EVENING, ALL...
CYRIL.
ROBIN, CYRIL SHELDRAKE, EARL OF WORDENSHIRE.
"ENGLAND'S KNIGHT."

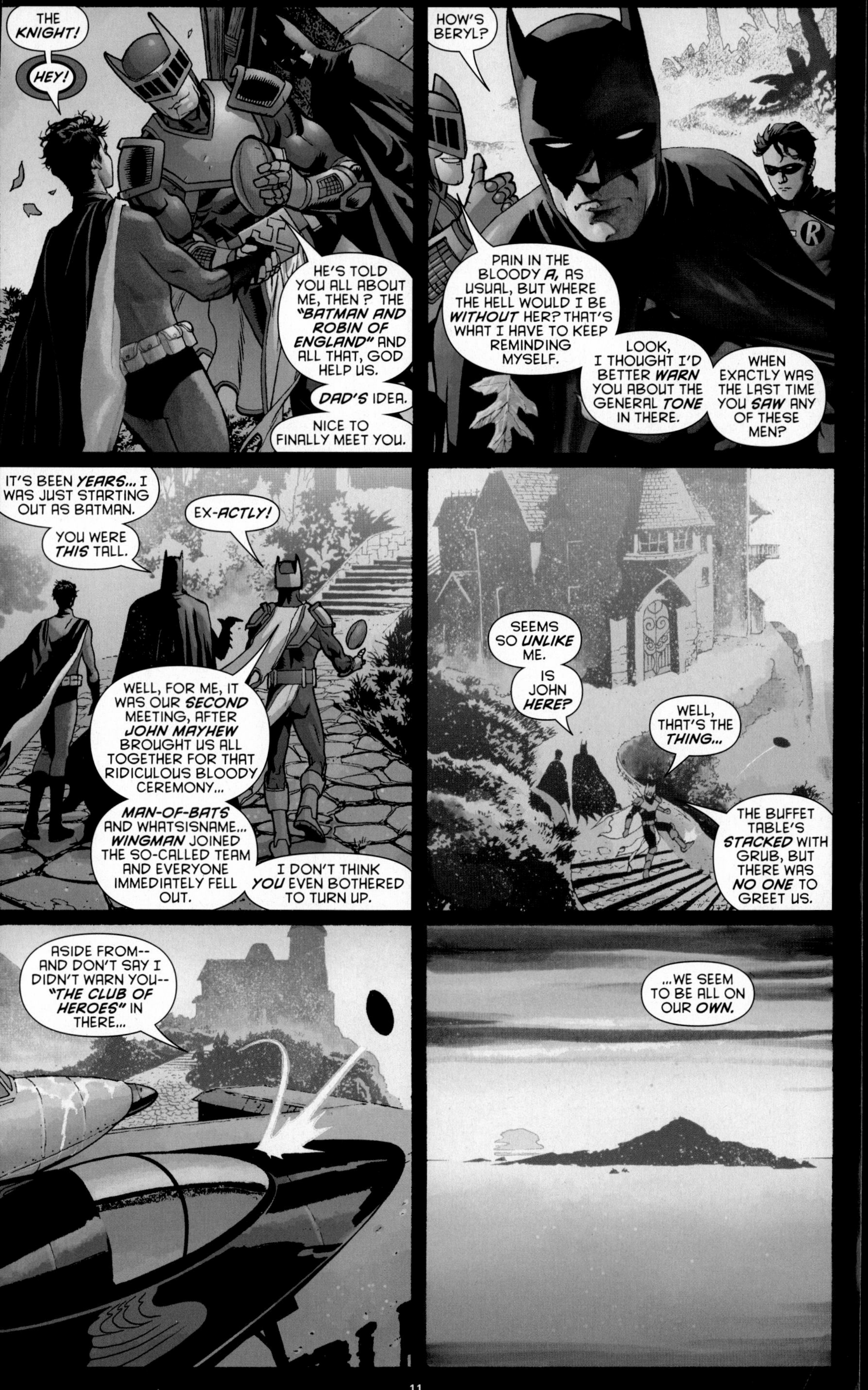

THE KNIGHT!
HEY!
HE'S TOLD YOU ALL ABOUT ME, THEN? THE "BATMAN AND ROBIN OF ENGLAND" AND ALL THAT, GOD HELP US.
DAD'S IDEA.
NICE TO FINALLY MEET YOU.
HOW'S BERYL?
PAIN IN THE BLOODY A, AS USUAL, BUT WHERE THE HELL WOULD I BE WITHOUT HER? THAT'S WHAT I HAVE TO KEEP REMINDING MYSELF.
LOOK, I THOUGHT I'D BETTER WARN YOU ABOUT THE GENERAL TONE IN THERE.
WHEN EXACTLY WAS THE LAST TIME YOU SAW ANY OF THESE MEN?
IT'S BEEN YEARS... I WAS JUST STARTING OUT AS BATMAN.
YOU WERE THIS TALL.
EX-ACTLY!
WELL, FOR ME, IT WAS OUR SECOND MEETING, AFTER JOHN MAYHEW BROUGHT US ALL TOGETHER FOR THAT RIDICULOUS BLOODY CEREMONY...
MAN-OF-BATS AND WHATSISNAME... WINGMAN JOINED THE SO-CALLED TEAM AND EVERYONE IMMEDIATELY FELL OUT.
I DON'T THINK YOU EVEN BOTHERED TO TURN UP.
SEEMS SO UNLIKE ME.
IS JOHN HERE?
WELL, THAT'S THE THING...
THE BUFFET TABLE'S STACKED WITH GRUB, BUT THERE WAS NO ONE TO GREET US.
ASIDE FROM-- AND DON'T SAY I DIDN'T WARN YOU-- "THE CLUB OF HEROES" IN THERE...
...WE SEEM TO BE ALL ON OUR OWN.

...THEN *HE* LUNGED, *I* PARRIED.

EN GARDE!

HE *BLINKED.*

I *STRUCK!*

WHAT HAPPENED THEN?

THE *TIP*, THE BLUNT TIP, OF MY FENCING FOIL HAD *BROKEN OFF* AT SOME POINT DURING OUR LUNATIC DUEL ACROSS THE ROOFTOPS OF *MONTMARTRE.*

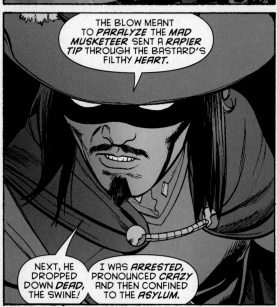

THE BLOW MEANT TO *PARALYZE* THE *MAD MUSKETEER* SENT A *RAPIER TIP* THROUGH THE BASTARD'S FILTHY *HEART.*

NEXT, HE DROPPED DOWN *DEAD,* THE *SWINE!*

I WAS *ARRESTED,* PRONOUNCED *CRAZY* AND THEN CONFINED TO THE *ASYLUM.*

AND WHO IS THERE? NOT ONE BUT TWO OF MY *GREATEST ENEMIES,* WAITING FOR ME, ALONGSIDE AN *ARMY* OF GIBBERING HOMICIDAL *FREAKS.*

I, THE FINEST SWORDSMAN *EN FRANCE, SANS* SWORD, IN *HELL.*

I ♥ ROME

THE *MORAL* OF MY *STORY?*

THERE'S *GOLD* IN THE *MINES* OF THE *UNDERWORLD.*

MY *BOOK* MADE ME *RICH* OVERNIGHT, AND NOW MY AGENT HAS SOLD THE *MOVIE RIGHTS* FOR GOD ONLY *KNOWS* HOW MANY *MILLIONS* OF *DOLLARS.*

I *NEVER* HAVE TO FIGHT CRIME AGAIN.

AND SINCE YOU ASK...THAT'S WHAT I OWE BATMAN.

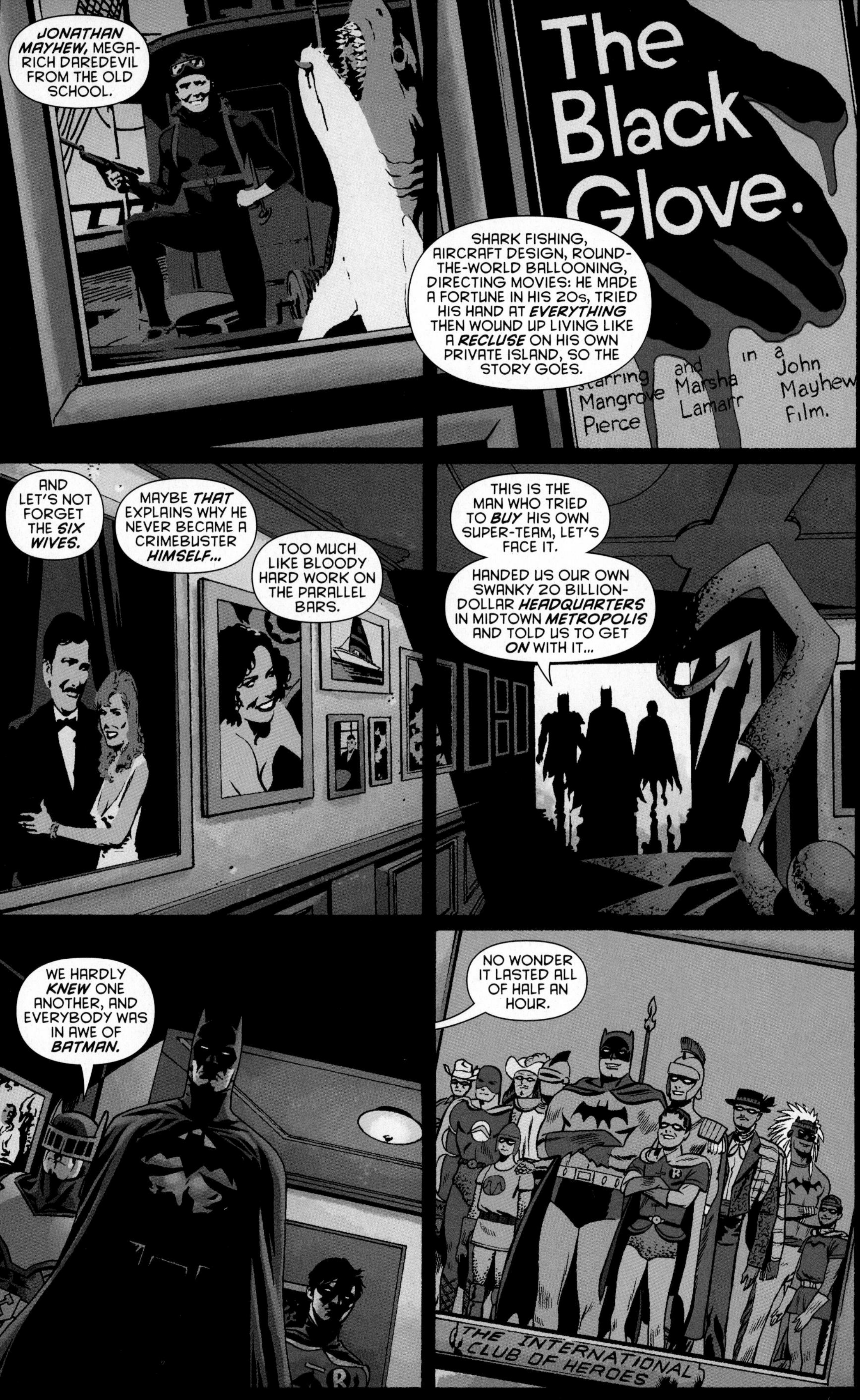
JONATHAN MAYHEW, MEGA-RICH DAREDEVIL FROM THE OLD SCHOOL.
The Black Glove.
SHARK FISHING, AIRCRAFT DESIGN, ROUND-THE-WORLD BALLOONING, DIRECTING MOVIES: HE MADE A FORTUNE IN HIS 20s, TRIED HIS HAND AT EVERYTHING THEN WOUND UP LIVING LIKE A RECLUSE ON HIS OWN PRIVATE ISLAND, SO THE STORY GOES.
starring Mangrove Pierce and Marsha Lamarr in a John Mayhew Film.
AND LET'S NOT FORGET THE SIX WIVES.
MAYBE THAT EXPLAINS WHY HE NEVER BECAME A CRIMEBUSTER HIMSELF...
TOO MUCH LIKE BLOODY HARD WORK ON THE PARALLEL BARS.
THIS IS THE MAN WHO TRIED TO BUY HIS OWN SUPER-TEAM, LET'S FACE IT.
HANDED US OUR OWN SWANKY 20 BILLION-DOLLAR HEADQUARTERS IN MIDTOWN METROPOLIS AND TOLD US TO GET ON WITH IT...
WE HARDLY KNEW ONE ANOTHER, AND EVERYBODY WAS IN AWE OF BATMAN.
NO WONDER IT LASTED ALL OF HALF AN HOUR.
THE INTERNATIONAL CLUB OF HEROES

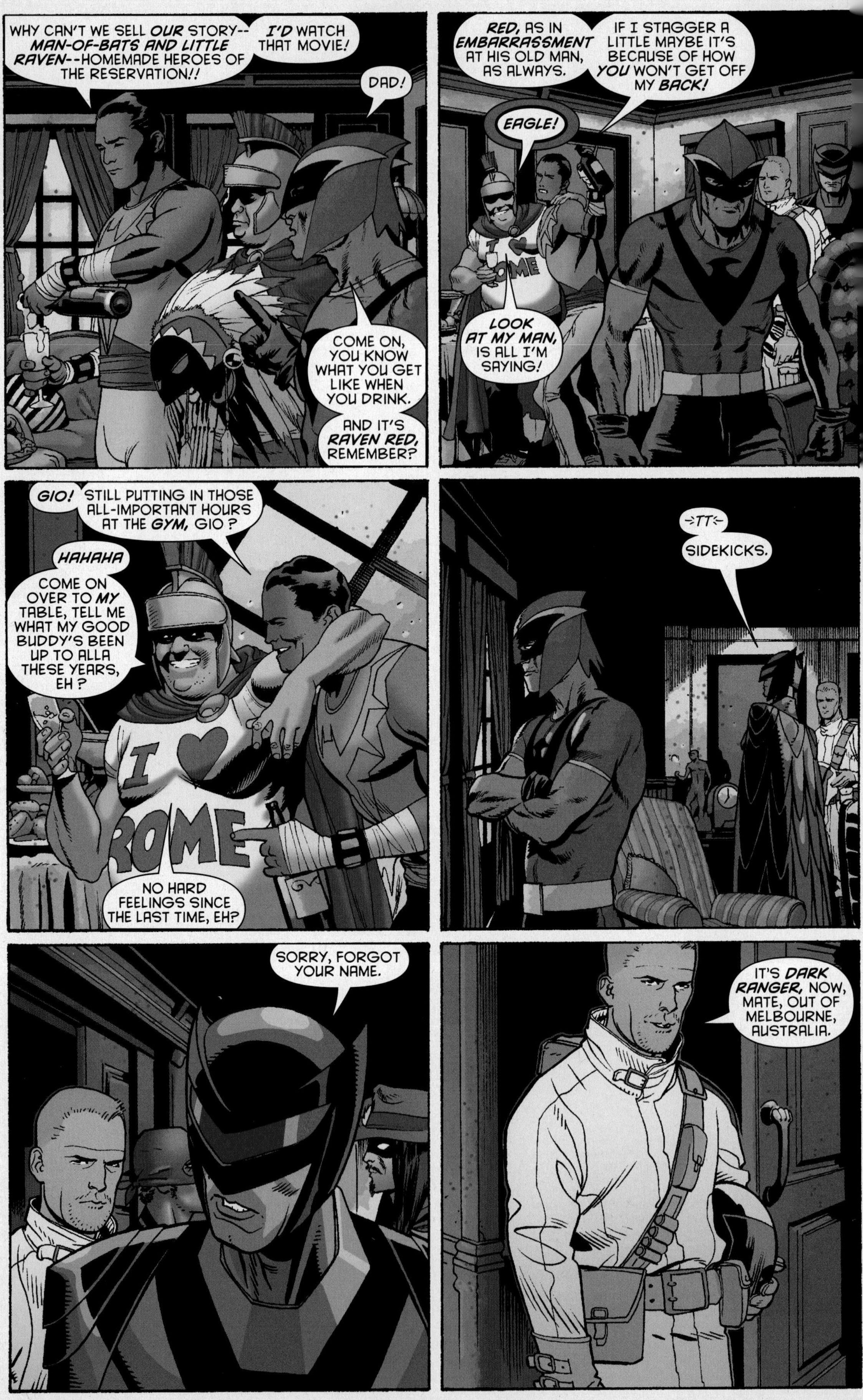
WHY CAN'T WE SELL OUR STORY-- MAN-OF-BATS AND LITTLE RAVEN--HOMEMADE HEROES OF THE RESERVATION!!
I'D WATCH THAT MOVIE!
DAD!
COME ON, YOU KNOW WHAT YOU GET LIKE WHEN YOU DRINK.
AND IT'S RAVEN RED, REMEMBER?
RED, AS IN EMBARRASSMENT AT HIS OLD MAN, AS ALWAYS.
IF I STAGGER A LITTLE MAYBE IT'S BECAUSE OF HOW YOU WON'T GET OFF MY BACK!
EAGLE!
LOOK AT MY MAN, IS ALL I'M SAYING!
GIO!
STILL PUTTING IN THOSE ALL-IMPORTANT HOURS AT THE GYM, GIO?
HAHAHA
COME ON OVER TO MY TABLE, TELL ME WHAT MY GOOD BUDDY'S BEEN UP TO ALLA THESE YEARS, EH?
NO HARD FEELINGS SINCE THE LAST TIME, EH?
-TT-
SIDEKICKS.
SORRY, FORGOT YOUR NAME.
IT'S DARK RANGER, NOW, MATE, OUT OF MELBOURNE, AUSTRALIA.

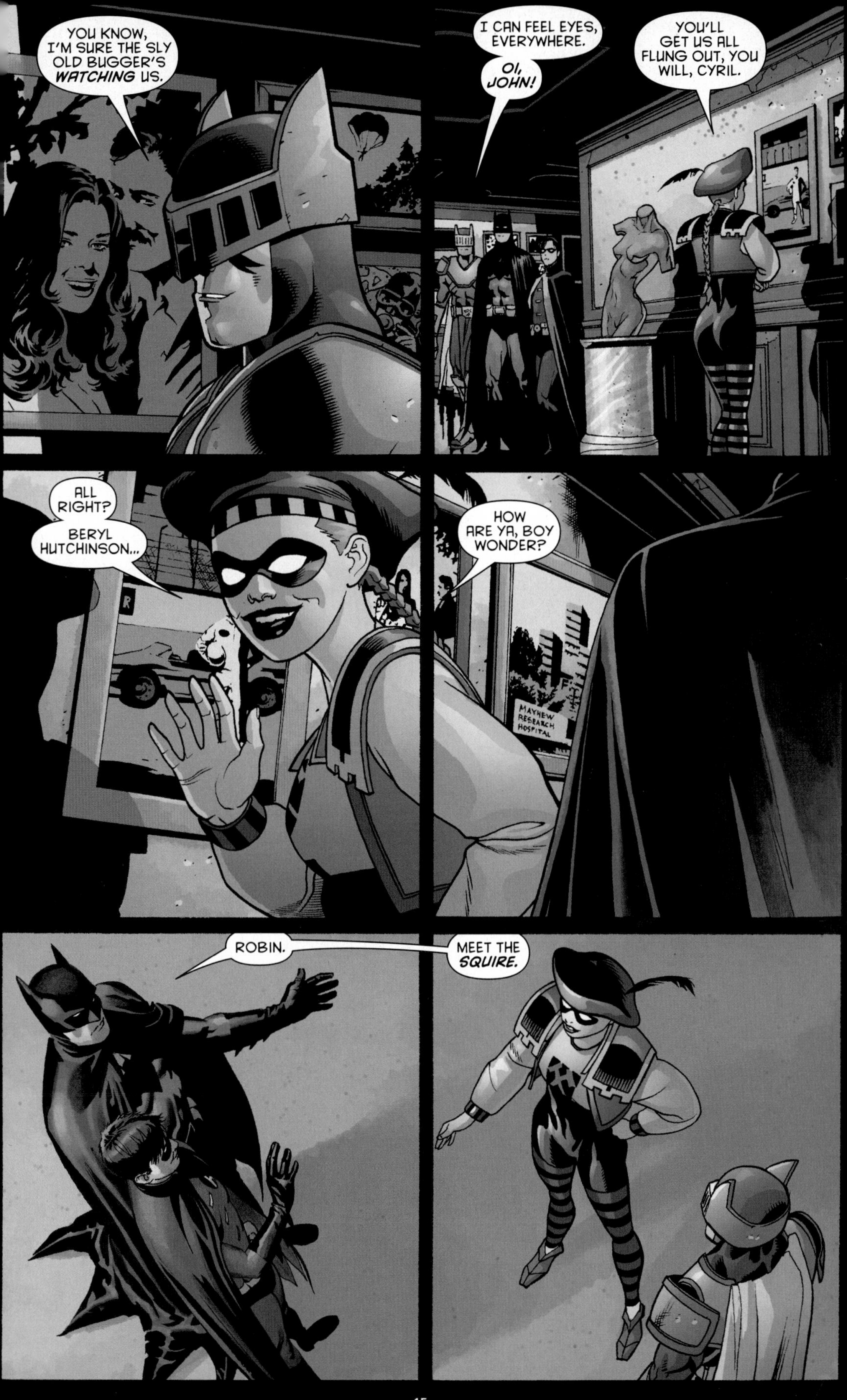
YOU KNOW, I'M SURE THE SLY OLD BUGGER'S WATCHING US.
I CAN FEEL EYES, EVERYWHERE.
OI, JOHN!
YOU'LL GET US ALL FLUNG OUT, YOU WILL, CYRIL.
ALL RIGHT?
BERYL HUTCHINSON...
HOW ARE YA, BOY WONDER?
MAYHEW RESEARCH HOSPITAL
ROBIN.
MEET THE SQUIRE.

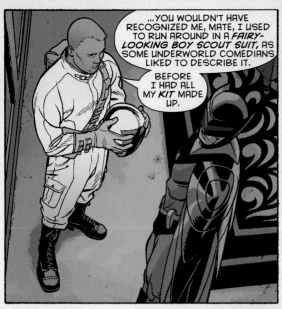

...YOU WOULDN'T HAVE RECOGNIZED ME, MATE, I USED TO RUN AROUND IN A *FAIRY-LOOKING BOY SCOUT SUIT,* AS SOME UNDERWORLD COMEDIANS LIKED TO DESCRIBE IT.

BEFORE I HAD ALL MY *KIT* MADE UP.

I STARTED OUT, I WAS JUST THE *RANGER...*

...BUT YOU KNOW HOW IT IS: THE BAD BLOKES GET TOUGHER AND MEANER EVERY TIME THEY SEE A NEW *GANGSTER* MOVIE...

...YOU'RE ALMOST *OBLIGED* TO GO THE *BAD ASS* ROUTE THESE DAYS, MATE.

HENCE THE *NED KELLY* STYLE PROTECTIVE *HEADGEAR* AND THE OLD *RIOT STREET* LOOK.

SO...SKY... NO, *WINGMAN,* RIGHT?

YOU'VE GOT THE WHOLE *DARK KNIGHT OF JUSTICE* THING GOING ON THERE YOURSELF.

TINK TINK

WHAT? I ACTUALLY CAME UP WITH THE *WINGMAN* CRIMEFIGHTING CONCEPT ABOUT A YEAR *BEFORE* BATMAN.

A WHOLE YEAR. POSSIBLY MORE.

WE WORKED TOGETHER ONCE, THAT'S ALL.

WHATEVER YOU SAY.

NO WORRIES. GOOD LUCK TO YOU, MATE.

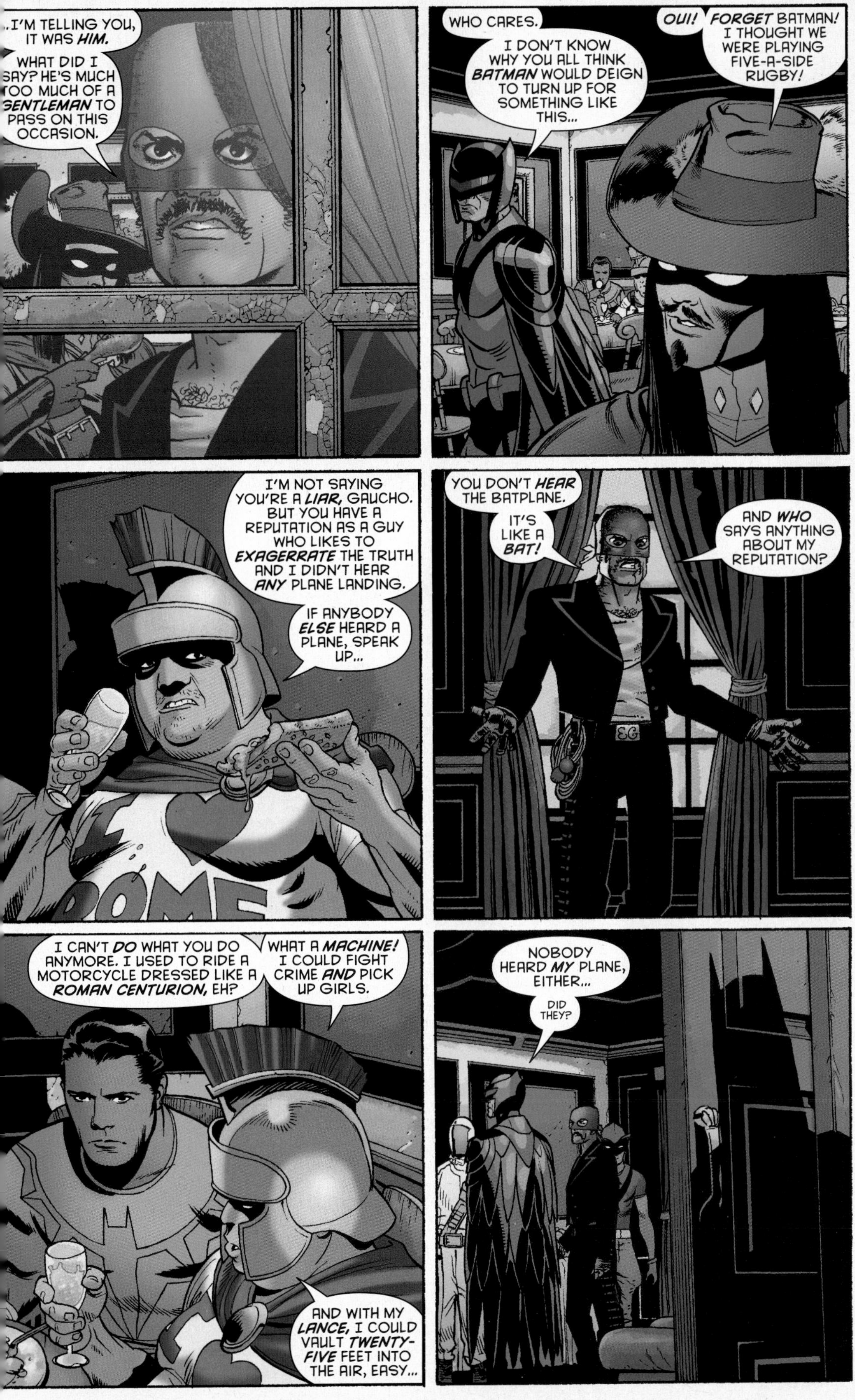
..I'M TELLING YOU, IT WAS HIM.
WHAT DID I SAY? HE'S MUCH TOO MUCH OF A GENTLEMAN TO PASS ON THIS OCCASION.
WHO CARES.
I DON'T KNOW WHY YOU ALL THINK BATMAN WOULD DEIGN TO TURN UP FOR SOMETHING LIKE THIS...
OUI!
FORGET BATMAN! I THOUGHT WE WERE PLAYING FIVE-A-SIDE RUGBY!
I'M NOT SAYING YOU'RE A LIAR, GAUCHO. BUT YOU HAVE A REPUTATION AS A GUY WHO LIKES TO EXAGERRATE THE TRUTH AND I DIDN'T HEAR ANY PLANE LANDING.
IF ANYBODY ELSE HEARD A PLANE, SPEAK UP...
YOU DON'T HEAR THE BATPLANE.
IT'S LIKE A BAT!
AND WHO SAYS ANYTHING ABOUT MY REPUTATION?
I CAN'T DO WHAT YOU DO ANYMORE. I USED TO RIDE A MOTORCYCLE DRESSED LIKE A ROMAN CENTURION, EH?
WHAT A MACHINE! I COULD FIGHT CRIME AND PICK UP GIRLS.
AND WITH MY LANCE, I COULD VAULT TWENTY-FIVE FEET INTO THE AIR, EASY...
NOBODY HEARD MY PLANE, EITHER...
DID THEY?

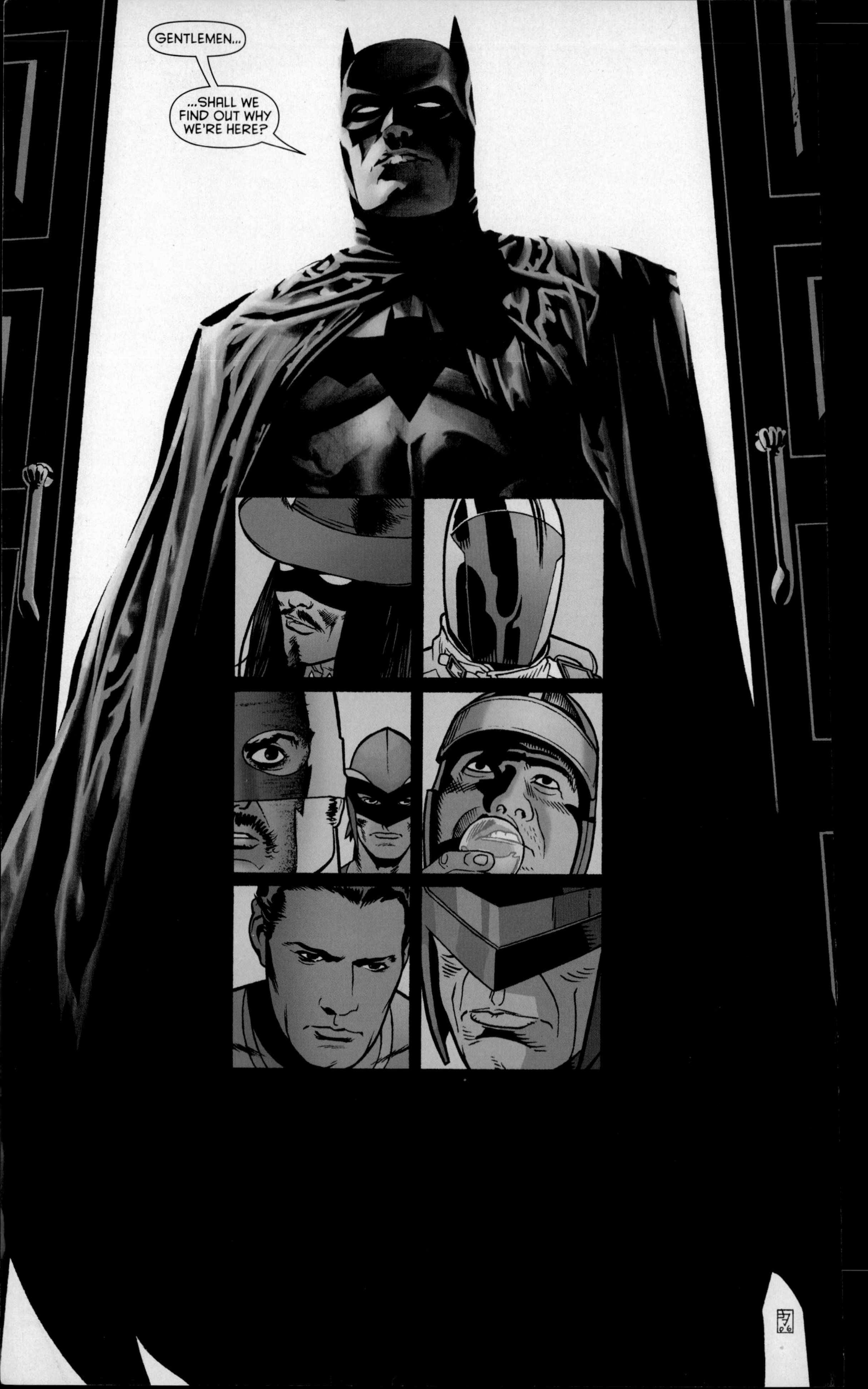
GENTLEMEN...
...SHALL WE FIND OUT WHY WE'RE HERE?

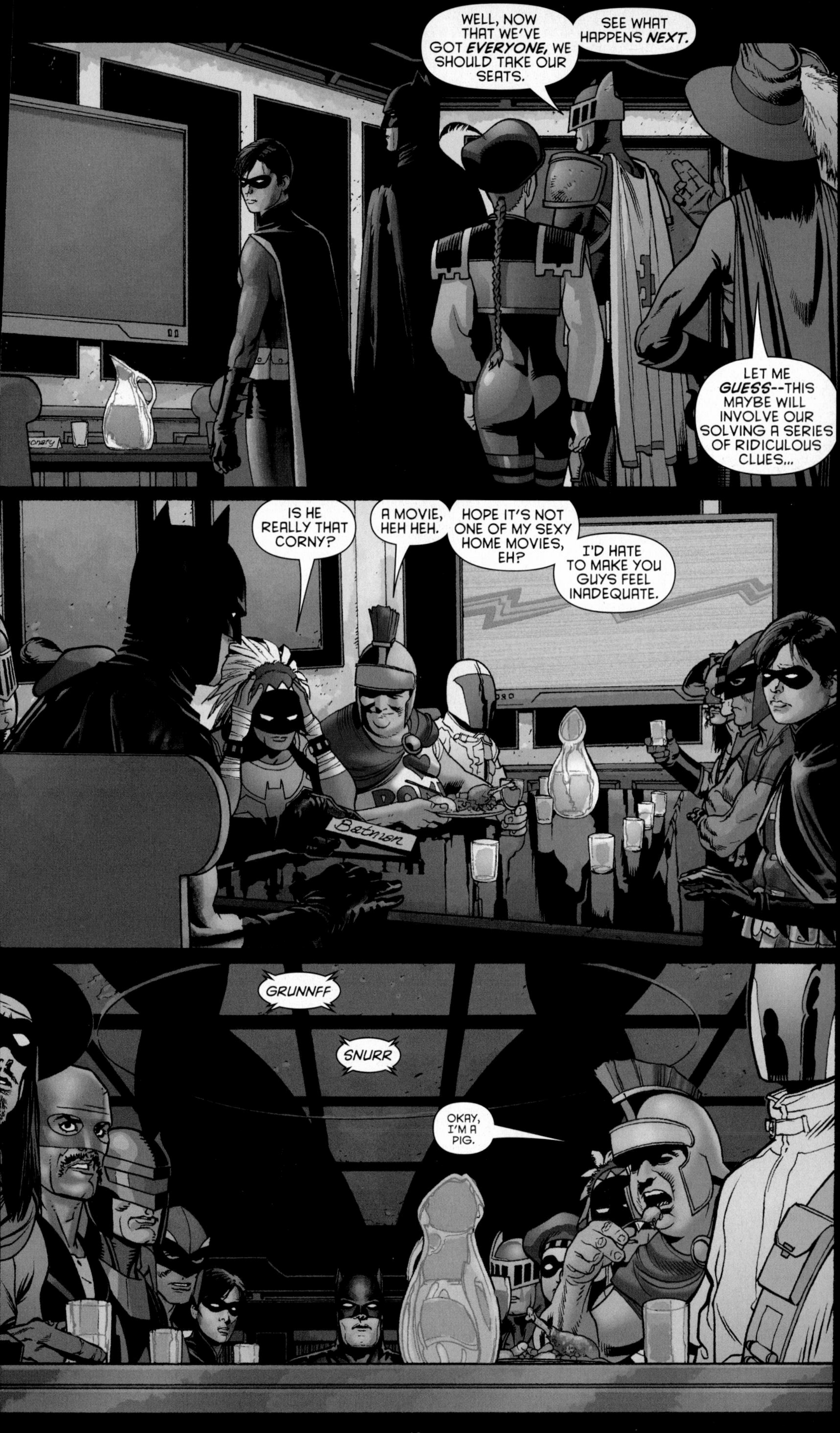
WELL, NOW THAT WE'VE GOT *EVERYONE,* WE SHOULD TAKE OUR SEATS.
SEE WHAT HAPPENS *NEXT.*
LET ME *GUESS*--THIS MAYBE WILL INVOLVE OUR SOLVING A SERIES OF RIDICULOUS CLUES...
IS HE REALLY THAT CORNY?
A MOVIE, HEH HEH.
HOPE IT'S NOT ONE OF MY SEXY HOME MOVIES, EH?
I'D HATE TO MAKE YOU GUYS FEEL INADEQUATE.
Batman
GRUNNFF
SNURR
OKAY, I'M A PIG.

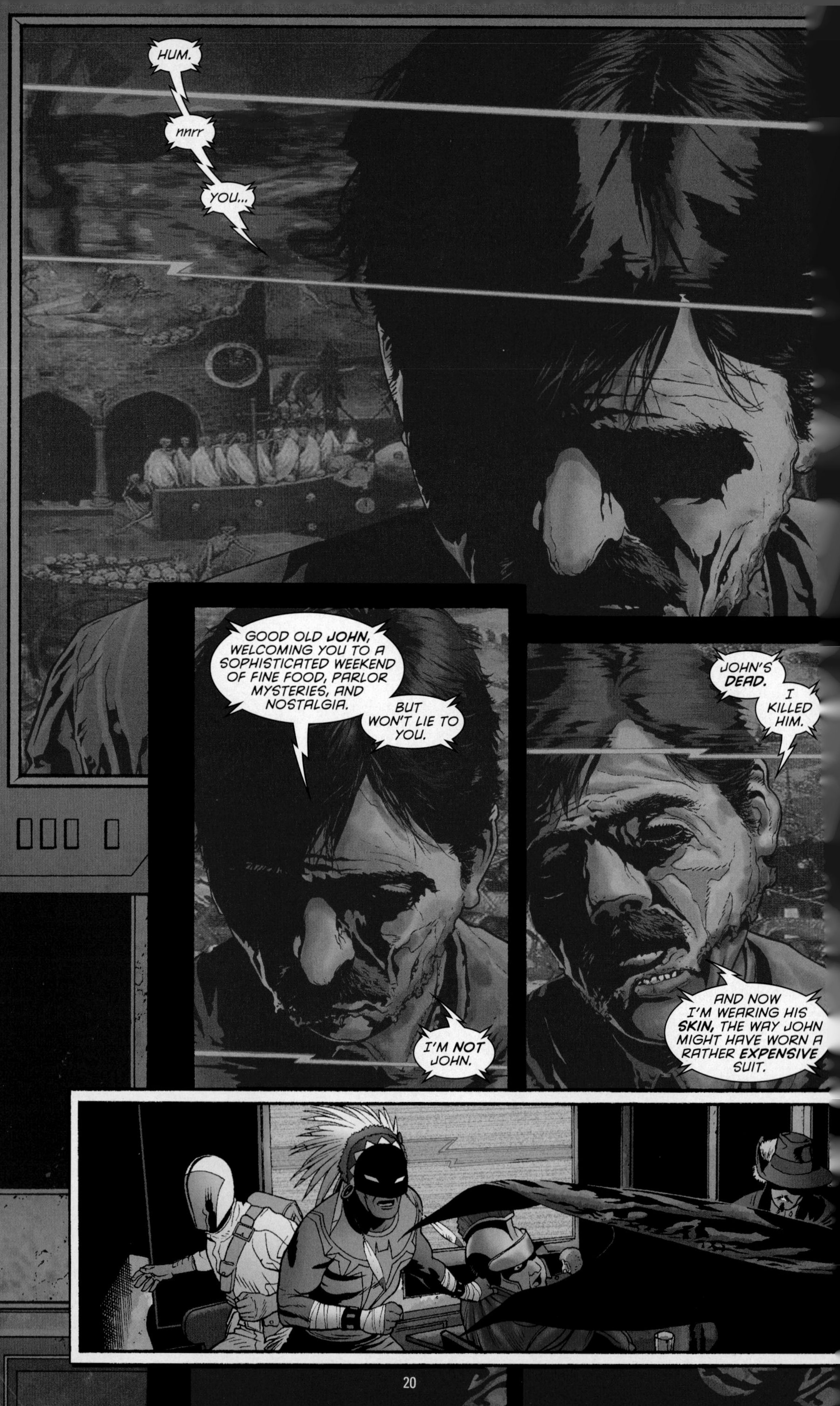
HUM.
nnrr
YOU...
GOOD OLD **JOHN**, WELCOMING YOU TO A SOPHISTICATED WEEKEND OF FINE FOOD, PARLOR MYSTERIES, AND NOSTALGIA.
BUT WON'T LIE TO YOU.
I'M **NOT** JOHN.
JOHN'S **DEAD.**
I KILLED HIM.
AND NOW I'M WEARING HIS **SKIN,** THE WAY JOHN MIGHT HAVE WORN A RATHER **EXPENSIVE** SUIT.

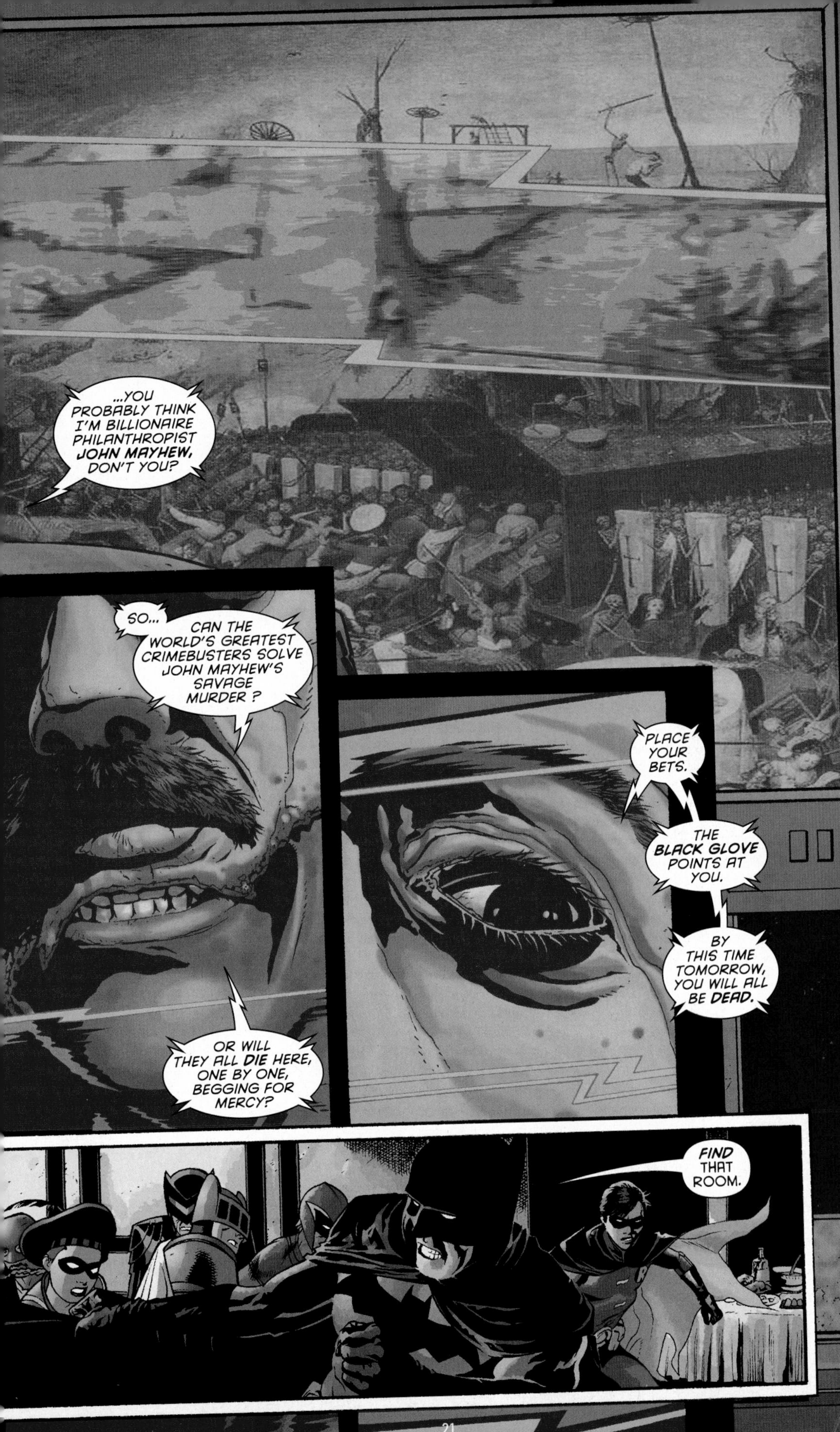
...YOU PROBABLY THINK I'M BILLIONAIRE PHILANTHROPIST JOHN MAYHEW, DON'T YOU?
SO...
CAN THE WORLD'S GREATEST CRIMEBUSTERS SOLVE JOHN MAYHEW'S SAVAGE MURDER ?
OR WILL THEY ALL DIE HERE, ONE BY ONE, BEGGING FOR MERCY?
PLACE YOUR BETS.
THE BLACK GLOVE POINTS AT YOU.
BY THIS TIME TOMORROW, YOU WILL ALL BE DEAD.
FIND THAT ROOM.

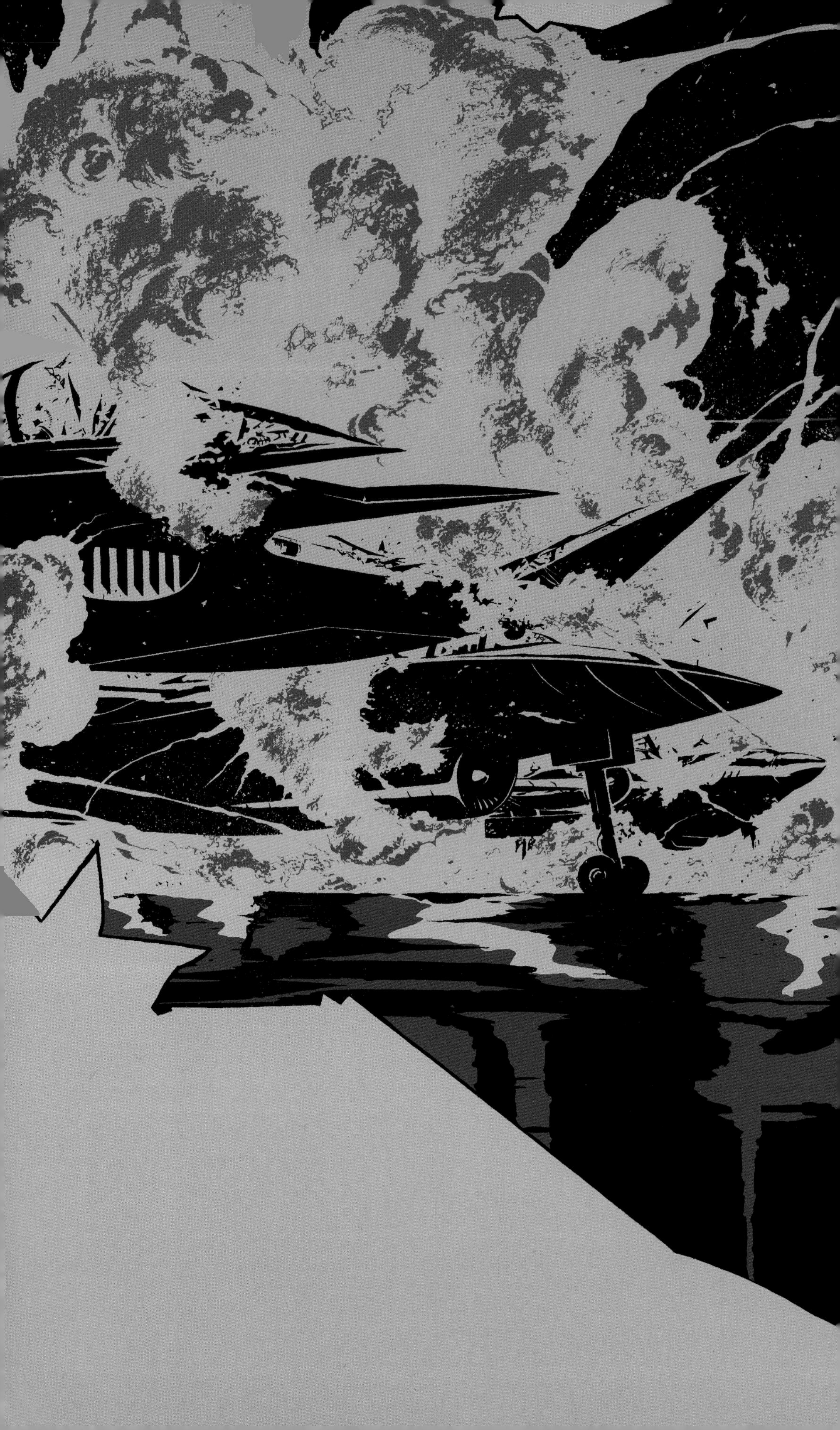

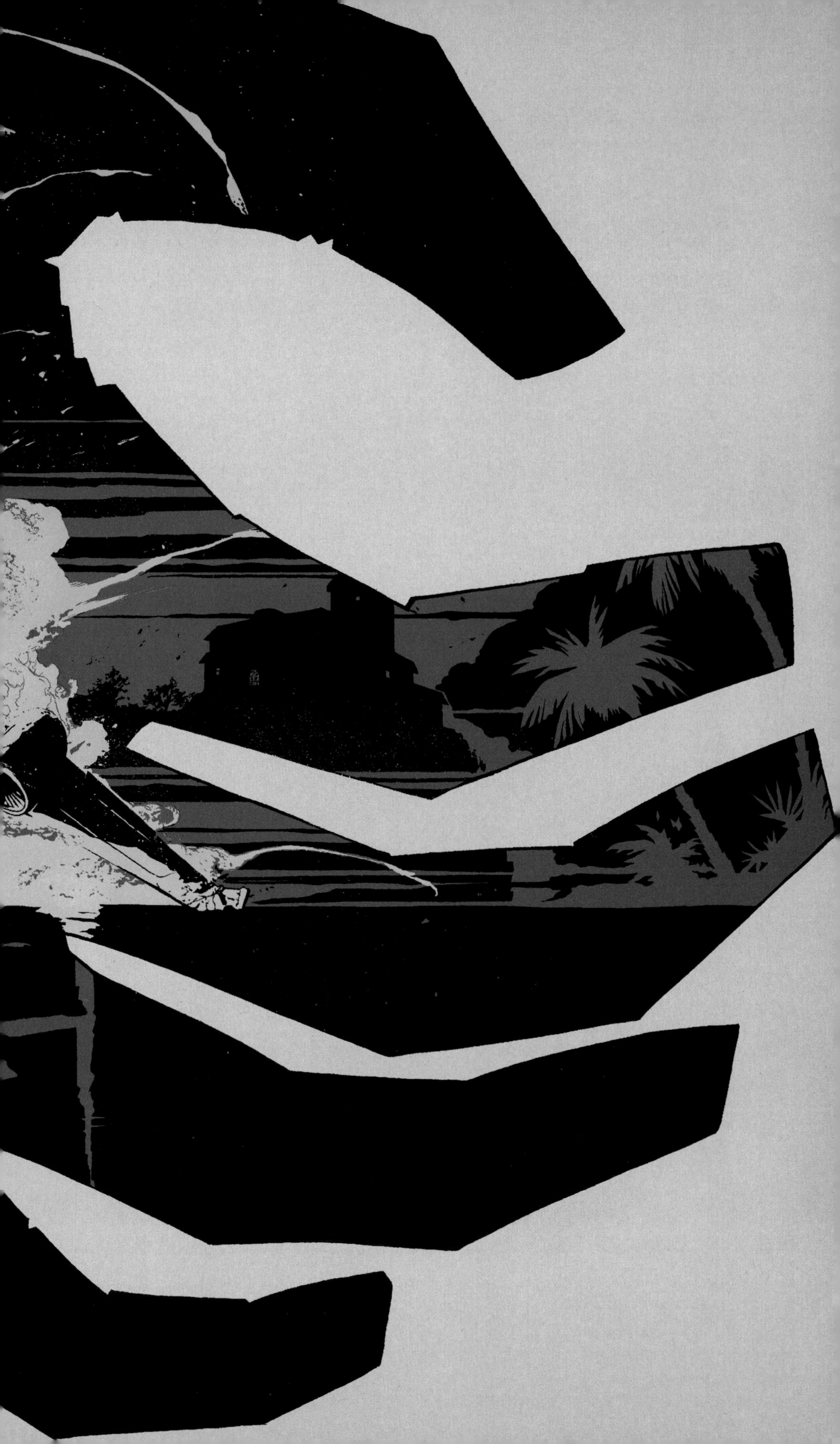

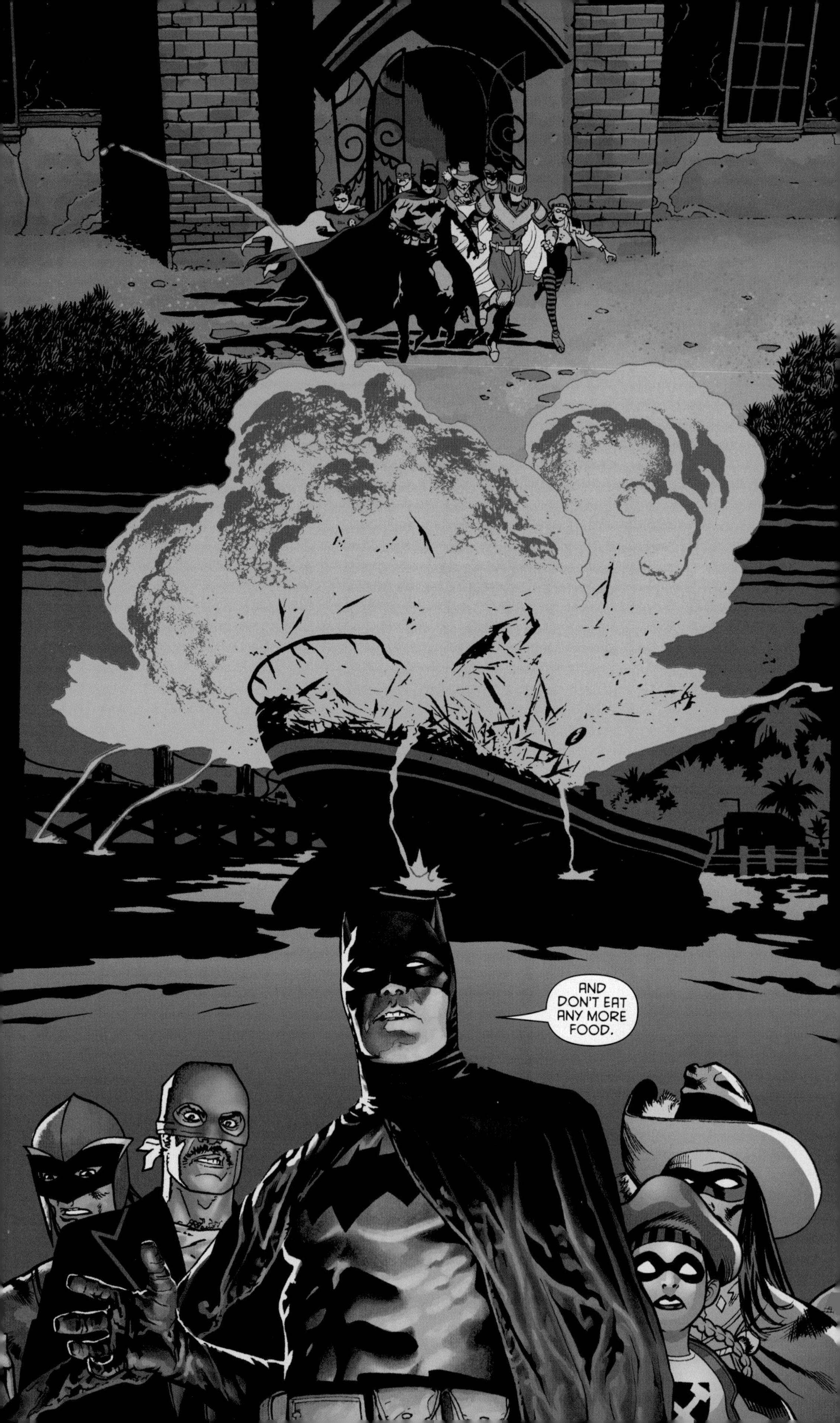
AND DON'T EAT ANY MORE FOOD.

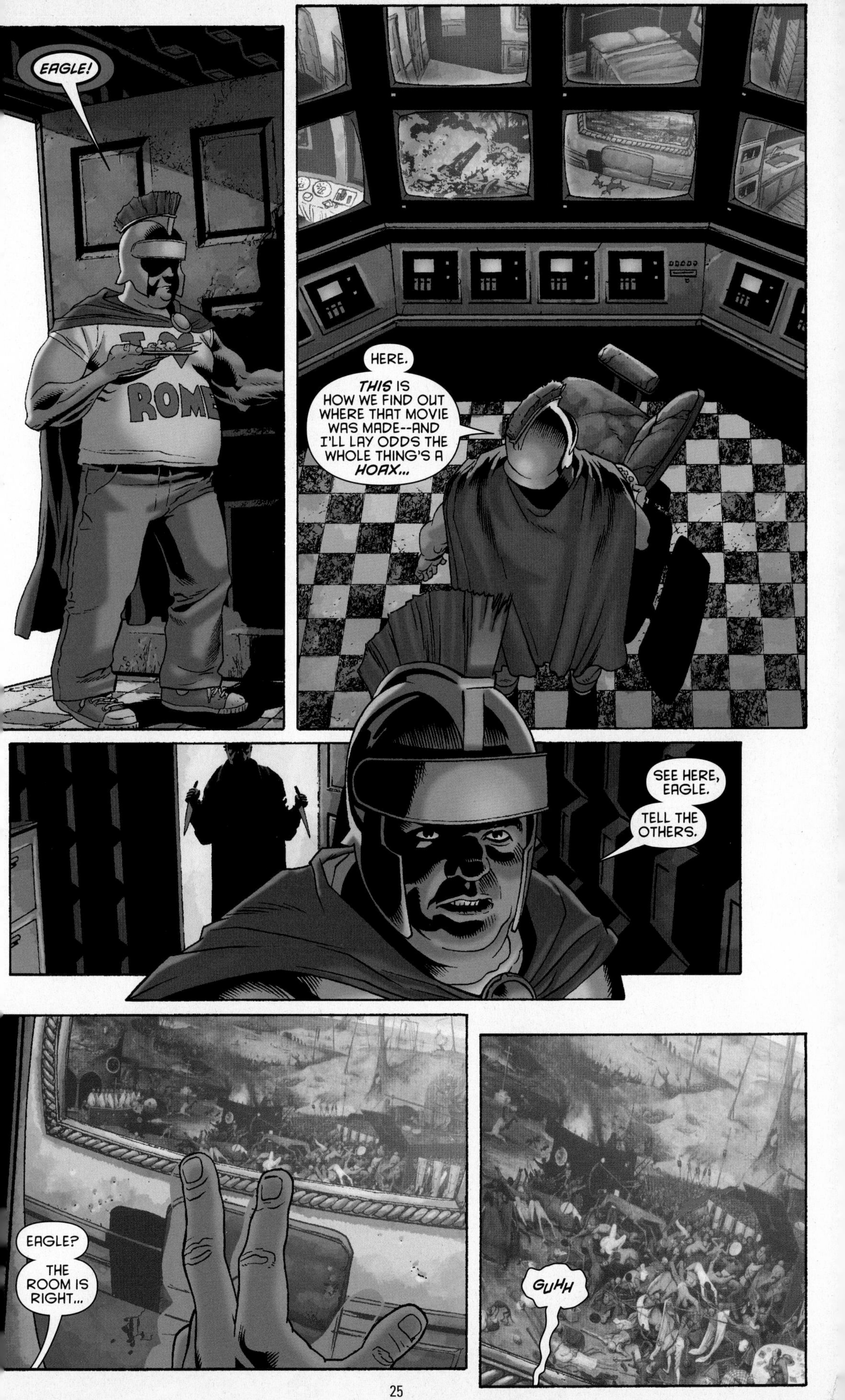
EAGLE!
HERE.
THIS IS HOW WE FIND OUT WHERE THAT MOVIE WAS MADE--AND I'LL LAY ODDS THE WHOLE THING'S A HOAX...
SEE HERE, EAGLE.
TELL THE OTHERS.
EAGLE?
THE ROOM IS RIGHT...
GUHH

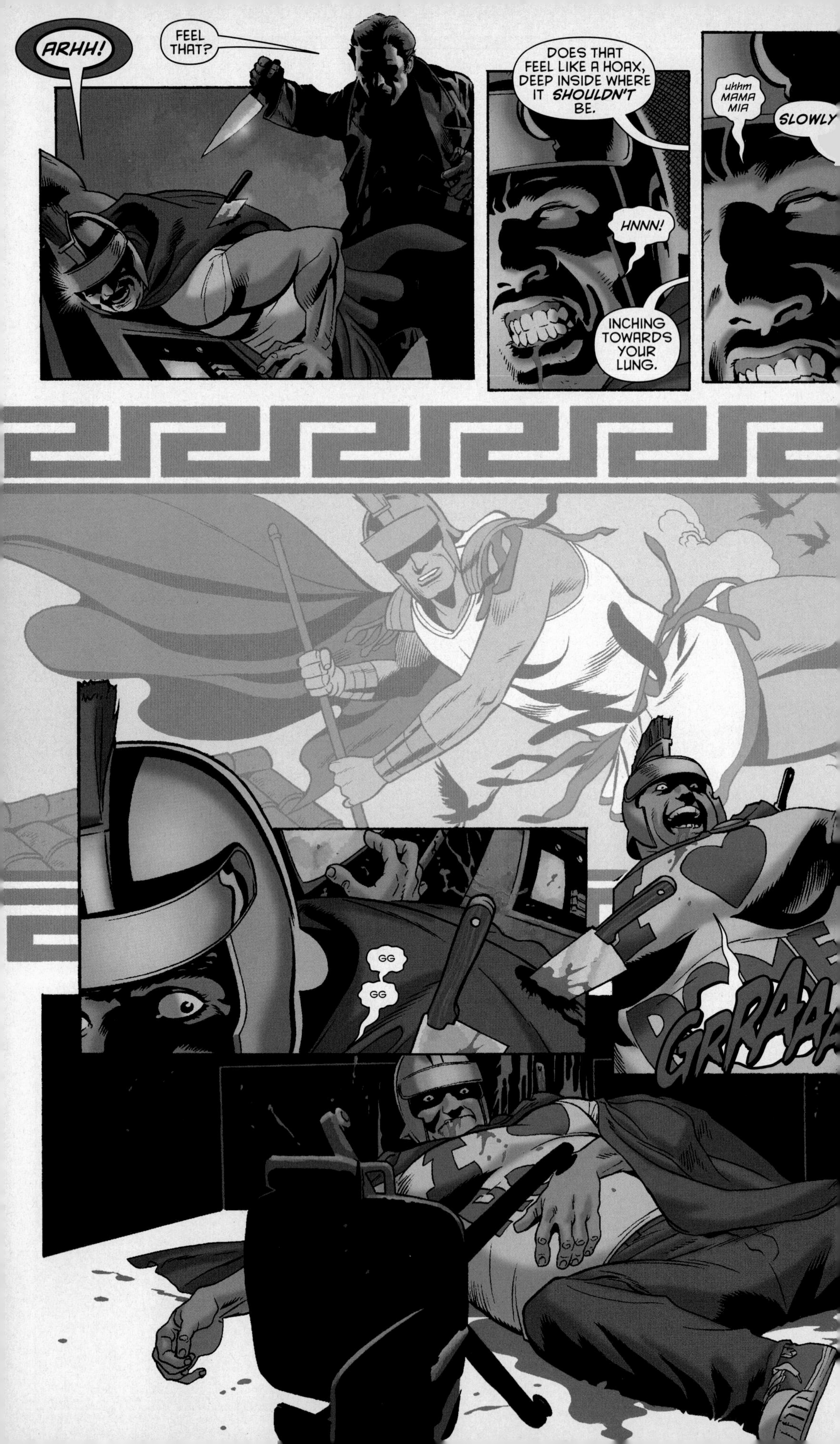
ARHH!
FEEL THAT?
DOES THAT FEEL LIKE A HOAX, DEEP INSIDE WHERE IT SHOULDN'T BE.
HNNN!
INCHING TOWARDS YOUR LUNG.
uhhm MAMA MIA
SLOWLY
GG
GG
GRRAA

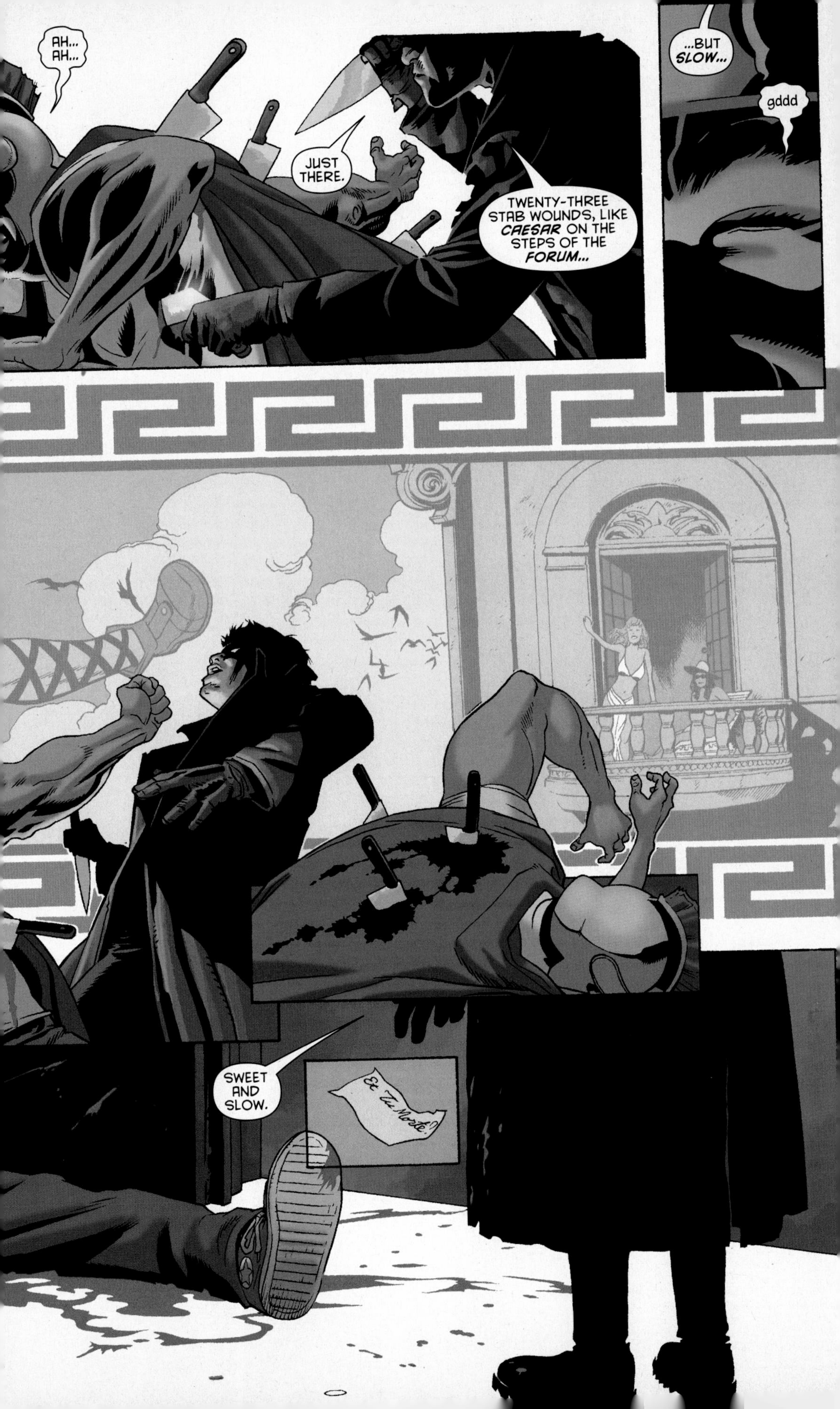
AH... AH...
JUST THERE.
TWENTY-THREE STAB WOUNDS, LIKE CAESAR ON THE STEPS OF THE FORUM...
...BUT SLOW...
gddd
SWEET AND SLOW.
Et Tu Morte?

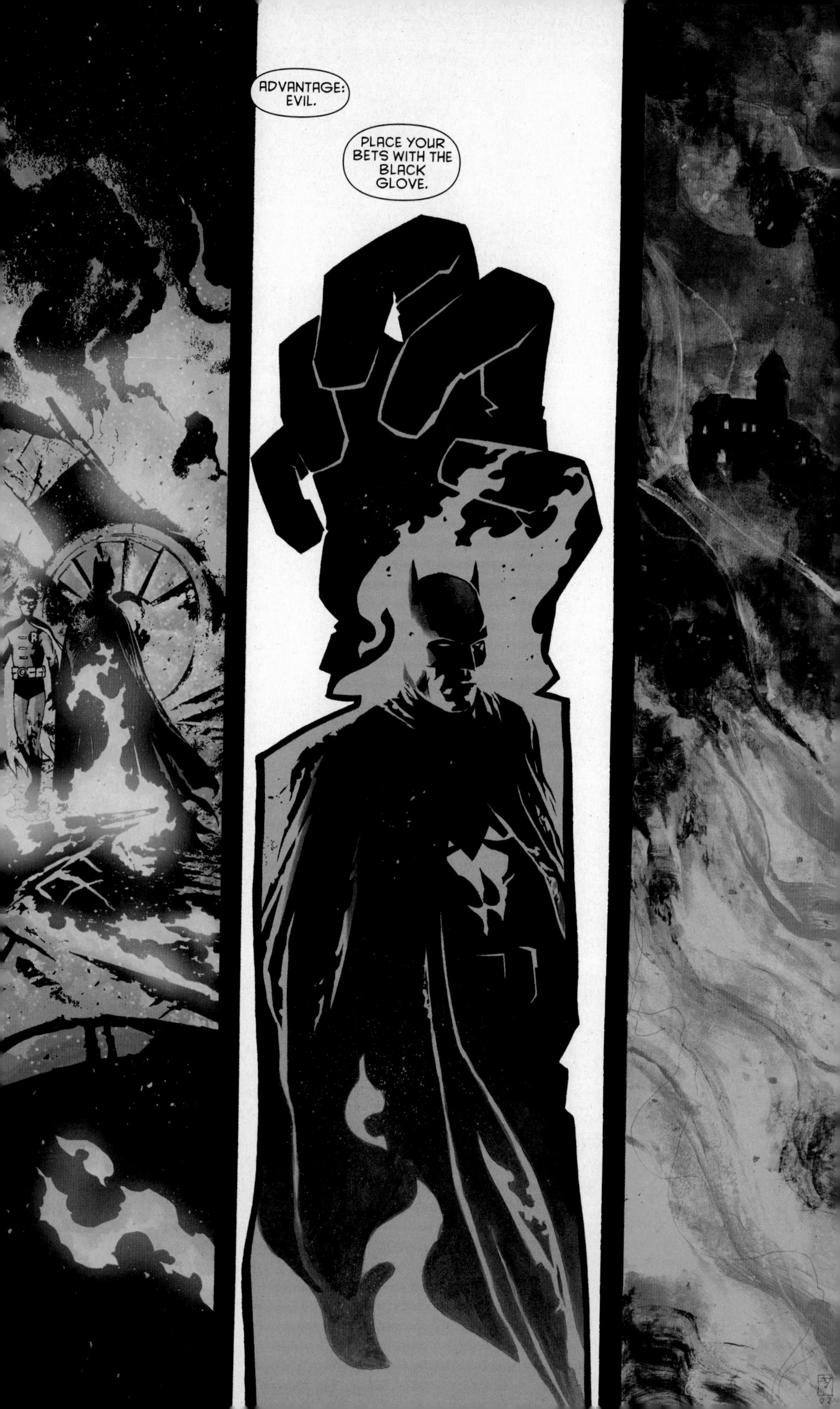
ADVANTAGE: EVIL.
PLACE YOUR BETS WITH THE BLACK GLOVE.

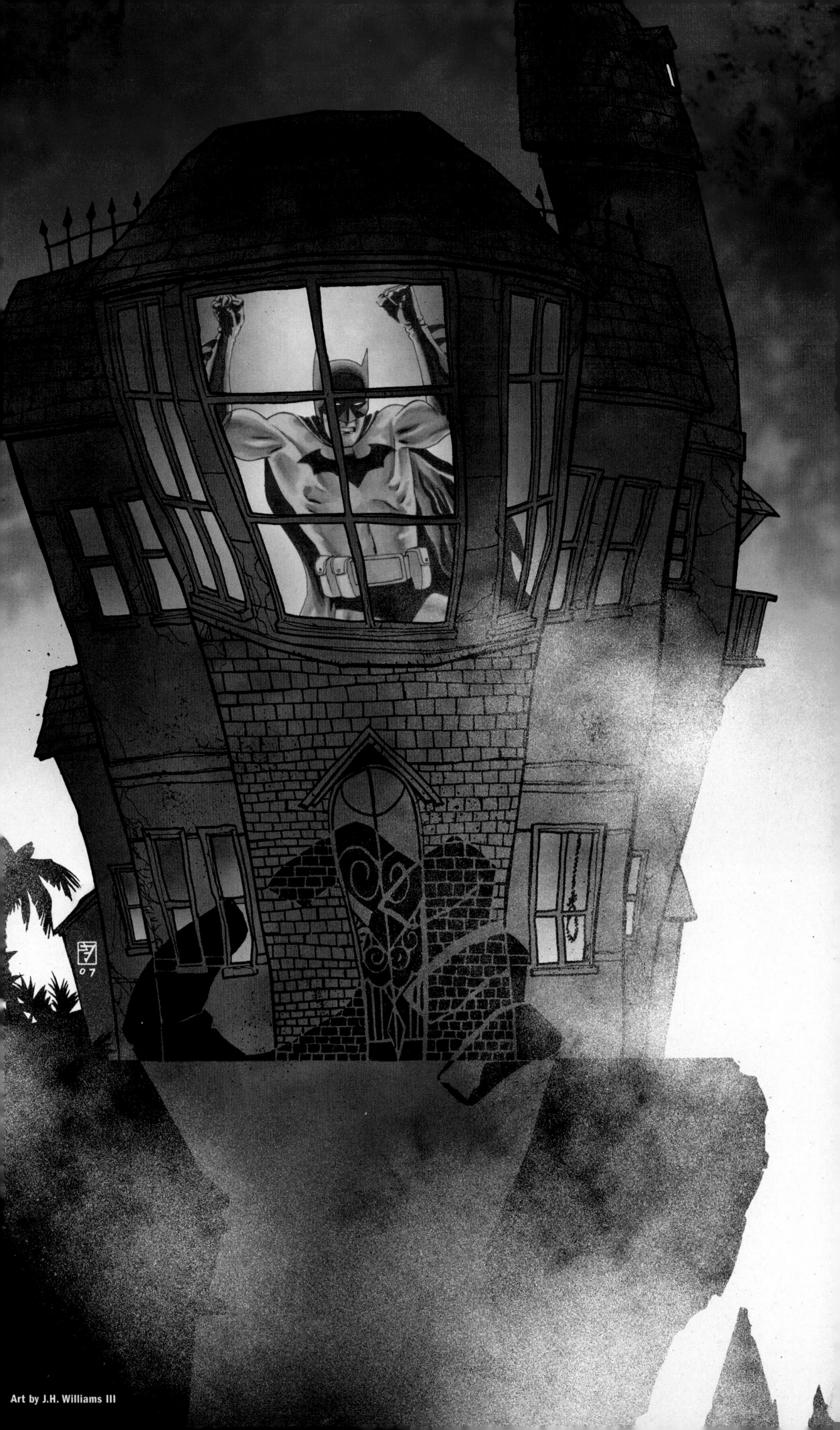

Art by J.H. Williams III

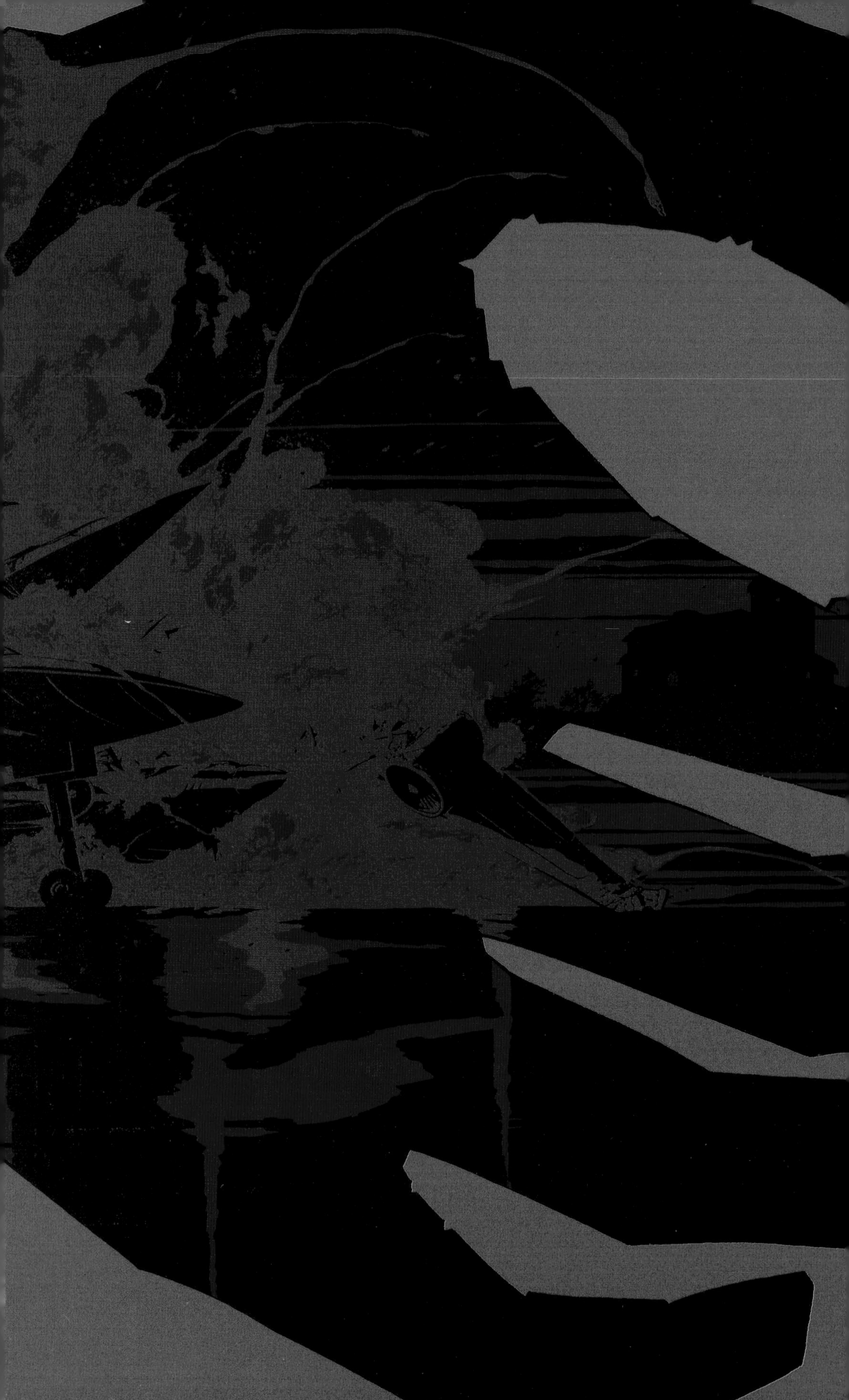

Chapter art by J.H. Williams III

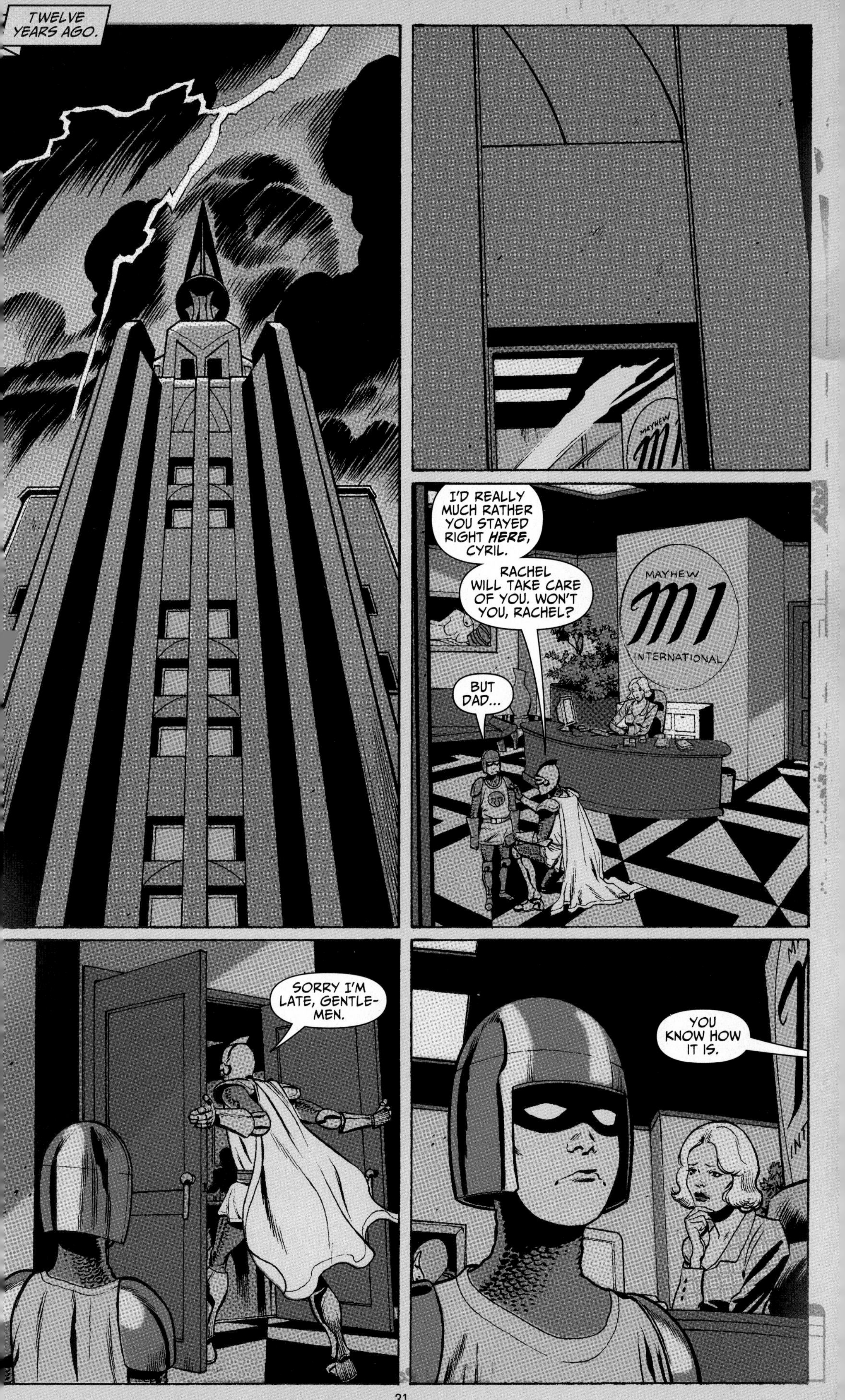
TWELVE YEARS AGO.
MAYHEW
I'D REALLY MUCH RATHER YOU STAYED RIGHT *HERE*, CYRIL.
RACHEL WILL TAKE CARE OF YOU. WON'T YOU, RACHEL?
MAYHEW
INTERNATIONAL
BUT DAD...
SORRY I'M LATE, GENTLE-MEN.
YOU KNOW HOW IT IS.

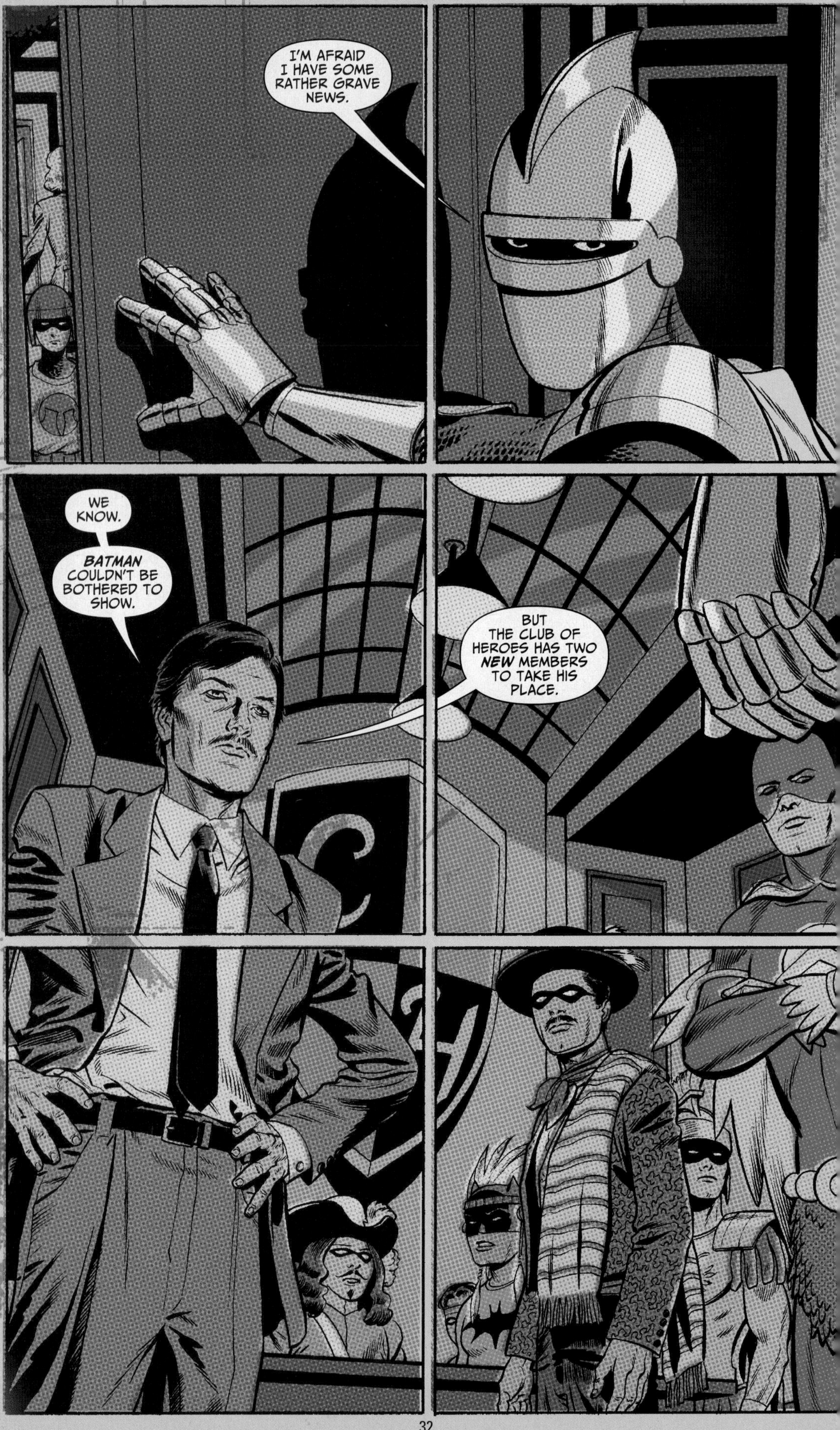
I'M AFRAID I HAVE SOME RATHER GRAVE NEWS.
WE KNOW.
BATMAN COULDN'T BE BOTHERED TO SHOW.
BUT THE CLUB OF HEROES HAS TWO *NEW* MEMBERS TO TAKE HIS PLACE.

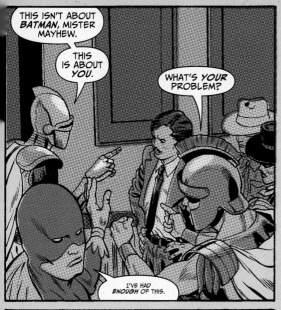

THIS ISN'T ABOUT *BATMAN*, MISTER MAYHEW.

THIS IS ABOUT *YOU*.

WHAT'S *YOUR* PROBLEM?

I'VE HAD *ENOUGH* OF THIS.

WHERE DO YOU THINK *YOU'RE* GOING?

OUT OF MY *WAY*, LEGIONARY!

AH, C'MON FELLAS, WE'RE HERE TO PROMOTE WORLD PEACE AND TRADE *CRIMEFIGHTING* METHODS.

I SAID *MOVE!*

HUTT!

YOU THINK I'M SCARED OF *YOU*, ENGLISH?

AUGHHHH!

DAD?

DAD!

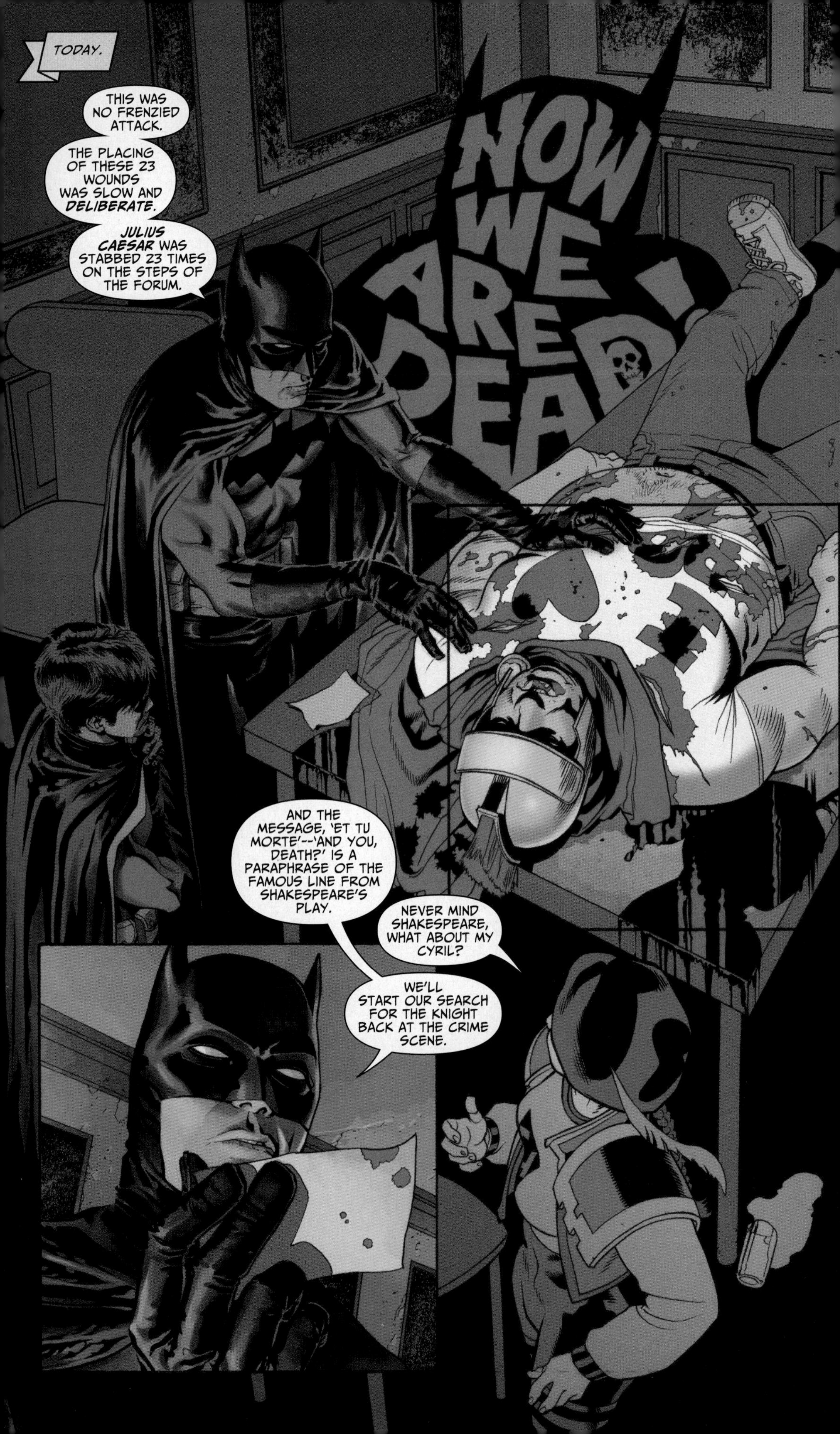
TODAY.
THIS WAS NO FRENZIED ATTACK.
THE PLACING OF THESE 23 WOUNDS WAS SLOW AND DELIBERATE.
JULIUS CAESAR WAS STABBED 23 TIMES ON THE STEPS OF THE FORUM.
NOW WE ARE DEAD
AND THE MESSAGE, 'ET TU MORTE'--'AND YOU, DEATH?' IS A PARAPHRASE OF THE FAMOUS LINE FROM SHAKESPEARE'S PLAY.
NEVER MIND SHAKESPEARE, WHAT ABOUT MY CYRIL?
WE'LL START OUR SEARCH FOR THE KNIGHT BACK AT THE CRIME SCENE.

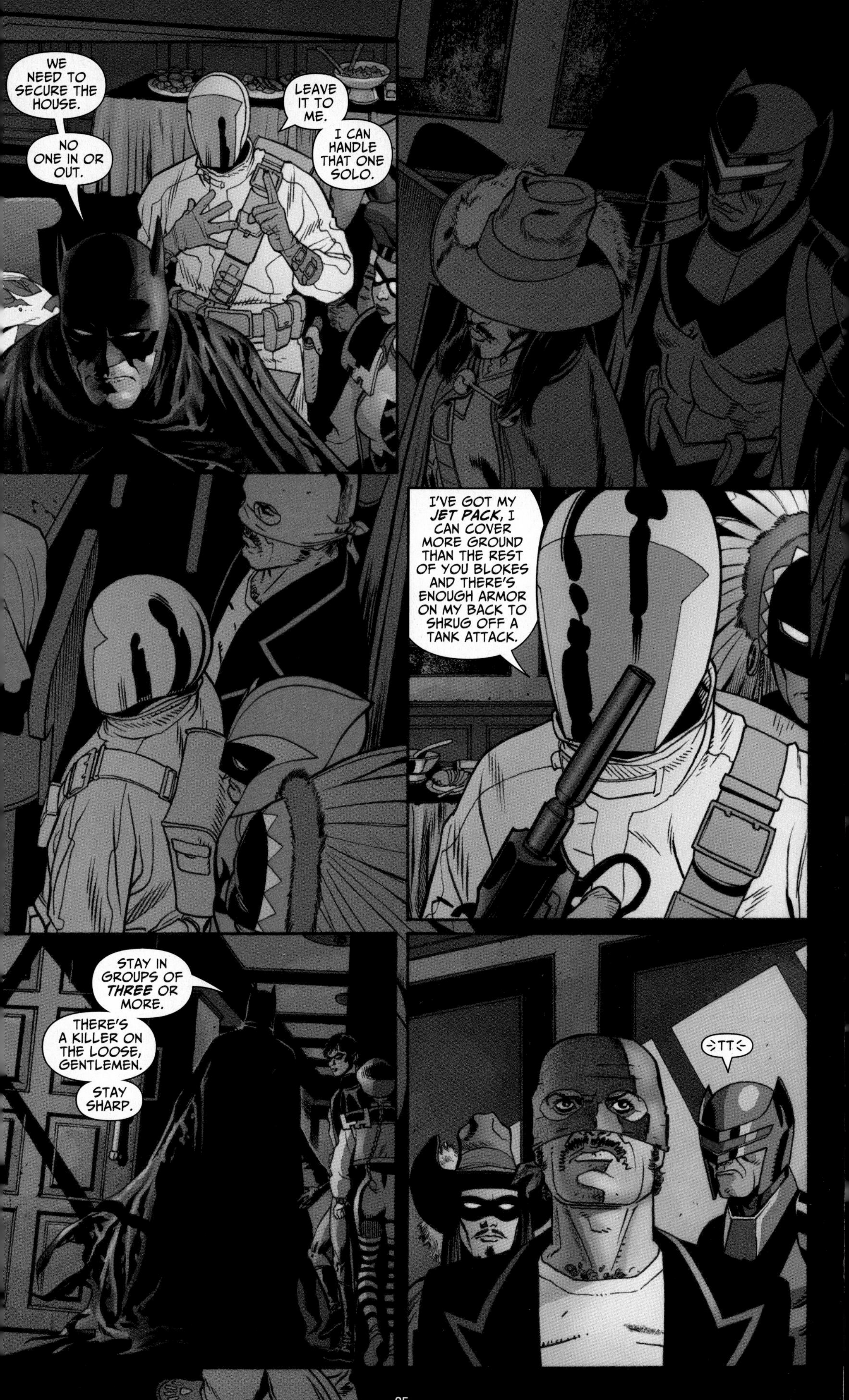
WE NEED TO SECURE THE HOUSE.
NO ONE IN OR OUT.
LEAVE IT TO ME.
I CAN HANDLE THAT ONE SOLO.
I'VE GOT MY JET PACK, I CAN COVER MORE GROUND THAN THE REST OF YOU BLOKES AND THERE'S ENOUGH ARMOR ON MY BACK TO SHRUG OFF A TANK ATTACK.
STAY IN GROUPS OF THREE OR MORE.
THERE'S A KILLER ON THE LOOSE, GENTLEMEN.
STAY SHARP.
TT

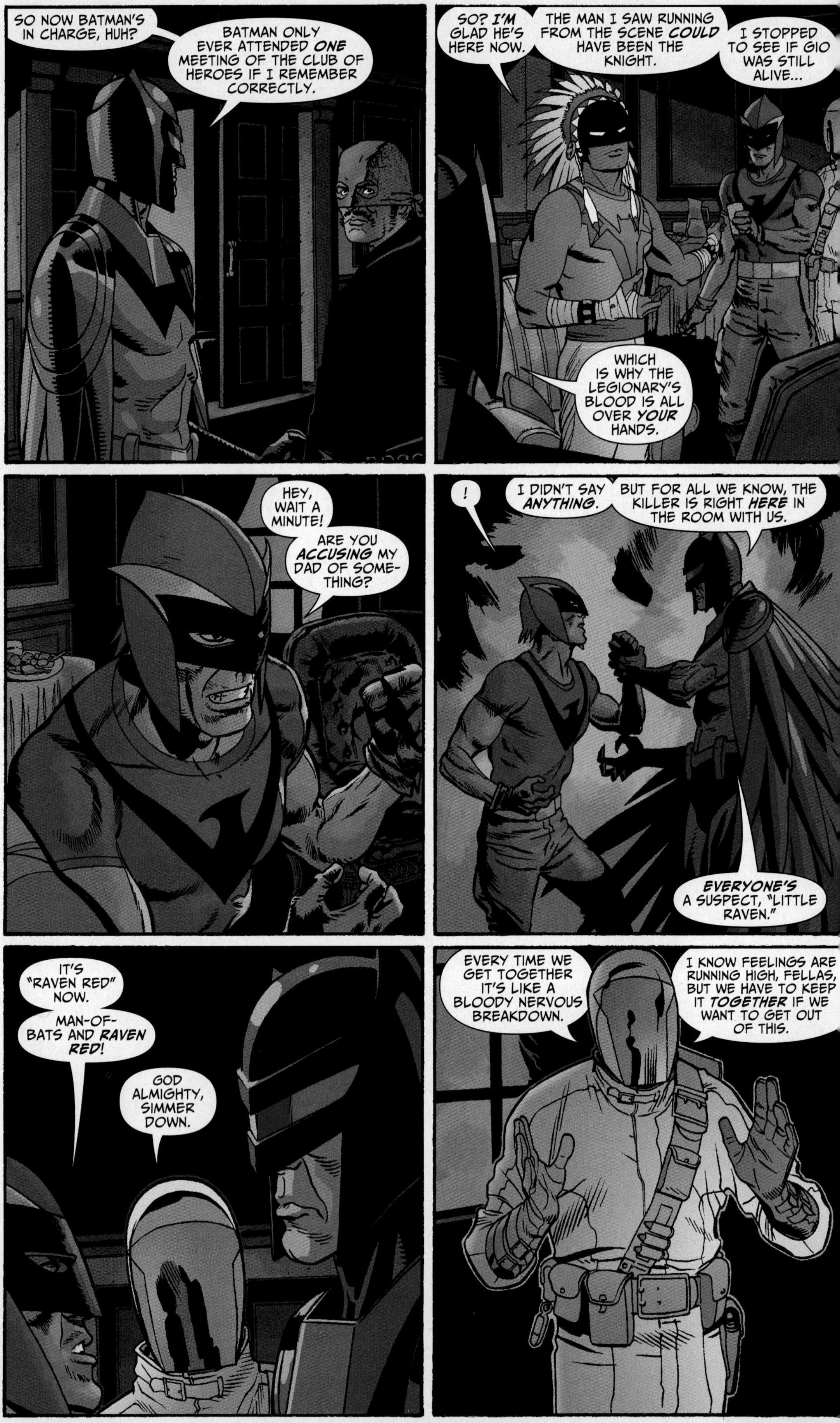
SO NOW BATMAN'S IN CHARGE, HUH?
BATMAN ONLY EVER ATTENDED *ONE* MEETING OF THE CLUB OF HEROES IF I REMEMBER CORRECTLY.
SO? *I'M* GLAD HE'S HERE NOW.
THE MAN I SAW RUNNING FROM THE SCENE *COULD* HAVE BEEN THE KNIGHT.
I STOPPED TO SEE IF GIO WAS STILL ALIVE...
WHICH IS WHY THE LEGIONARY'S BLOOD IS ALL OVER *YOUR* HANDS.
HEY, WAIT A MINUTE!
ARE YOU *ACCUSING* MY DAD OF SOME-THING?
!
I DIDN'T SAY *ANYTHING*.
BUT FOR ALL WE KNOW, THE KILLER IS RIGHT *HERE* IN THE ROOM WITH US.
EVERYONE'S A SUSPECT, "LITTLE RAVEN."
IT'S "RAVEN RED" NOW.
MAN-OF-BATS AND *RAVEN RED*!
GOD ALMIGHTY, SIMMER DOWN.
EVERY TIME WE GET TOGETHER IT'S LIKE A BLOODY NERVOUS BREAKDOWN.
I KNOW FEELINGS ARE RUNNING HIGH, FELLAS, BUT WE HAVE TO KEEP IT *TOGETHER* IF WE WANT TO GET OUT OF THIS.

NOM DE--!

I WAS STARTING TO *ENJOY* MY LIFE FOR THE FIRST TIME AFTER THOSE YEARS IN PRISON...

...NOW I'M TRAPPED ON AN *ISLAND* IN THE MIDDLE OF A TROPICAL STORM, BY A *MADMAN* WHO HAS KILLED AND *SKINNED* OUR HOST.

THE MADMAN COULD BE *ONE* OF US.

THEY SAY THE *KNIGHT'S* A RECOVERING DRUG ADDICT.

I HEARD ON HIS LAST CASE HE WAS MIND-CONTROLLED BY A *GORILLA!*

CYRIL'S AWAYS BEEN A GOOD KID. YOU'D BETTER PRAY NOTHING'S HAPPENED TO HIM OR WE'RE DOWN ONE FIGHTER I WOULD RATHER HAVE AT MY SIDE.

ANYWAY, WHAT'S SO *FUNNY?*

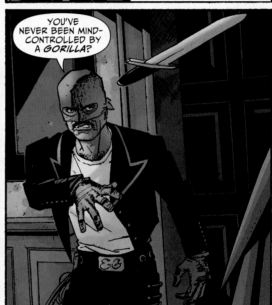

YOU'VE NEVER BEEN MIND-CONTROLLED BY A *GORILLA?*

THOK

NOT REALLY.

WE KNOW HE HAD THE *MOTIVE.*

YOU SAW IT.

WE *ALL* SAW WHAT HAPPENED THAT DAY.

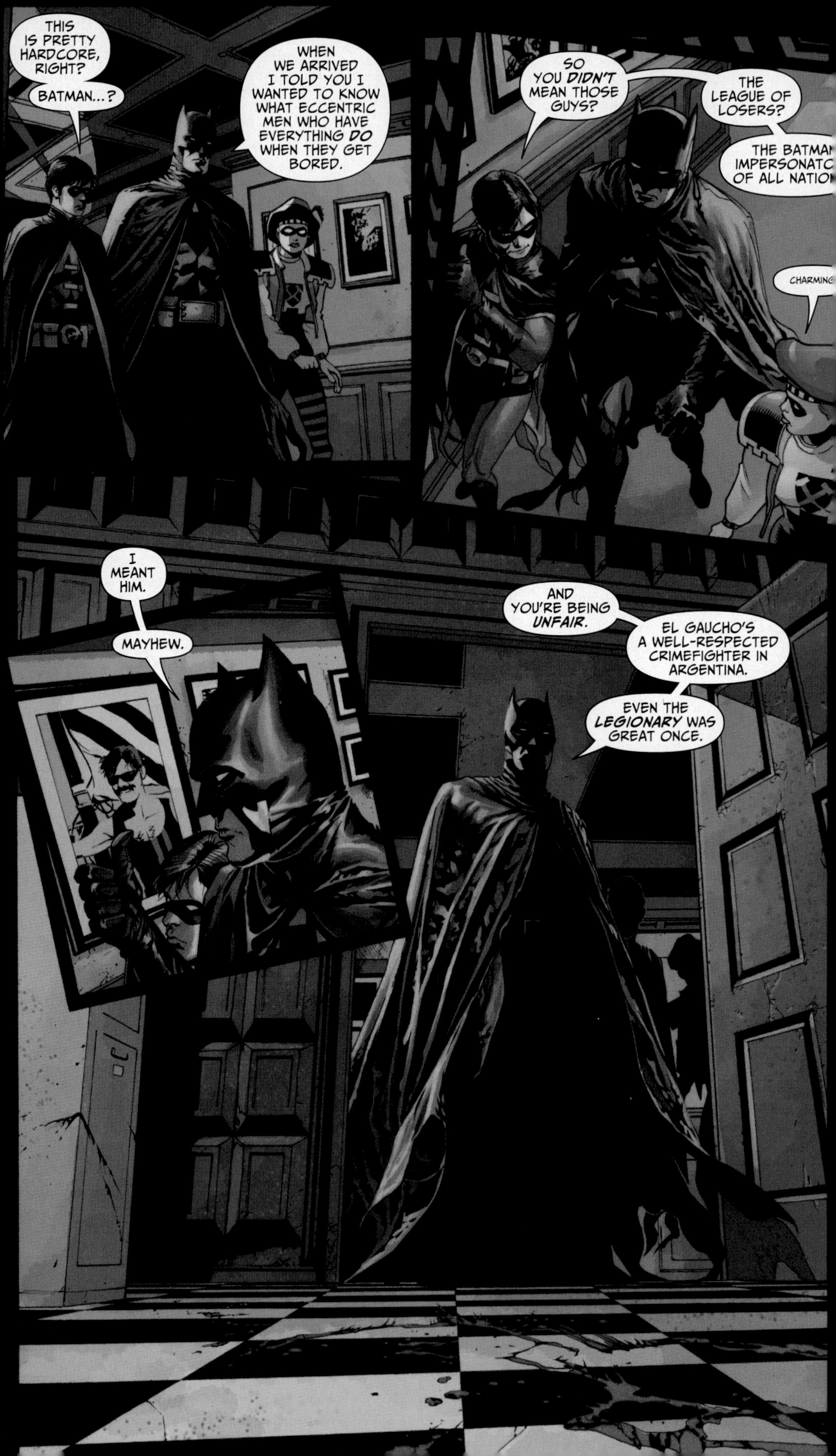
THIS IS PRETTY HARDCORE, RIGHT?
BATMAN...?
WHEN WE ARRIVED I TOLD YOU I WANTED TO KNOW WHAT ECCENTRIC MEN WHO HAVE EVERYTHING DO WHEN THEY GET BORED.
SO YOU DIDN'T MEAN THOSE GUYS?
THE LEAGUE OF LOSERS?
THE BATMAN IMPERSONATO OF ALL NATIO
CHARMING
I MEANT HIM.
MAYHEW.
AND YOU'RE BEING UNFAIR.
EL GAUCHO'S A WELL-RESPECTED CRIMEFIGHTER IN ARGENTINA.
EVEN THE LEGIONARY WAS GREAT ONCE.

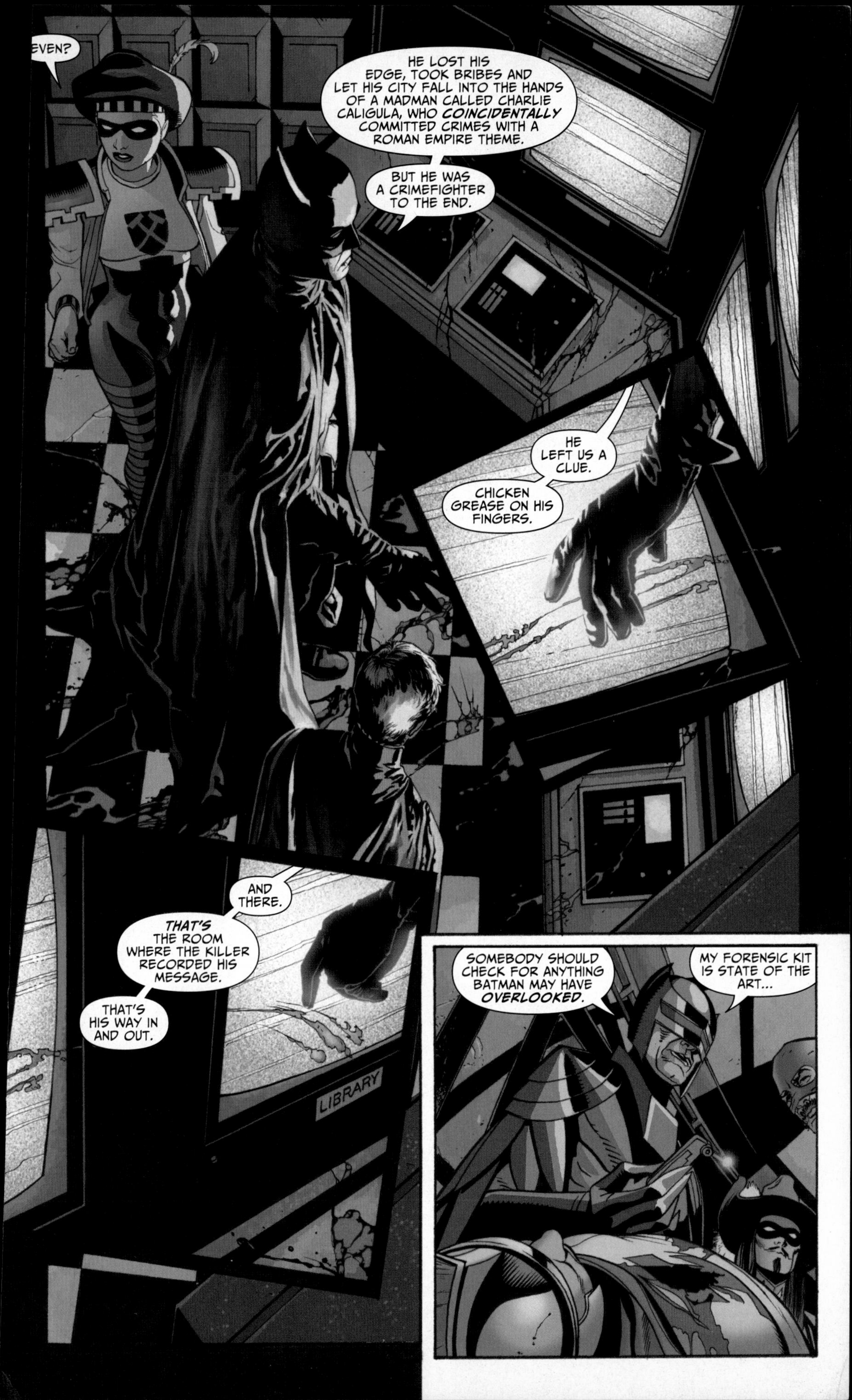
EVEN?
HE LOST HIS EDGE, TOOK BRIBES AND LET HIS CITY FALL INTO THE HANDS OF A MADMAN CALLED CHARLIE CALIGULA, WHO COINCIDENTALLY COMMITTED CRIMES WITH A ROMAN EMPIRE THEME.
BUT HE WAS A CRIMEFIGHTER TO THE END.
HE LEFT US A CLUE.
CHICKEN GREASE ON HIS FINGERS.
AND THERE.
THAT'S THE ROOM WHERE THE KILLER RECORDED HIS MESSAGE.
THAT'S HIS WAY IN AND OUT.
LIBRARY
SOMEBODY SHOULD CHECK FOR ANYTHING BATMAN MAY HAVE OVERLOOKED.
MY FORENSIC KIT IS STATE OF THE ART...

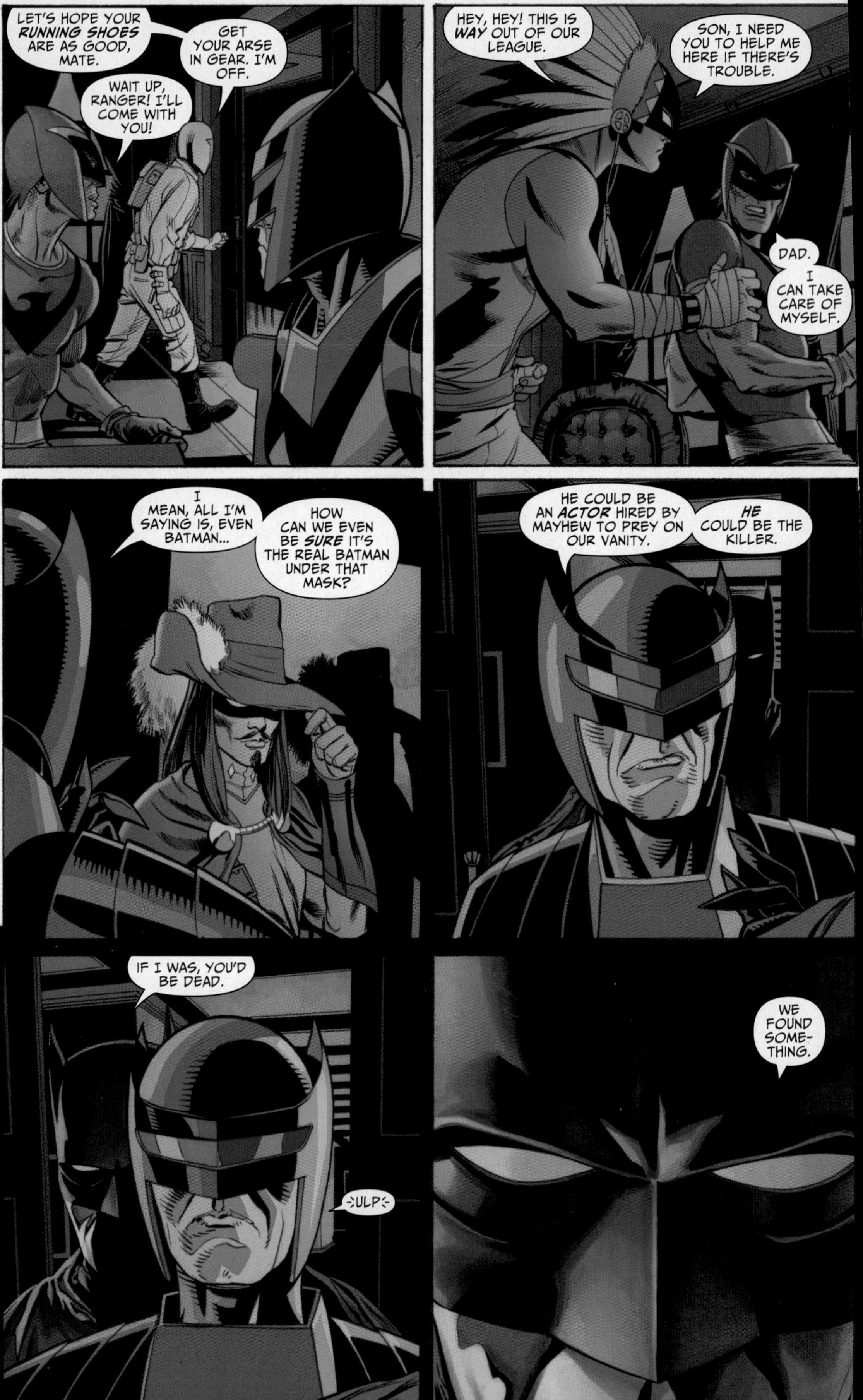
LET'S HOPE YOUR RUNNING SHOES ARE AS GOOD, MATE.
GET YOUR ARSE IN GEAR. I'M OFF.
WAIT UP, RANGER! I'LL COME WITH YOU!
HEY, HEY! THIS IS WAY OUT OF OUR LEAGUE.
SON, I NEED YOU TO HELP ME HERE IF THERE'S TROUBLE.
DAD.
I CAN TAKE CARE OF MYSELF.
I MEAN, ALL I'M SAYING IS, EVEN BATMAN...
HOW CAN WE EVEN BE SURE IT'S THE REAL BATMAN UNDER THAT MASK?
HE COULD BE AN ACTOR HIRED BY MAYHEW TO PREY ON OUR VANITY.
HE COULD BE THE KILLER.
IF I WAS, YOU'D BE DEAD.
ULP
WE FOUND SOME-THING.

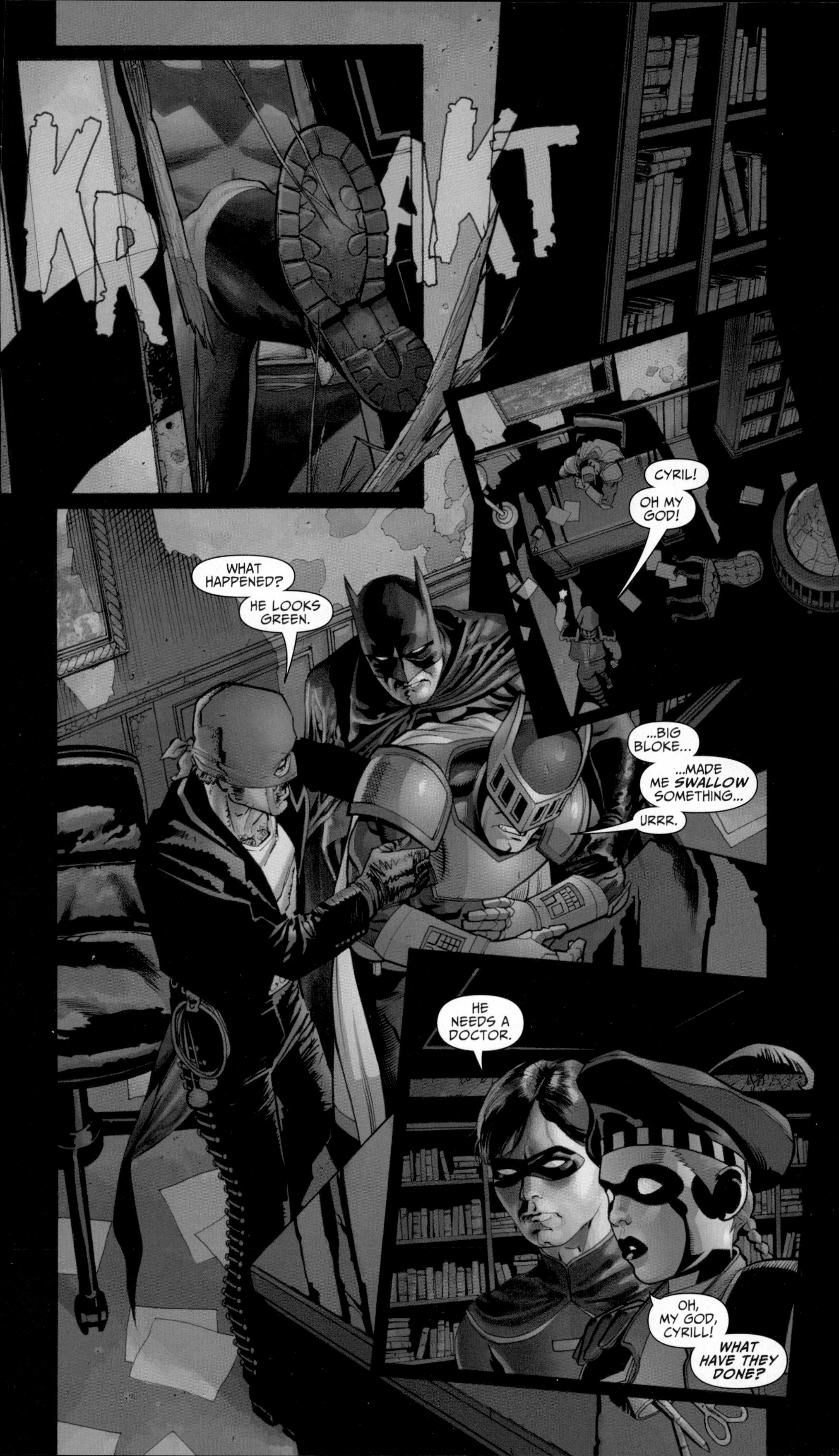
KRAKT
CYRIL!
OH MY GOD!
WHAT HAPPENED?
HE LOOKS GREEN.
...BIG BLOKE...
...MADE ME SWALLOW SOMETHING...
URRR.
HE NEEDS A DOCTOR.
OH, MY GOD, CYRILL!
WHAT HAVE THEY DONE?

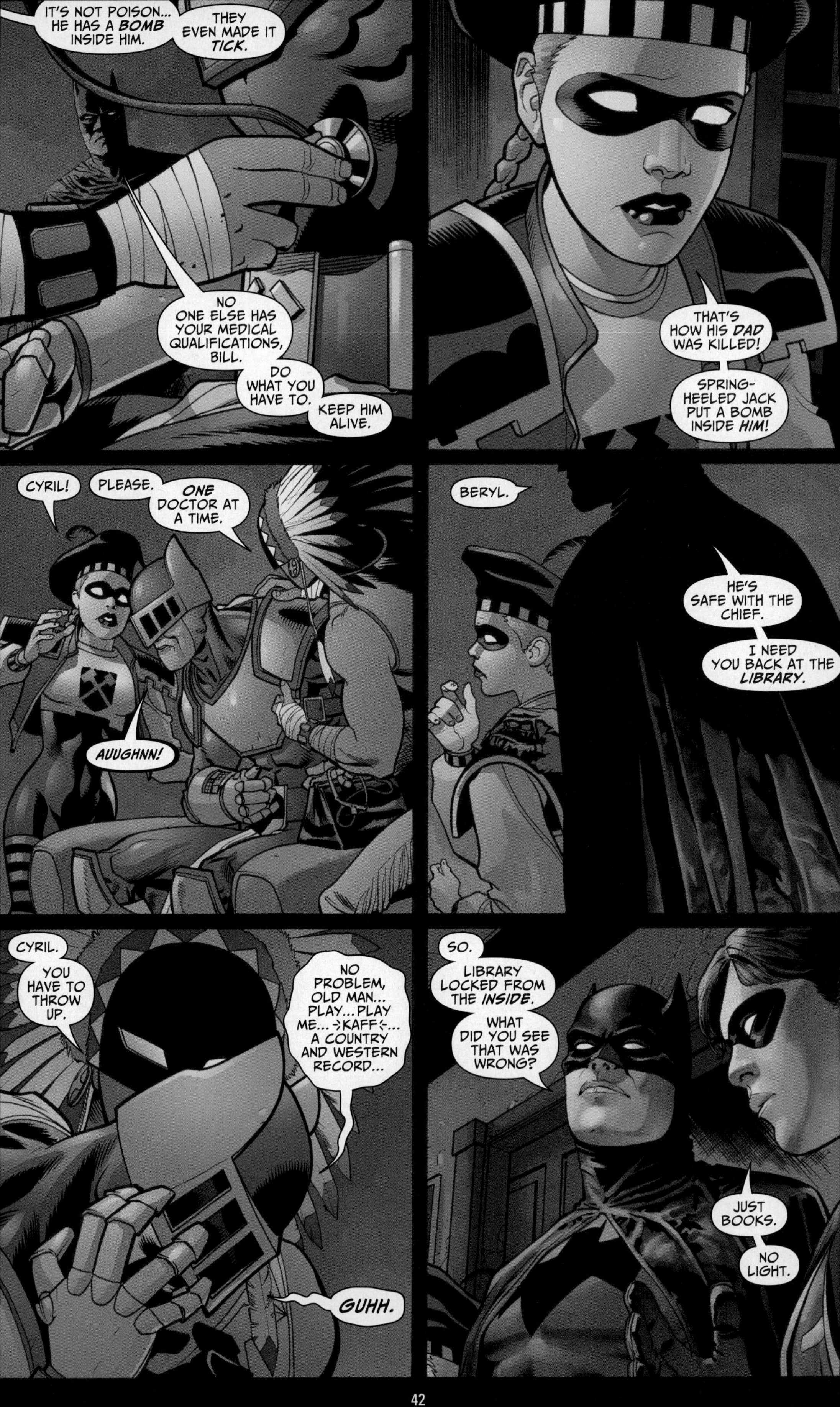
IT'S NOT POISON... HE HAS A BOMB INSIDE HIM.
THEY EVEN MADE IT TICK.
NO ONE ELSE HAS YOUR MEDICAL QUALIFICATIONS, BILL.
DO WHAT YOU HAVE TO.
KEEP HIM ALIVE.
THAT'S HOW HIS DAD WAS KILLED!
SPRING-HEELED JACK PUT A BOMB INSIDE HIM!
CYRIL!
PLEASE. ONE DOCTOR AT A TIME.
AUUGHNN!
BERYL.
HE'S SAFE WITH THE CHIEF.
I NEED YOU BACK AT THE LIBRARY.
CYRIL.
YOU HAVE TO THROW UP.
NO PROBLEM, OLD MAN... PLAY...PLAY ME... KAFF... A COUNTRY AND WESTERN RECORD...
GUHH.
SO.
LIBRARY LOCKED FROM THE INSIDE.
WHAT DID YOU SEE THAT WAS WRONG?
JUST BOOKS.
NO LIGHT.

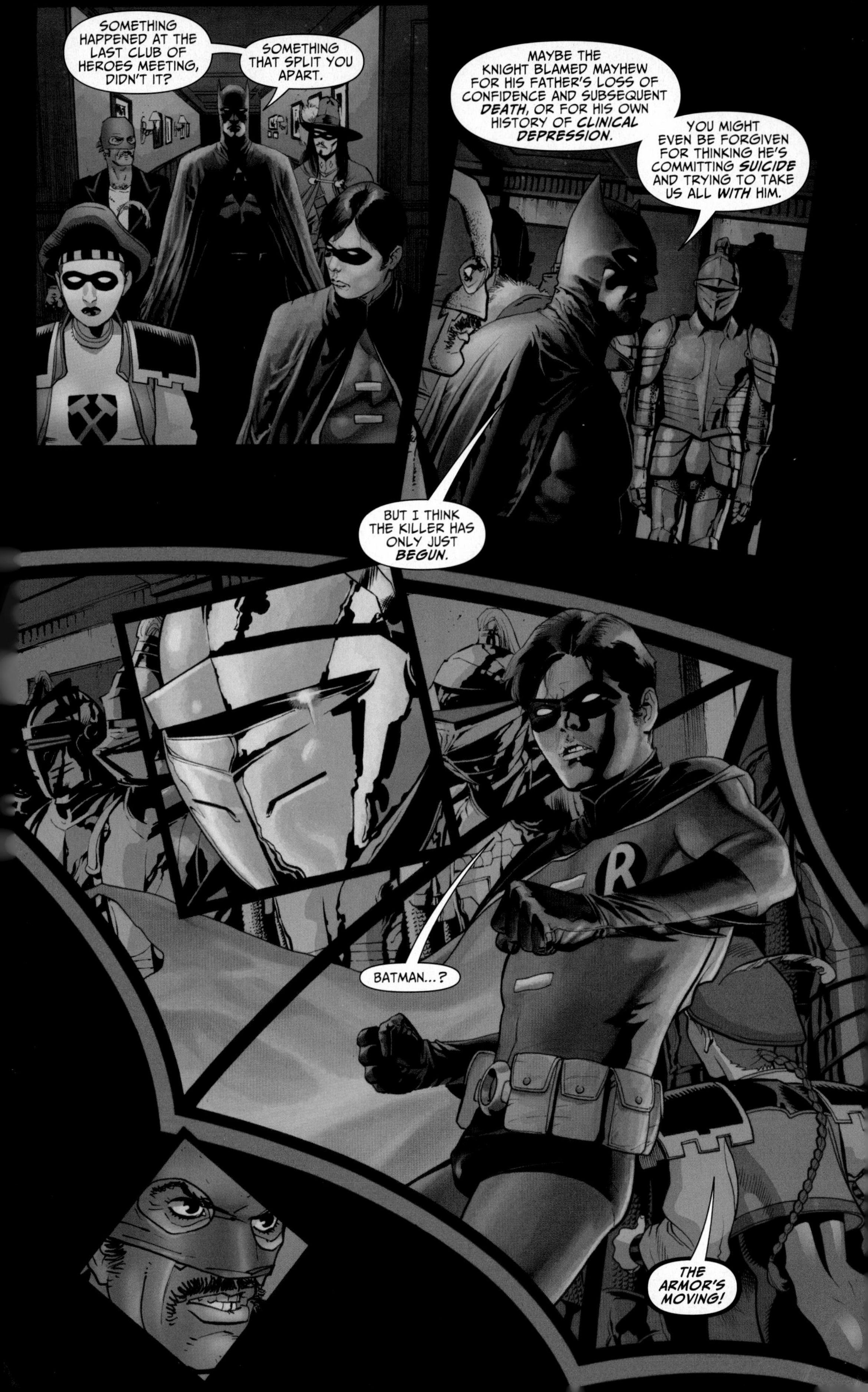
SOMETHING HAPPENED AT THE LAST CLUB OF HEROES MEETING, DIDN'T IT?
SOMETHING THAT SPLIT YOU APART.
MAYBE THE KNIGHT BLAMED MAYHEW FOR HIS FATHER'S LOSS OF CONFIDENCE AND SUBSEQUENT DEATH, OR FOR HIS OWN HISTORY OF CLINICAL DEPRESSION.
YOU MIGHT EVEN BE FORGIVEN FOR THINKING HE'S COMMITTING SUICIDE AND TRYING TO TAKE US ALL WITH HIM.
BUT I THINK THE KILLER HAS ONLY JUST BEGUN.
BATMAN...?
THE ARMOR'S MOVING!

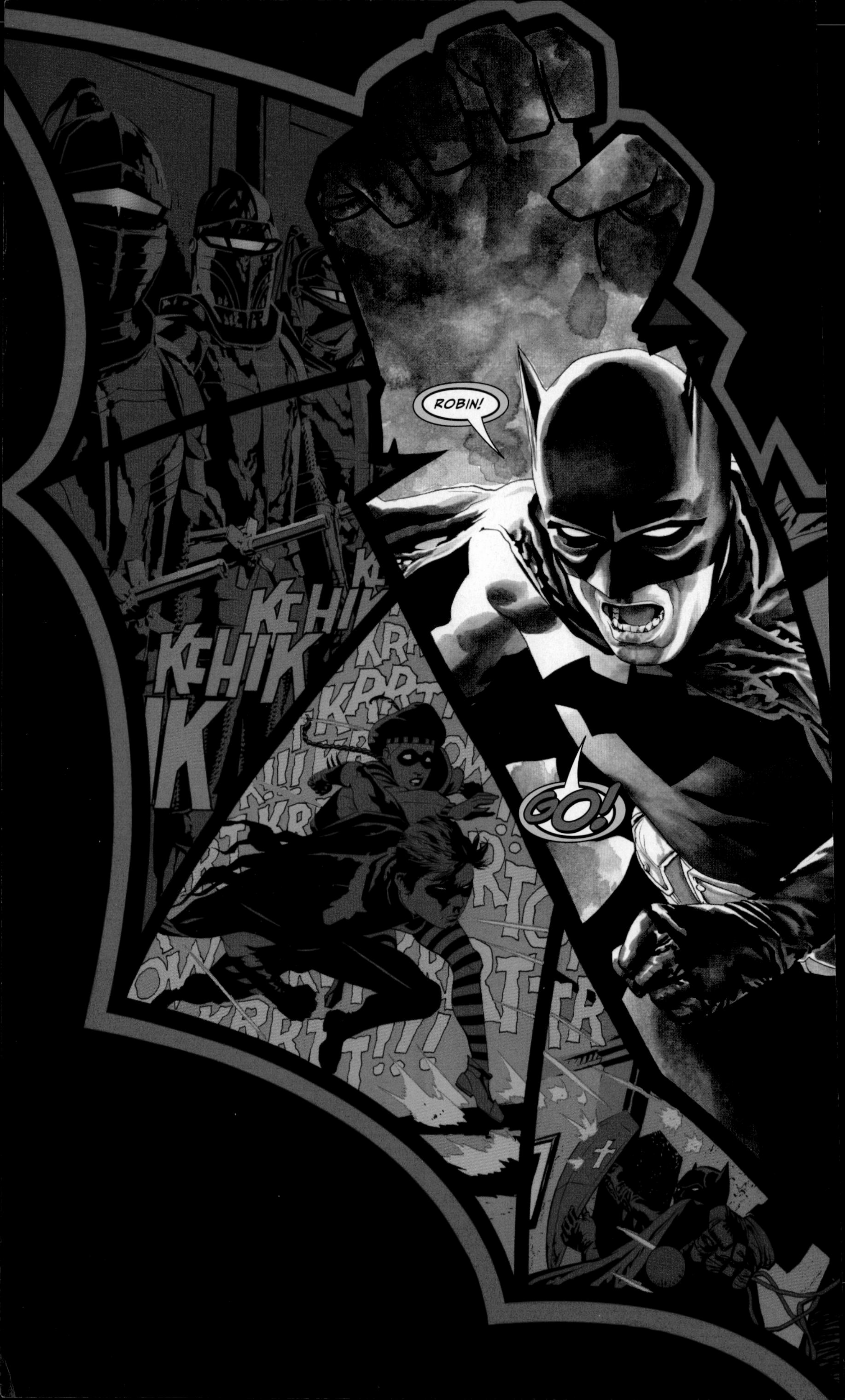
ROBIN!
GO!

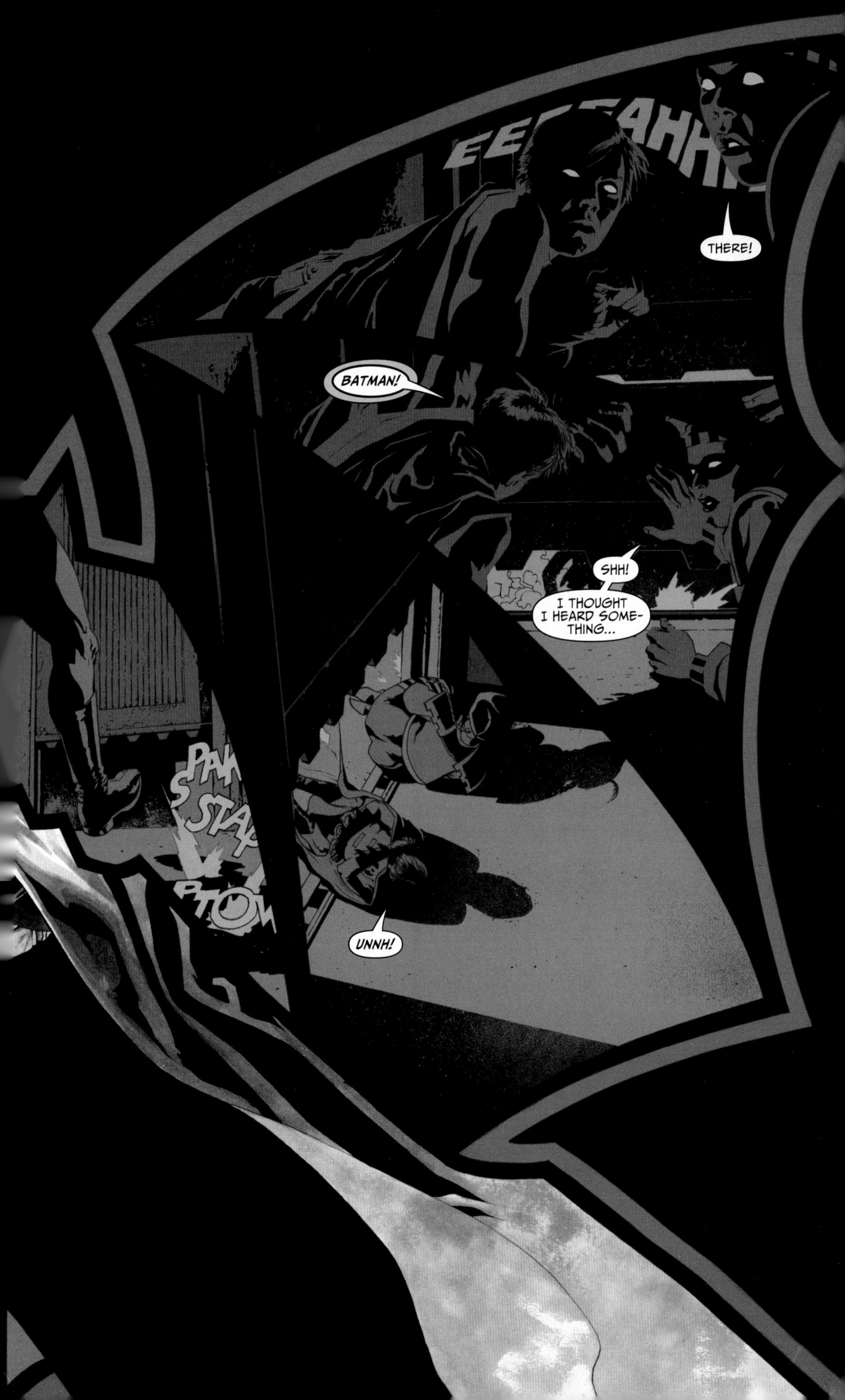
THERE!
BATMAN!
SHH!
I THOUGHT I HEARD SOME-THING...
UNNH!

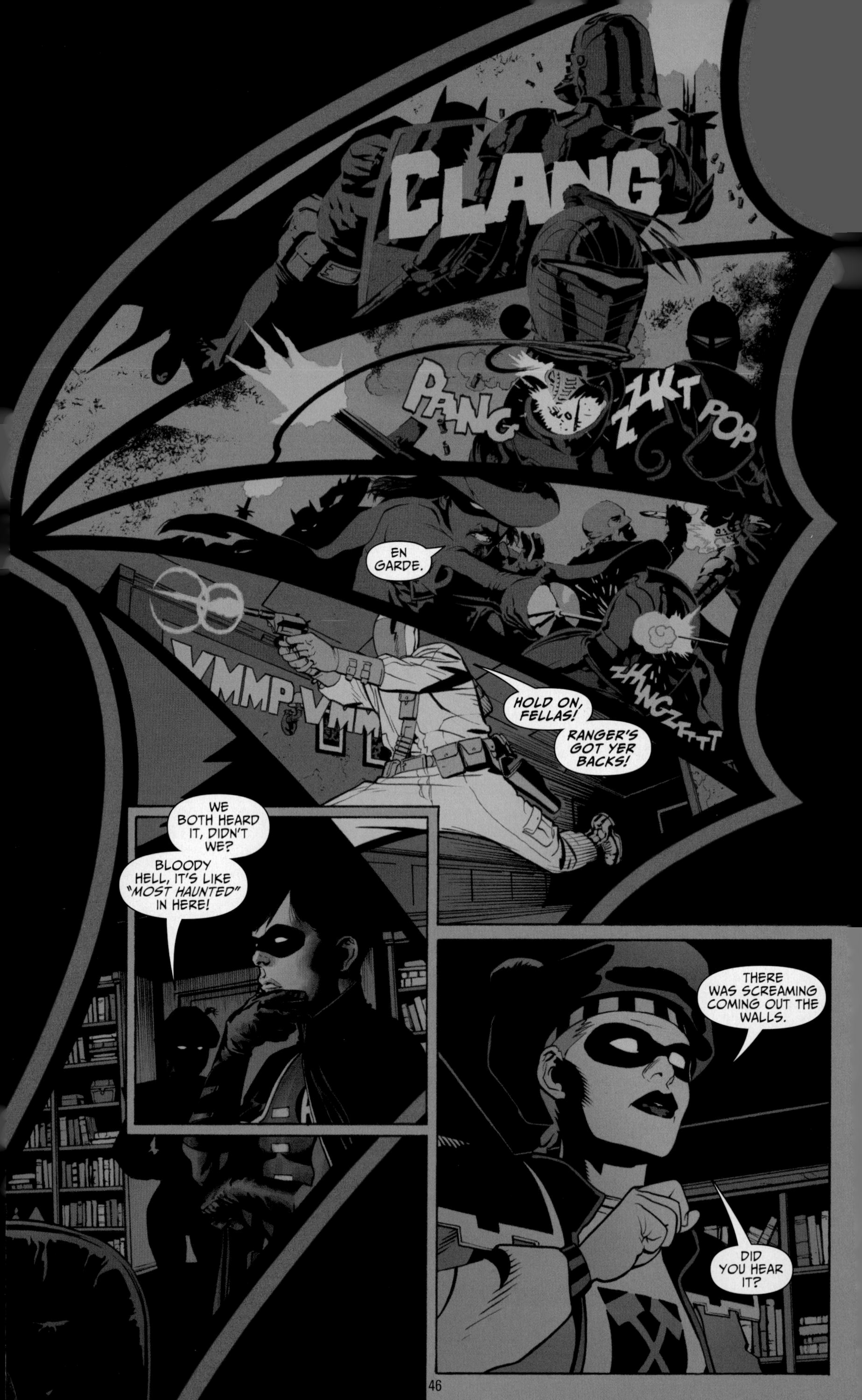
CLANG
PANG
ZZKT
POP
EN GARDE.
VMMP-VMM
ZHNGZKTTT
HOLD ON, FELLAS!
RANGER'S GOT YER BACKS!
WE BOTH HEARD IT, DIDN'T WE?
BLOODY HELL, IT'S LIKE *"MOST HAUNTED"* IN HERE!
THERE WAS SCREAMING COMING OUT THE WALLS.
DID YOU HEAR IT?

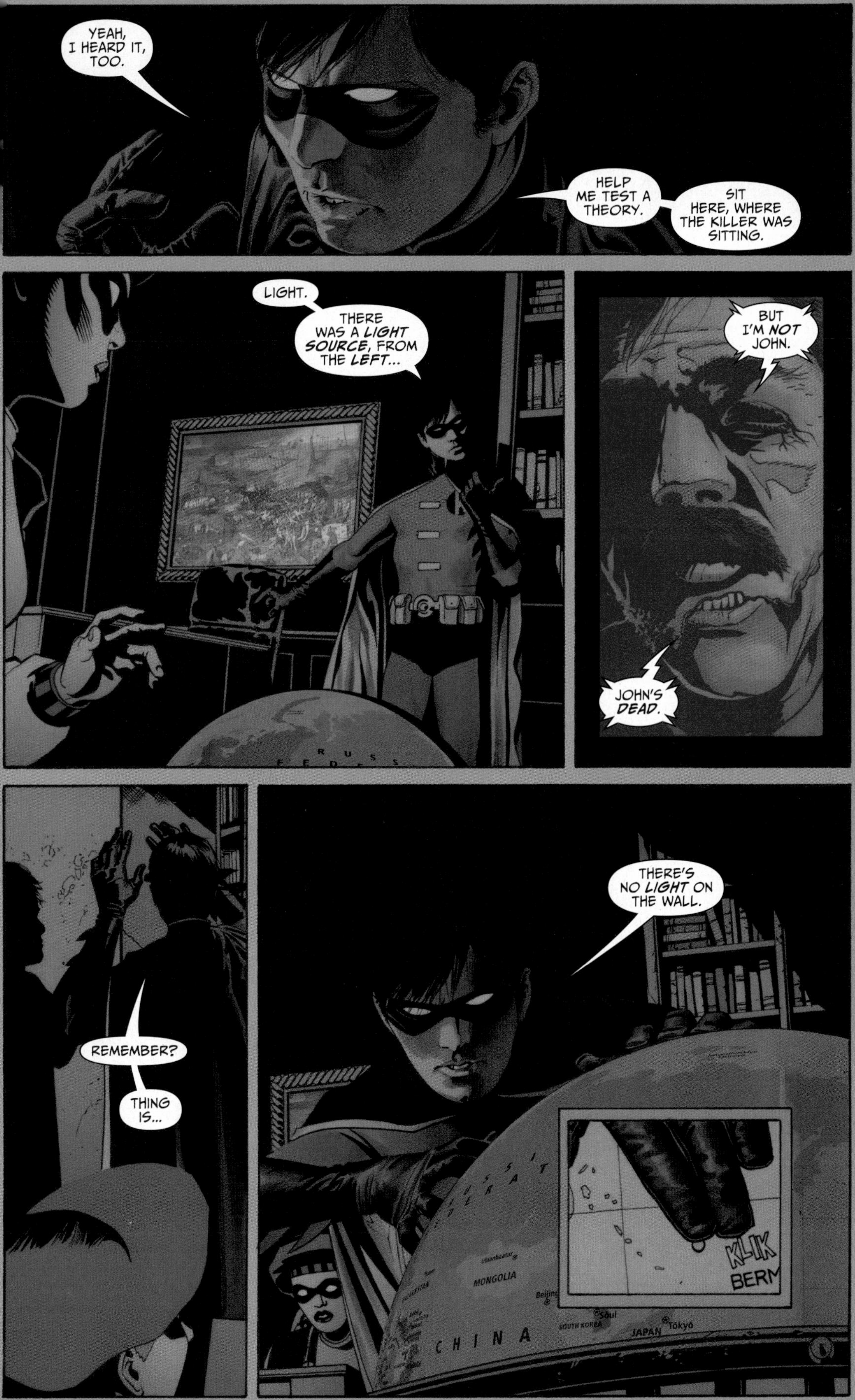

YEAH, I HEARD IT, TOO.
HELP ME TEST A THEORY.
SIT HERE, WHERE THE KILLER WAS SITTING.
LIGHT.
THERE WAS A LIGHT SOURCE, FROM THE LEFT...
BUT I'M NOT JOHN.
JOHN'S DEAD.
REMEMBER?
THING IS...
THERE'S NO LIGHT ON THE WALL.
MONGOLIA
CHINA
SOUTH KOREA
JAPAN
KLIK
BERM

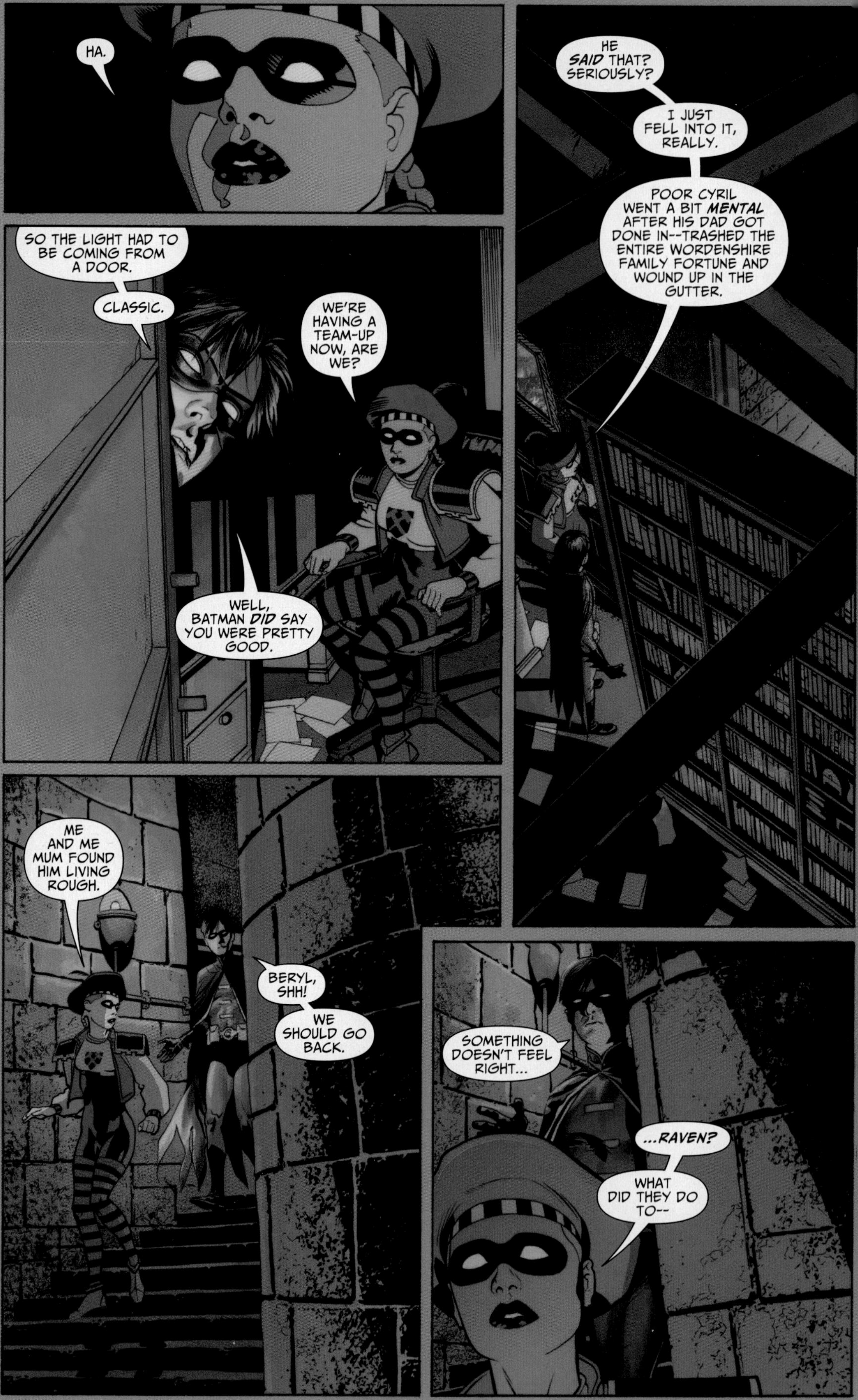
HA.
HE SAID THAT? SERIOUSLY?
I JUST FELL INTO IT, REALLY.
POOR CYRIL WENT A BIT MENTAL AFTER HIS DAD GOT DONE IN--TRASHED THE ENTIRE WORDENSHIRE FAMILY FORTUNE AND WOUND UP IN THE GUTTER.
SO THE LIGHT HAD TO BE COMING FROM A DOOR.
CLASSIC.
WE'RE HAVING A TEAM-UP NOW, ARE WE?
WELL, BATMAN DID SAY YOU WERE PRETTY GOOD.
ME AND ME MUM FOUND HIM LIVING ROUGH.
BERYL, SHH!
WE SHOULD GO BACK.
SOMETHING DOESN'T FEEL RIGHT...
...RAVEN?
WHAT DID THEY DO TO--

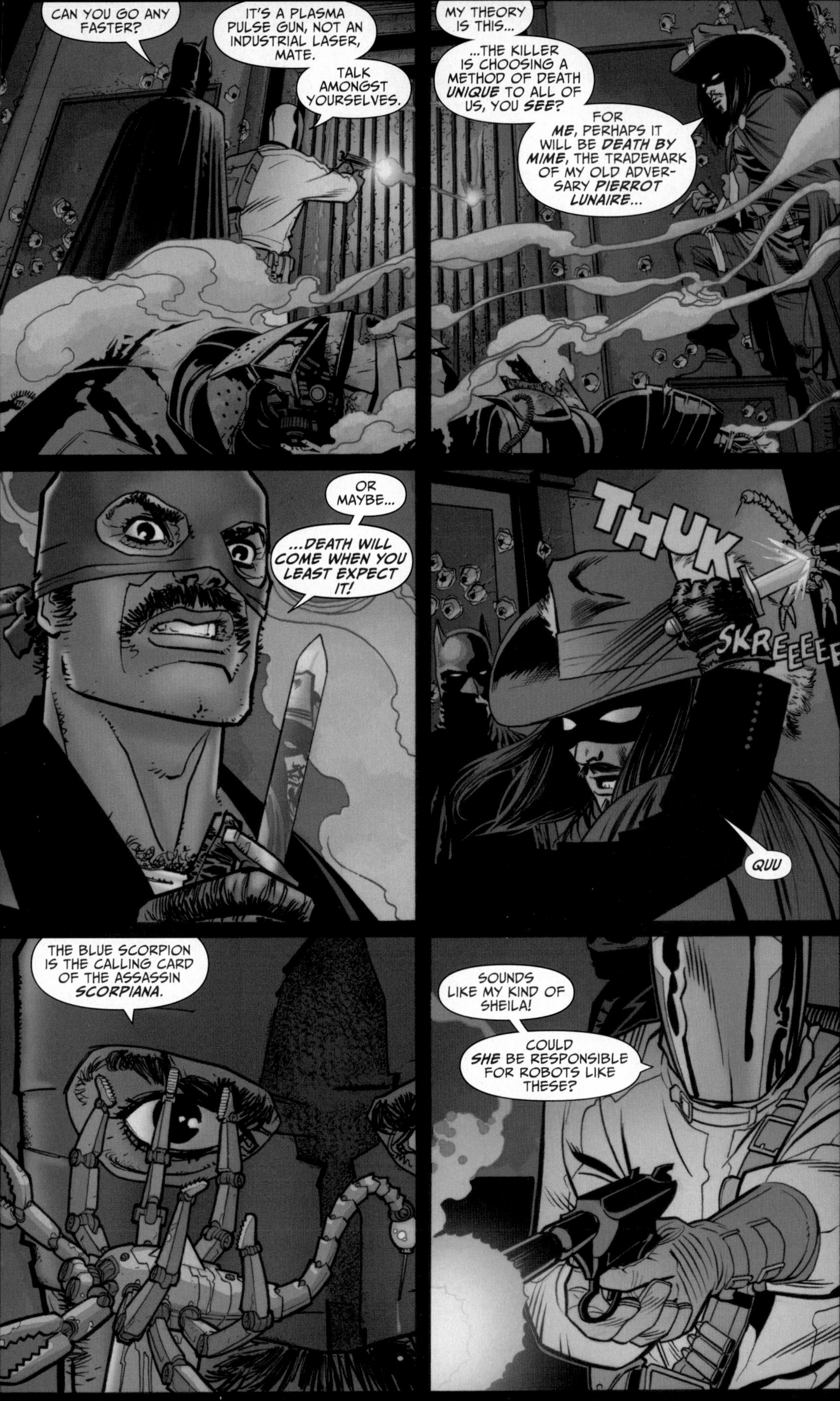
CAN YOU GO ANY FASTER?
IT'S A PLASMA PULSE GUN, NOT AN INDUSTRIAL LASER, MATE.
TALK AMONGST YOURSELVES.
MY THEORY IS THIS...
...THE KILLER IS CHOOSING A METHOD OF DEATH UNIQUE TO ALL OF US, YOU SEE?
FOR ME, PERHAPS IT WILL BE DEATH BY MIME, THE TRADEMARK OF MY OLD ADVER-SARY PIERROT LUNAIRE...
OR MAYBE...
...DEATH WILL COME WHEN YOU LEAST EXPECT IT!
THUK
SKREEEEE
QUU
THE BLUE SCORPION IS THE CALLING CARD OF THE ASSASSIN SCORPIANA.
SOUNDS LIKE MY KIND OF SHEILA!
COULD SHE BE RESPONSIBLE FOR ROBOTS LIKE THESE?

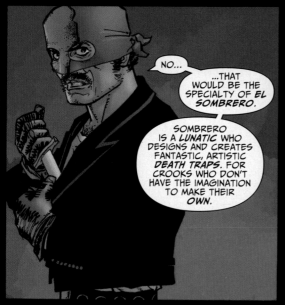

NO... ...THAT WOULD BE THE SPECIALTY OF *EL SOMBRERO.*

SOMBRERO IS A *LUNATIC* WHO DESIGNS AND CREATES FANTASTIC, ARTISTIC *DEATH TRAPS.* FOR CROOKS WHO DON'T HAVE THE IMAGINATION TO MAKE THEIR *OWN.*

YOU THINK HE COULD BUILD A DEATH TRAP AS BIG AS THIS *HOUSE?*

ALL HE NEEDS IS *MONEY* AND *TIME.*

THIS WHOLE *ISLAND* COULD BE HIS WORK.

YOU KNOW WHAT HAPPENED THAT DAY, BATMAN?

SOME MEN WHO LIKED TO FIGHT HAD A *FIGHT.* PAHFF!

JOHN MAYHEW'S "CLUB OF HEROES" WAS EXPOSED AS A SHAM.

AND SOMETHING THAT MIGHT HAVE LED TO GLOBAL MEDIA *EXPOSURE,* MAYBE EVEN *JUSTICE LEAGUE* STATUS, LED NOWHERE.

WE HAVE TO WONDER WHO HAD THE MOST TO LOSE WHEN THE CLUB OF HEROES WENT DOWN.

YOU STILL THINK *ONE MAN* IS DOING THIS?

MAYHEW *FAILED* WITH HIS CLUB OF *HEROES.* WHO CAN SAY...?

MAYBE HE THOUGHT HE COULD SUCCEED WITH A CLUB OF VILLAINS?

MOTHER OF GOD.

WINGMAN!

50

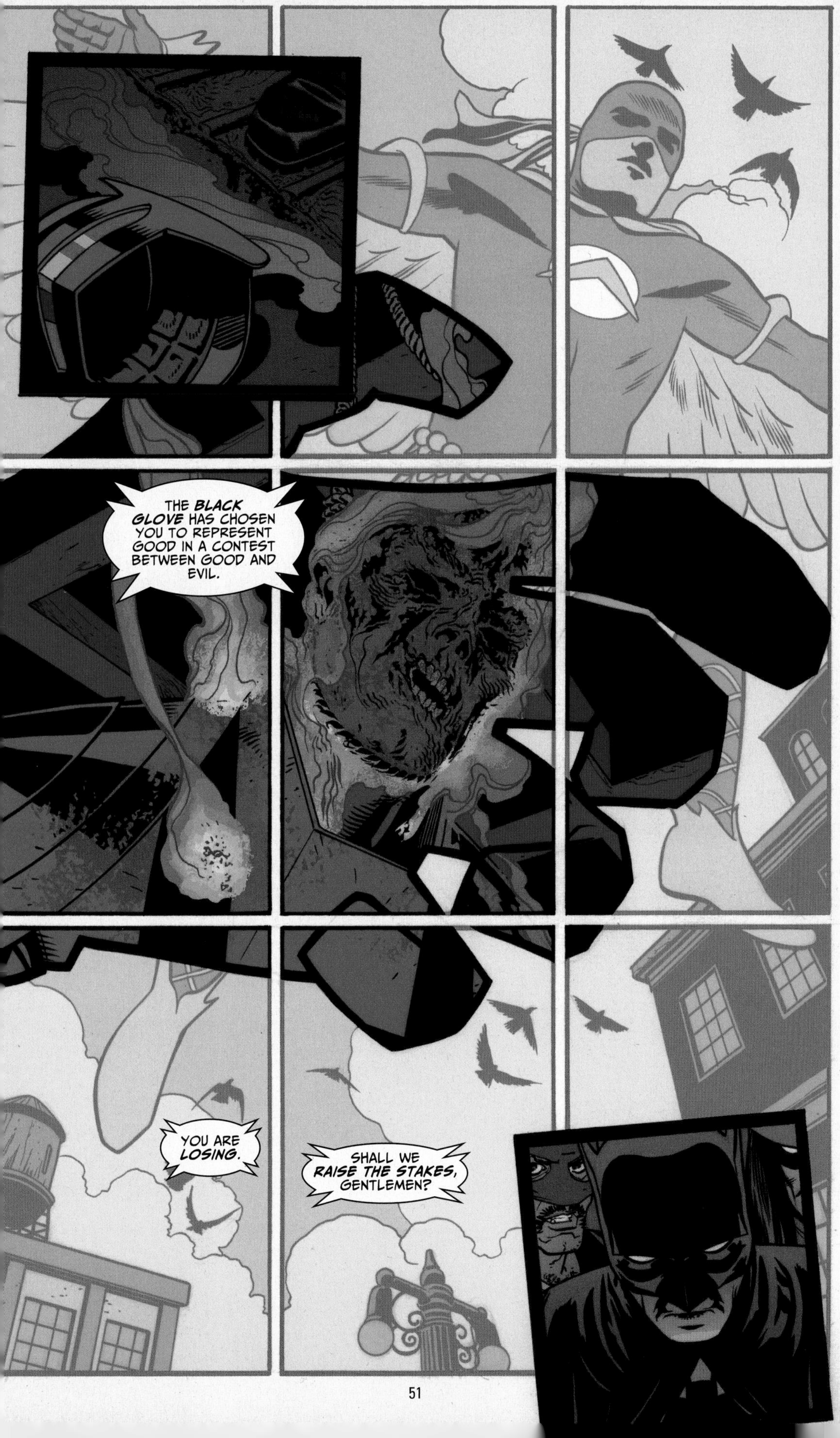
THE BLACK GLOVE HAS CHOSEN YOU TO REPRESENT GOOD IN A CONTEST BETWEEN GOOD AND EVIL.
YOU ARE LOSING.
SHALL WE RAISE THE STAKES, GENTLEMEN?

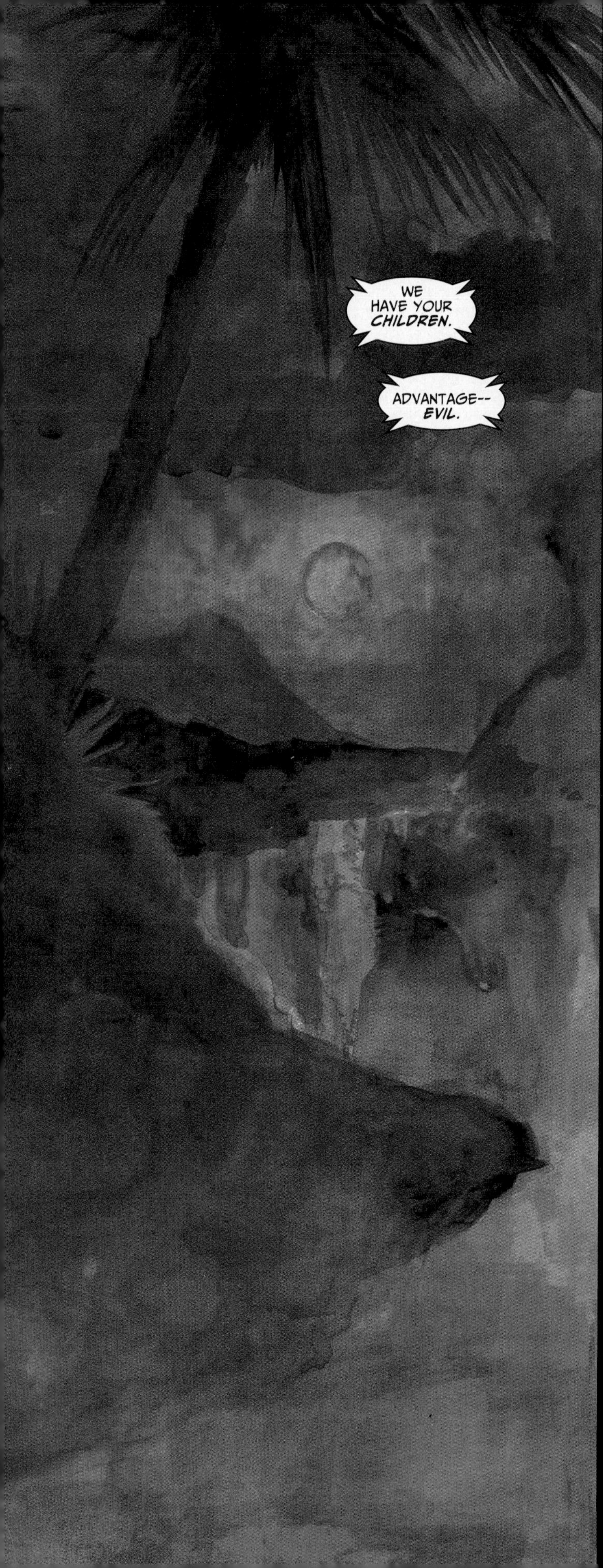
WE HAVE YOUR CHILDREN.
ADVANTAGE-- EVIL.
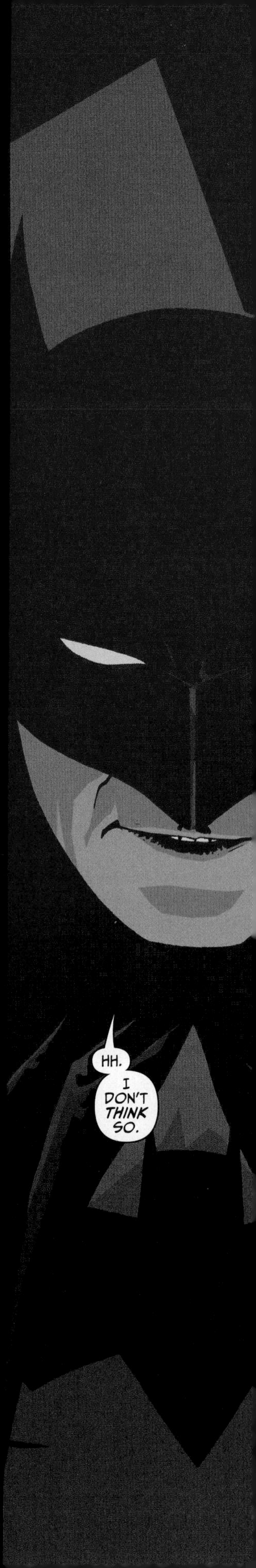
HH. I DON'T THINK SO.

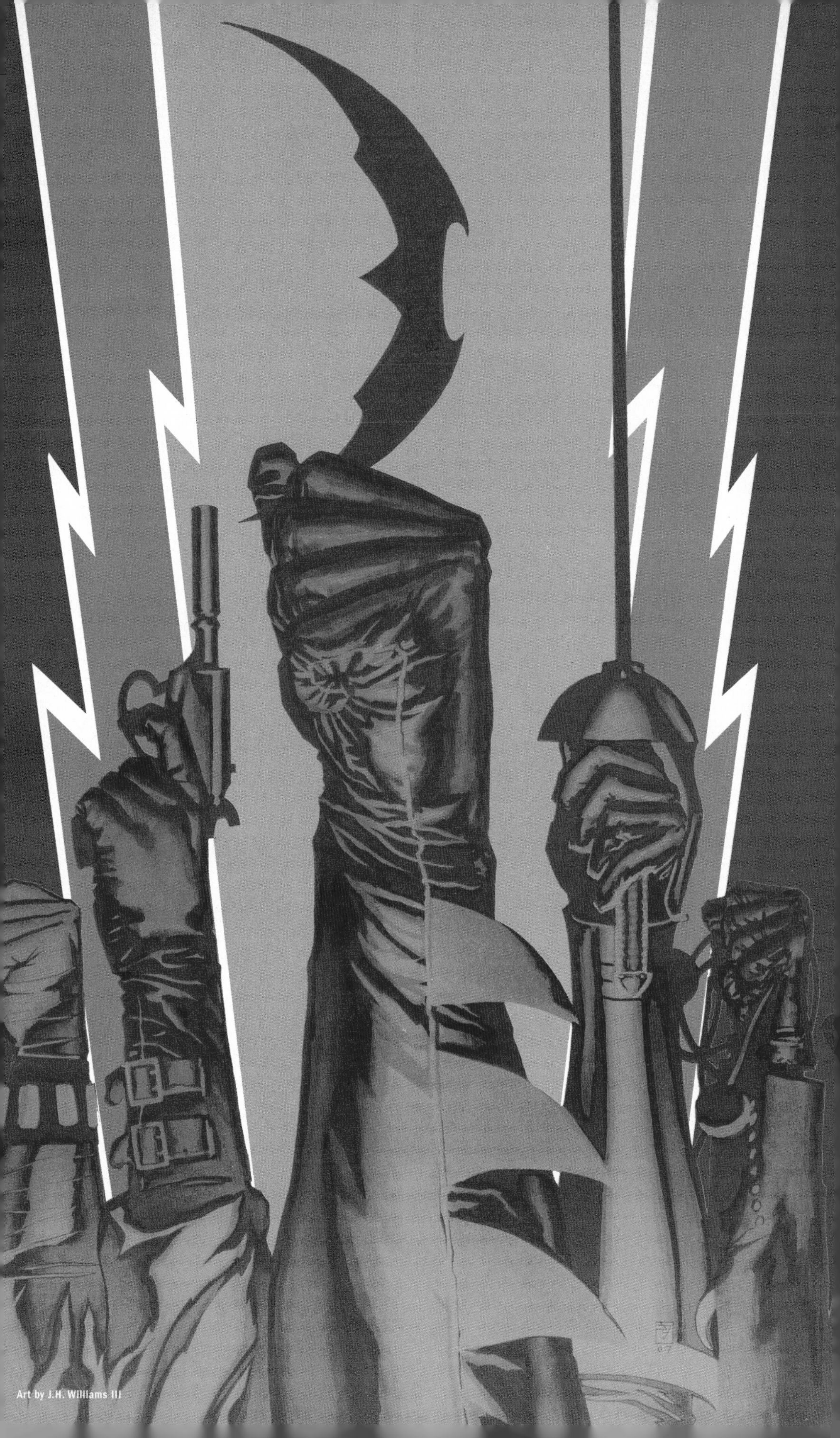

Art by J.H. Williams III

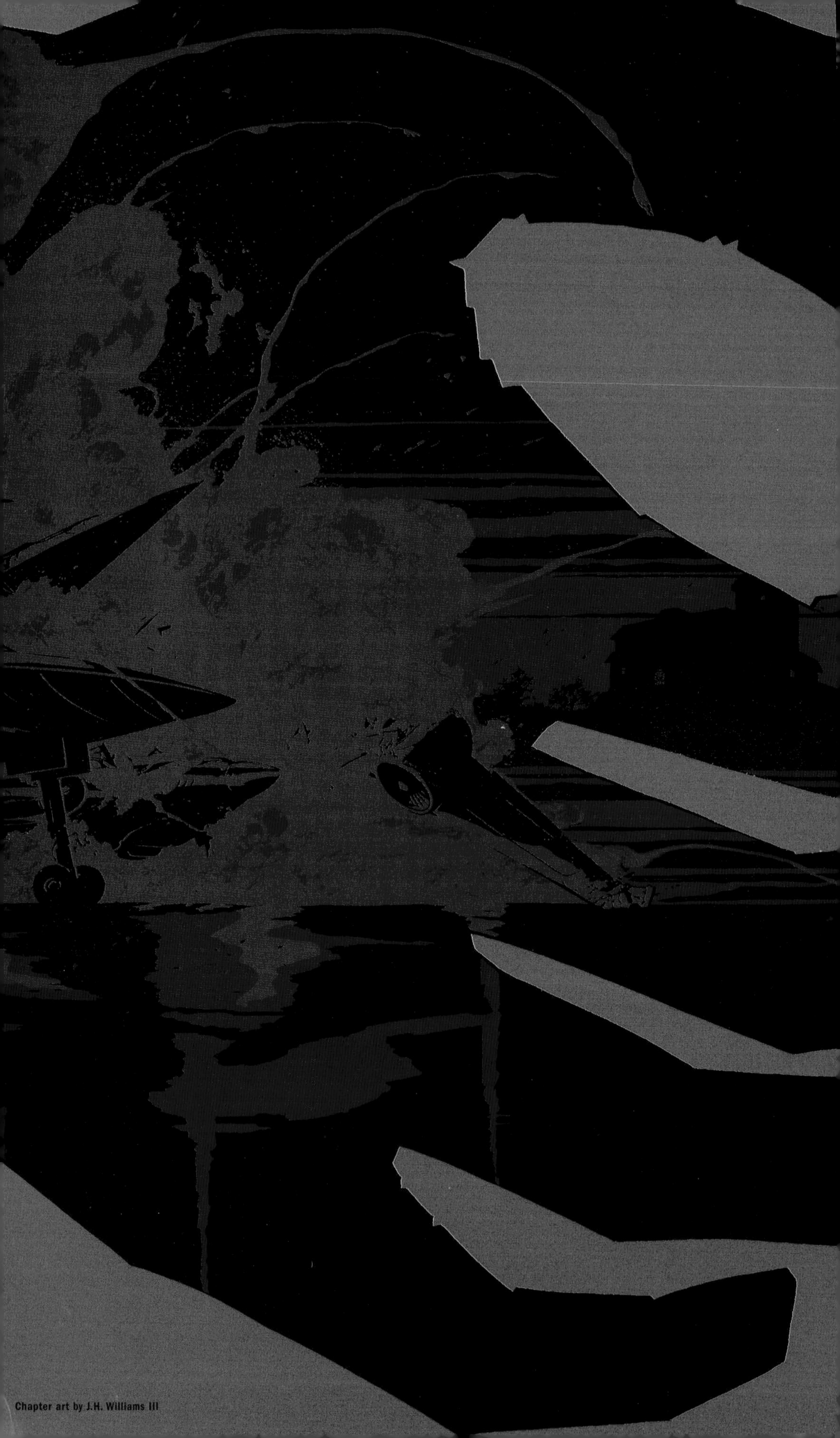

Chapter art by J.H. Williams III

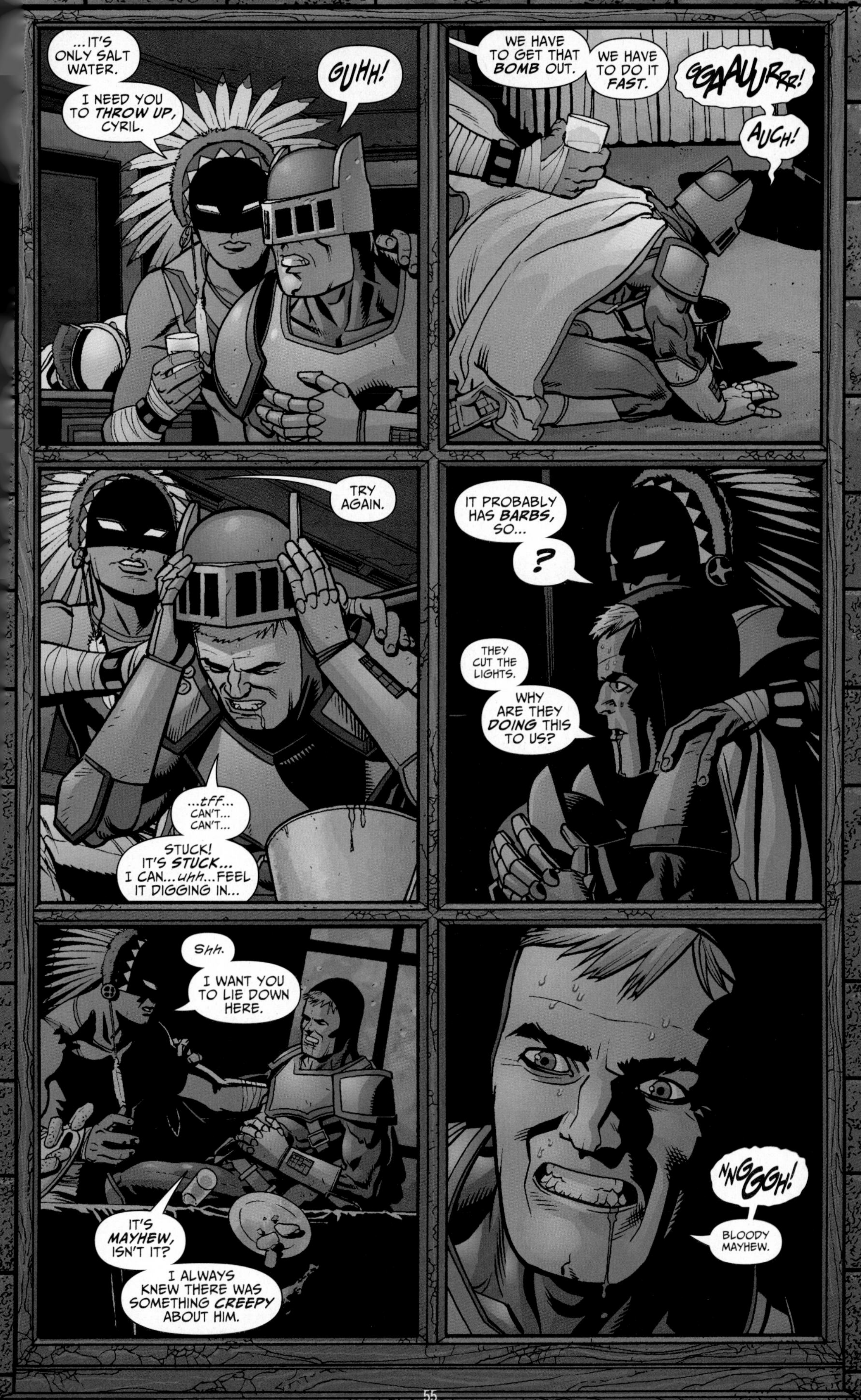
...IT'S ONLY SALT WATER.
I NEED YOU TO THROW UP, CYRIL.
GUHH!
WE HAVE TO GET THAT BOMB OUT.
WE HAVE TO DO IT FAST.
GGAAAUURRRR!
AUCH!
TRY AGAIN.
...tff... CAN'T... CAN'T...
STUCK! IT'S STUCK... I CAN...uhh...FEEL IT DIGGING IN...
IT PROBABLY HAS BARBS, SO...
?
THEY CUT THE LIGHTS.
WHY ARE THEY DOING THIS TO US?
Shh.
I WANT YOU TO LIE DOWN HERE.
IT'S MAYHEW, ISN'T IT?
I ALWAYS KNEW THERE WAS SOMETHING CREEPY ABOUT HIM.
NNGGGH!
BLOODY MAYHEW.

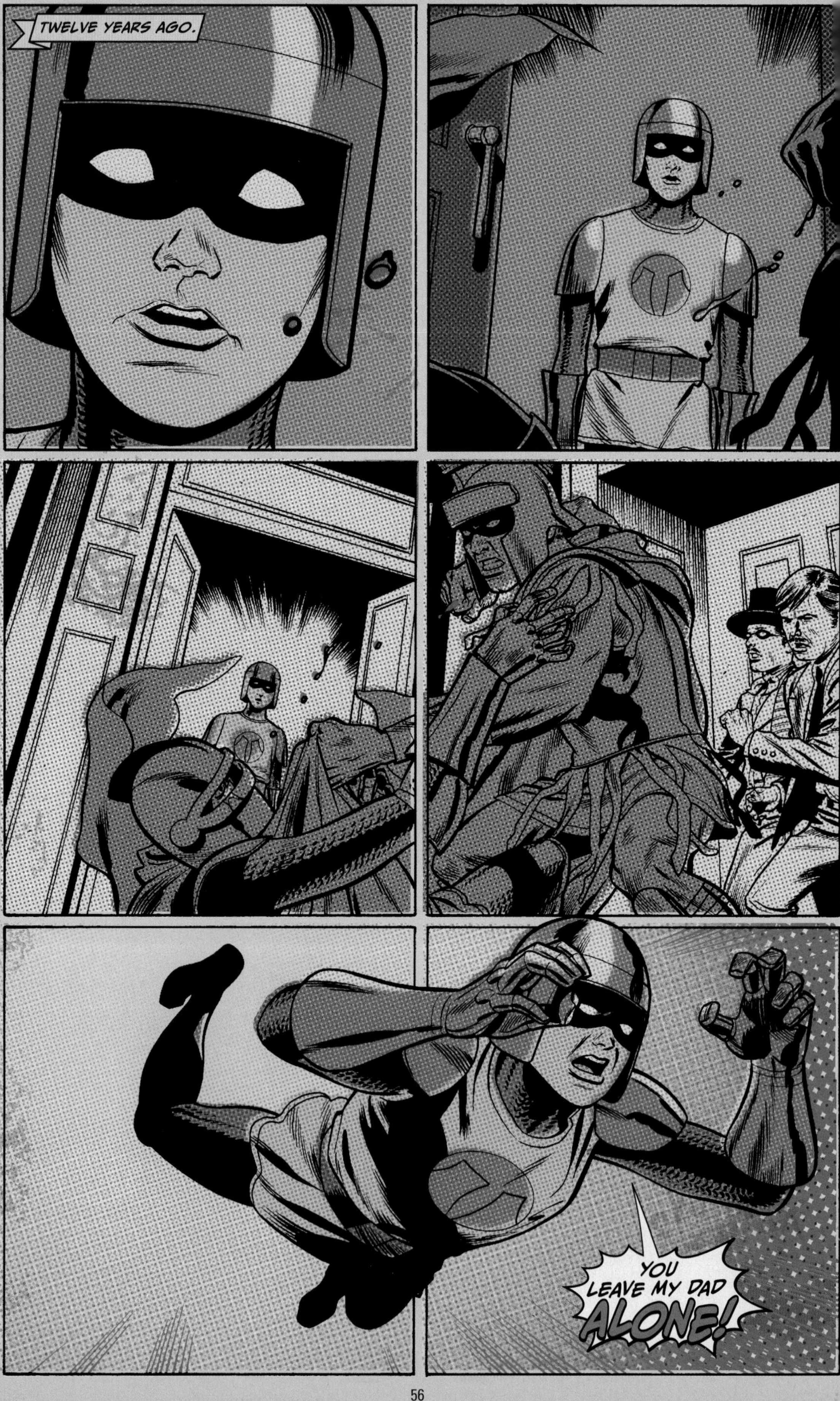
TWELVE YEARS AGO.
YOU LEAVE MY DAD ALONE!

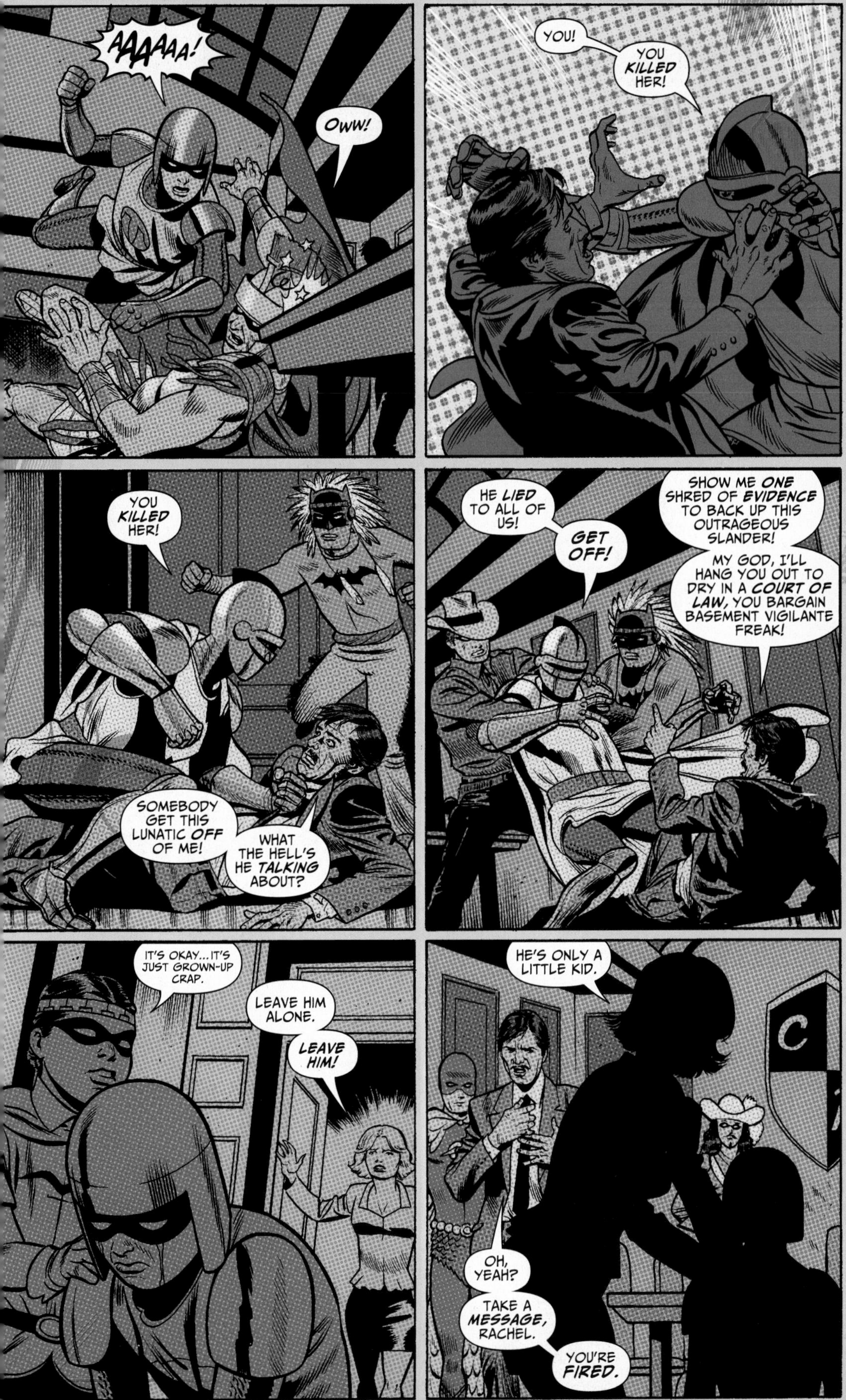
AAAAAA!
OWW!
YOU!
YOU KILLED HER!
YOU KILLED HER!
SOMEBODY GET THIS LUNATIC OFF OF ME!
WHAT THE HELL'S HE TALKING ABOUT?
HE LIED TO ALL OF US!
GET OFF!
SHOW ME ONE SHRED OF EVIDENCE TO BACK UP THIS OUTRAGEOUS SLANDER!
MY GOD, I'LL HANG YOU OUT TO DRY IN A COURT OF LAW, YOU BARGAIN BASEMENT VIGILANTE FREAK!
IT'S OKAY... IT'S JUST GROWN-UP CRAP.
LEAVE HIM ALONE.
LEAVE HIM!
HE'S ONLY A LITTLE KID.
OH, YEAH?
TAKE A MESSAGE, RACHEL.
YOU'RE FIRED.

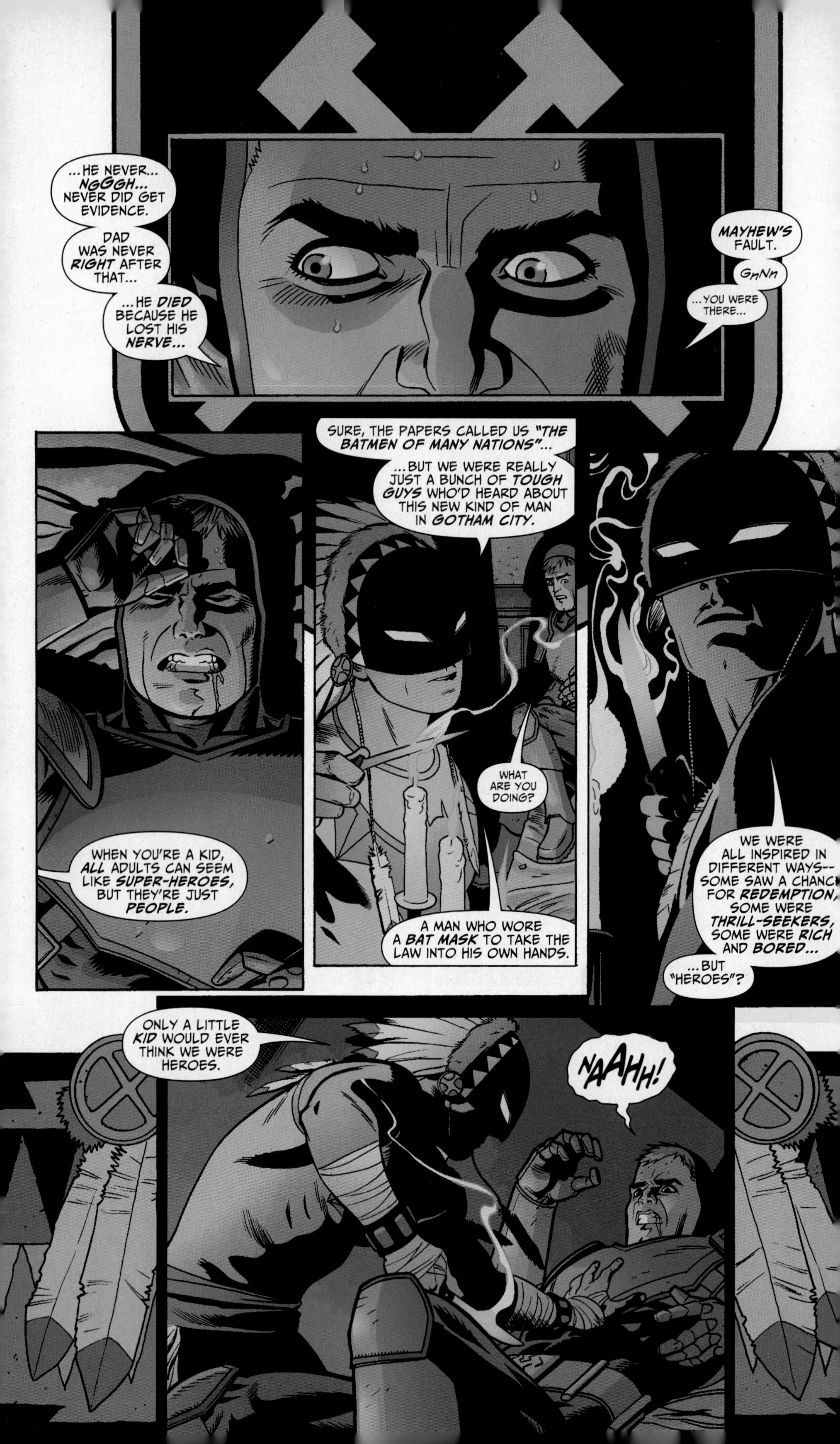

...HE NEVER... NGGGH... NEVER DID GET EVIDENCE.
DAD WAS NEVER RIGHT AFTER THAT...
...HE DIED BECAUSE HE LOST HIS NERVE...
MAYHEW'S FAULT.
GnNn
...YOU WERE THERE...
WHEN YOU'RE A KID, ALL ADULTS CAN SEEM LIKE SUPER-HEROES, BUT THEY'RE JUST PEOPLE.
SURE, THE PAPERS CALLED US "THE BATMEN OF MANY NATIONS"...
...BUT WE WERE REALLY JUST A BUNCH OF TOUGH GUYS WHO'D HEARD ABOUT THIS NEW KIND OF MAN IN GOTHAM CITY.
WHAT ARE YOU DOING?
A MAN WHO WORE A BAT MASK TO TAKE THE LAW INTO HIS OWN HANDS.
WE WERE ALL INSPIRED IN DIFFERENT WAYS-- SOME SAW A CHANC FOR REDEMPTION, SOME WERE THRILL-SEEKERS, SOME WERE RICH AND BORED...
...BUT "HEROES"?
ONLY A LITTLE KID WOULD EVER THINK WE WERE HEROES.
NAAHH!

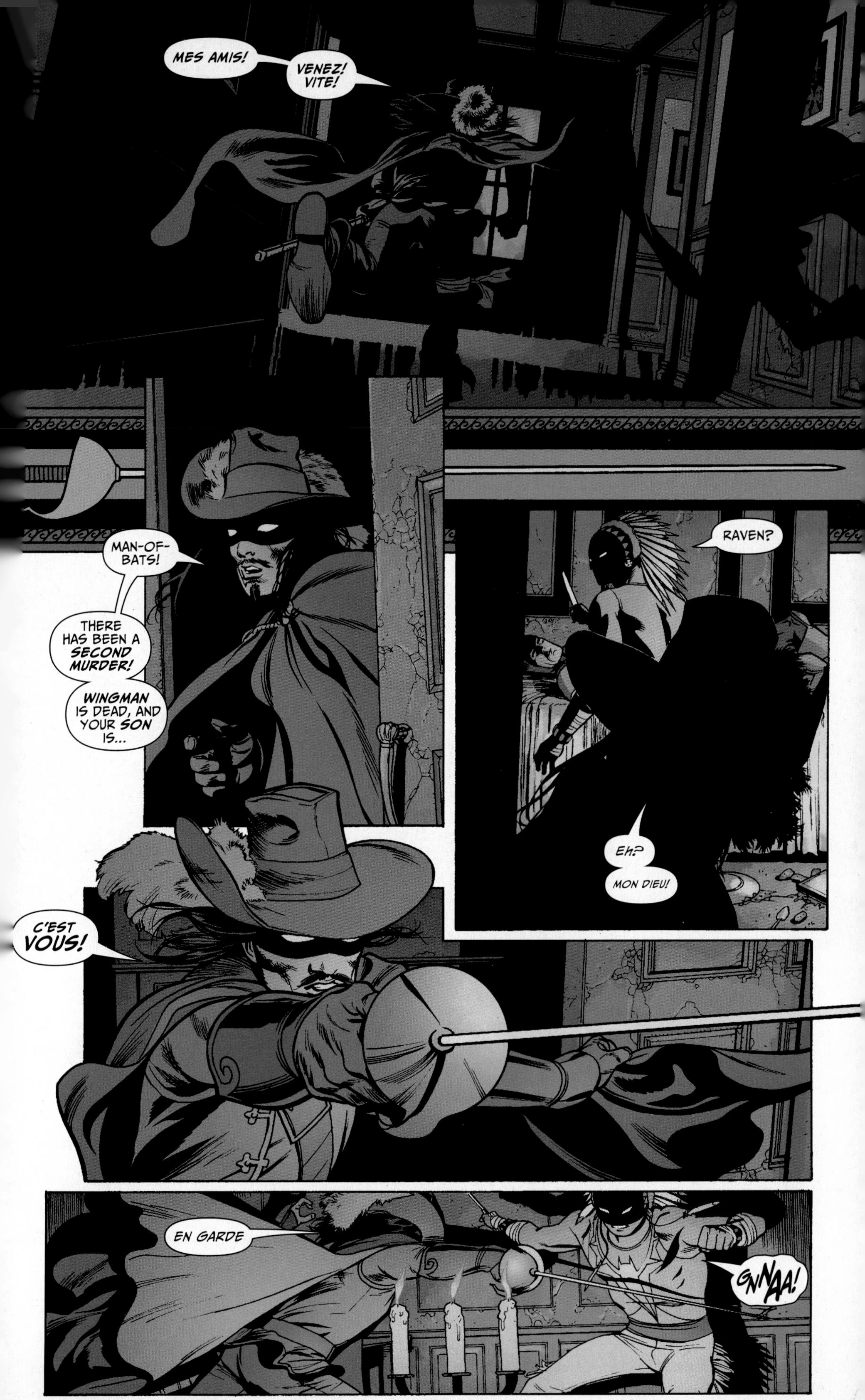
MES AMIS!
VENEZ! VITE!
MAN-OF-BATS!
THERE HAS BEEN A SECOND MURDER!
WINGMAN IS DEAD, AND YOUR SON IS...
RAVEN?
Eh?
MON DIEU!
C'EST VOUS!
EN GARDE
GNNAA!

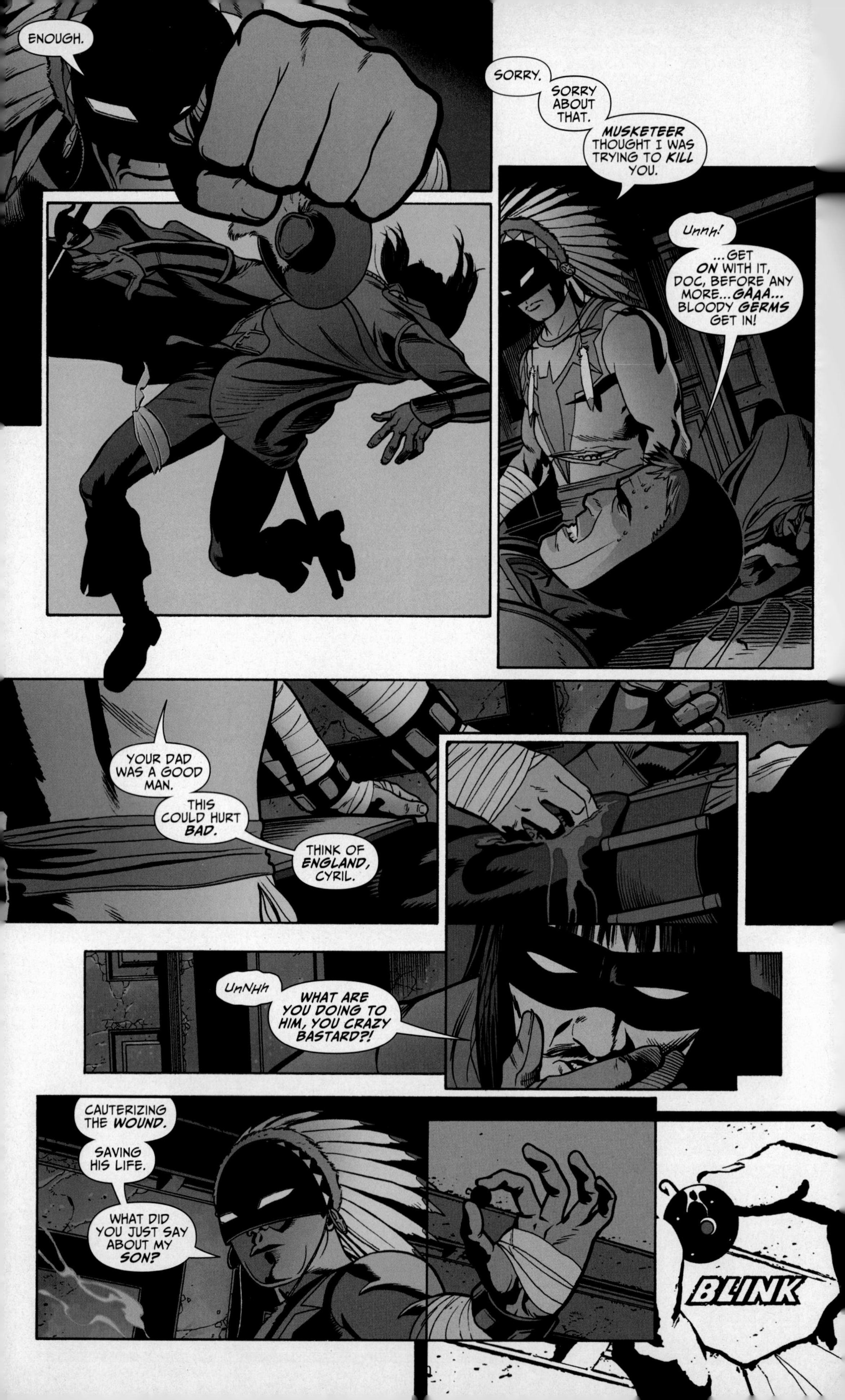
ENOUGH.
SORRY.
SORRY ABOUT THAT.
MUSKETEER THOUGHT I WAS TRYING TO KILL YOU.
Unnh!
...GET ON WITH IT, DOC, BEFORE ANY MORE...GAAA... BLOODY GERMS GET IN!
YOUR DAD WAS A GOOD MAN.
THIS COULD HURT BAD.
THINK OF ENGLAND, CYRIL.
UnNhh
WHAT ARE YOU DOING TO HIM, YOU CRAZY BASTARD?!
CAUTERIZING THE WOUND.
SAVING HIS LIFE.
WHAT DID YOU JUST SAY ABOUT MY SON?
BLINK

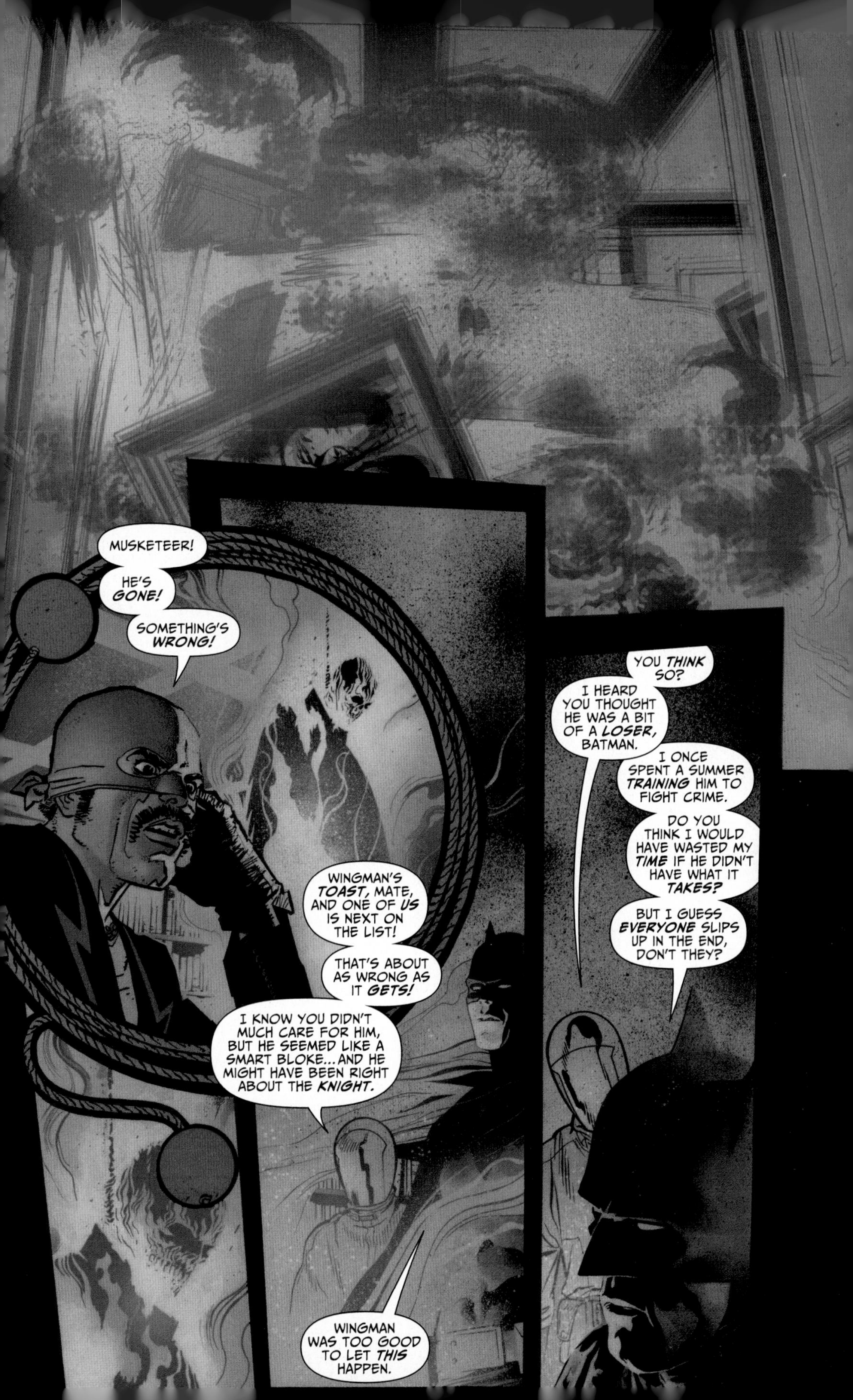
MUSKETEER!
HE'S GONE!
SOMETHING'S WRONG!
WINGMAN'S TOAST, MATE, AND ONE OF US IS NEXT ON THE LIST!
THAT'S ABOUT AS WRONG AS IT GETS!
I KNOW YOU DIDN'T MUCH CARE FOR HIM, BUT HE SEEMED LIKE A SMART BLOKE... AND HE MIGHT HAVE BEEN RIGHT ABOUT THE KNIGHT.
WINGMAN WAS TOO GOOD TO LET THIS HAPPEN.
YOU THINK SO?
I HEARD YOU THOUGHT HE WAS A BIT OF A LOSER, BATMAN.
I ONCE SPENT A SUMMER TRAINING HIM TO FIGHT CRIME.
DO YOU THINK I WOULD HAVE WASTED MY TIME IF HE DIDN'T HAVE WHAT IT TAKES?
BUT I GUESS EVERYONE SLIPS UP IN THE END, DON'T THEY?

WINGMAN HAD A FEW RUN-INS WITH A DISFIGURED DEEPSEA DIVER TURNED *PIRATE.*
THEY CALLED HIM *KING KRAKEN.*
KRAKEN'S WEAPON OF CHOICE WAS A HIGH VOLTAGE *ELECTRICAL RIFLE* WHICH COULD EASILY CREATE THE KIND OF TRAUMA WE SEE HERE.
MORE EVIDENCE FOR THE *CLUB OF VILLAINS* THEORY?
OR ANOTHER RED HERRING?
THE DARK KNIGHT MUST DIE!

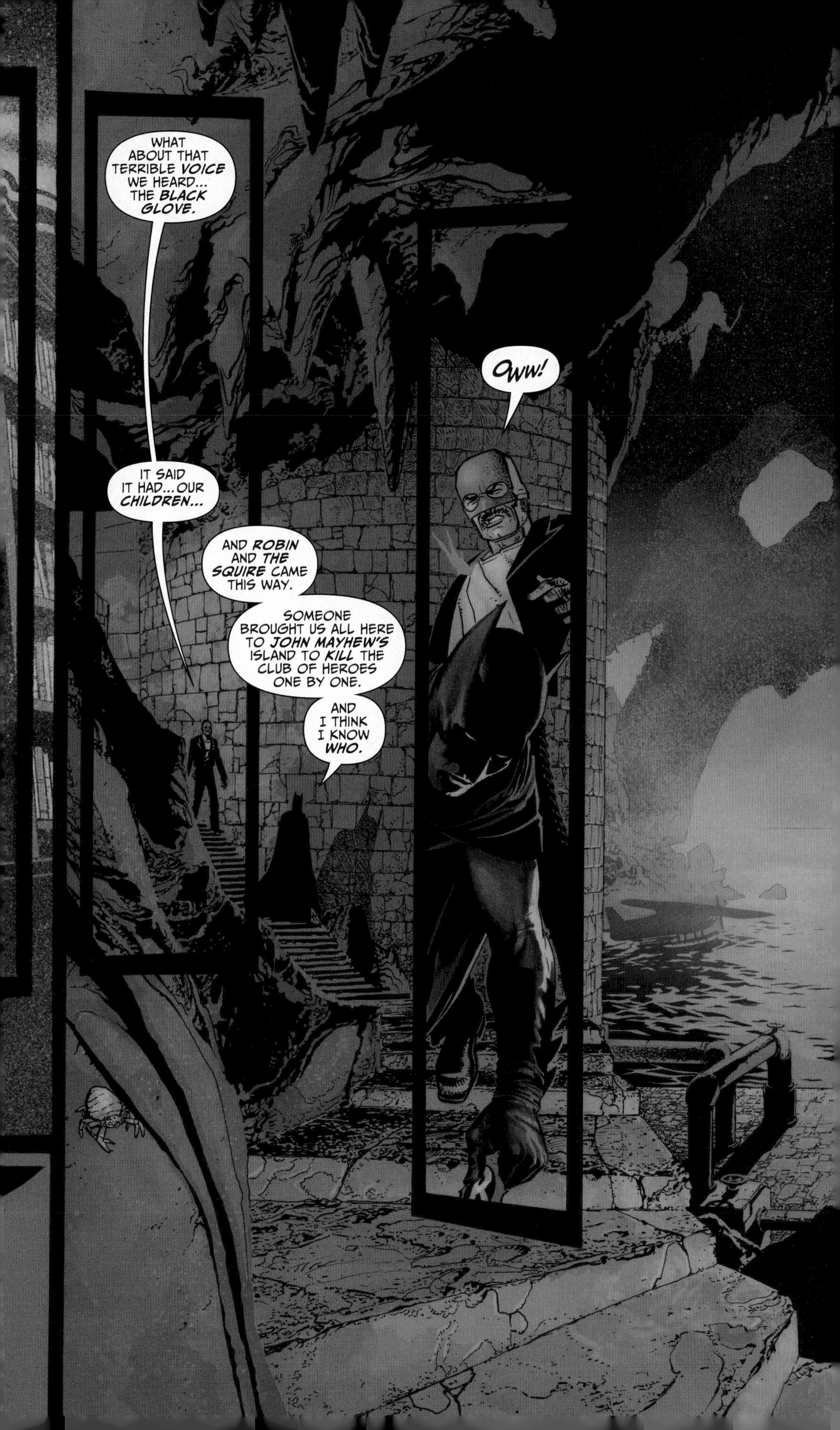
WHAT ABOUT THAT TERRIBLE VOICE WE HEARD... THE BLACK GLOVE.
IT SAID IT HAD...OUR CHILDREN...
AND ROBIN AND THE SQUIRE CAME THIS WAY.
SOMEONE BROUGHT US ALL HERE TO JOHN MAYHEW'S ISLAND TO KILL THE CLUB OF HEROES ONE BY ONE.
AND I THINK I KNOW WHO.
OWW!

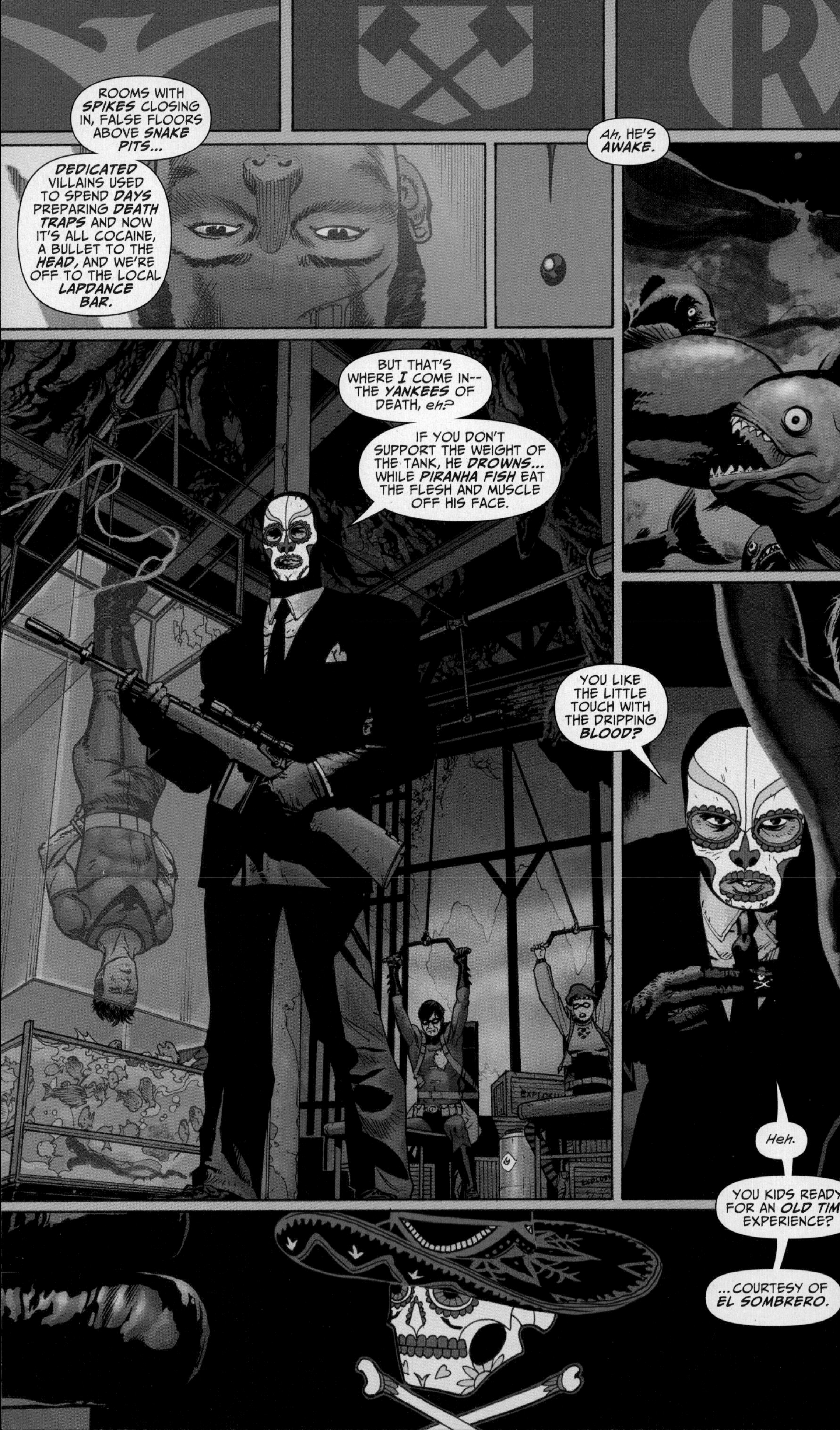
ROOMS WITH SPIKES CLOSING IN, FALSE FLOORS ABOVE SNAKE PITS...
DEDICATED VILLAINS USED TO SPEND DAYS PREPARING DEATH TRAPS AND NOW IT'S ALL COCAINE, A BULLET TO THE HEAD, AND WE'RE OFF TO THE LOCAL LAPDANCE BAR.
Ah, HE'S AWAKE.
BUT THAT'S WHERE I COME IN-- THE YANKEES OF DEATH, eh?
IF YOU DON'T SUPPORT THE WEIGHT OF THE TANK, HE DROWNS... WHILE PIRANHA FISH EAT THE FLESH AND MUSCLE OFF HIS FACE.
YOU LIKE THE LITTLE TOUCH WITH THE DRIPPING BLOOD?
Heh.
YOU KIDS READY FOR AN OLD TIM EXPERIENCE?
...COURTESY OF EL SOMBRERO.

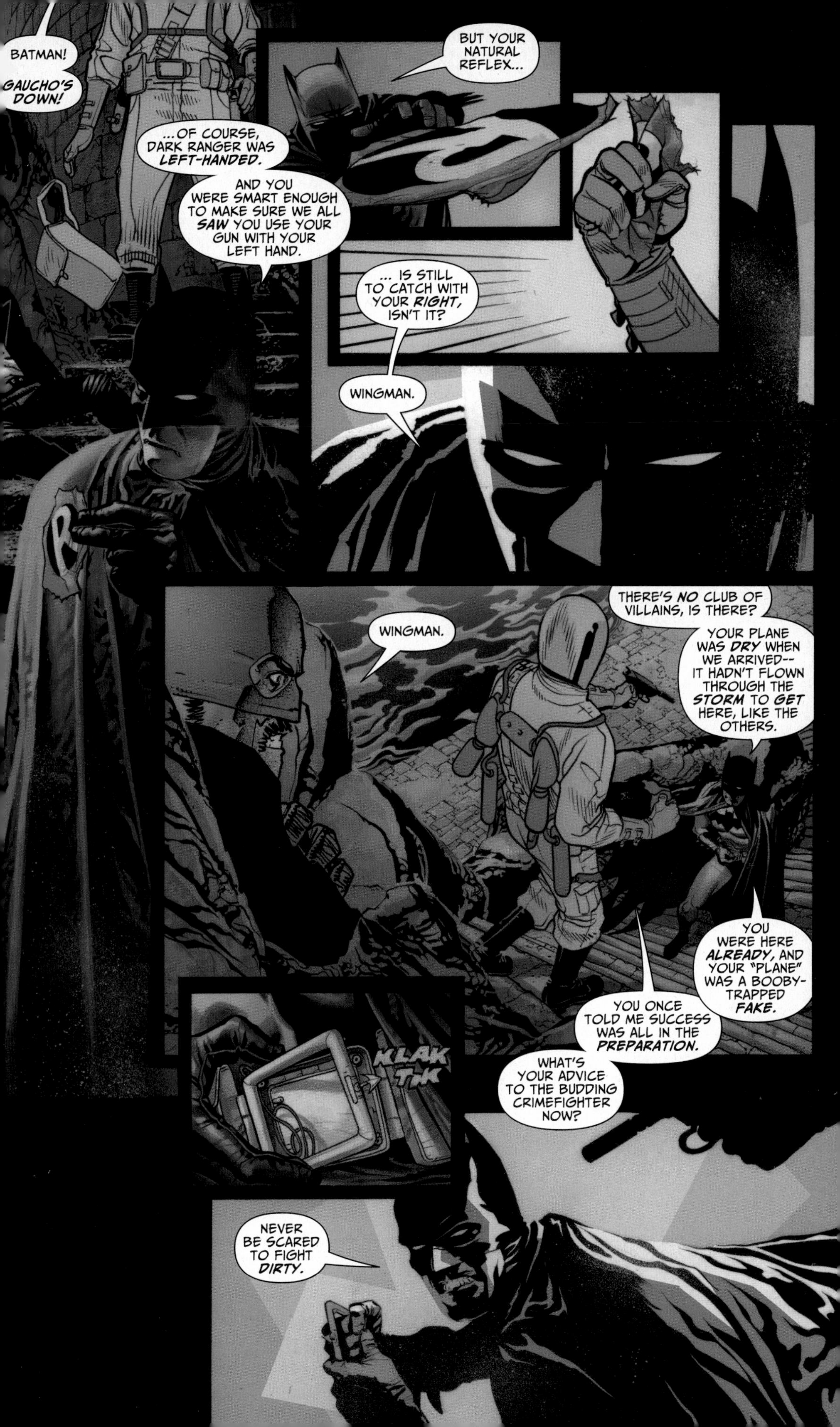
BATMAN!
GAUCHO'S DOWN!
...OF COURSE, DARK RANGER WAS LEFT-HANDED.
AND YOU WERE SMART ENOUGH TO MAKE SURE WE ALL SAW YOU USE YOUR GUN WITH YOUR LEFT HAND.
BUT YOUR NATURAL REFLEX...
... IS STILL TO CATCH WITH YOUR RIGHT, ISN'T IT?
WINGMAN.
WINGMAN.
THERE'S NO CLUB OF VILLAINS, IS THERE?
YOUR PLANE WAS DRY WHEN WE ARRIVED-- IT HADN'T FLOWN THROUGH THE STORM TO GET HERE, LIKE THE OTHERS.
YOU WERE HERE ALREADY, AND YOUR "PLANE" WAS A BOOBY-TRAPPED FAKE.
YOU ONCE TOLD ME SUCCESS WAS ALL IN THE PREPARATION.
WHAT'S YOUR ADVICE TO THE BUDDING CRIMEFIGHTER NOW?
KLAK TIK
NEVER BE SCARED TO FIGHT DIRTY.

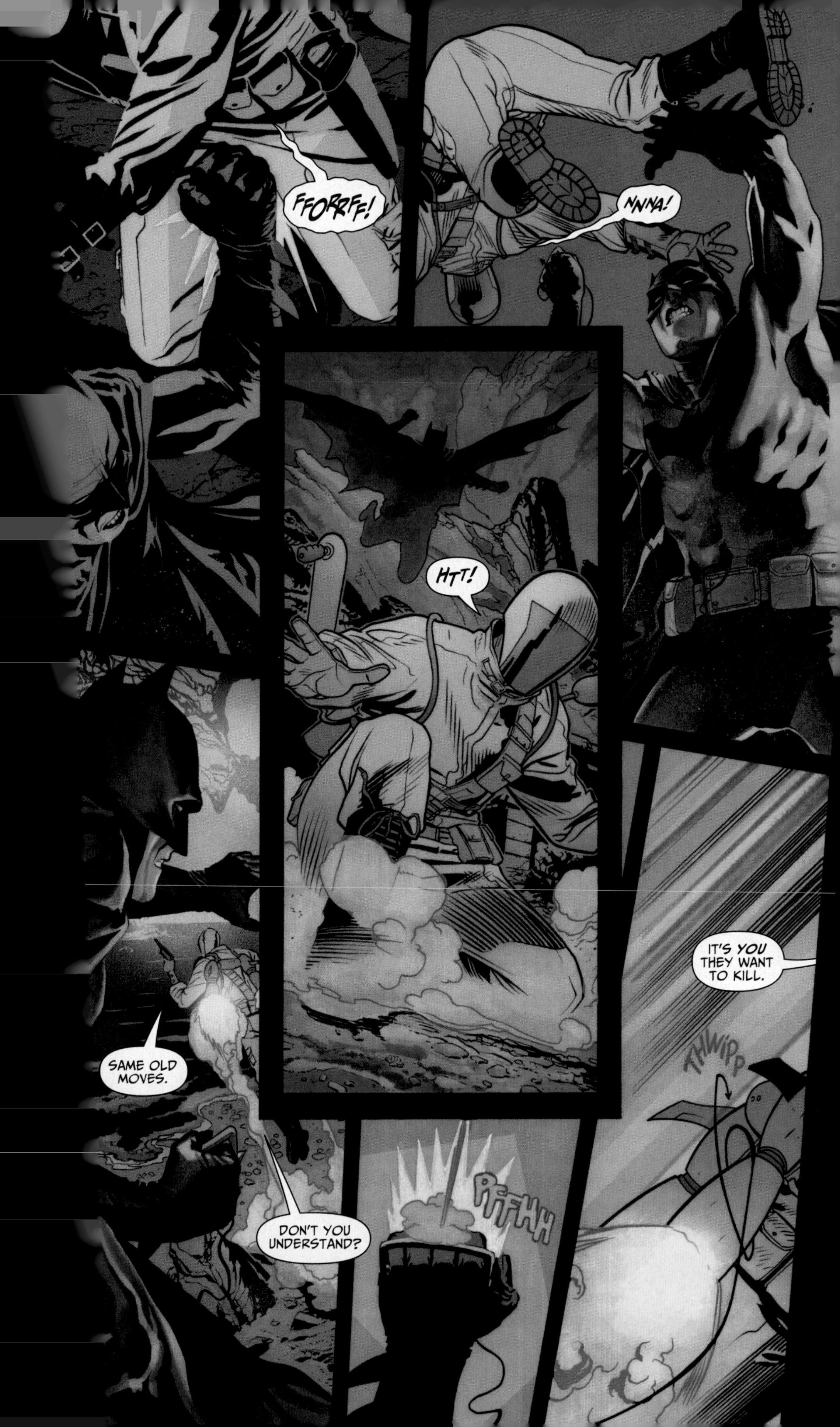
FFORRFF!
NNNA!
HTT!
IT'S YOU THEY WANT TO KILL.
THWIPP
SAME OLD MOVES.
PFFHH
DON'T YOU UNDERSTAND?

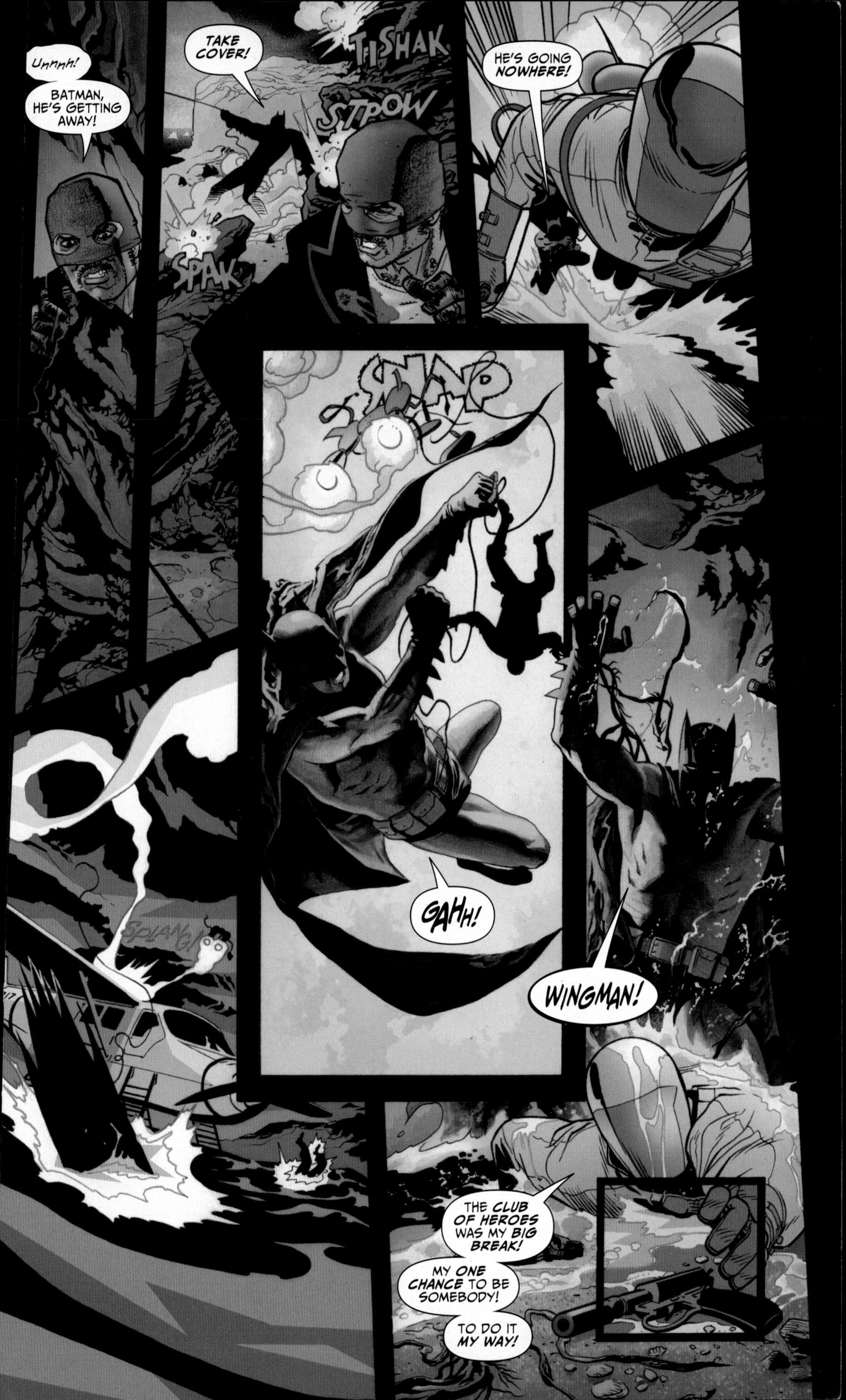
Unnnh!
BATMAN, HE'S GETTING AWAY!
TAKE COVER!
TI SHAK
STPOW
SPAK
HE'S GOING NOWHERE!
SNAP
SPLANG!
GAHH!
WINGMAN!
THE CLUB OF HEROES WAS MY BIG BREAK!
MY ONE CHANCE TO BE SOMEBODY!
TO DO IT MY WAY!

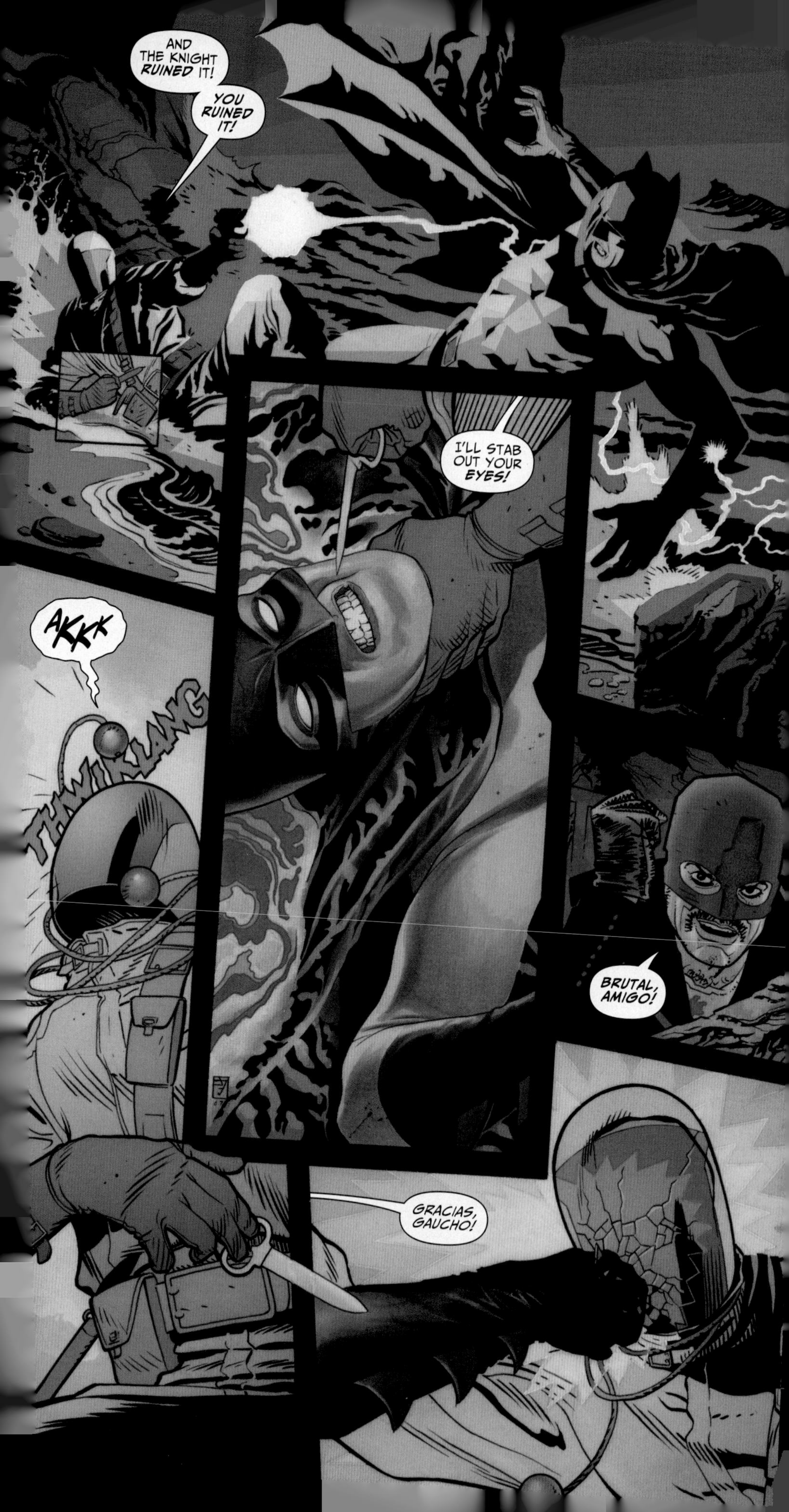
AND THE KNIGHT RUINED IT!
YOU RUINED IT!
I'LL STAB OUT YOUR EYES!
AKKK
THWAKLANG
BRUTAL, AMIGO!
GRACIAS, GAUCHO!

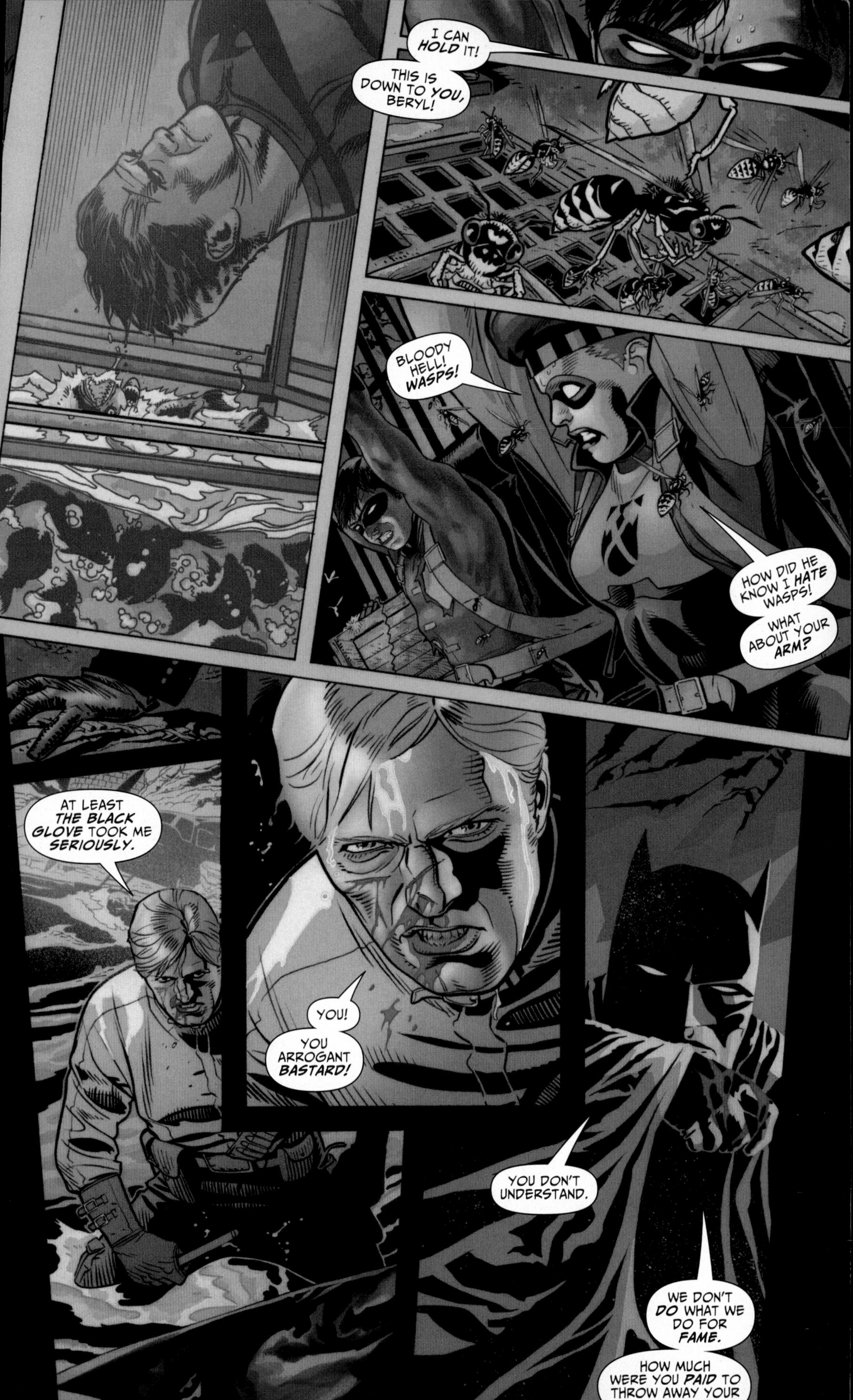
I CAN HOLD IT!
THIS IS DOWN TO YOU, BERYL!
BLOODY HELL! WASPS!
HOW DID HE KNOW I HATE WASPS!
WHAT ABOUT YOUR ARM?
AT LEAST THE BLACK GLOVE TOOK ME SERIOUSLY.
YOU!
YOU ARROGANT BASTARD!
YOU DON'T UNDERSTAND.
WE DON'T DO WHAT WE DO FOR FAME.
HOW MUCH WERE YOU PAID TO THROW AWAY YOUR MORALS?

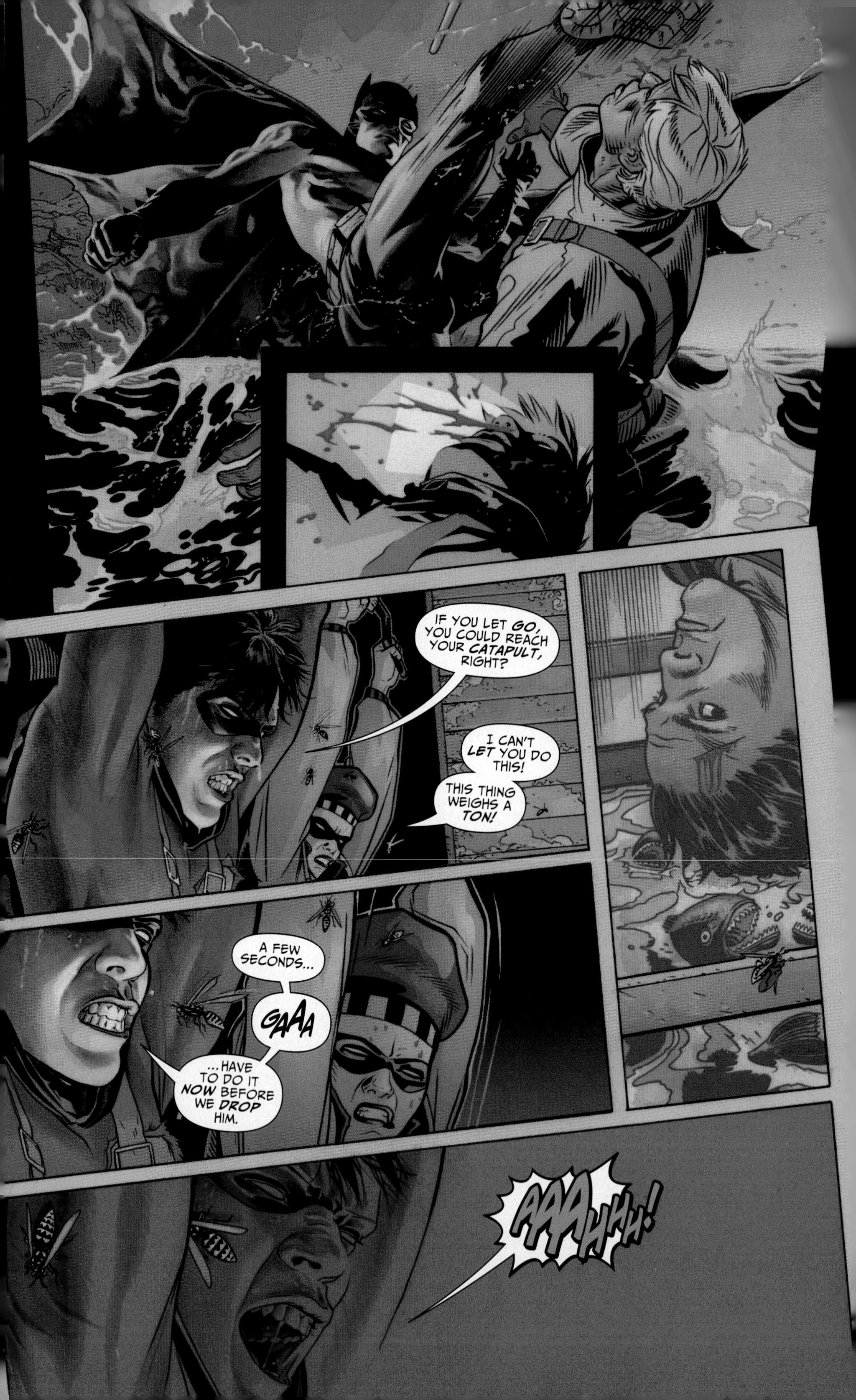

IF YOU LET GO, YOU COULD REACH YOUR CATAPULT, RIGHT?
I CAN'T LET YOU DO THIS!
THIS THING WEIGHS A TON!
A FEW SECONDS...
GAAA
...HAVE TO DO IT NOW BEFORE WE DROP HIM.
AAAAHHH!

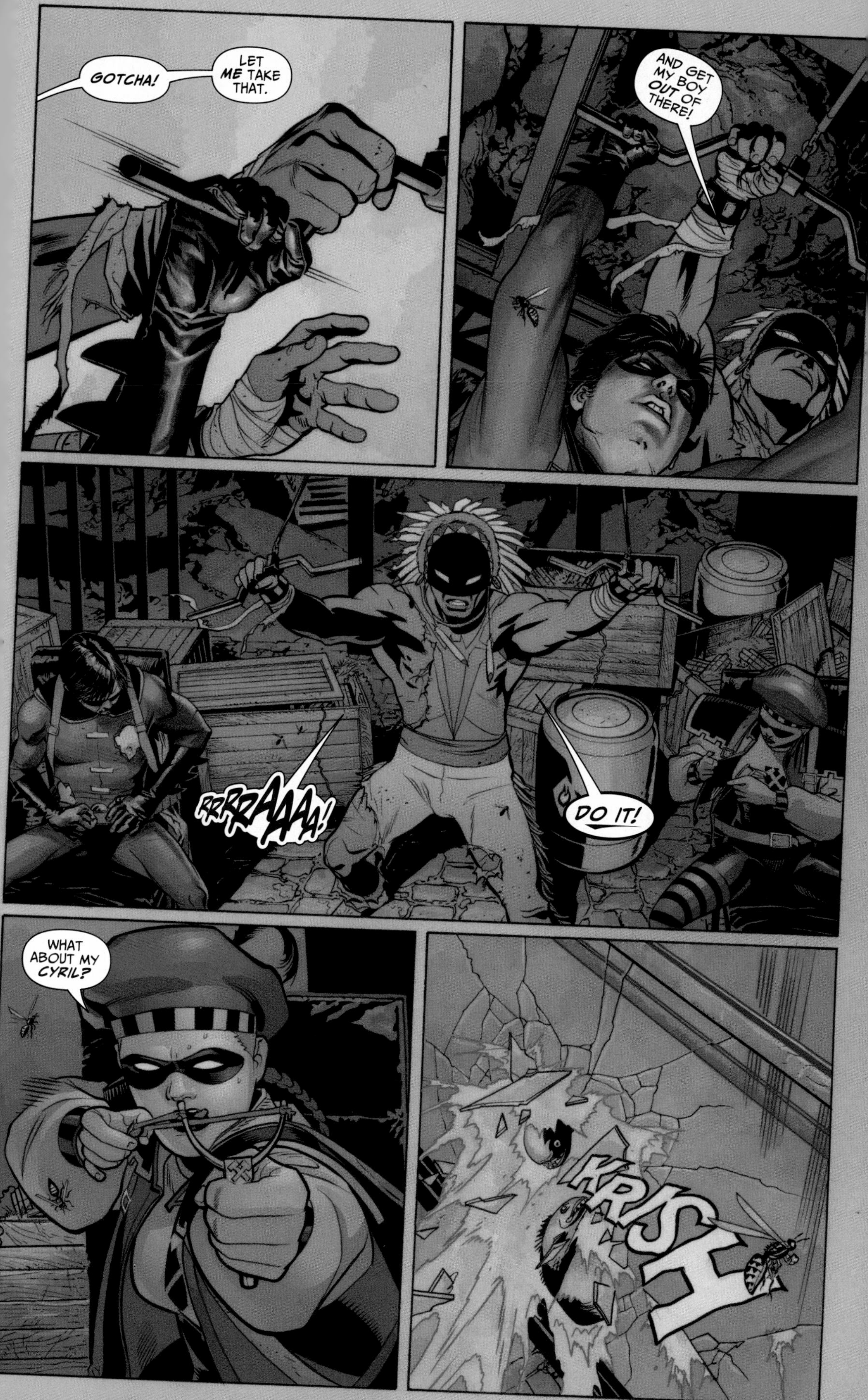
GOTCHA!
LET ME TAKE THAT.
AND GET MY BOY OUT OF THERE!
RRRRAAAAA!
DO IT!
WHAT ABOUT MY CYRIL?
KRISH

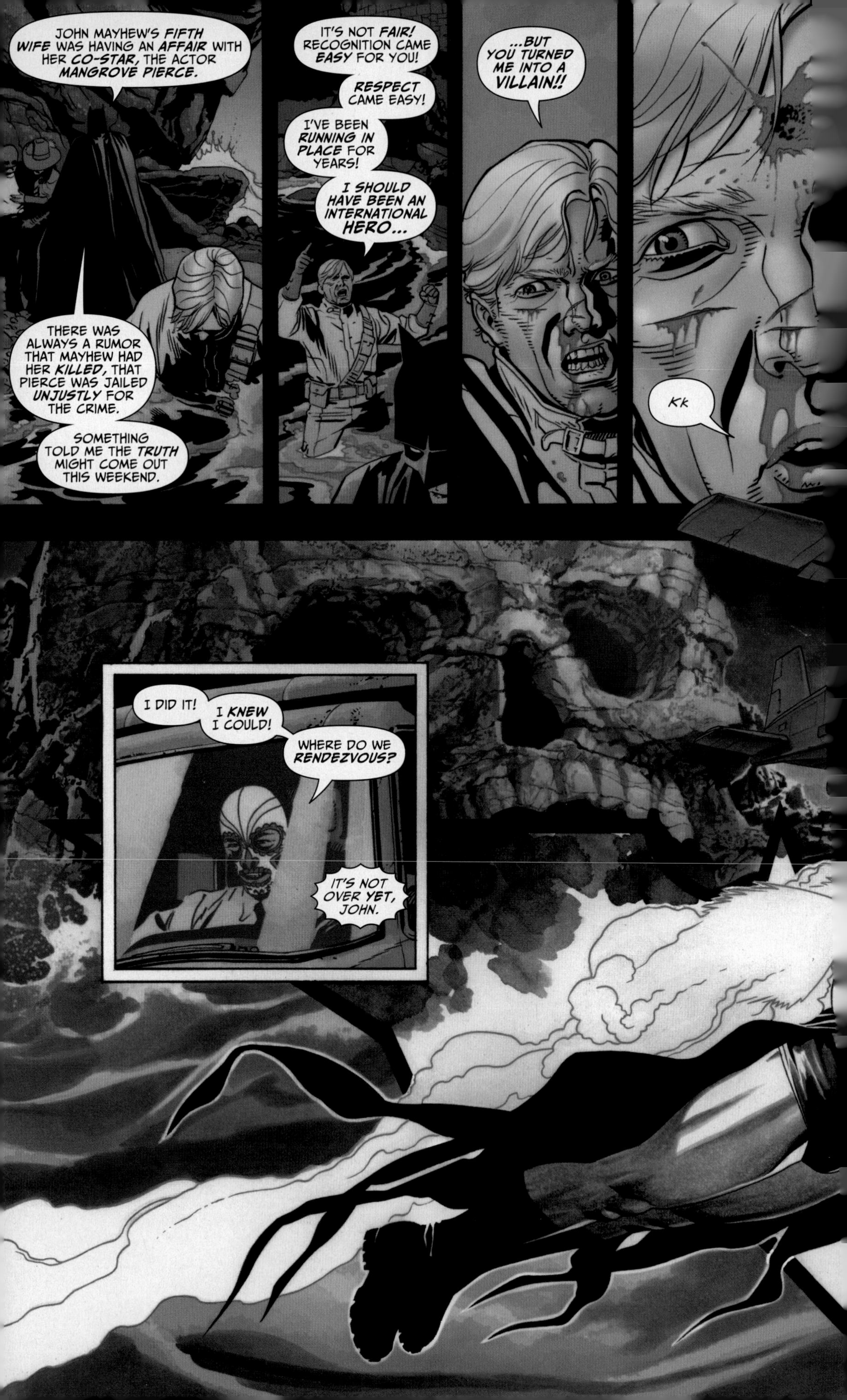

JOHN MAYHEW'S FIFTH WIFE WAS HAVING AN AFFAIR WITH HER CO-STAR, THE ACTOR MANGROVE PIERCE.
THERE WAS ALWAYS A RUMOR THAT MAYHEW HAD HER KILLED, THAT PIERCE WAS JAILED UNJUSTLY FOR THE CRIME.
SOMETHING TOLD ME THE TRUTH MIGHT COME OUT THIS WEEKEND.
IT'S NOT FAIR! RECOGNITION CAME EASY FOR YOU!
RESPECT CAME EASY!
I'VE BEEN RUNNING IN PLACE FOR YEARS!
I SHOULD HAVE BEEN AN INTERNATIONAL HERO...
...BUT YOU TURNED ME INTO A VILLAIN!!
KK
I DID IT!
I KNEW I COULD!
WHERE DO WE RENDEZVOUS?
IT'S NOT OVER YET, JOHN.

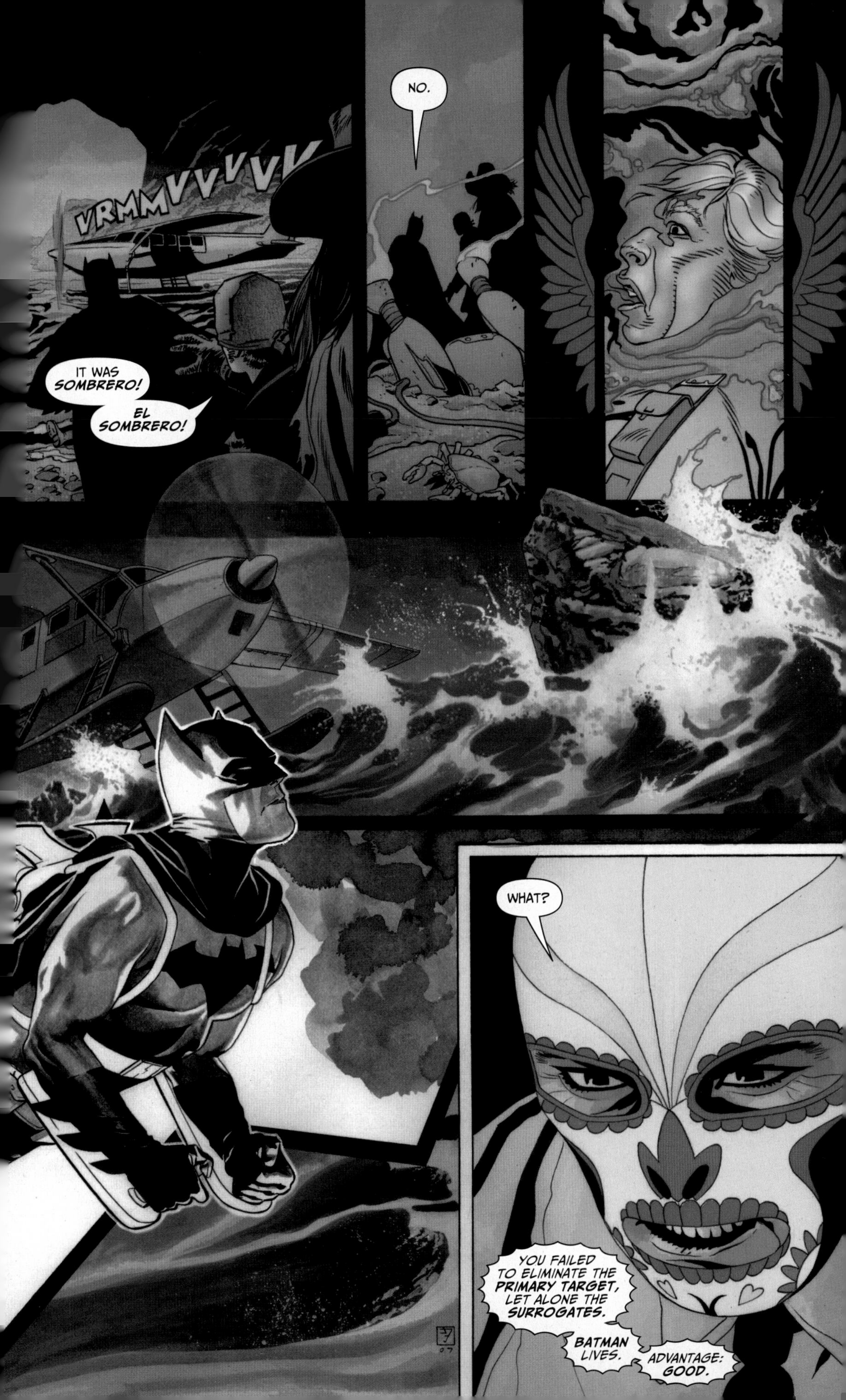
VRMMVVVVVK
IT WAS SOMBRERO!
EL SOMBRERO!
NO.
WHAT?
YOU FAILED TO ELIMINATE THE PRIMARY TARGET, LET ALONE THE SURROGATES.
BATMAN LIVES.
ADVANTAGE: GOOD.

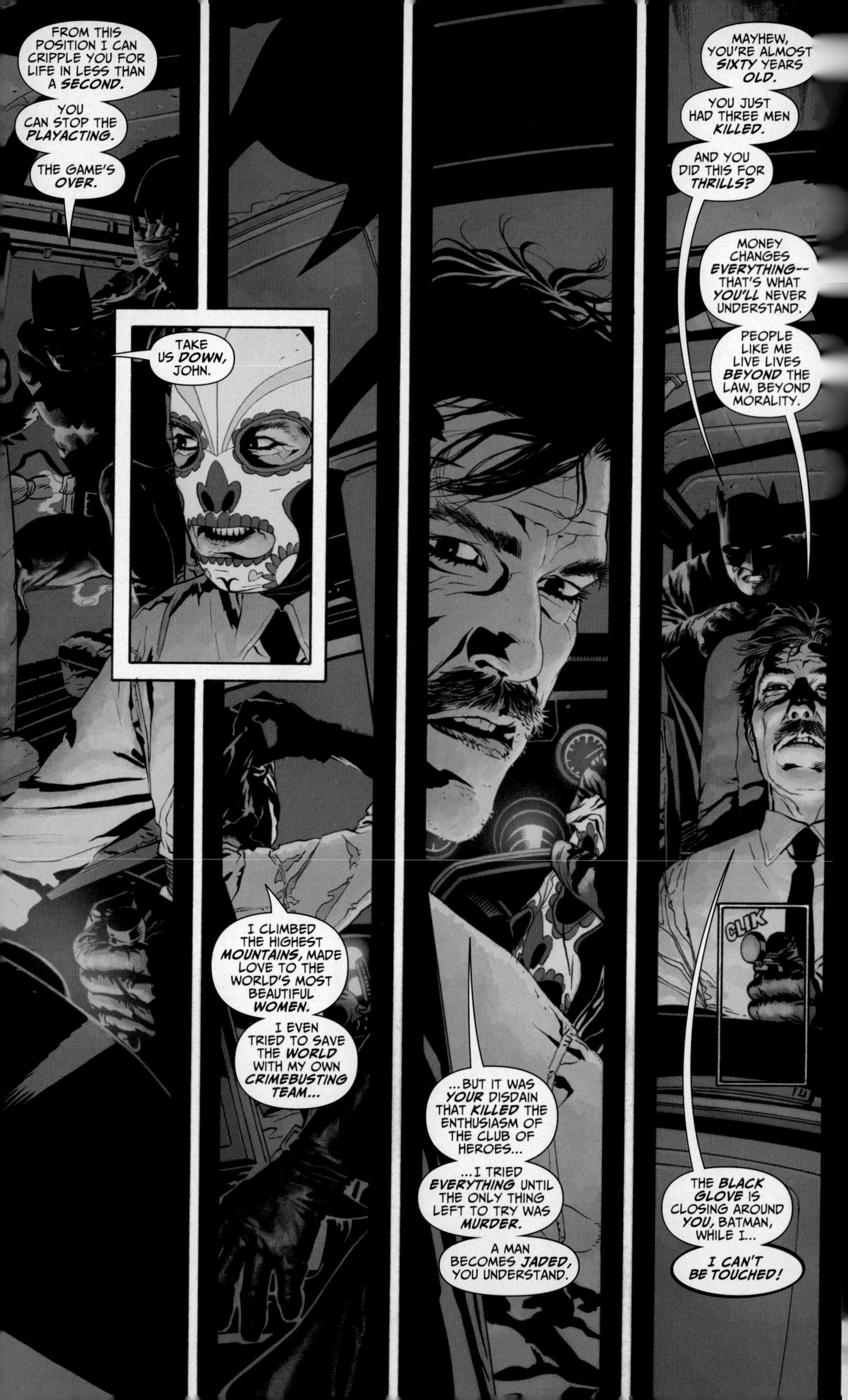
FROM THIS POSITION I CAN CRIPPLE YOU FOR LIFE IN LESS THAN A SECOND.
YOU CAN STOP THE PLAYACTING.
THE GAME'S OVER.
TAKE US DOWN, JOHN.
I CLIMBED THE HIGHEST MOUNTAINS, MADE LOVE TO THE WORLD'S MOST BEAUTIFUL WOMEN.
I EVEN TRIED TO SAVE THE WORLD WITH MY OWN CRIMEBUSTING TEAM...
...BUT IT WAS YOUR DISDAIN THAT KILLED THE ENTHUSIASM OF THE CLUB OF HEROES...
...I TRIED EVERYTHING UNTIL THE ONLY THING LEFT TO TRY WAS MURDER.
A MAN BECOMES JADED, YOU UNDERSTAND.
MAYHEW, YOU'RE ALMOST SIXTY YEARS OLD.
YOU JUST HAD THREE MEN KILLED.
AND YOU DID THIS FOR THRILLS?
MONEY CHANGES EVERYTHING--THAT'S WHAT YOU'LL NEVER UNDERSTAND.
PEOPLE LIKE ME LIVE LIVES BEYOND THE LAW, BEYOND MORALITY.
CLIK
THE BLACK GLOVE IS CLOSING AROUND YOU, BATMAN, WHILE I...
I CAN'T BE TOUCHED!

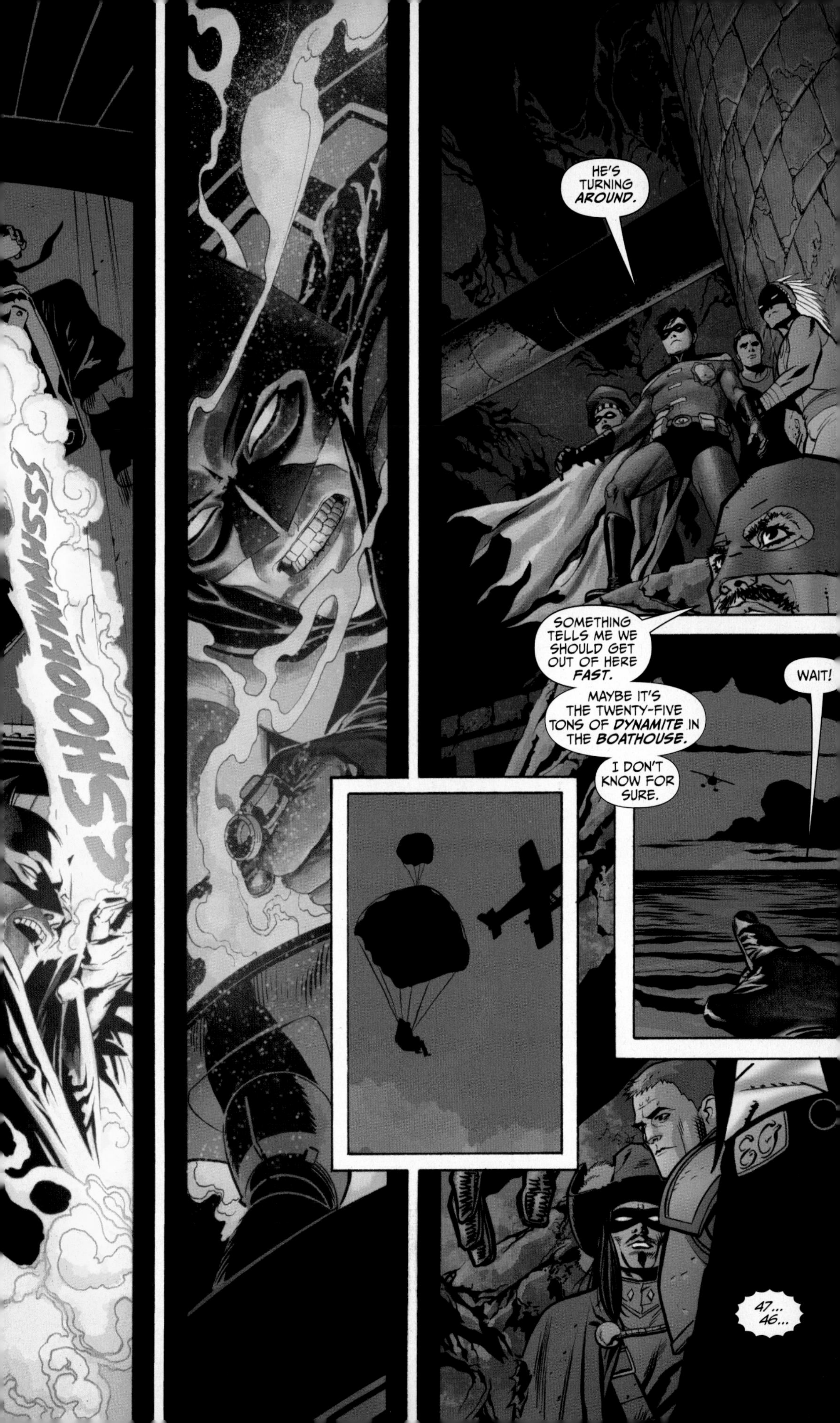
SSHOOOOWHHSSS
HE'S TURNING AROUND.
SOMETHING TELLS ME WE SHOULD GET OUT OF HERE FAST.
MAYBE IT'S THE TWENTY-FIVE TONS OF DYNAMITE IN THE BOATHOUSE.
I DON'T KNOW FOR SURE.
WAIT!
47... 46...

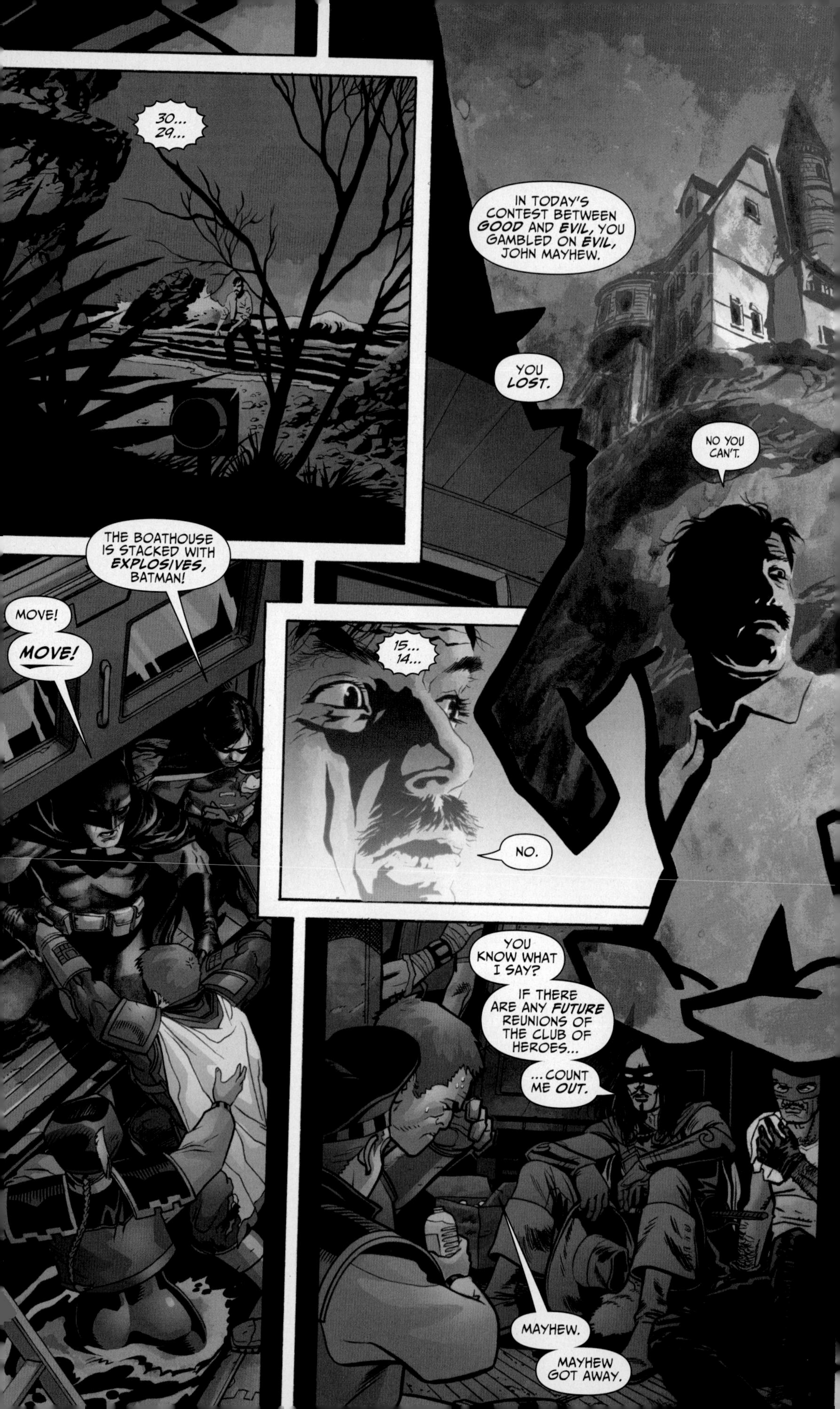
30...
29...
IN TODAY'S CONTEST BETWEEN GOOD AND EVIL, YOU GAMBLED ON EVIL, JOHN MAYHEW.
YOU LOST.
NO YOU CAN'T.
THE BOATHOUSE IS STACKED WITH EXPLOSIVES, BATMAN!
MOVE!
MOVE!
15...
14...
NO.
YOU KNOW WHAT I SAY?
IF THERE ARE ANY FUTURE REUNIONS OF THE CLUB OF HEROES...
...COUNT ME OUT.
MAYHEW.
MAYHEW GOT AWAY.

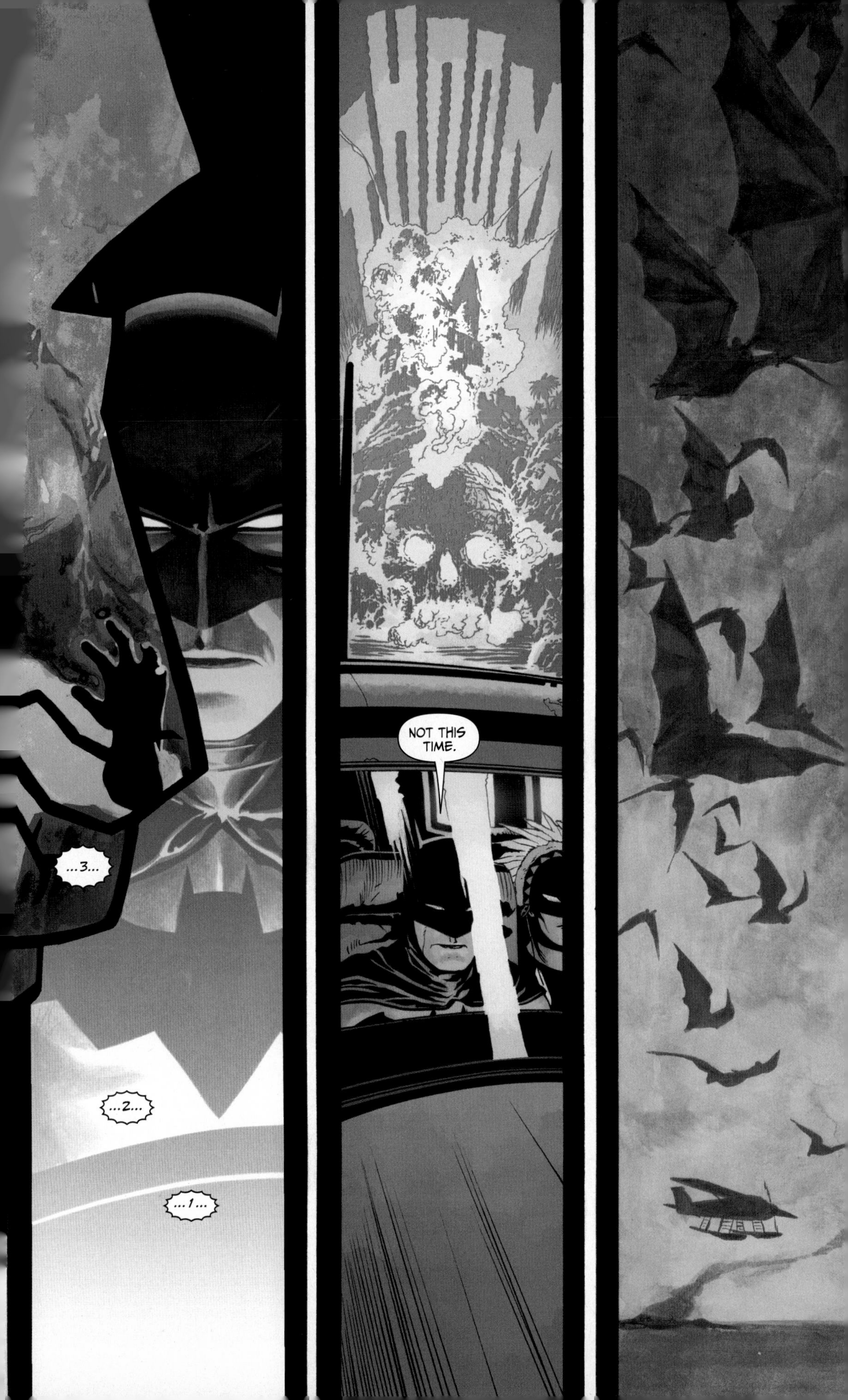
...3...
...2...
...1...
THOOM
NOT THIS TIME.

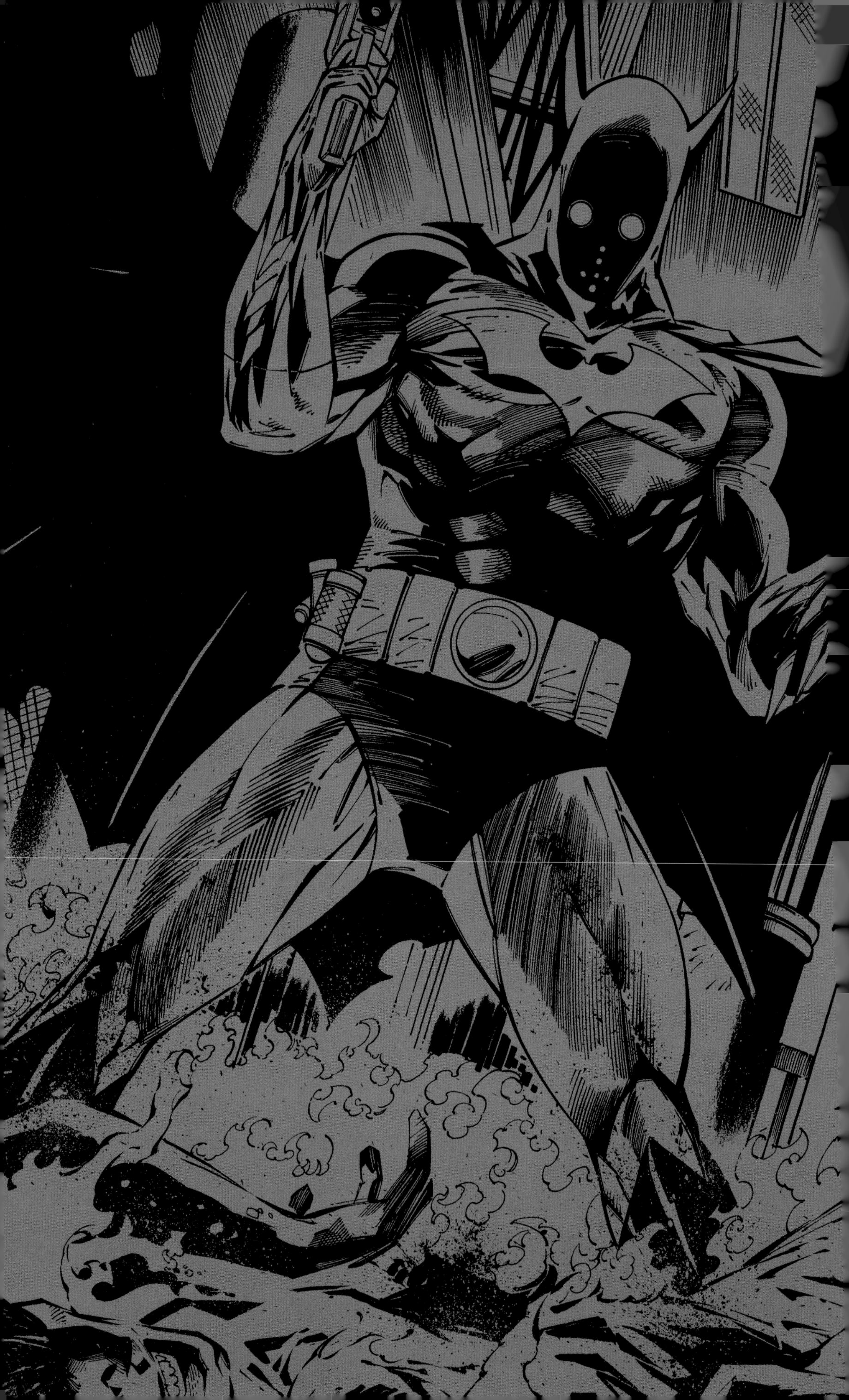

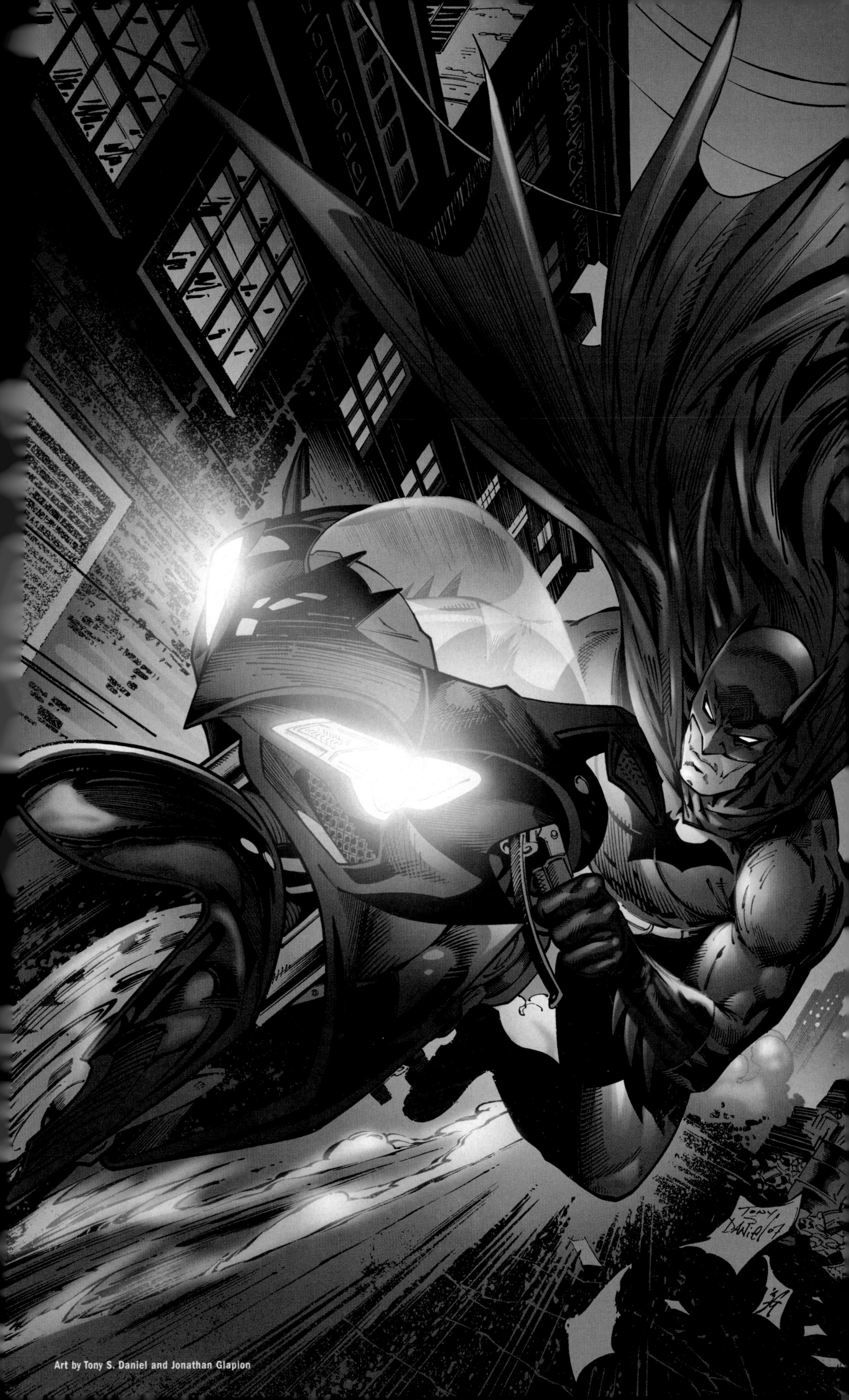

Art by Tony S. Daniel and Jonathan Glapion

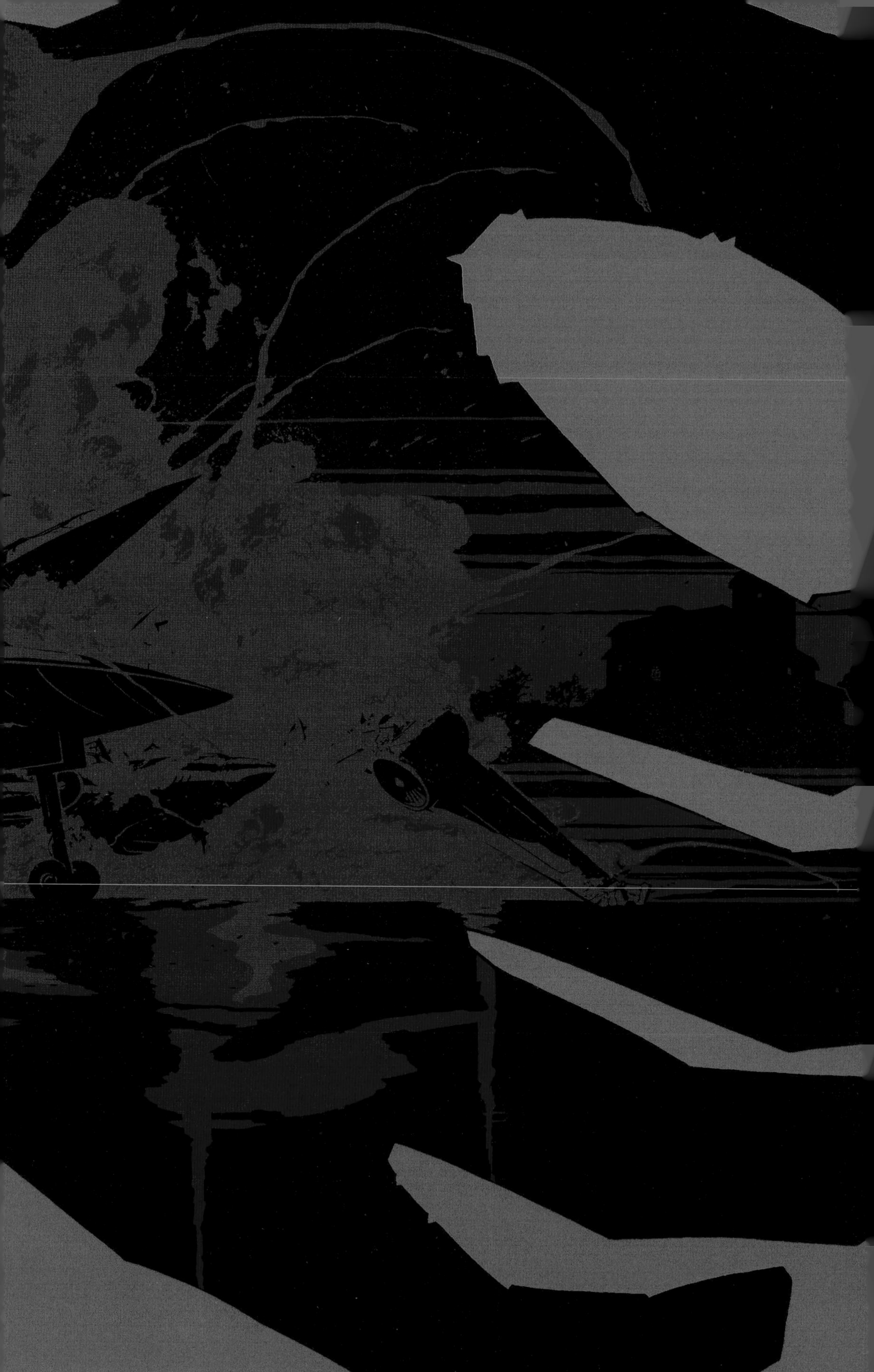

Chapter pencils by Tony S. Daniel
Chapter inks by Tony S. Daniel, Sandu Florea, Jonathan Glapion and Mark Irwin

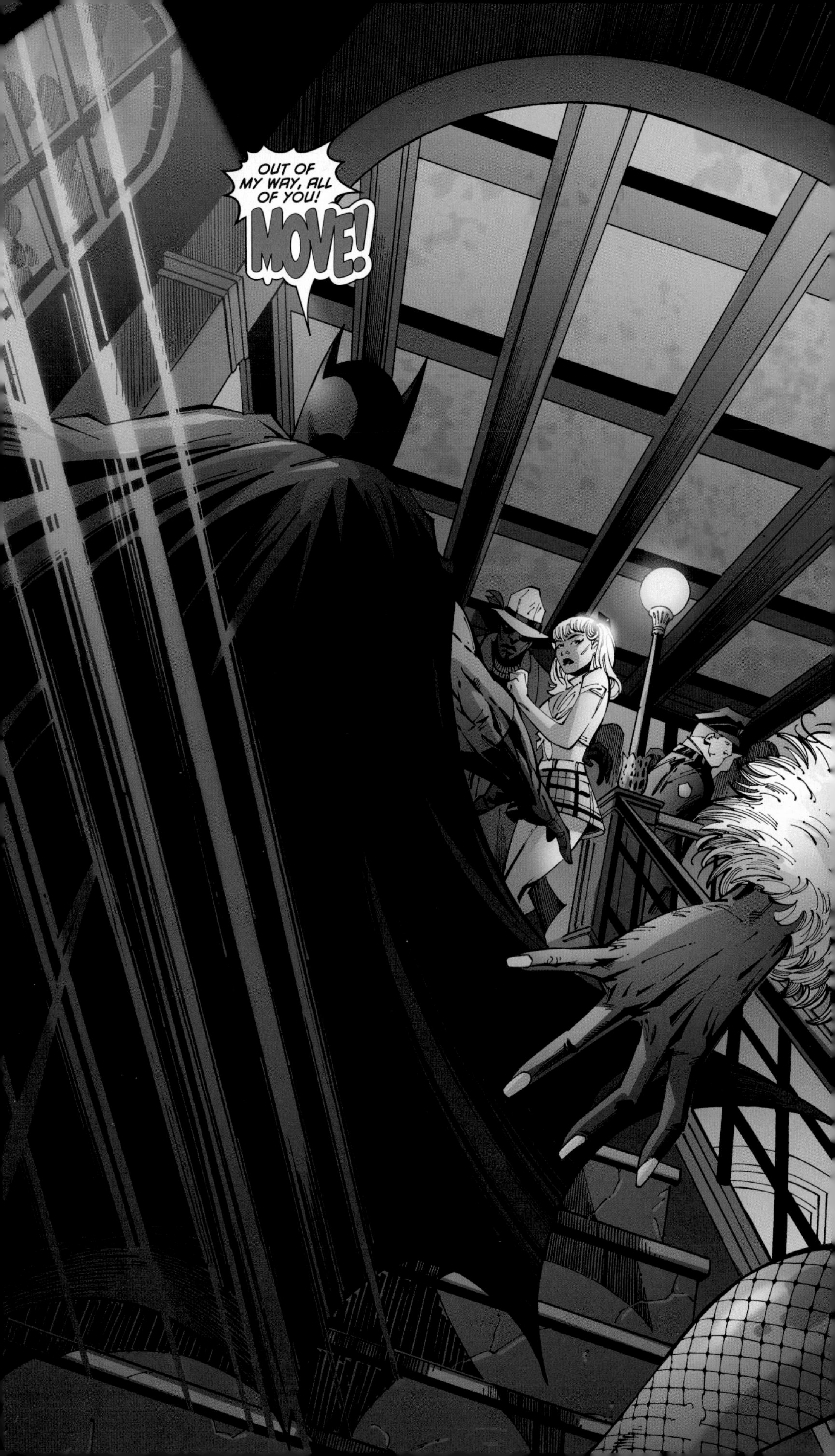
OUT OF MY WAY, ALL OF YOU!
MOVE!

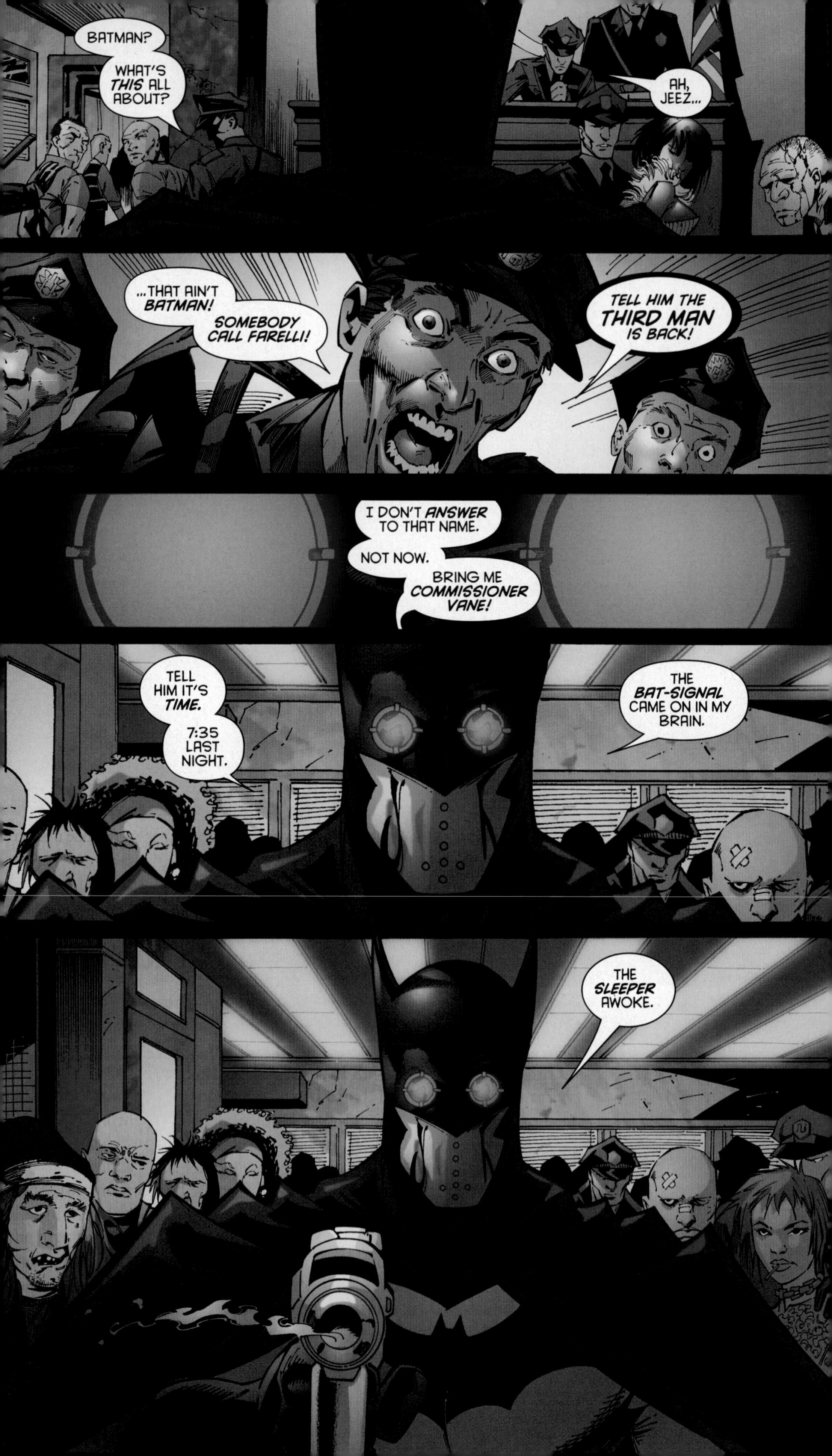
BATMAN?
WHAT'S THIS ALL ABOUT?
AH, JEEZ...
...THAT AIN'T BATMAN!
SOMEBODY CALL FARELLI!
TELL HIM THE THIRD MAN IS BACK!
I DON'T ANSWER TO THAT NAME.
NOT NOW.
BRING ME COMMISSIONER VANE!
TELL HIM IT'S TIME.
7:35 LAST NIGHT.
THE BAT-SIGNAL CAME ON IN MY BRAIN.
THE SLEEPER AWOKE.

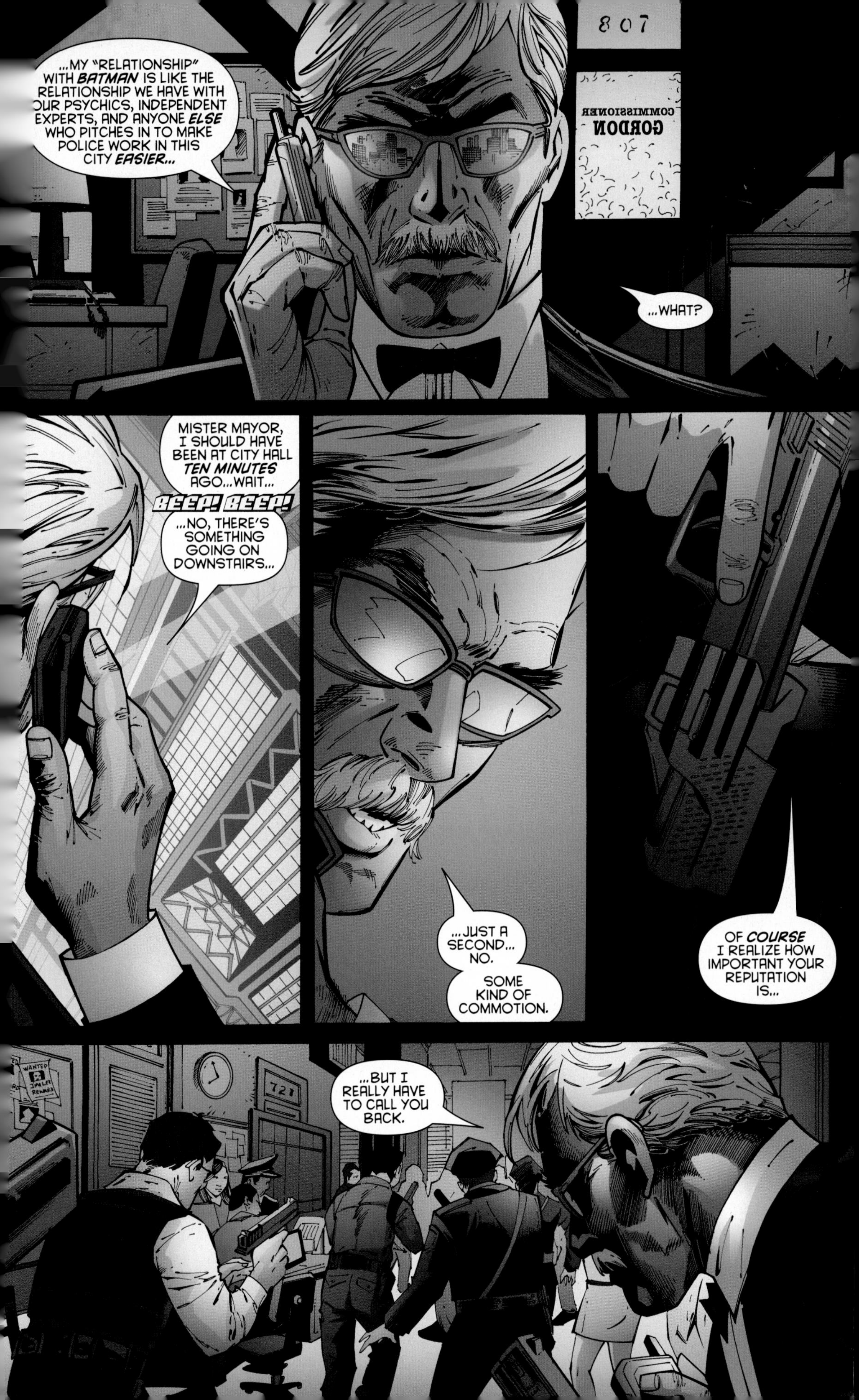
807
...MY "RELATIONSHIP" WITH BATMAN IS LIKE THE RELATIONSHIP WE HAVE WITH OUR PSYCHICS, INDEPENDENT EXPERTS, AND ANYONE ELSE WHO PITCHES IN TO MAKE POLICE WORK IN THIS CITY EASIER...
...WHAT?
MISTER MAYOR, I SHOULD HAVE BEEN AT CITY HALL TEN MINUTES AGO...WAIT...
BEEP! BEEP!
...NO, THERE'S SOMETHING GOING ON DOWNSTAIRS...
...JUST A SECOND... NO.
SOME KIND OF COMMOTION.
OF COURSE I REALIZE HOW IMPORTANT YOUR REPUTATION IS...
WANTED
721
...BUT I REALLY HAVE TO CALL YOU BACK.

I WALKED ALL THE WAY FROM HELL.
WITH A SECRET TO TELL.
ABOUT BATMAN AND ME.
space medicine

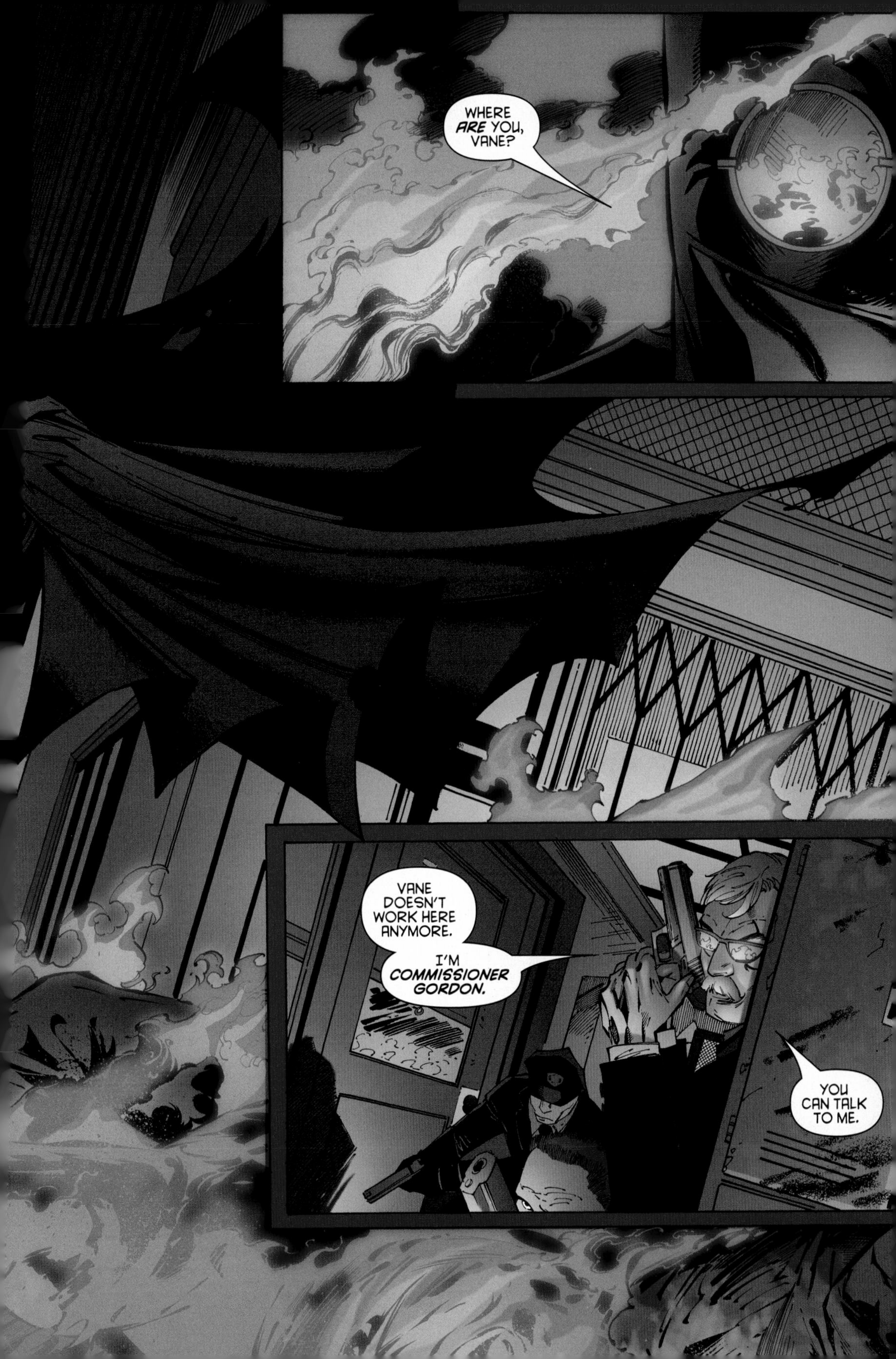
WHERE ARE YOU, VANE?
VANE DOESN'T WORK HERE ANYMORE.
I'M COMMISSIONER GORDON.
YOU CAN TALK TO ME.

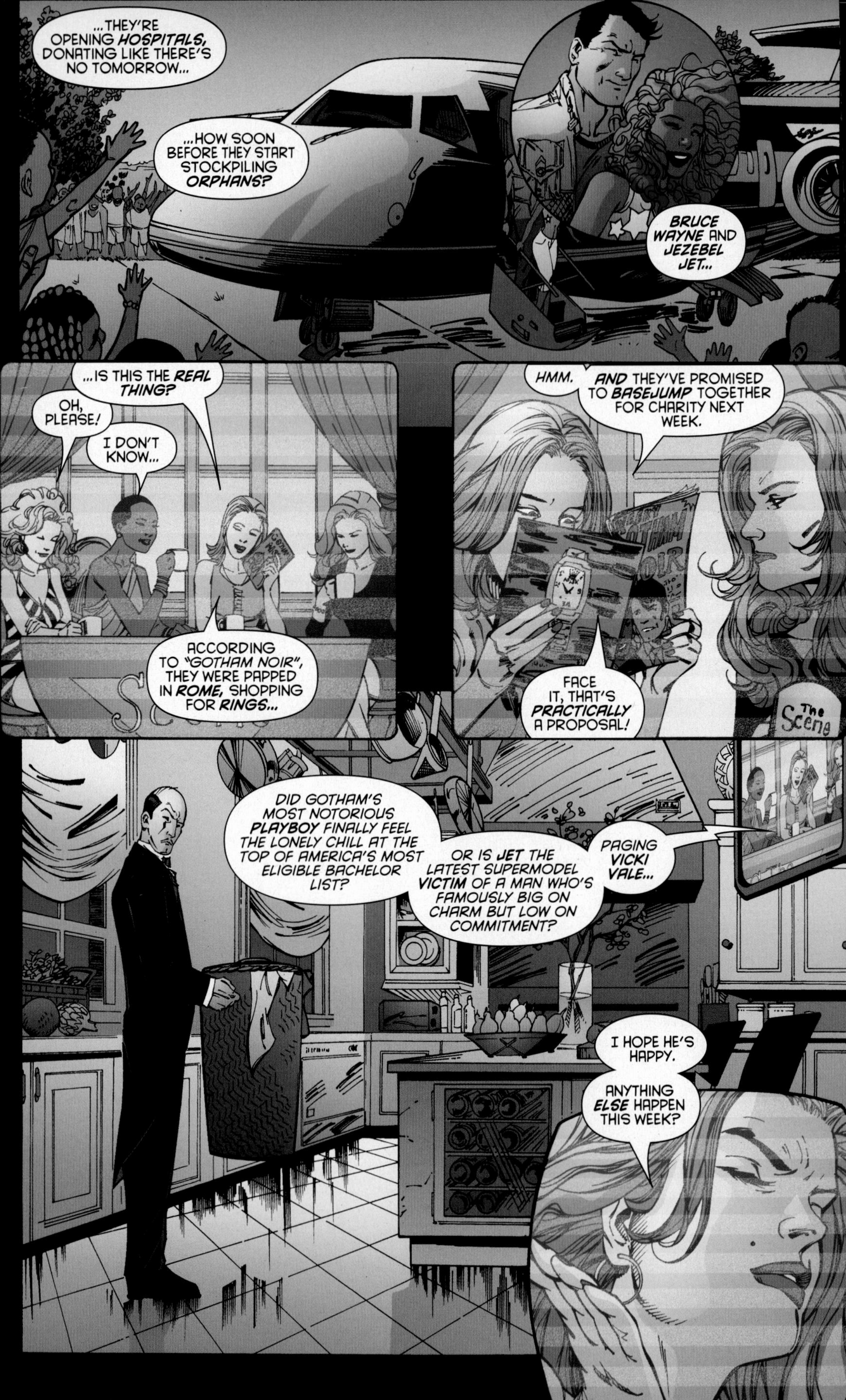
...THEY'RE OPENING HOSPITALS, DONATING LIKE THERE'S NO TOMORROW...
...HOW SOON BEFORE THEY START STOCKPILING ORPHANS?
BRUCE WAYNE AND JEZEBEL JET...
...IS THIS THE REAL THING?
OH, PLEASE!
I DON'T KNOW...
ACCORDING TO "GOTHAM NOIR", THEY WERE PAPPED IN ROME, SHOPPING FOR RINGS...
HMM.
AND THEY'VE PROMISED TO BASEJUMP TOGETHER FOR CHARITY NEXT WEEK.
FACE IT, THAT'S PRACTICALLY A PROPOSAL!
The Scene
DID GOTHAM'S MOST NOTORIOUS PLAYBOY FINALLY FEEL THE LONELY CHILL AT THE TOP OF AMERICA'S MOST ELIGIBLE BACHELOR LIST?
OR IS JET THE LATEST SUPERMODEL VICTIM OF A MAN WHO'S FAMOUSLY BIG ON CHARM BUT LOW ON COMMITMENT?
PAGING VICKI VALE...
I HOPE HE'S HAPPY.
ANYTHING ELSE HAPPEN THIS WEEK?

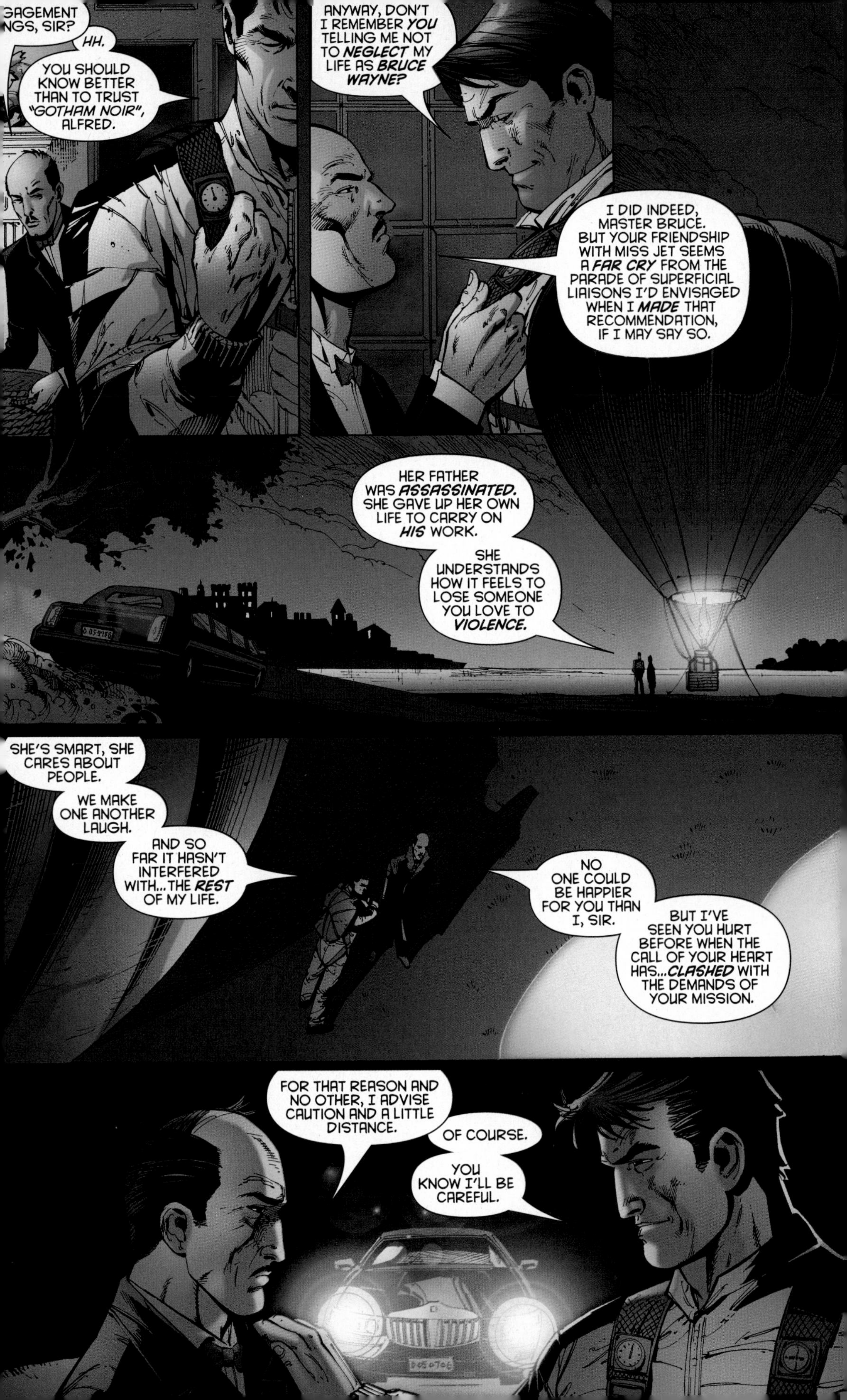
GAGEMENT
NGS, SIR?
HH.
YOU SHOULD KNOW BETTER THAN TO TRUST "GOTHAM NOIR", ALFRED.
ANYWAY, DON'T I REMEMBER YOU TELLING ME NOT TO NEGLECT MY LIFE AS BRUCE WAYNE?
I DID INDEED, MASTER BRUCE. BUT YOUR FRIENDSHIP WITH MISS JET SEEMS A FAR CRY FROM THE PARADE OF SUPERFICIAL LIAISONS I'D ENVISAGED WHEN I MADE THAT RECOMMENDATION, IF I MAY SAY SO.
HER FATHER WAS ASSASSINATED. SHE GAVE UP HER OWN LIFE TO CARRY ON HIS WORK.
SHE UNDERSTANDS HOW IT FEELS TO LOSE SOMEONE YOU LOVE TO VIOLENCE.
SHE'S SMART, SHE CARES ABOUT PEOPLE.
WE MAKE ONE ANOTHER LAUGH.
AND SO FAR IT HASN'T INTERFERED WITH...THE REST OF MY LIFE.
NO ONE COULD BE HAPPIER FOR YOU THAN I, SIR.
BUT I'VE SEEN YOU HURT BEFORE WHEN THE CALL OF YOUR HEART HAS...CLASHED WITH THE DEMANDS OF YOUR MISSION.
FOR THAT REASON AND NO OTHER, I ADVISE CAUTION AND A LITTLE DISTANCE.
OF COURSE.
YOU KNOW I'LL BE CAREFUL.

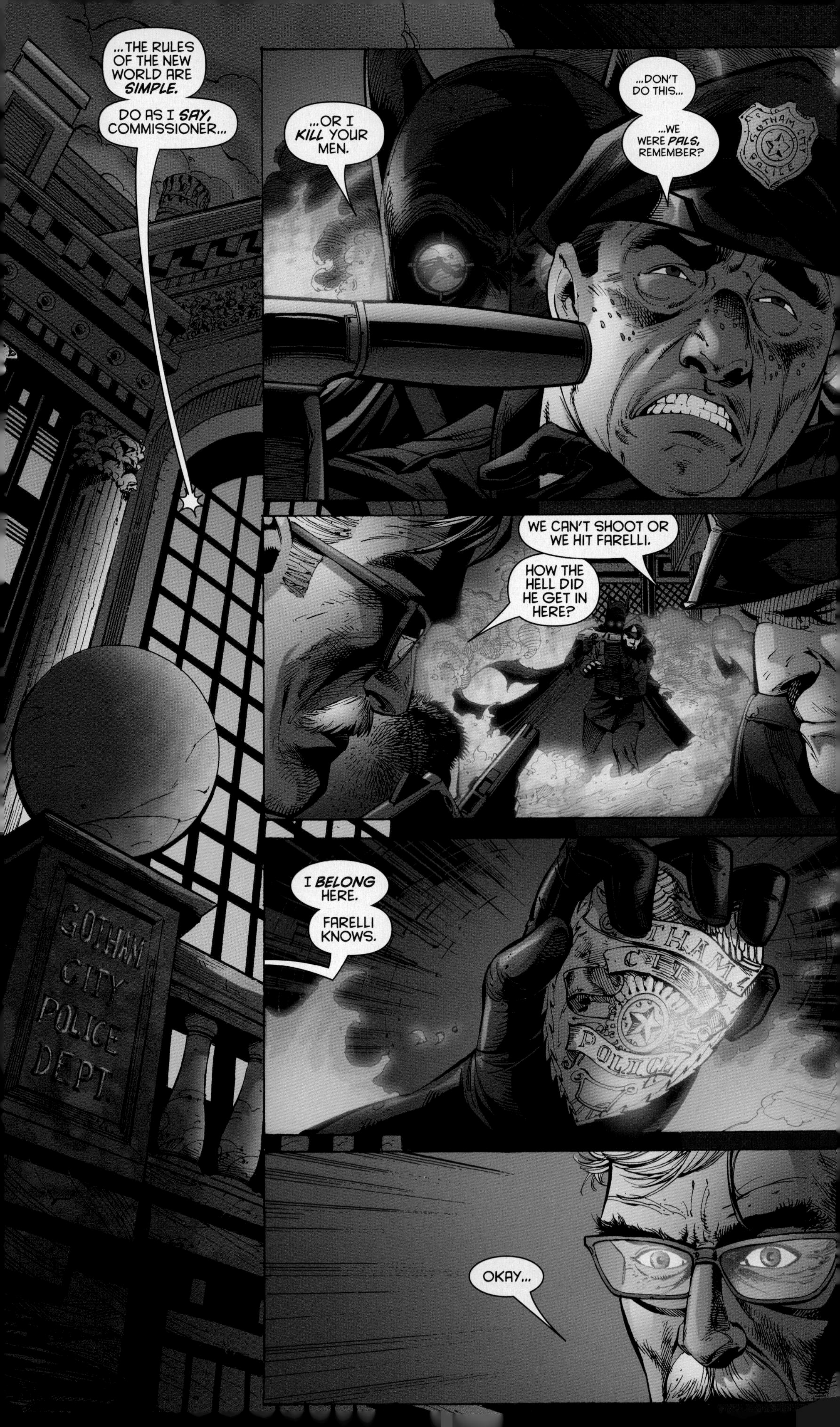
...THE RULES OF THE NEW WORLD ARE *SIMPLE.*
DO AS I *SAY,* COMMISSIONER...
...OR I *KILL* YOUR MEN.
...DON'T DO THIS...
...WE WERE *PALS,* REMEMBER?
GOTHAM CITY POLICE
WE CAN'T SHOOT OR WE HIT FARELLI.
HOW THE HELL DID HE GET IN HERE?
GOTHAM CITY POLICE DEPT.
I *BELONG* HERE.
FARELLI KNOWS.
GOTHAM CITY POLICE
OKAY...

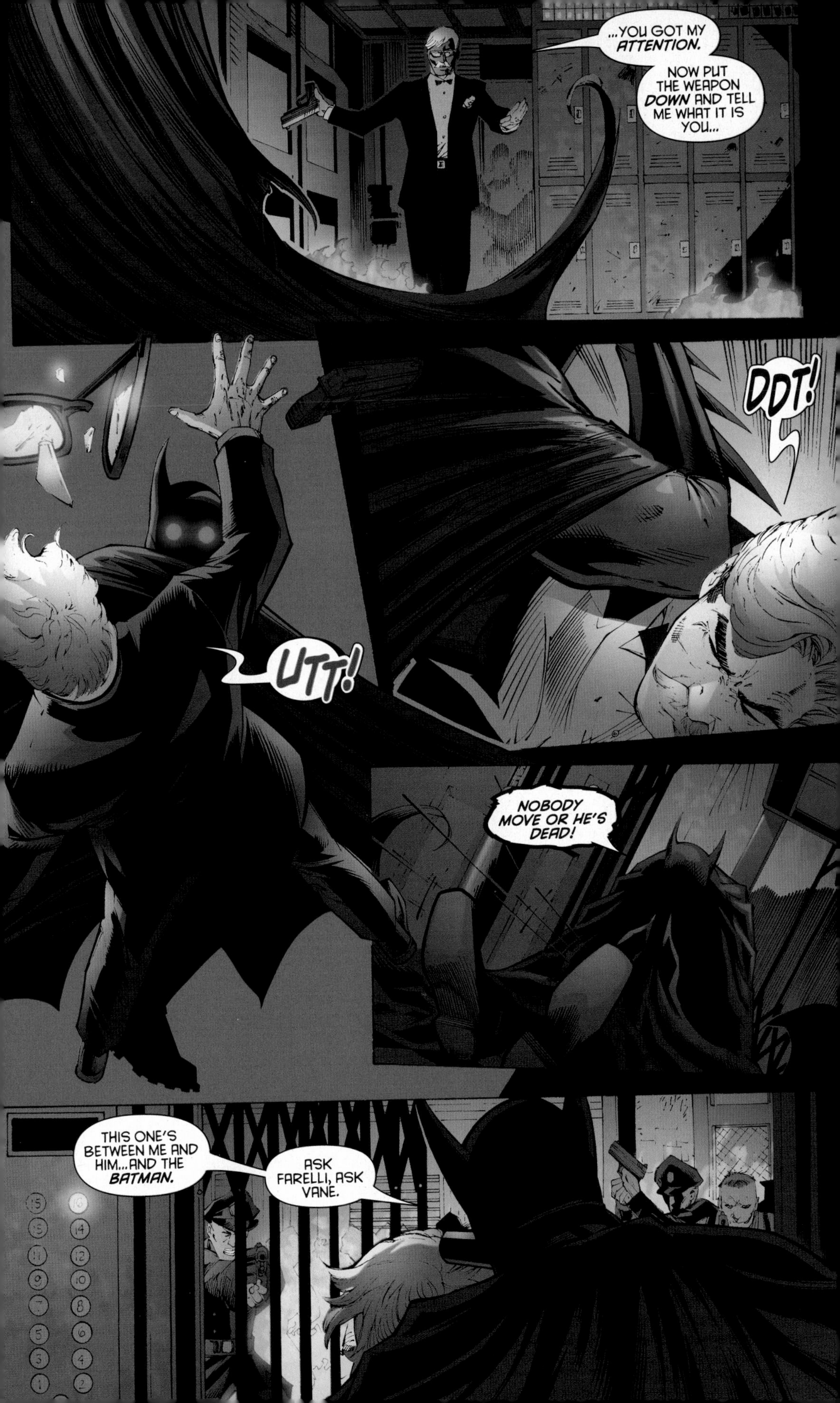
...YOU GOT MY ATTENTION.
NOW PUT THE WEAPON DOWN AND TELL ME WHAT IT IS YOU...
DDT!
UTT!
NOBODY MOVE OR HE'S DEAD!
THIS ONE'S BETWEEN ME AND HIM...AND THE BATMAN.
ASK FARELLI, ASK VANE.

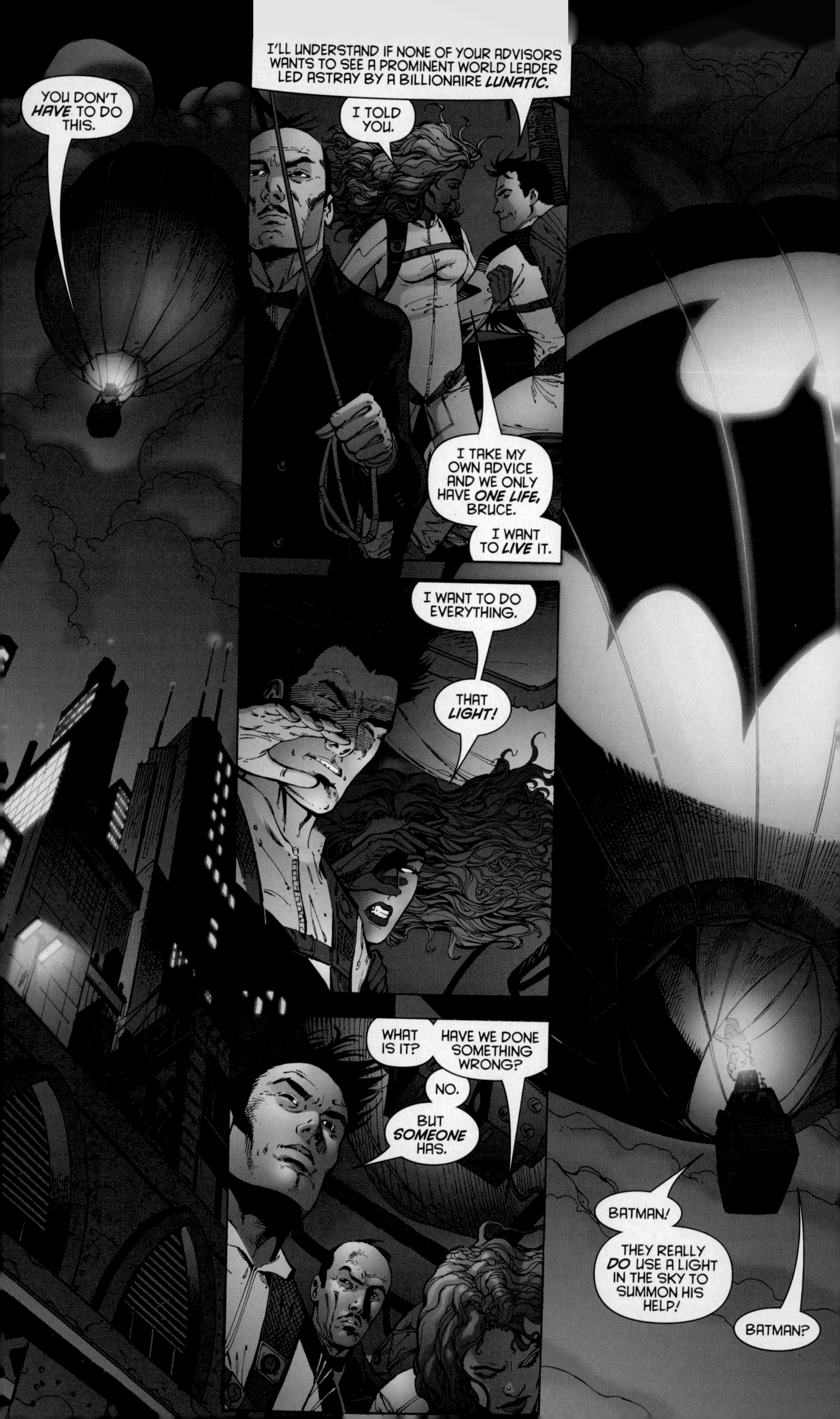
YOU DON'T HAVE TO DO THIS.
I'LL UNDERSTAND IF NONE OF YOUR ADVISORS WANTS TO SEE A PROMINENT WORLD LEADER LED ASTRAY BY A BILLIONAIRE LUNATIC.
I TOLD YOU.
I TAKE MY OWN ADVICE AND WE ONLY HAVE ONE LIFE, BRUCE.
I WANT TO LIVE IT.
I WANT TO DO EVERYTHING.
THAT LIGHT!
WHAT IS IT?
HAVE WE DONE SOMETHING WRONG?
NO.
BUT SOMEONE HAS.
BATMAN!
THEY REALLY DO USE A LIGHT IN THE SKY TO SUMMON HIS HELP!
BATMAN?

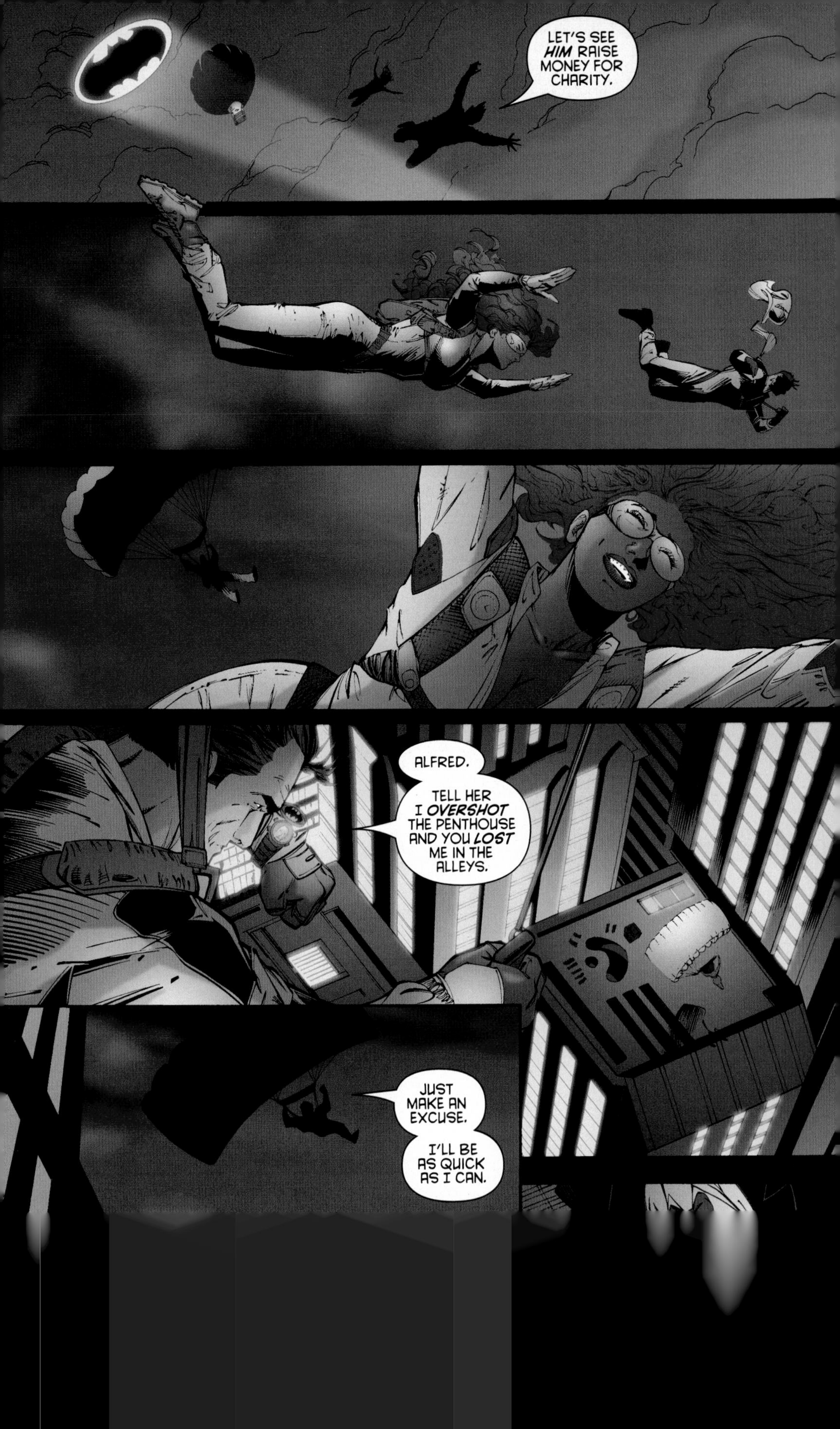
LET'S SEE *HIM* RAISE MONEY FOR CHARITY.
ALFRED.
TELL HER I *OVERSHOT* THE PENTHOUSE AND YOU *LOST* ME IN THE ALLEYS.
JUST MAKE AN EXCUSE.
I'LL BE AS QUICK AS I CAN.

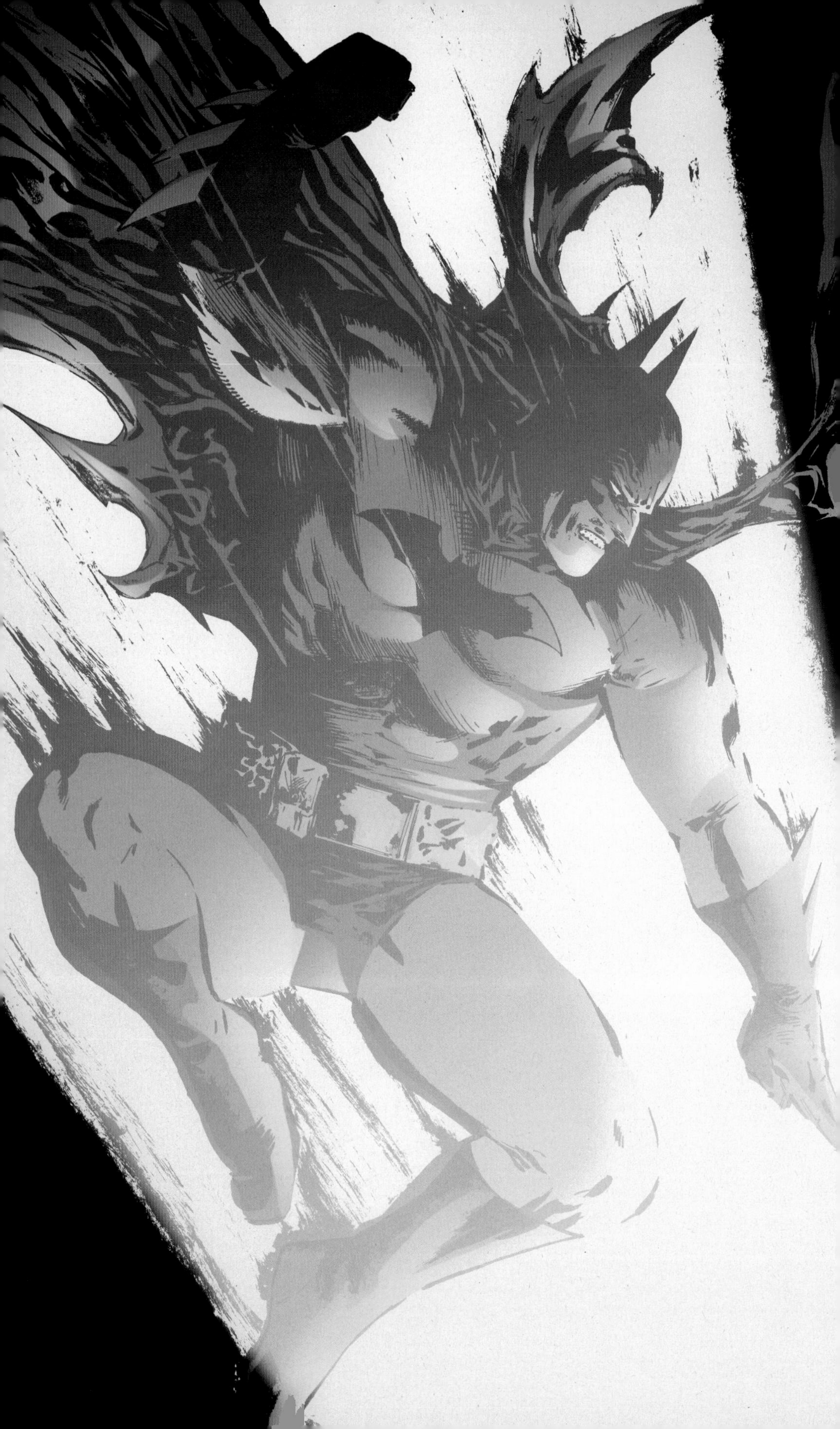

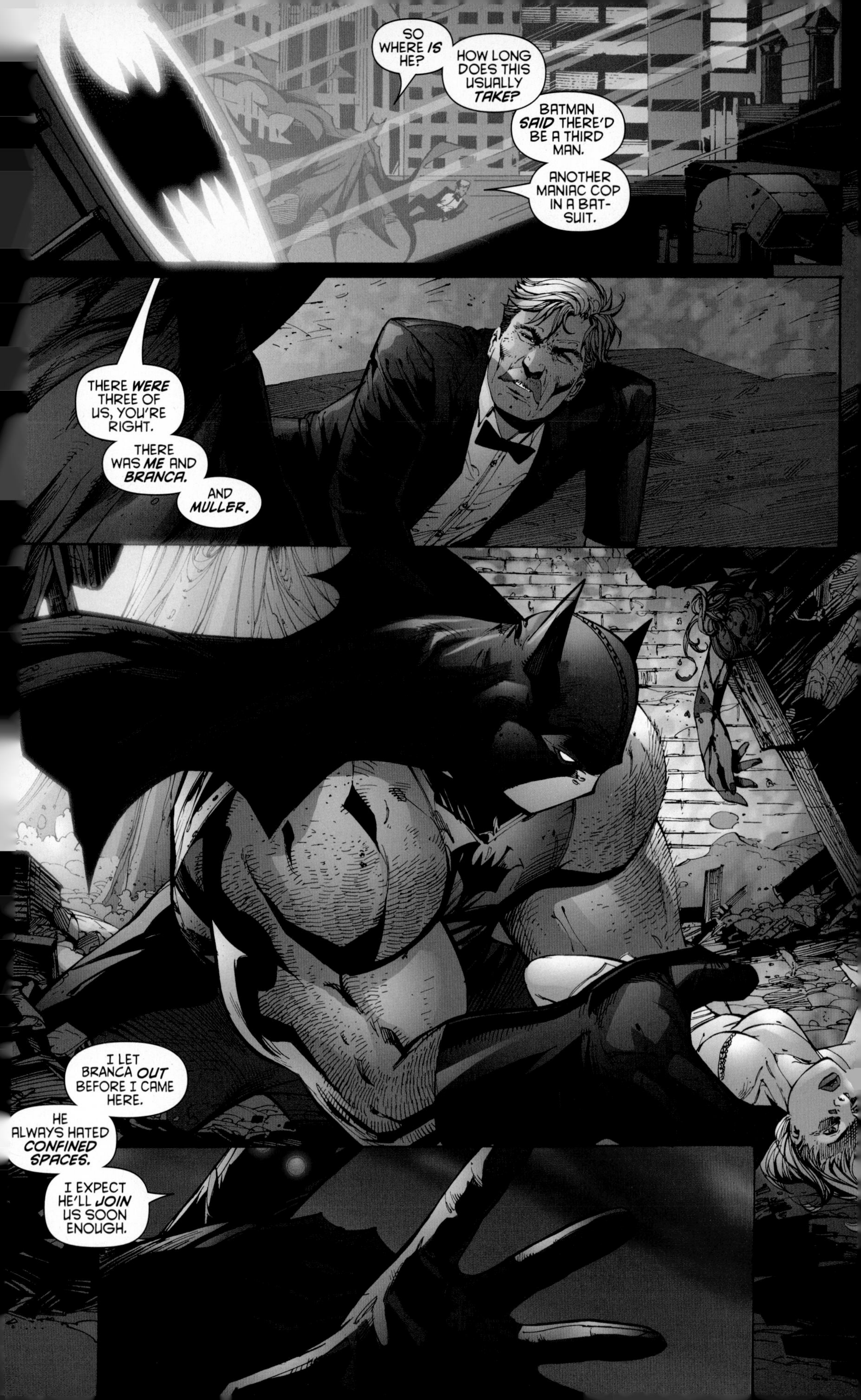
SO WHERE IS HE?
HOW LONG DOES THIS USUALLY TAKE?
BATMAN SAID THERE'D BE A THIRD MAN.
ANOTHER MANIAC COP IN A BAT-SUIT.
THERE WERE THREE OF US, YOU'RE RIGHT.
THERE WAS ME AND BRANCA.
AND MULLER.
I LET BRANCA OUT BEFORE I CAME HERE.
HE ALWAYS HATED CONFINED SPACES.
I EXPECT HE'LL JOIN US SOON ENOUGH.

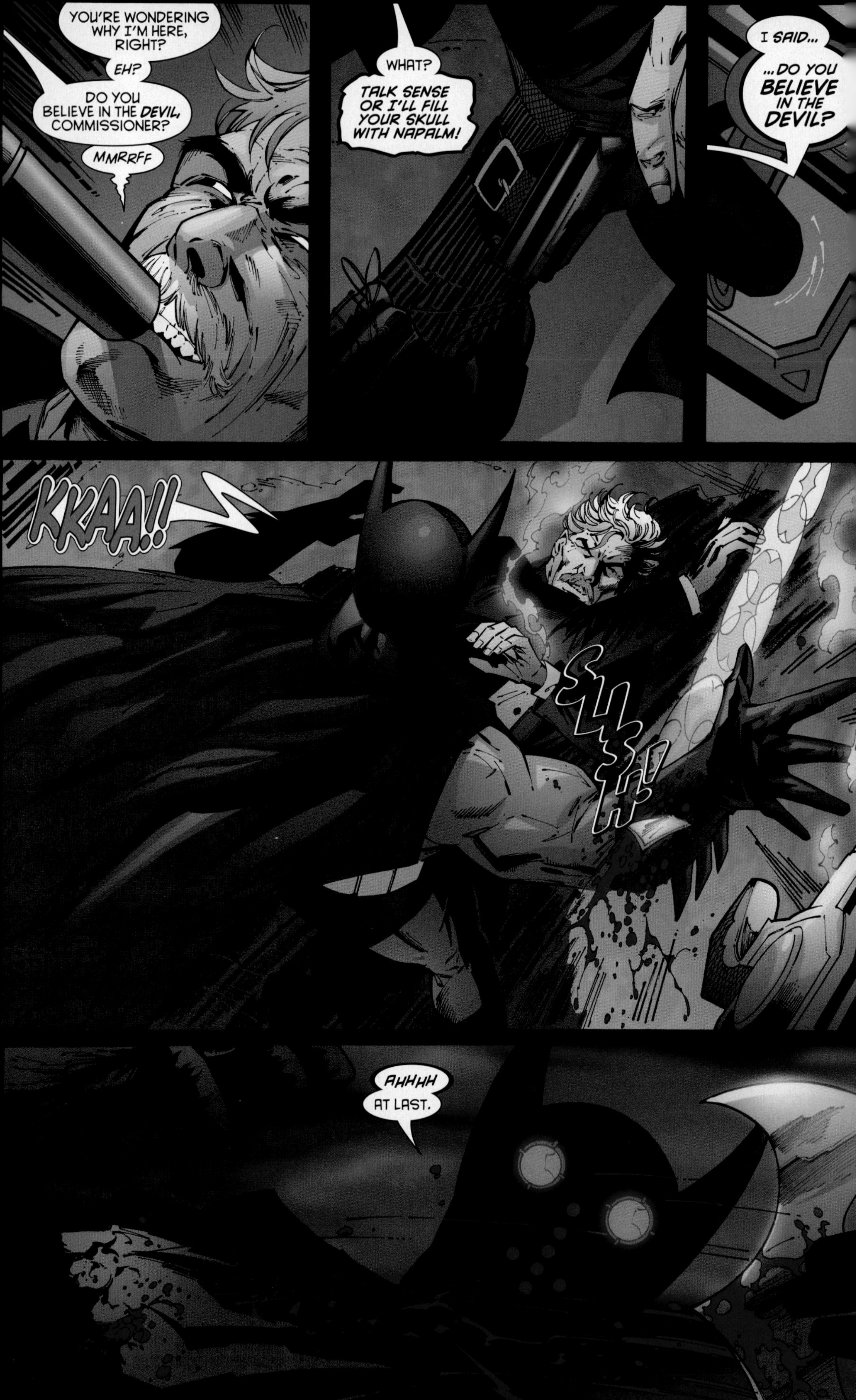
YOU'RE WONDERING WHY I'M HERE, RIGHT?
EH?
DO YOU BELIEVE IN THE DEVIL, COMMISSIONER?
MMRRFF
WHAT? TALK SENSE OR I'LL FILL YOUR SKULL WITH NAPALM!
I SAID...
...DO YOU BELIEVE IN THE DEVIL?
KKAA!!
SHLUK!
AHHHH
AT LAST.

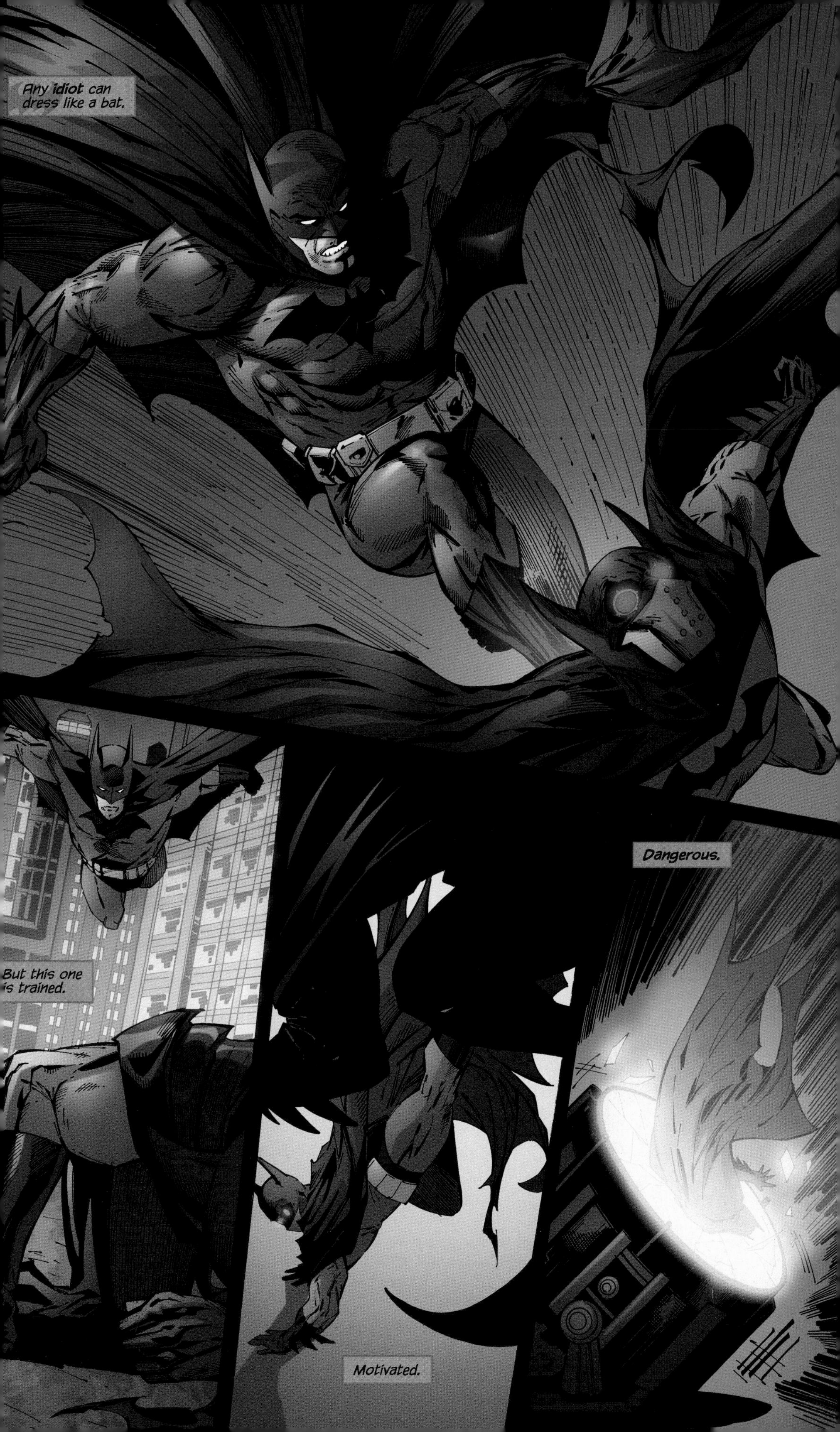
Any idiot can dress like a bat.
But this one is trained.
Dangerous.
Motivated.

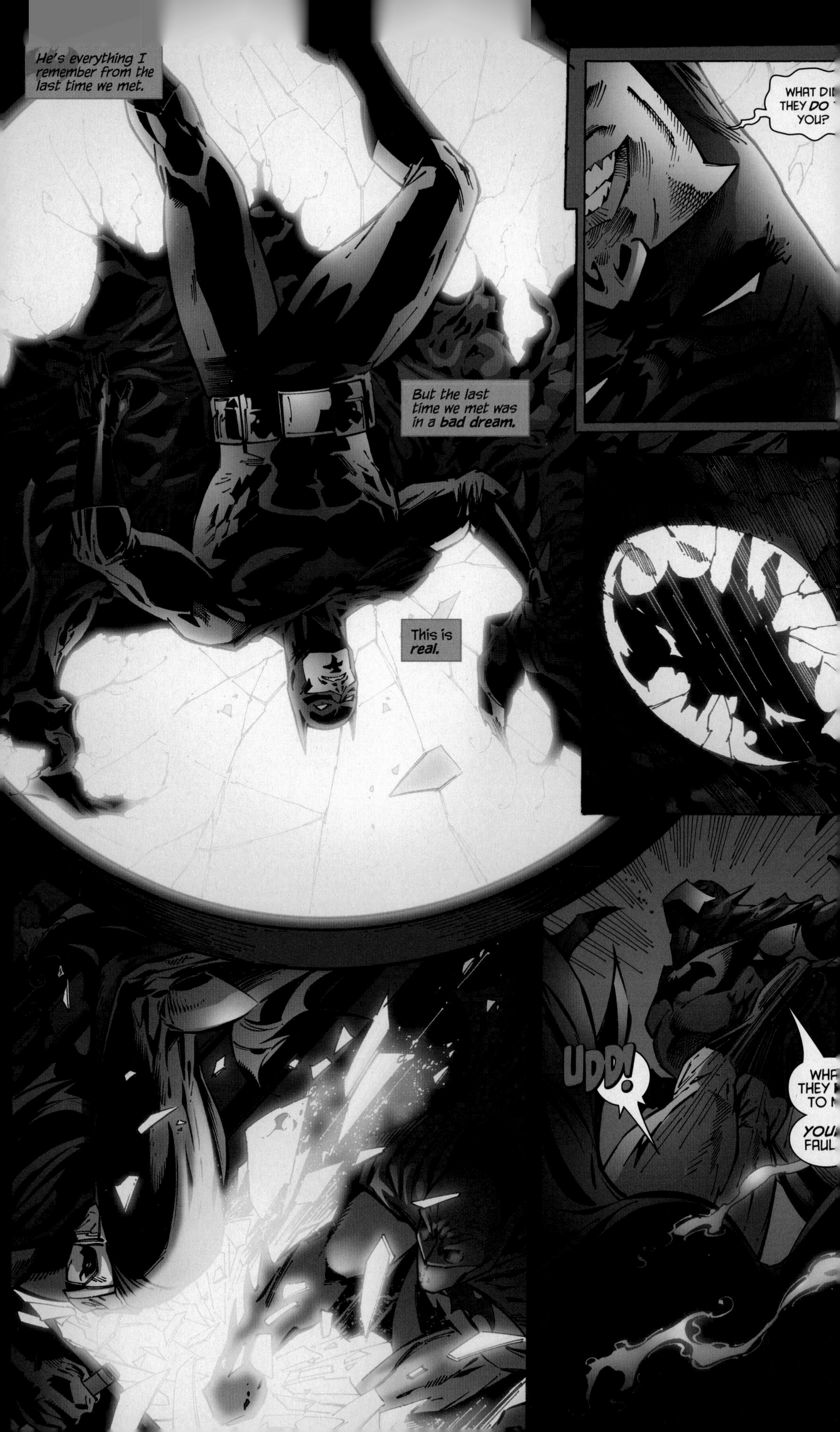
He's everything I remember from the last time we met.
WHAT DI
THEY DO
YOU?
But the last time we met was in a bad dream.
This is real.
UDD!
WHA
THEY
TO M
YOU
FAUL

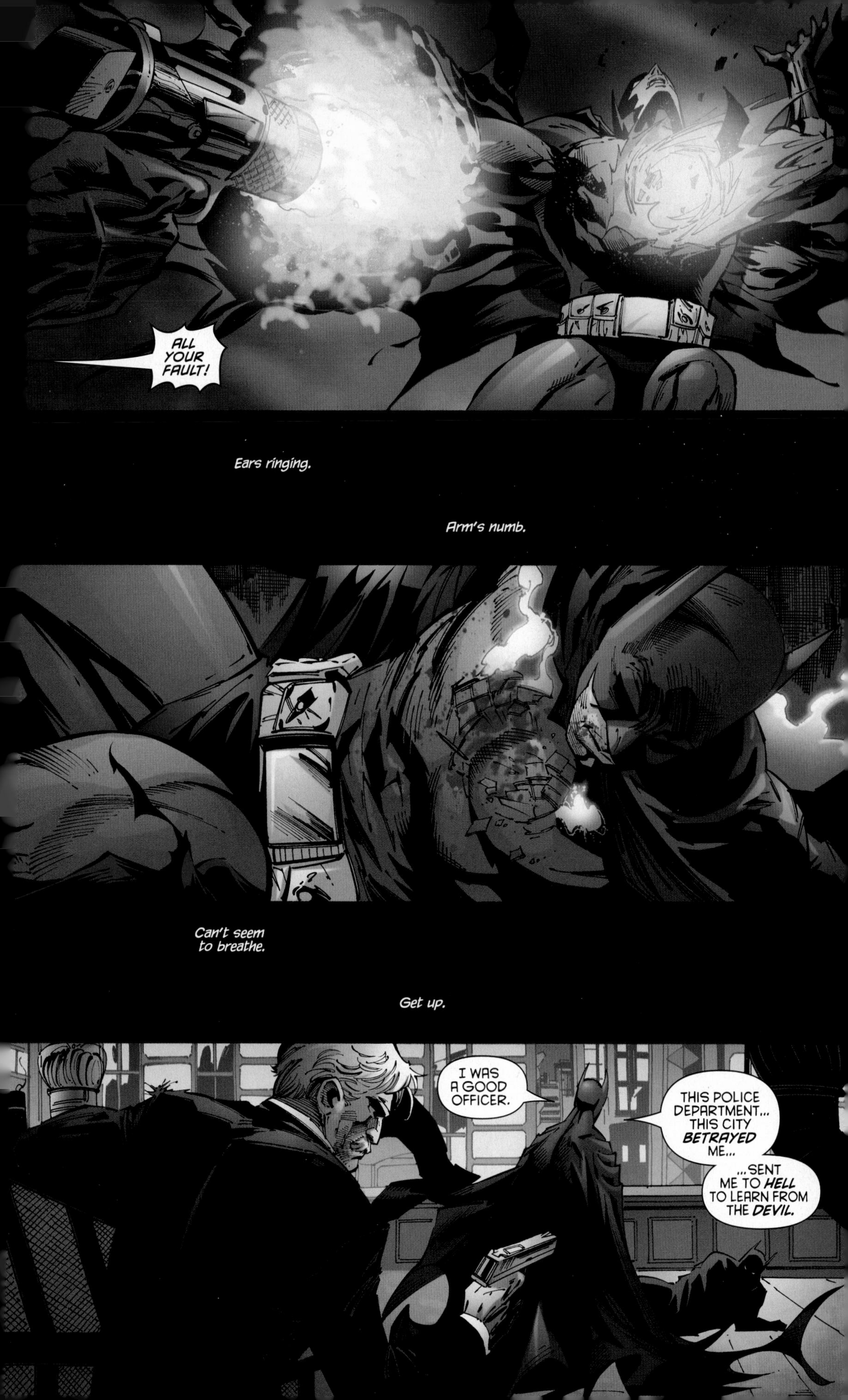
ALL YOUR FAULT!
Ears ringing.
Arm's numb.
Can't seem to breathe.
Get up.
I WAS A GOOD OFFICER.
THIS POLICE DEPARTMENT... THIS CITY BETRAYED ME...
...SENT ME TO HELL TO LEARN FROM THE DEVIL.

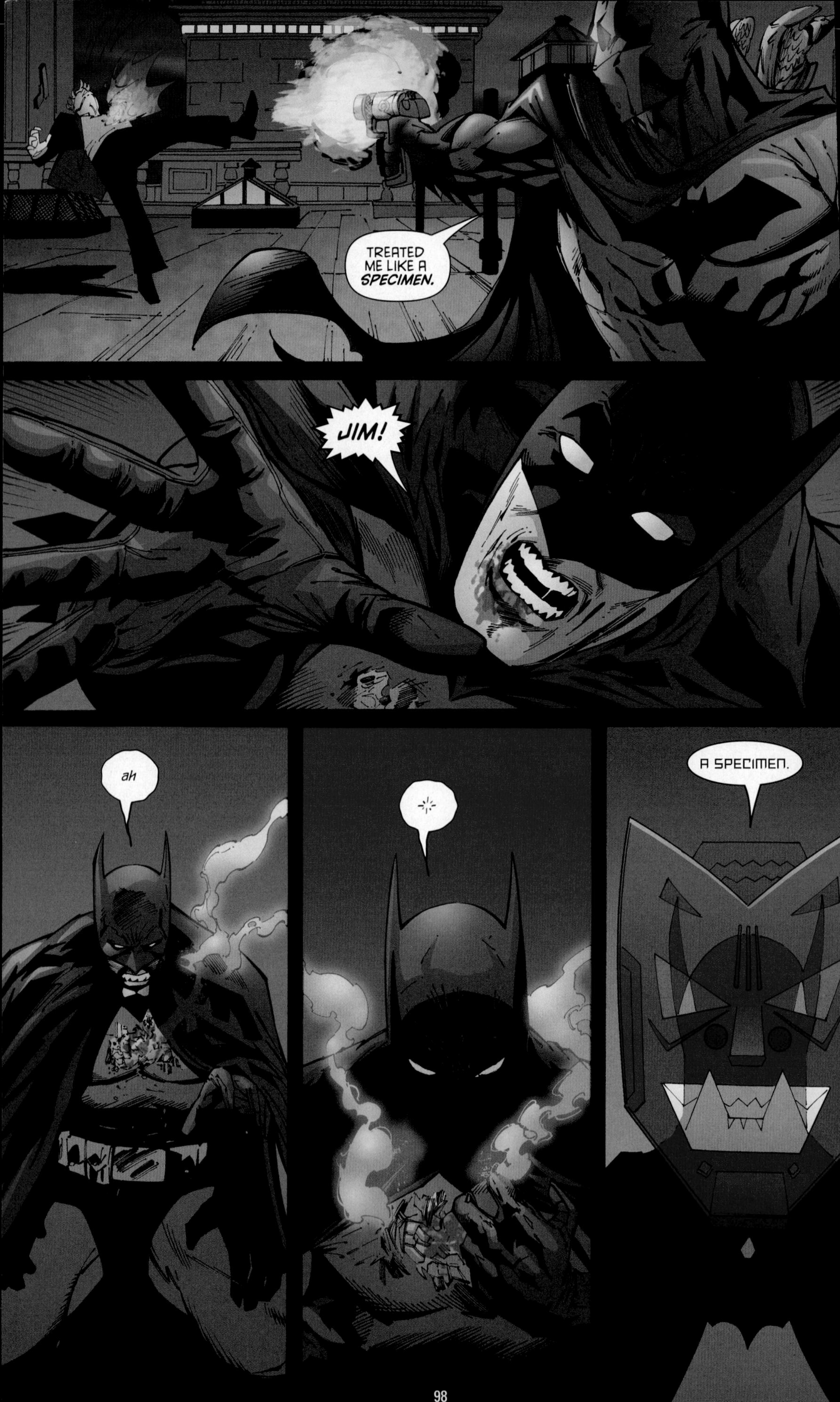
TREATED ME LIKE A *SPECIMEN.*
JIM!
ah
A SPECIMEN.

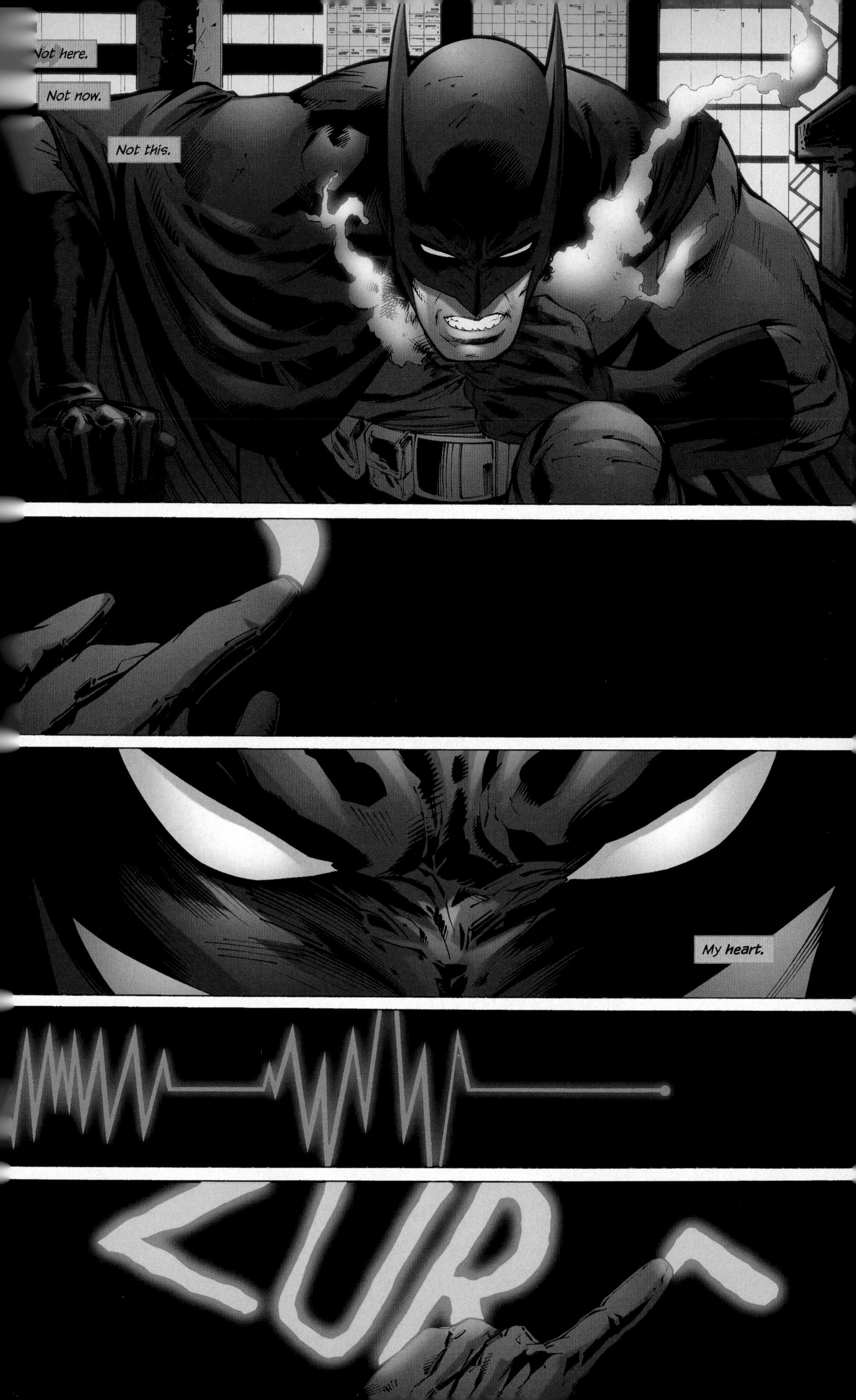

Not here.
Not now.
Not this.
My heart.
ZURR

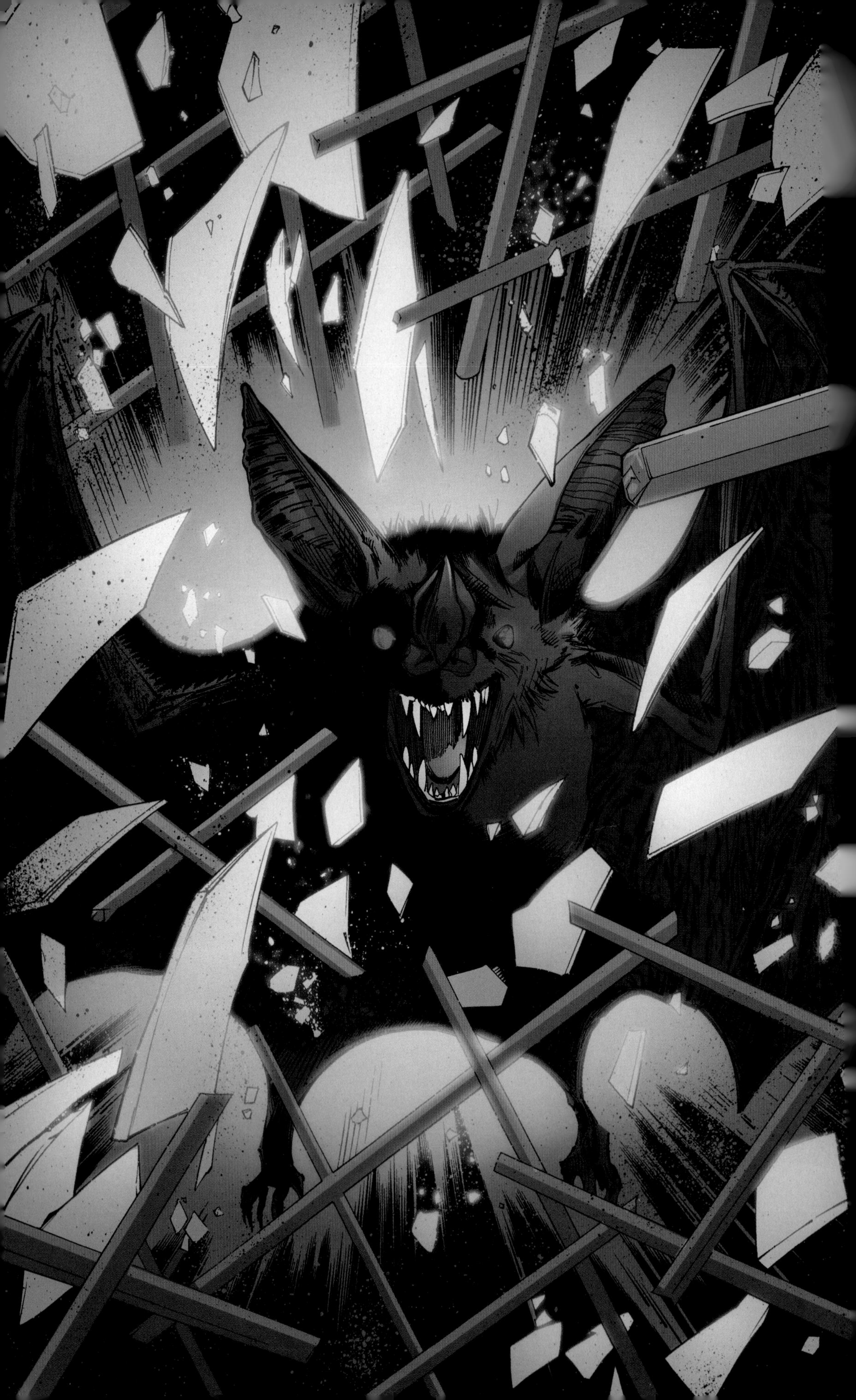

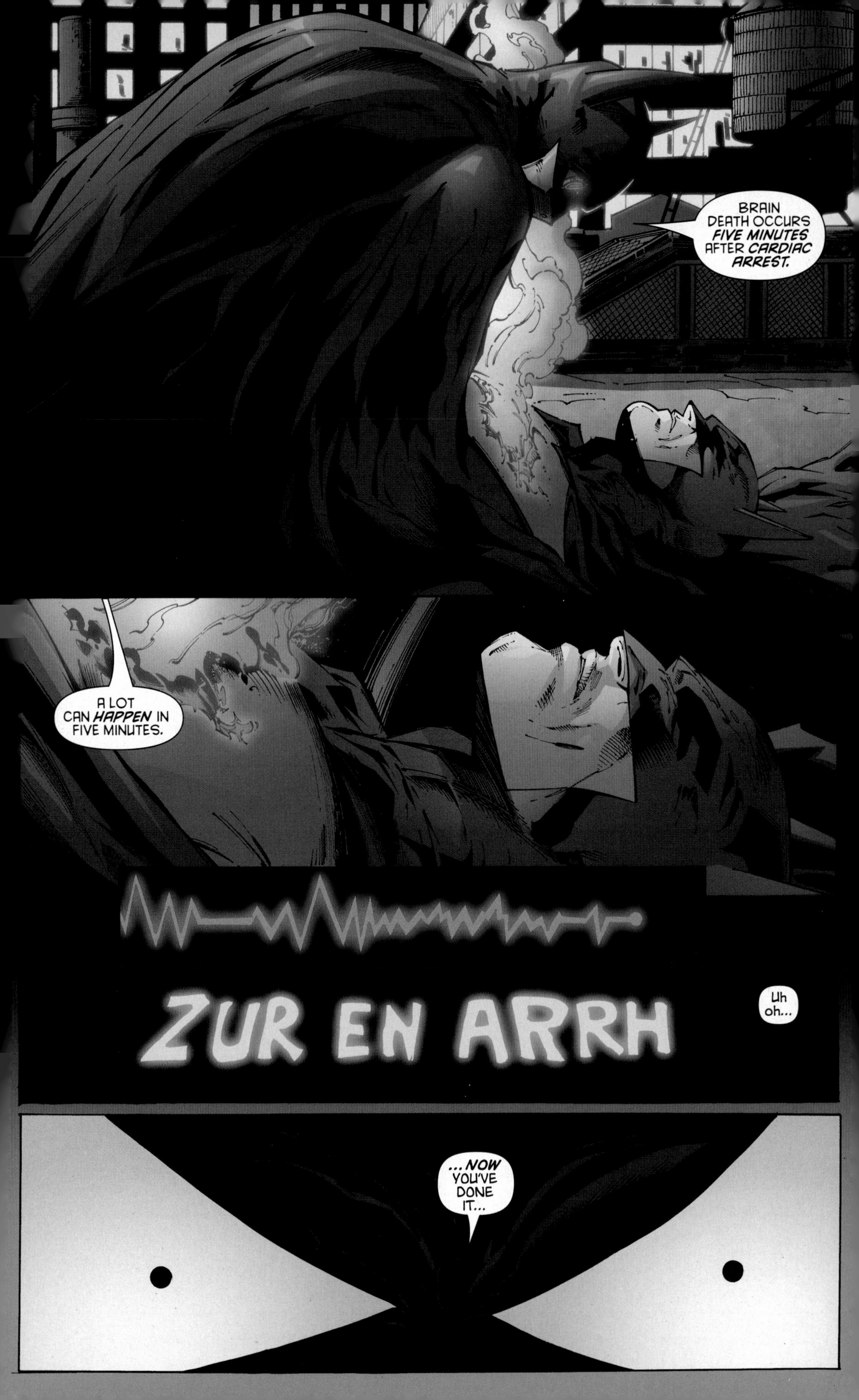
BRAIN DEATH OCCURS FIVE MINUTES AFTER CARDIAC ARREST.
A LOT CAN HAPPEN IN FIVE MINUTES.
ZUR EN ARRH
Uh oh...
...NOW YOU'VE DONE IT...

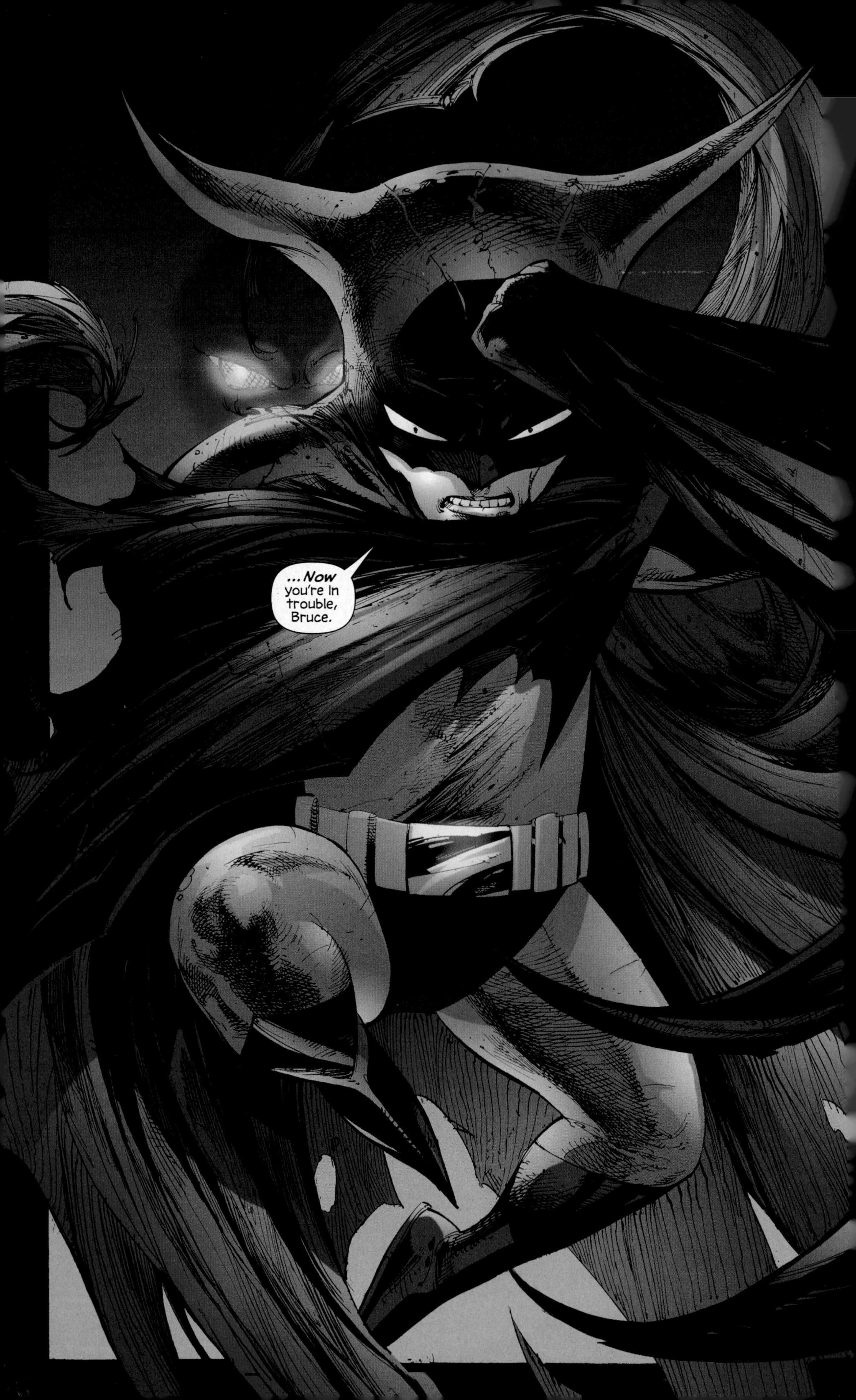
...Now you're in trouble, Bruce.

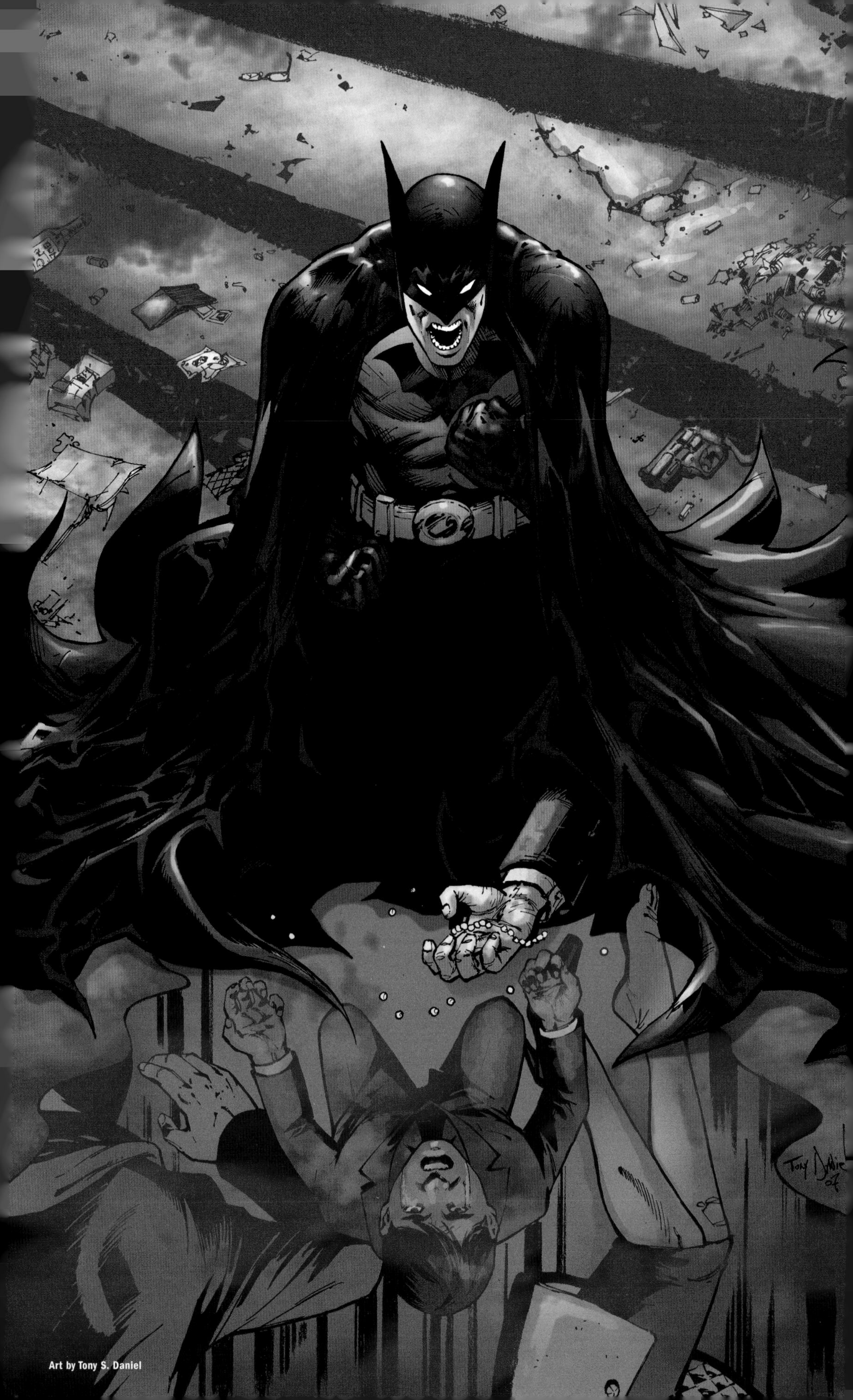

Art by Tony S. Daniel

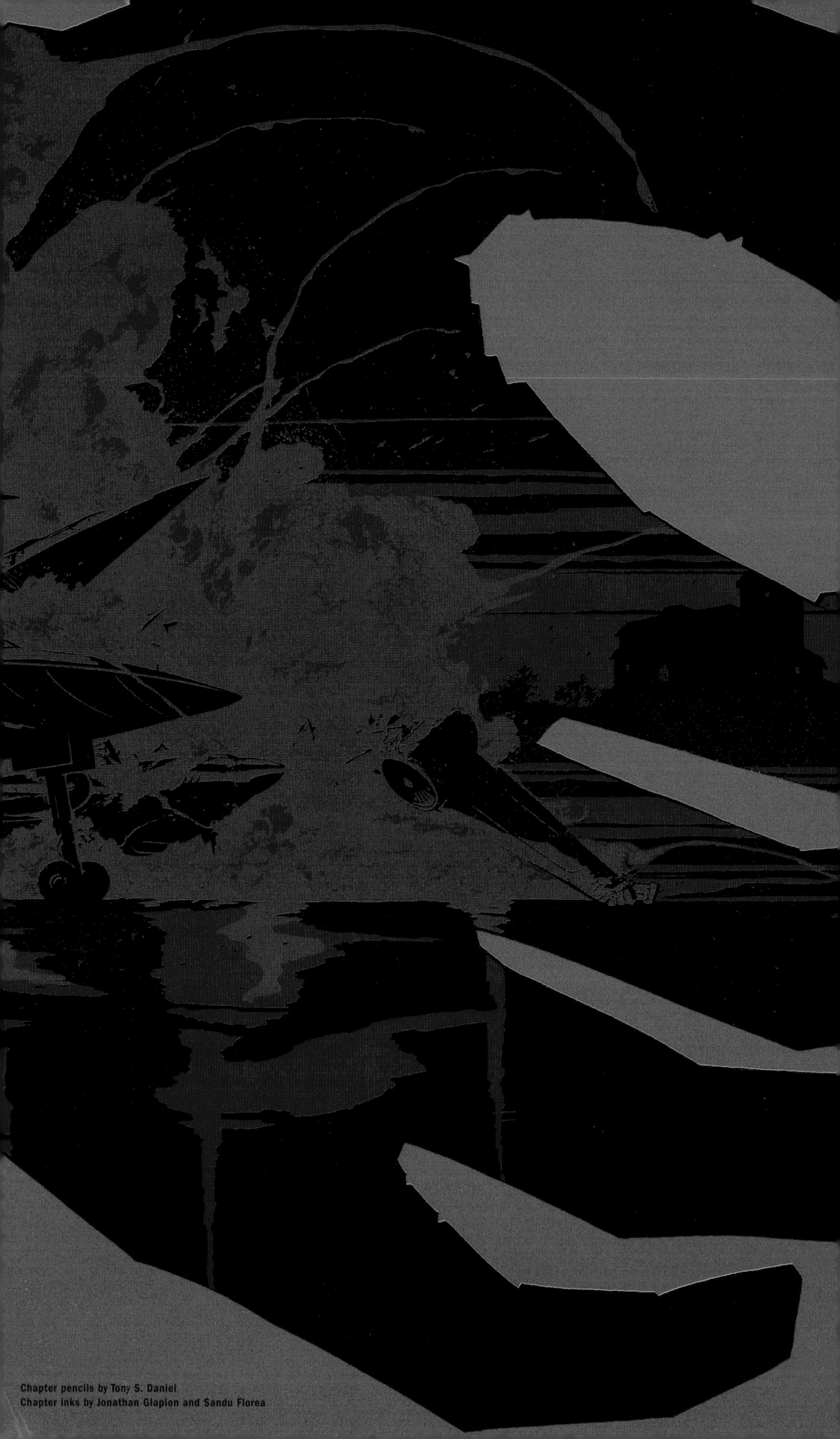

Chapter pencils by Tony S. Daniel
Chapter inks by Jonathan Glapion and Sandu Florea

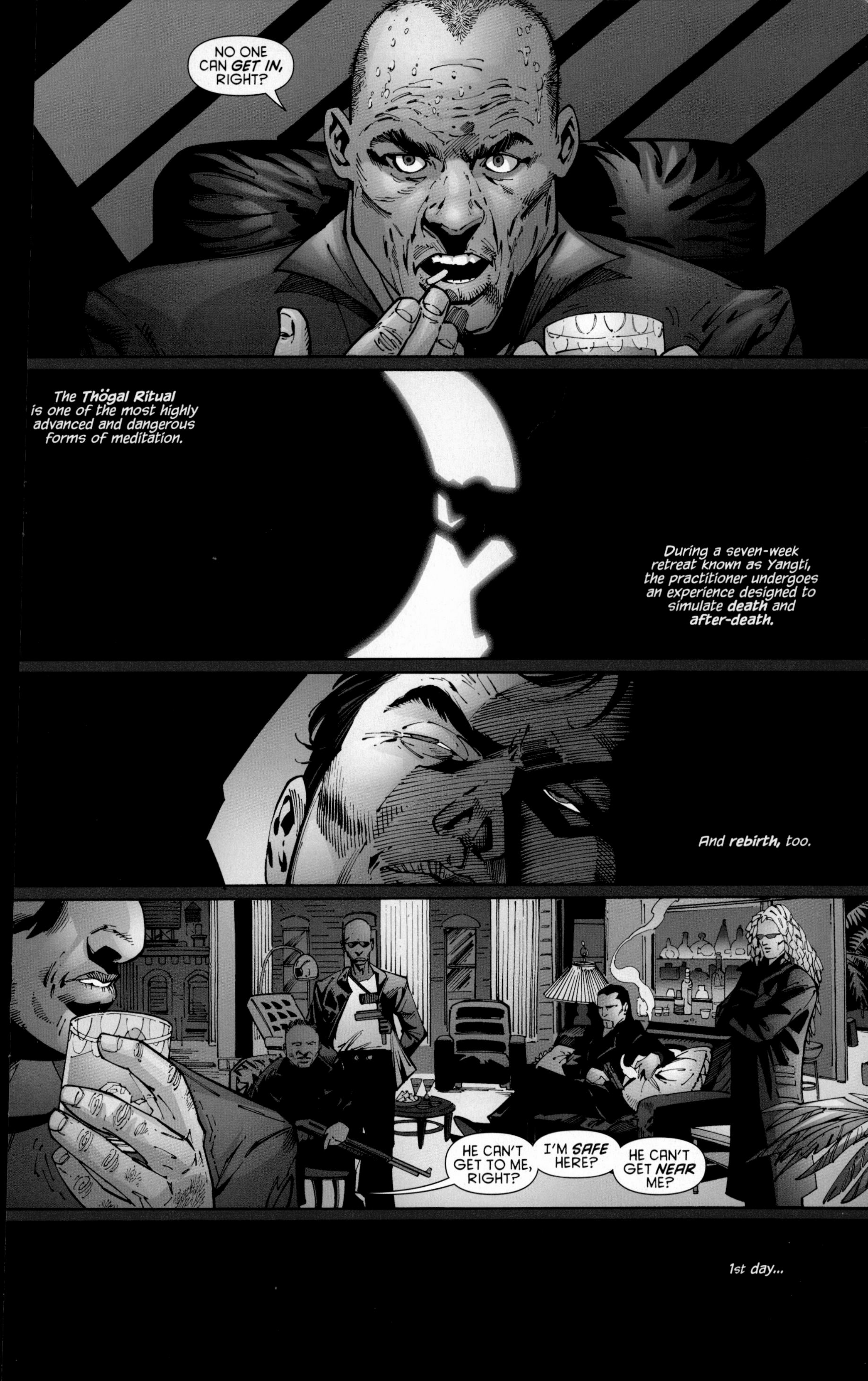
NO ONE CAN GET IN, RIGHT?
The Thögal Ritual is one of the most highly advanced and dangerous forms of meditation.
During a seven-week retreat known as Yangti, the practitioner undergoes an experience designed to simulate death and after-death.
And rebirth, too.
HE CAN'T GET TO ME, RIGHT?
I'M SAFE HERE?
HE CAN'T GET NEAR ME?
1st day...

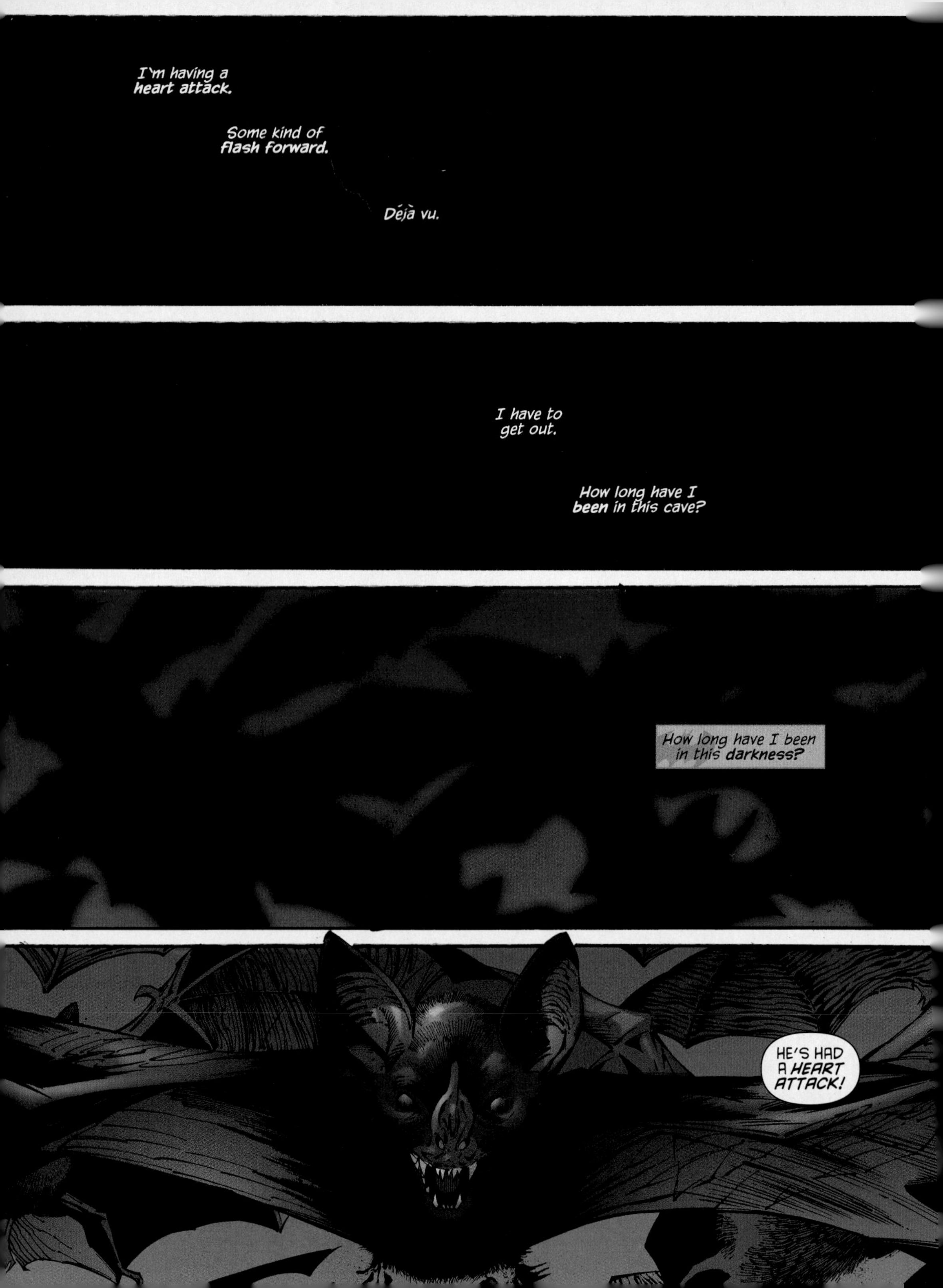
I'm having a heart attack.
Some kind of flash forward.
Déjà vu.
I have to get out.
How long have I been in this cave?
How long have I been in this darkness?
HE'S HAD A HEART ATTACK!

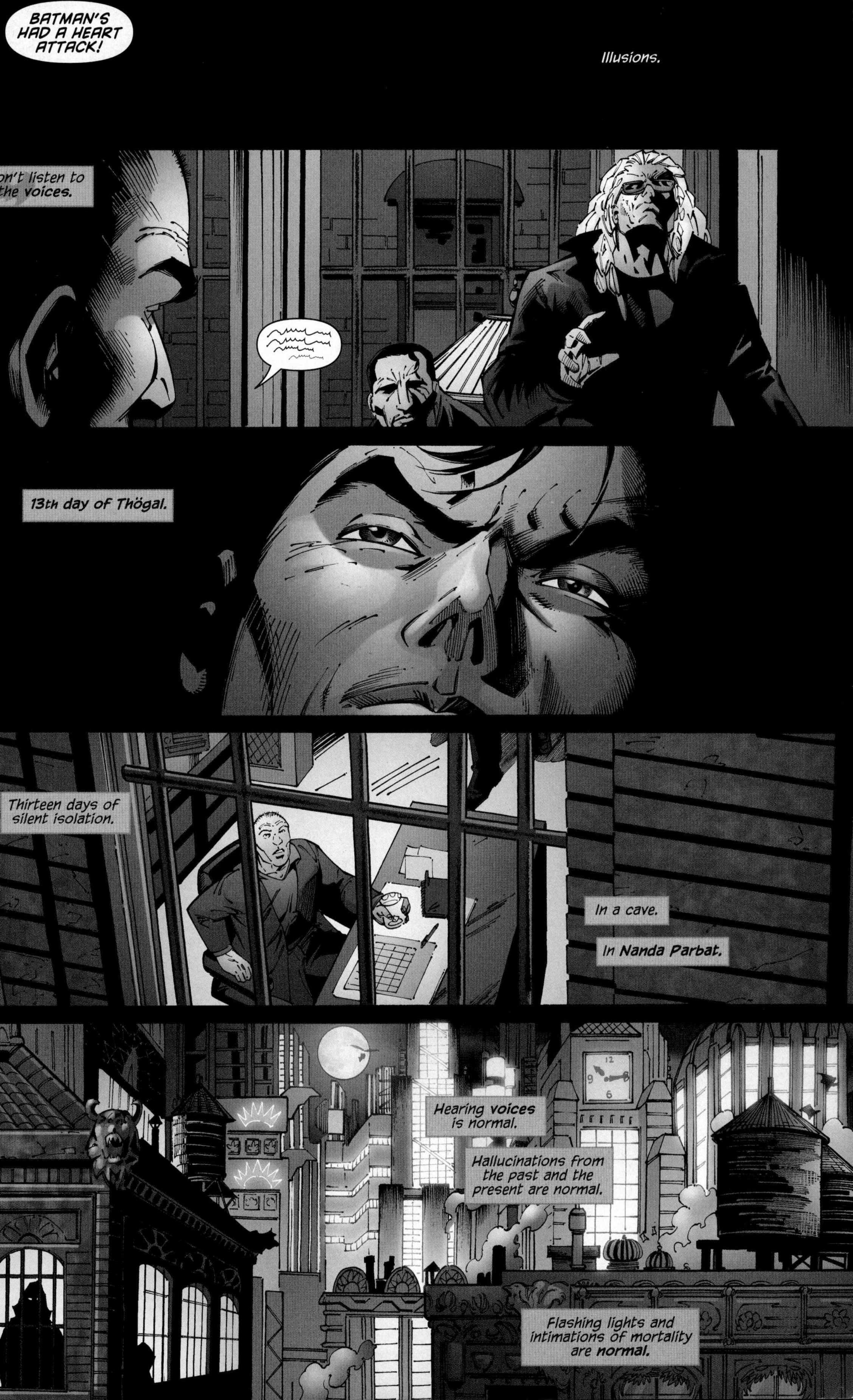

BATMAN'S HAD A HEART ATTACK!
Illusions.
on't listen to the voices.
13th day of Thögal.
Thirteen days of silent isolation.
In a cave.
In Nanda Parbat.
Hearing voices is normal.
Hallucinations from the past and the present are normal.
Flashing lights and intimations of mortality are normal.

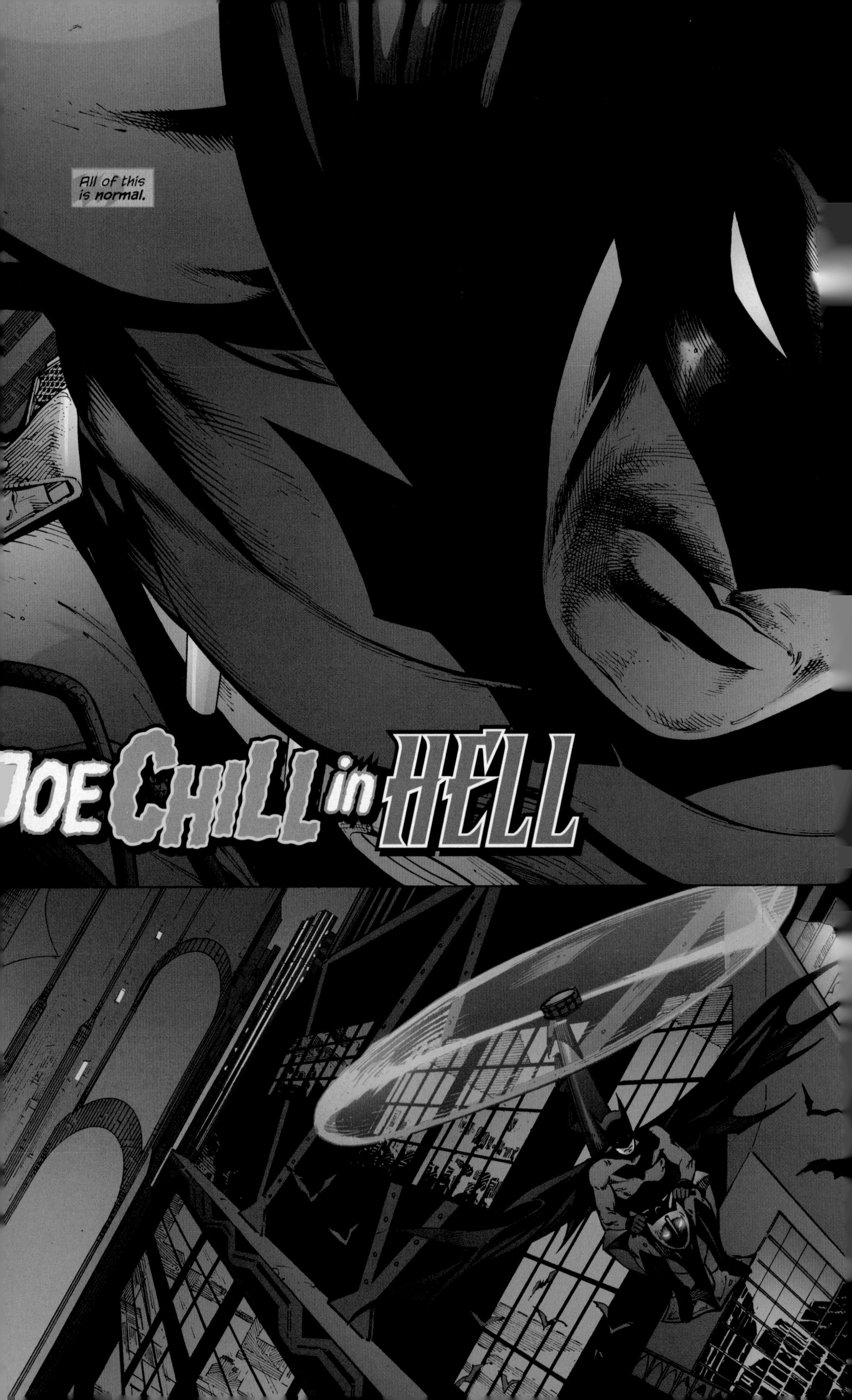
All of this is normal.
JOE CHILL in HELL

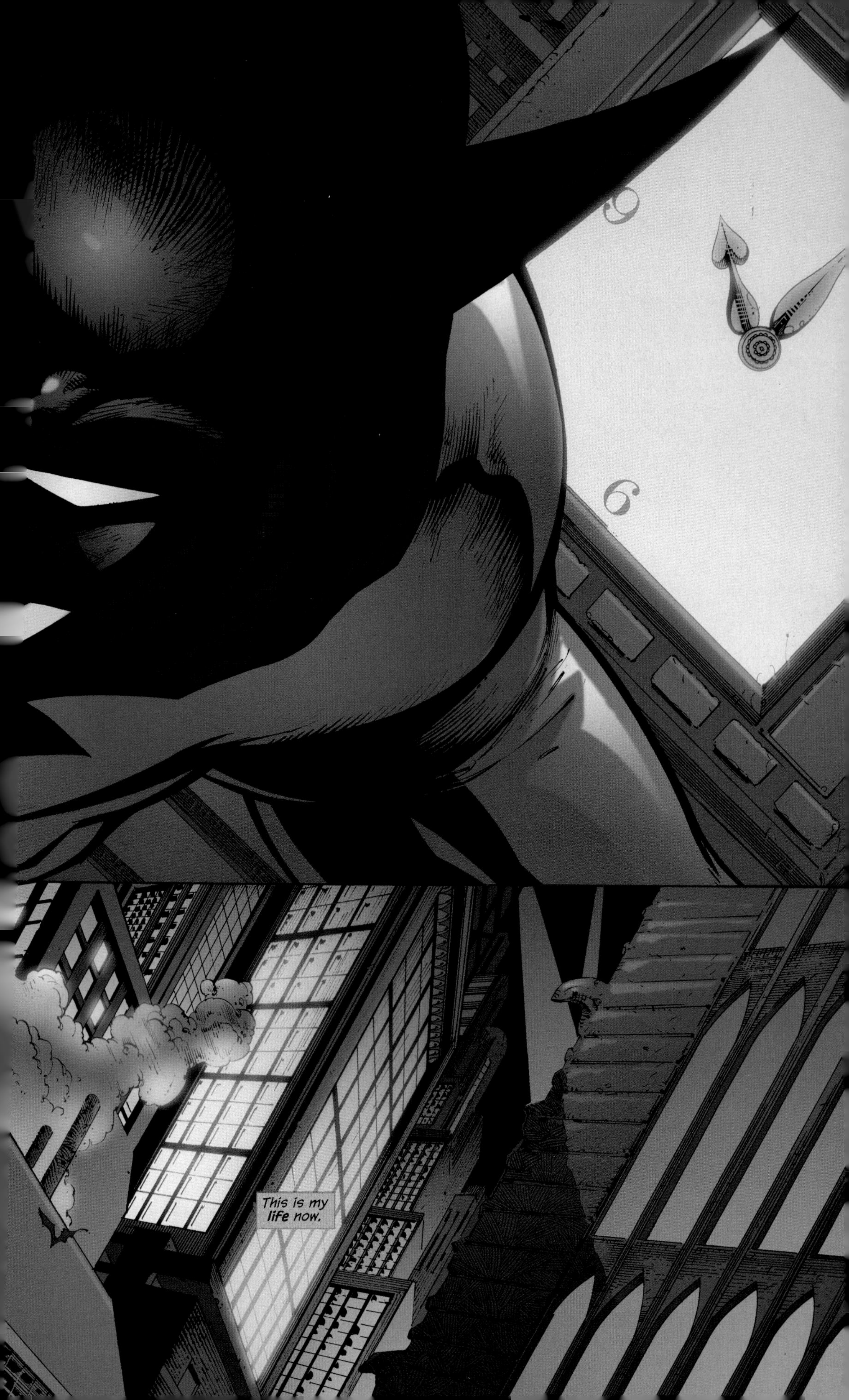
This is my life now.

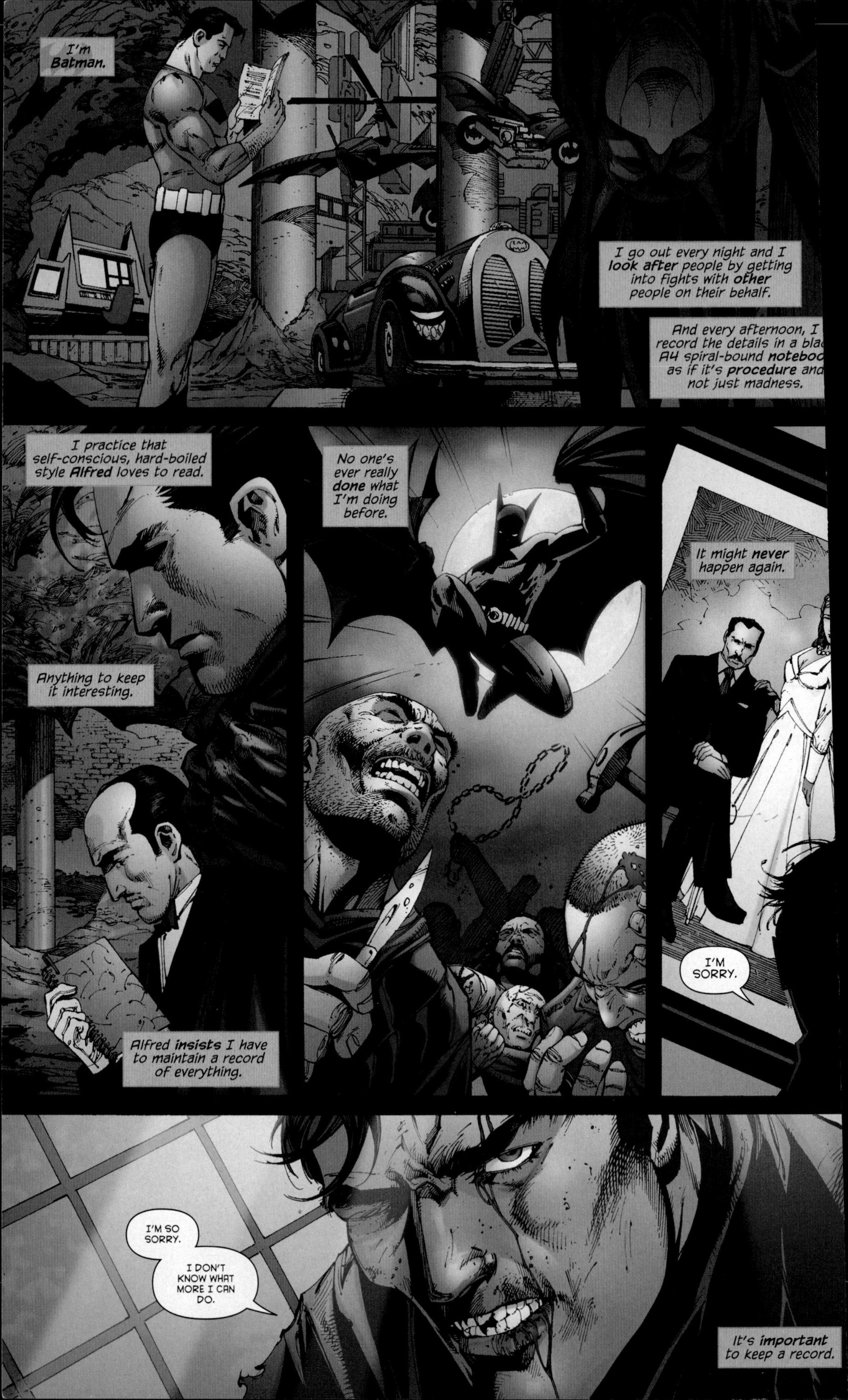
I'm Batman.
I go out every night and I look after people by getting into fights with other people on their behalf.
And every afternoon, I record the details in a blac A4 spiral-bound notebo as if it's procedure and not just madness.
I practice that self-conscious, hard-boiled style Alfred loves to read.
Anything to keep it interesting.
Alfred insists I have to maintain a record of everything.
No one's ever really done what I'm doing before.
It might never happen again.
I'M SORRY.
I'M SO SORRY.
I DON'T KNOW WHAT MORE I CAN DO.
It's important to keep a record.

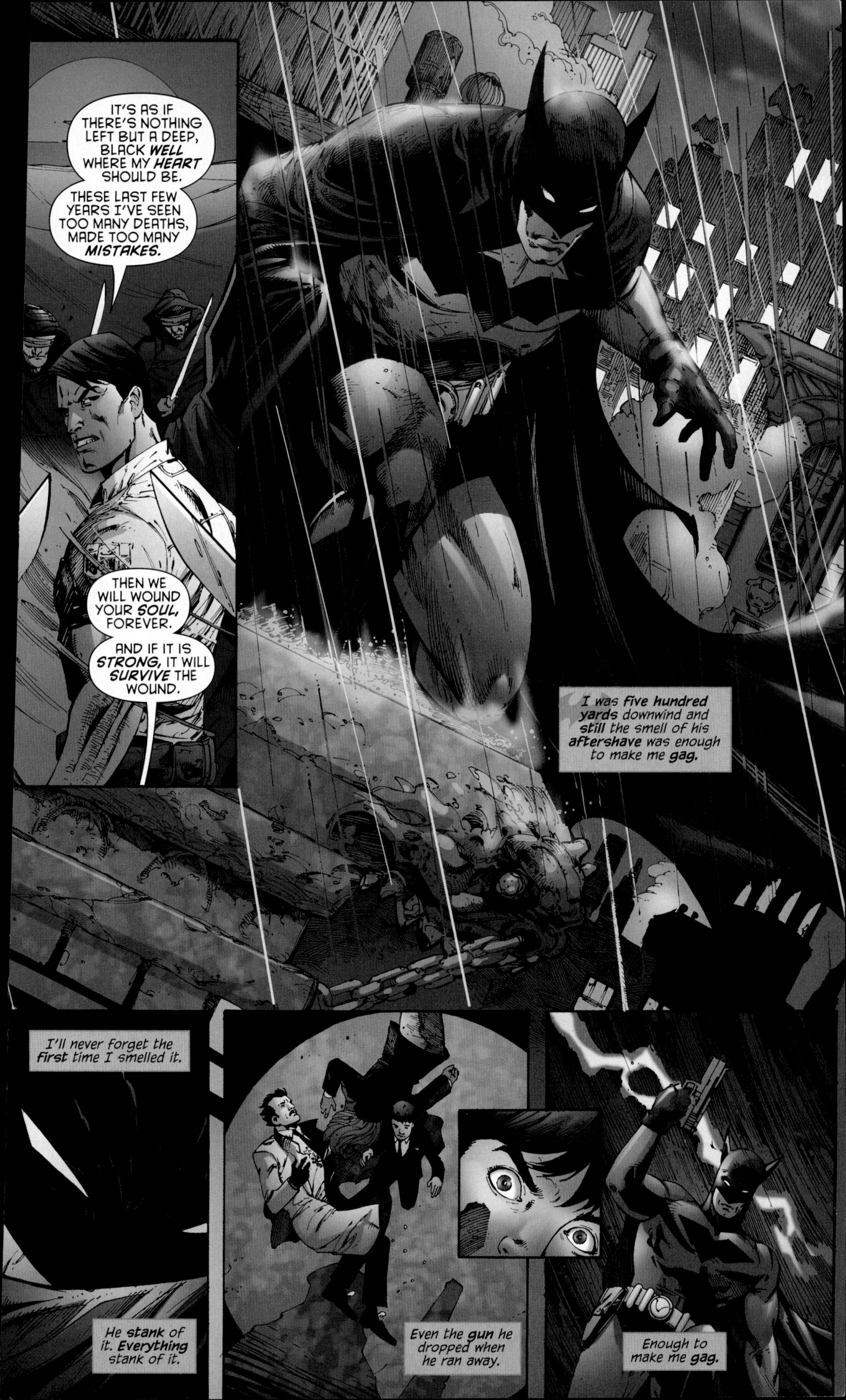
IT'S AS IF THERE'S NOTHING LEFT BUT A DEEP, BLACK WELL WHERE MY HEART SHOULD BE.
THESE LAST FEW YEARS I'VE SEEN TOO MANY DEATHS, MADE TOO MANY MISTAKES.
THEN WE WILL WOUND YOUR SOUL, FOREVER.
AND IF IT IS STRONG, IT WILL SURVIVE THE WOUND.
I was five hundred yards downwind and still the smell of his aftershave was enough to make me gag.
I'll never forget the first time I smelled it.
He stank of it. Everything stank of it.
Even the gun he dropped when he ran away.
Enough to make me gag.

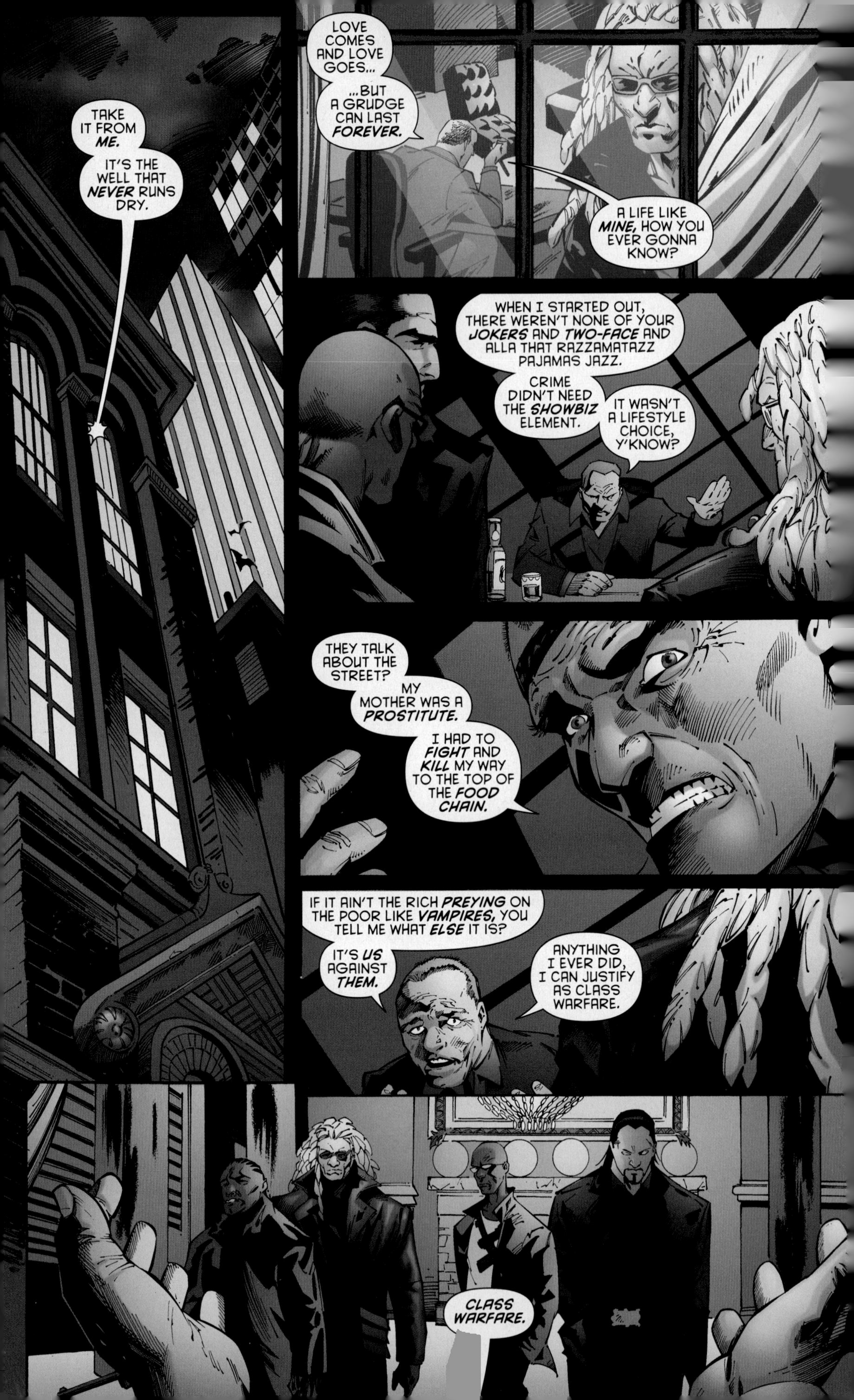
TAKE IT FROM ME.
IT'S THE WELL THAT NEVER RUNS DRY.
LOVE COMES AND LOVE GOES...
...BUT A GRUDGE CAN LAST FOREVER.
A LIFE LIKE MINE, HOW YOU EVER GONNA KNOW?
WHEN I STARTED OUT, THERE WEREN'T NONE OF YOUR JOKERS AND TWO-FACE AND ALLA THAT RAZZAMATAZZ PAJAMAS JAZZ.
CRIME DIDN'T NEED THE SHOWBIZ ELEMENT.
IT WASN'T A LIFESTYLE CHOICE, Y'KNOW?
THEY TALK ABOUT THE STREET?
MY MOTHER WAS A PROSTITUTE.
I HAD TO FIGHT AND KILL MY WAY TO THE TOP OF THE FOOD CHAIN.
IF IT AIN'T THE RICH PREYING ON THE POOR LIKE VAMPIRES, YOU TELL ME WHAT ELSE IT IS?
IT'S US AGAINST THEM.
ANYTHING I EVER DID, I CAN JUSTIFY AS CLASS WARFARE.
CLASS WARFARE.

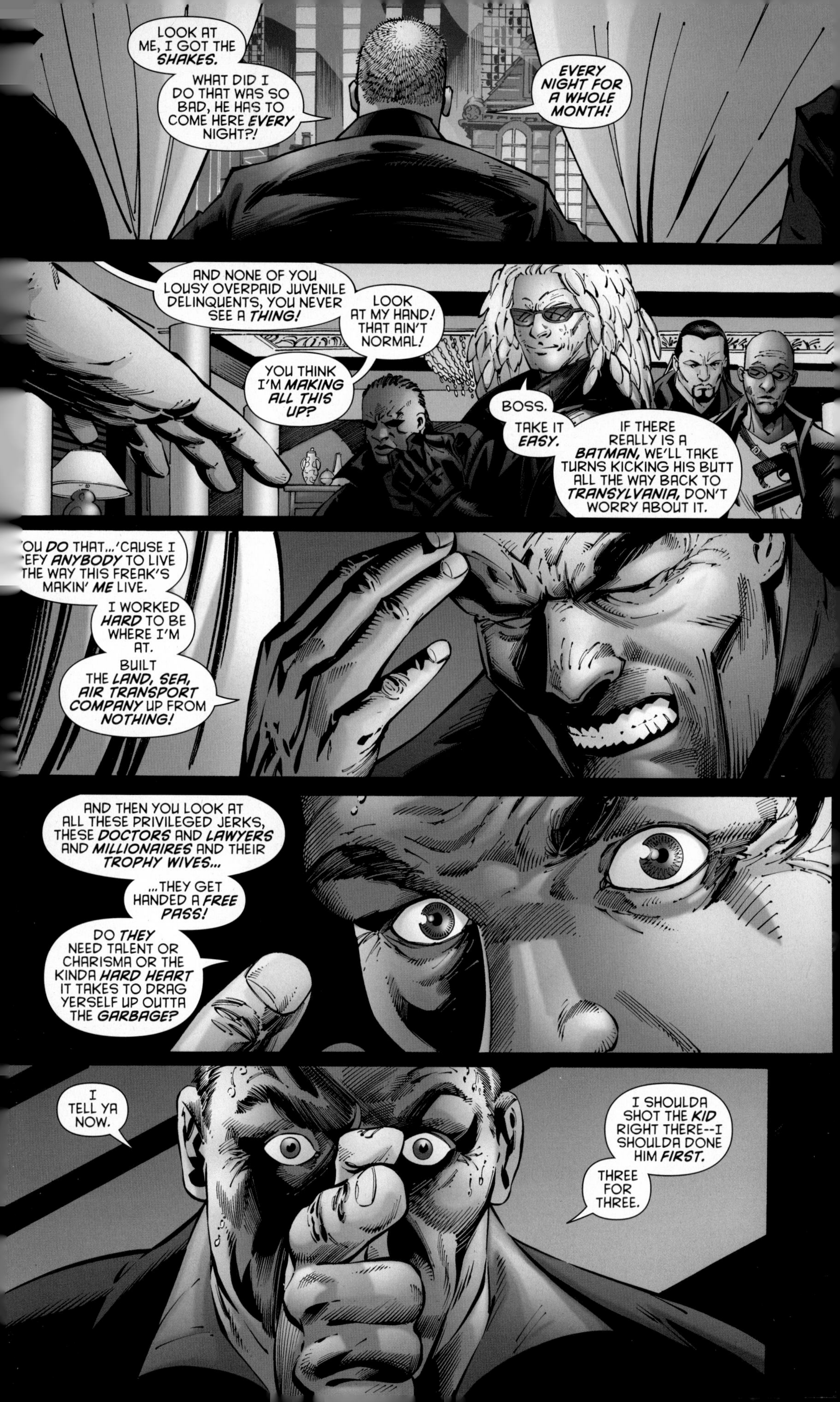
LOOK AT ME, I GOT THE SHAKES.
WHAT DID I DO THAT WAS SO BAD, HE HAS TO COME HERE EVERY NIGHT?!
EVERY NIGHT FOR A WHOLE MONTH!
AND NONE OF YOU LOUSY OVERPAID JUVENILE DELINQUENTS, YOU NEVER SEE A THING!
LOOK AT MY HAND! THAT AIN'T NORMAL!
YOU THINK I'M MAKING ALL THIS UP?
BOSS.
TAKE IT EASY.
IF THERE REALLY IS A BATMAN, WE'LL TAKE TURNS KICKING HIS BUTT ALL THE WAY BACK TO TRANSYLVANIA, DON'T WORRY ABOUT IT.
OU DO THAT...'CAUSE I EFY ANYBODY TO LIVE THE WAY THIS FREAK'S MAKIN' ME LIVE.
I WORKED HARD TO BE WHERE I'M AT.
BUILT THE LAND, SEA, AIR TRANSPORT COMPANY UP FROM NOTHING!
AND THEN YOU LOOK AT ALL THESE PRIVILEGED JERKS, THESE DOCTORS AND LAWYERS AND MILLIONAIRES AND THEIR TROPHY WIVES...
...THEY GET HANDED A FREE PASS!
DO THEY NEED TALENT OR CHARISMA OR THE KINDA HARD HEART IT TAKES TO DRAG YERSELF UP OUTTA THE GARBAGE?
I TELL YA NOW.
I SHOULDA SHOT THE KID RIGHT THERE--I SHOULDA DONE HIM FIRST.
THREE FOR THREE.

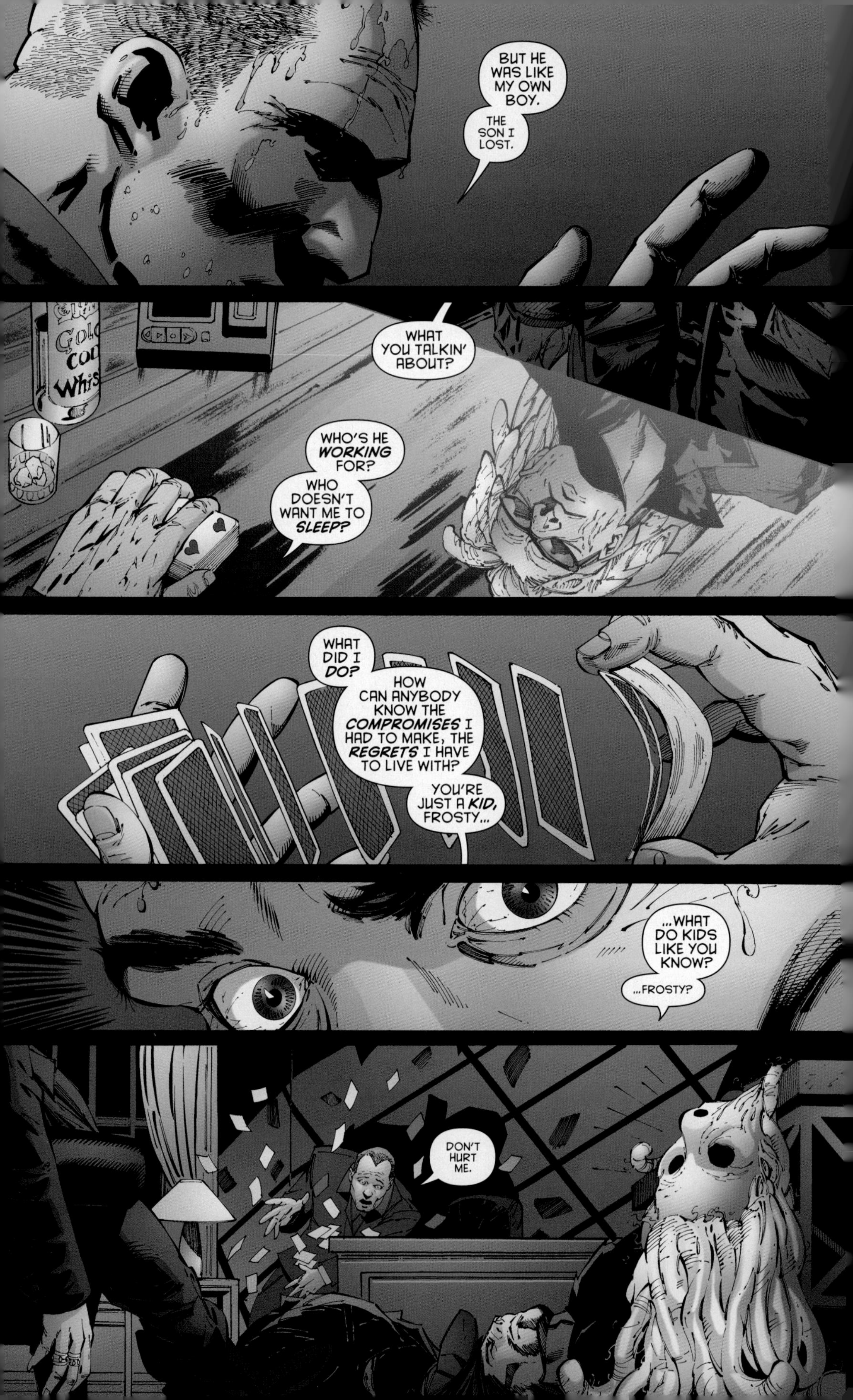
BUT HE WAS LIKE MY OWN BOY.
THE SON I LOST.
WHAT YOU TALKIN' ABOUT?
WHO'S HE **WORKING** FOR?
WHO DOESN'T WANT ME TO **SLEEP?**
WHAT DID I **DO?**
HOW CAN ANYBODY KNOW THE **COMPROMISES** I HAD TO MAKE, THE **REGRETS** I HAVE TO LIVE WITH?
YOU'RE JUST A **KID,** FROSTY...
...WHAT DO KIDS LIKE YOU KNOW?
...FROSTY?
DON'T HURT ME.

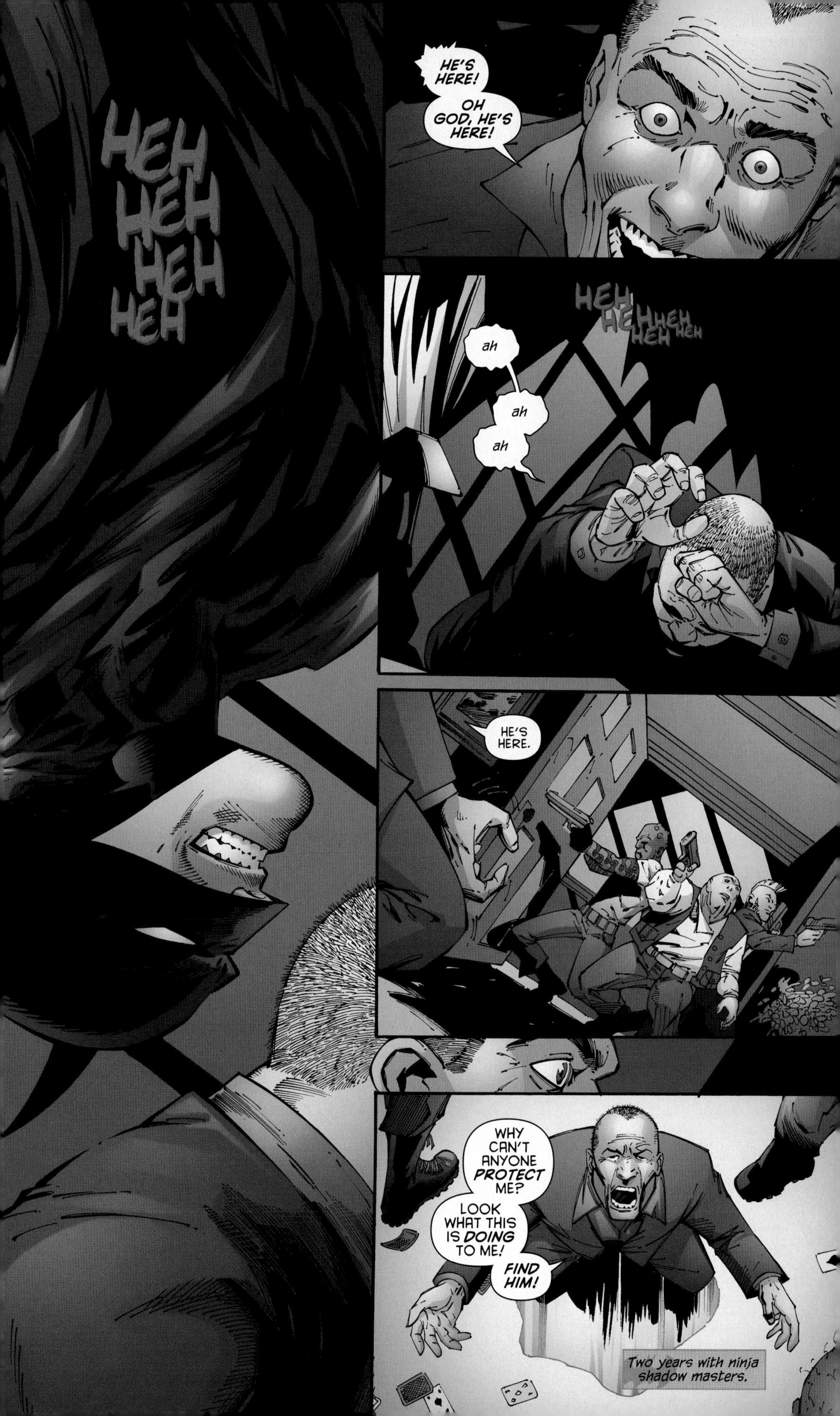
HEH HEH HEH HEH
HE'S HERE!
OH GOD, HE'S HERE!
HEH HEH HEH HEH HEH
ah
ah
ah
HE'S HERE.
WHY CAN'T ANYONE *PROTECT* ME?
LOOK WHAT THIS IS *DOING* TO ME!
FIND HIM!
Two years with ninja shadow masters.

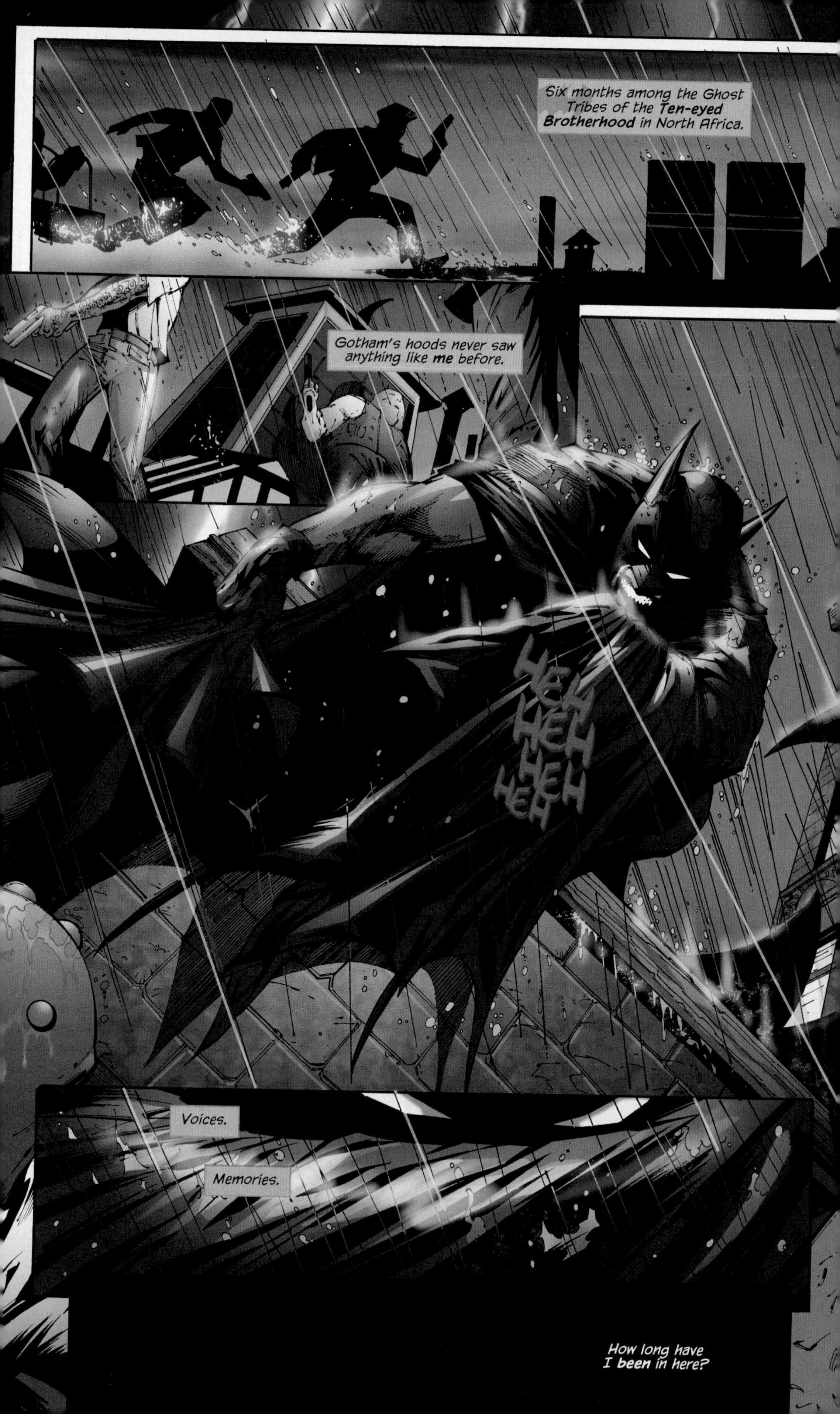

Six months among the Ghost Tribes of the Ten-eyed Brotherhood in North Africa.
Gotham's hoods never saw anything like me before.
HEH HEH HEH HEH
Voices.
Memories.
How long have I been in here?

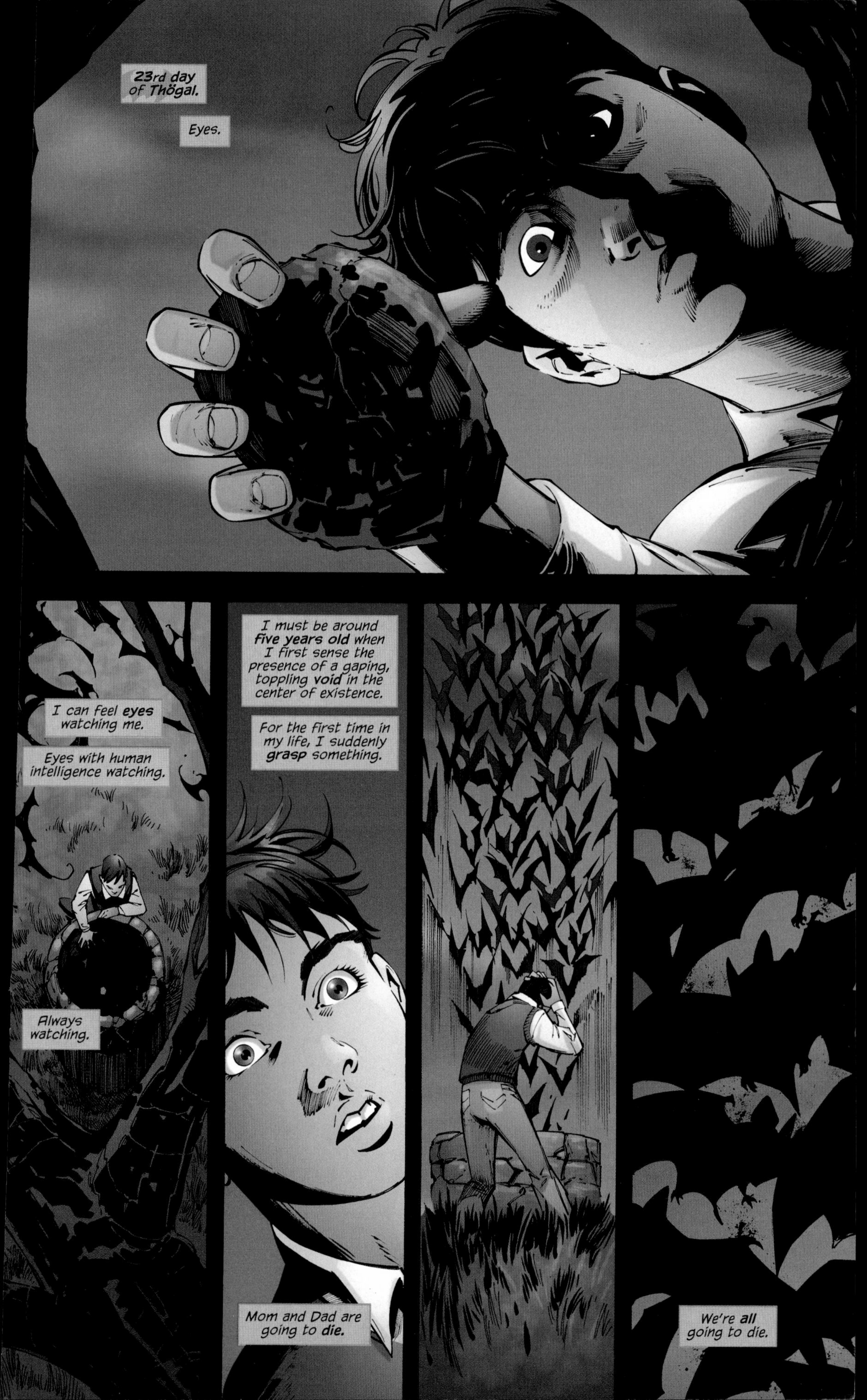
23rd day of Thögal.
Eyes.
I can feel eyes watching me.
Eyes with human intelligence watching.
Always watching.
I must be around five years old when I first sense the presence of a gaping, toppling void in the center of existence.
For the first time in my life, I suddenly grasp something.
Mom and Dad are going to die.
We're all going to die.

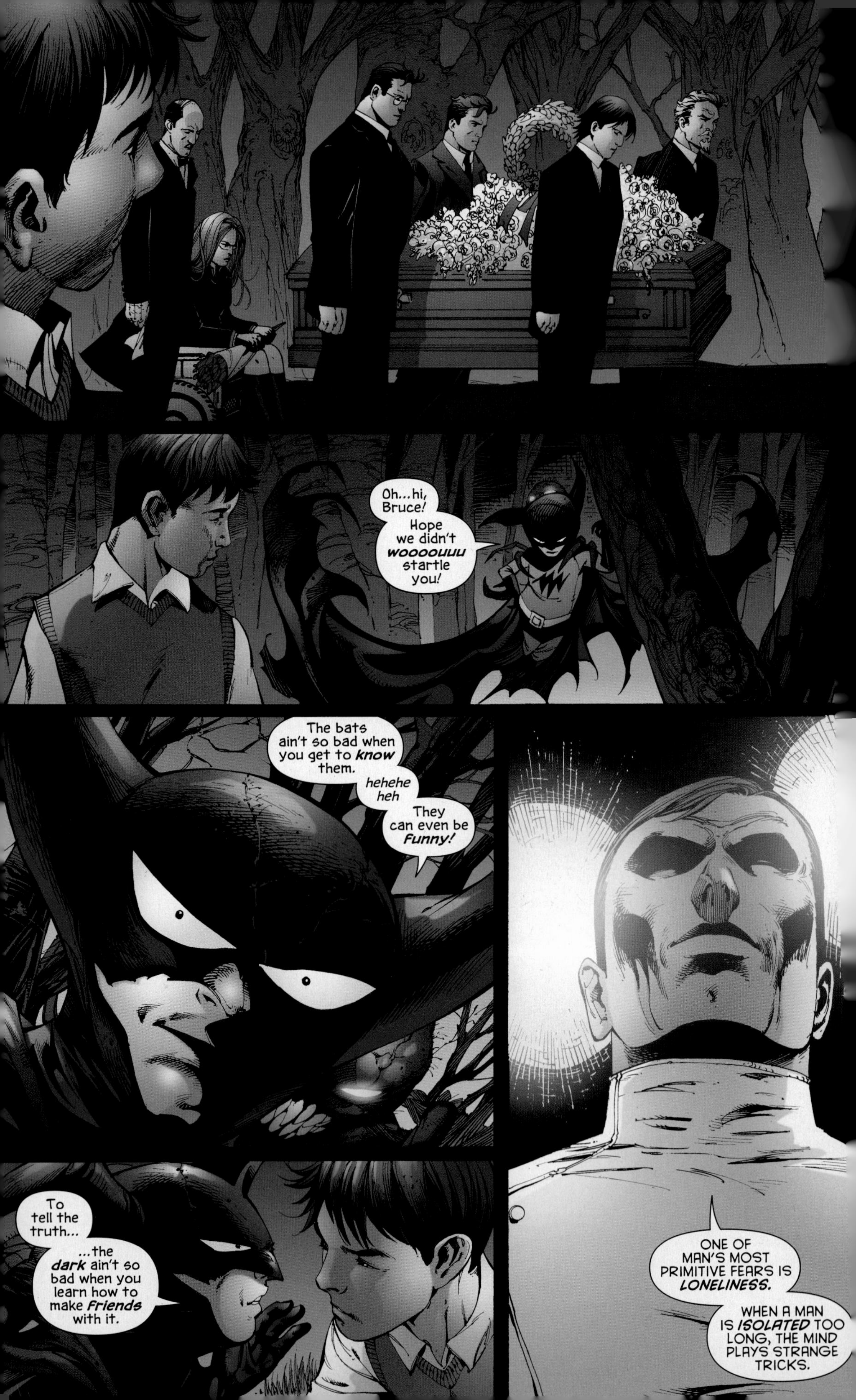
Oh...hi, Bruce! Hope we didn't *woooouuu* startle you!
The bats ain't so bad when you get to *know* them.
hehehe heh
They can even be *Funny!*
To tell the truth...
...the *dark* ain't so bad when you learn how to make *friends* with it.
ONE OF MAN'S MOST PRIMITIVE FEARS IS *LONELINESS.*
WHEN A MAN IS *ISOLATED* TOO LONG, THE MIND PLAYS STRANGE TRICKS.

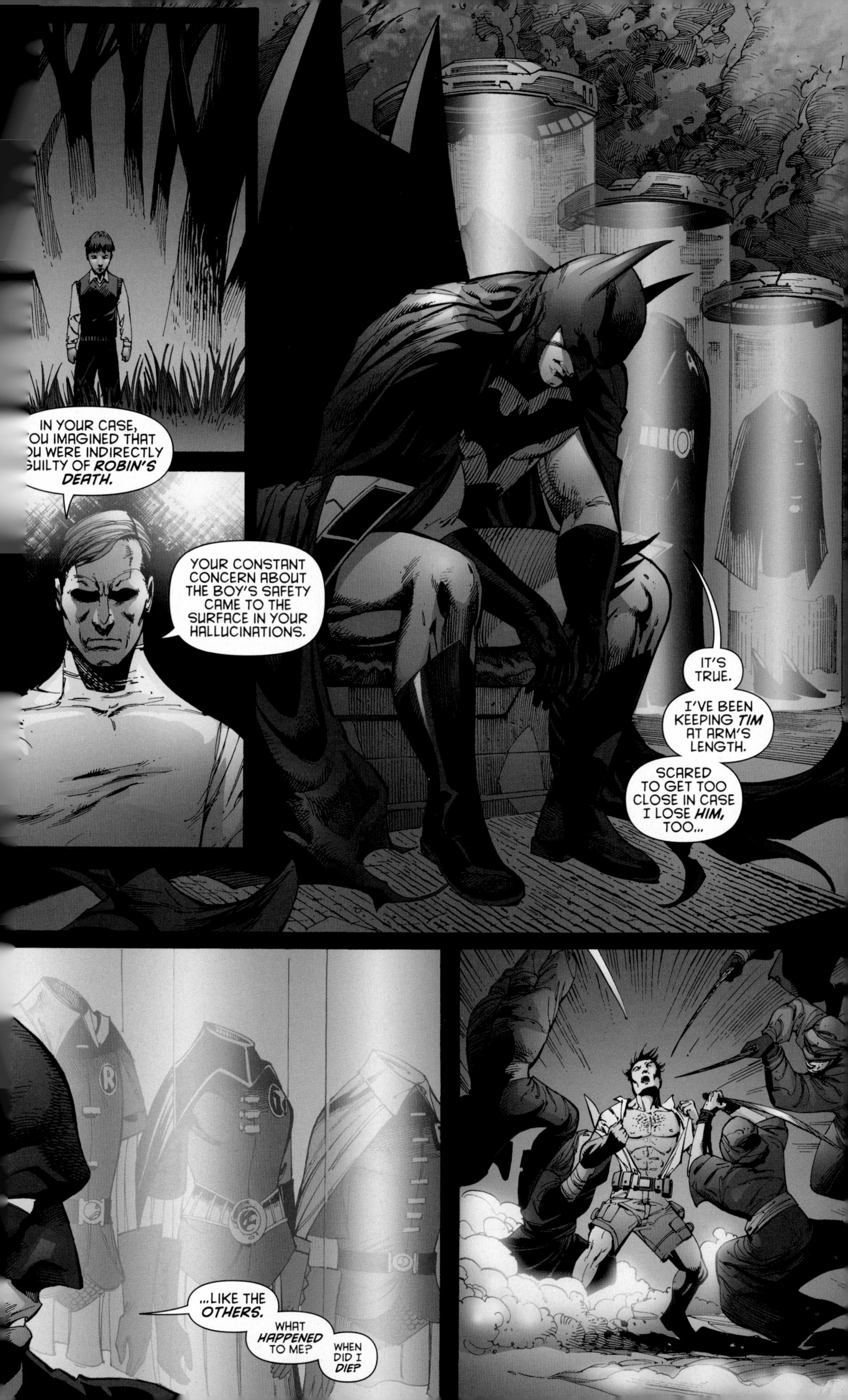
IN YOUR CASE, YOU IMAGINED THAT YOU WERE INDIRECTLY GUILTY OF ROBIN'S DEATH.
YOUR CONSTANT CONCERN ABOUT THE BOY'S SAFETY CAME TO THE SURFACE IN YOUR HALLUCINATIONS.
IT'S TRUE.
I'VE BEEN KEEPING TIM AT ARM'S LENGTH.
SCARED TO GET TOO CLOSE IN CASE I LOSE HIM, TOO...
...LIKE THE OTHERS.
WHAT HAPPENED TO ME?
WHEN DID I DIE?

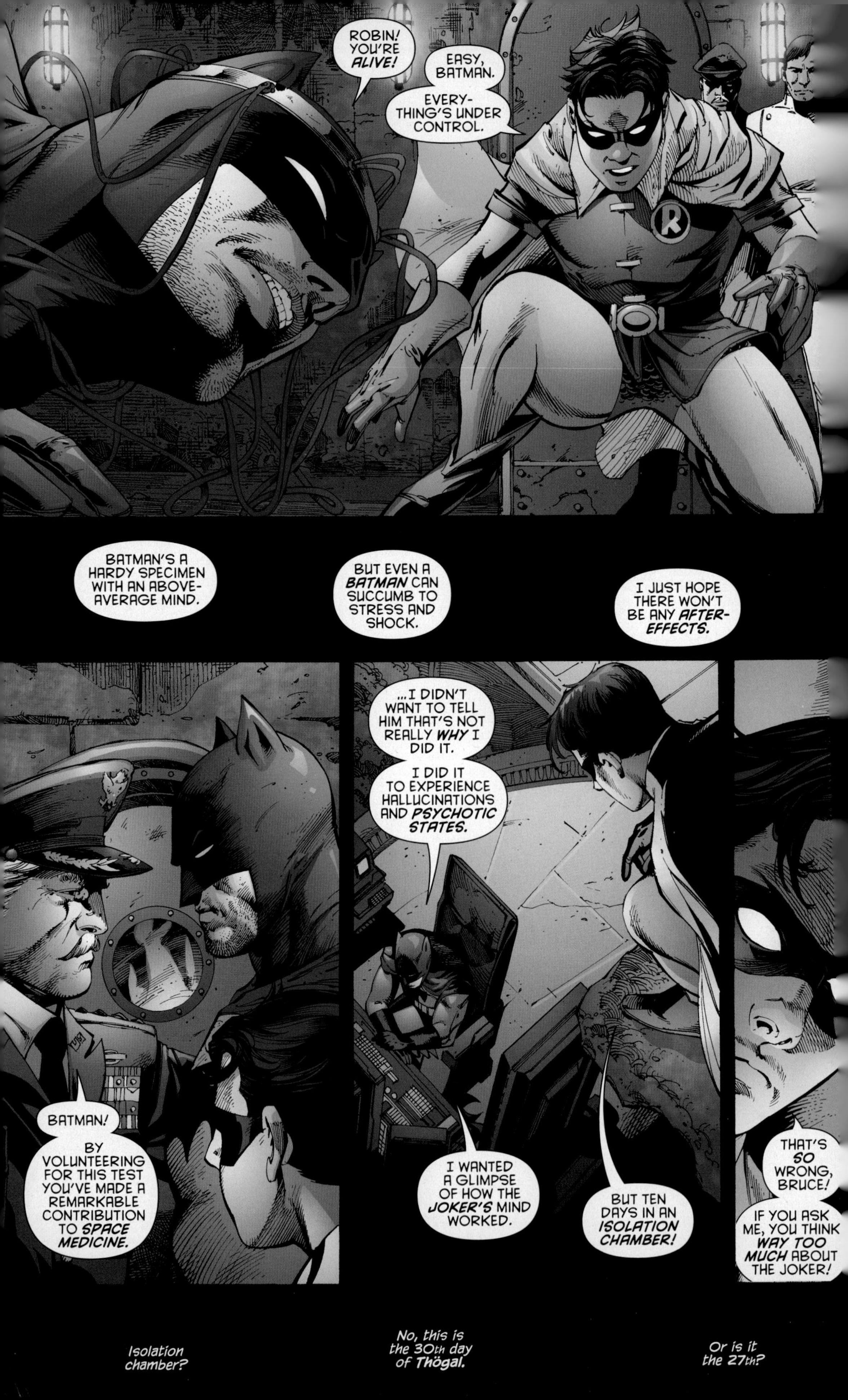
ROBIN! YOU'RE ALIVE!
EASY, BATMAN.
EVERYTHING'S UNDER CONTROL.
BATMAN'S A HARDY SPECIMEN WITH AN ABOVE-AVERAGE MIND.
BUT EVEN A BATMAN CAN SUCCUMB TO STRESS AND SHOCK.
I JUST HOPE THERE WON'T BE ANY AFTER-EFFECTS.
BATMAN!
BY VOLUNTEERING FOR THIS TEST YOU'VE MADE A REMARKABLE CONTRIBUTION TO SPACE MEDICINE.
...I DIDN'T WANT TO TELL HIM THAT'S NOT REALLY WHY I DID IT.
I DID IT TO EXPERIENCE HALLUCINATIONS AND PSYCHOTIC STATES.
I WANTED A GLIMPSE OF HOW THE JOKER'S MIND WORKED.
BUT TEN DAYS IN AN ISOLATION CHAMBER!
THAT'S SO WRONG, BRUCE!
IF YOU ASK ME, YOU THINK WAY TOO MUCH ABOUT THE JOKER!
Isolation chamber?
No, this is the 30th day of Thögal.
Or is it the 27th?

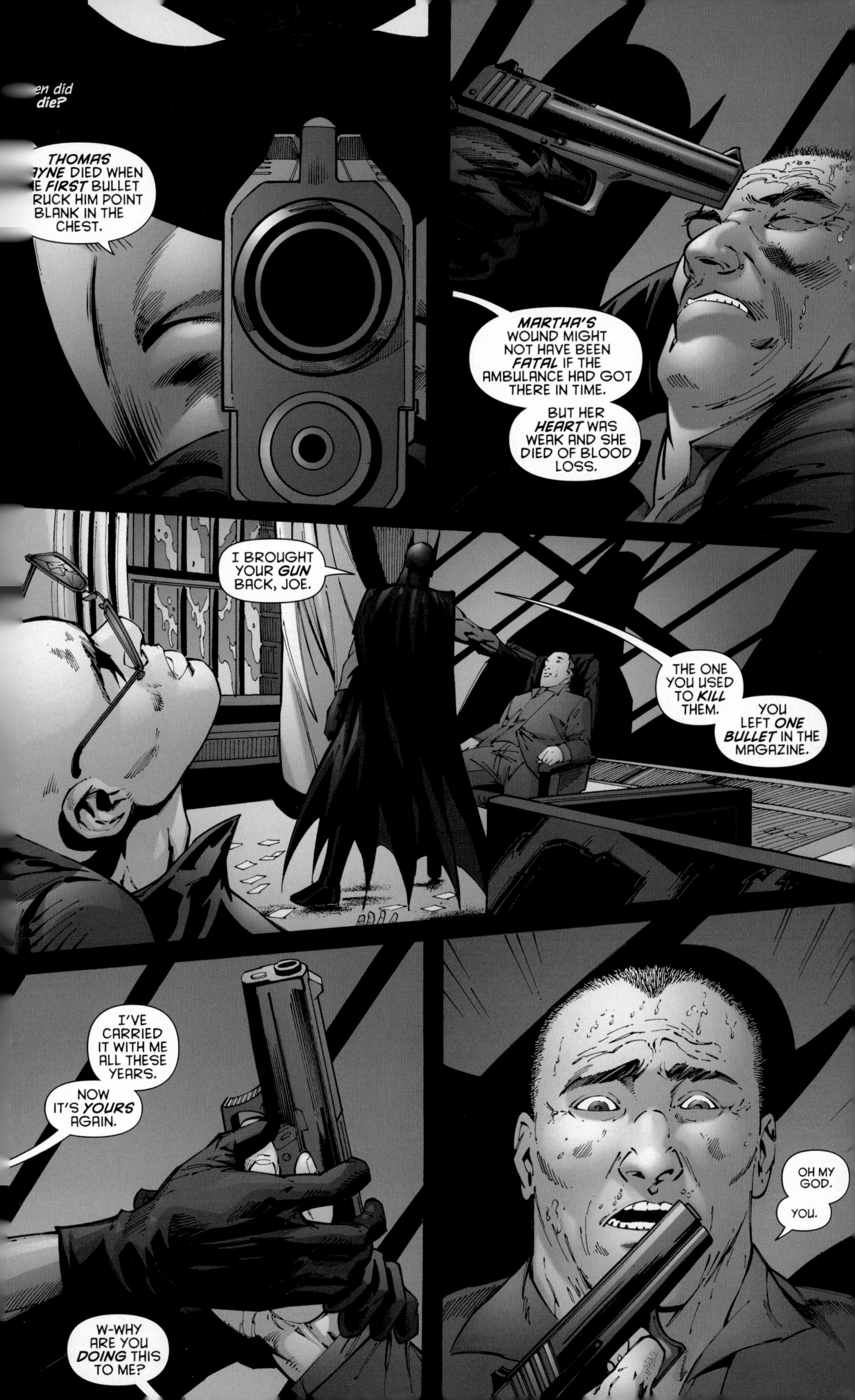

en did
die?
THOMAS AYNE DIED WHEN E FIRST BULLET RUCK HIM POINT BLANK IN THE CHEST.
MARTHA'S WOUND MIGHT NOT HAVE BEEN FATAL IF THE AMBULANCE HAD GOT THERE IN TIME.
BUT HER HEART WAS WEAK AND SHE DIED OF BLOOD LOSS.
I BROUGHT YOUR GUN BACK, JOE.
THE ONE YOU USED TO KILL THEM.
YOU LEFT ONE BULLET IN THE MAGAZINE.
I'VE CARRIED IT WITH ME ALL THESE YEARS.
NOW IT'S YOURS AGAIN.
W-WHY ARE YOU DOING THIS TO ME?
OH MY GOD.
YOU.

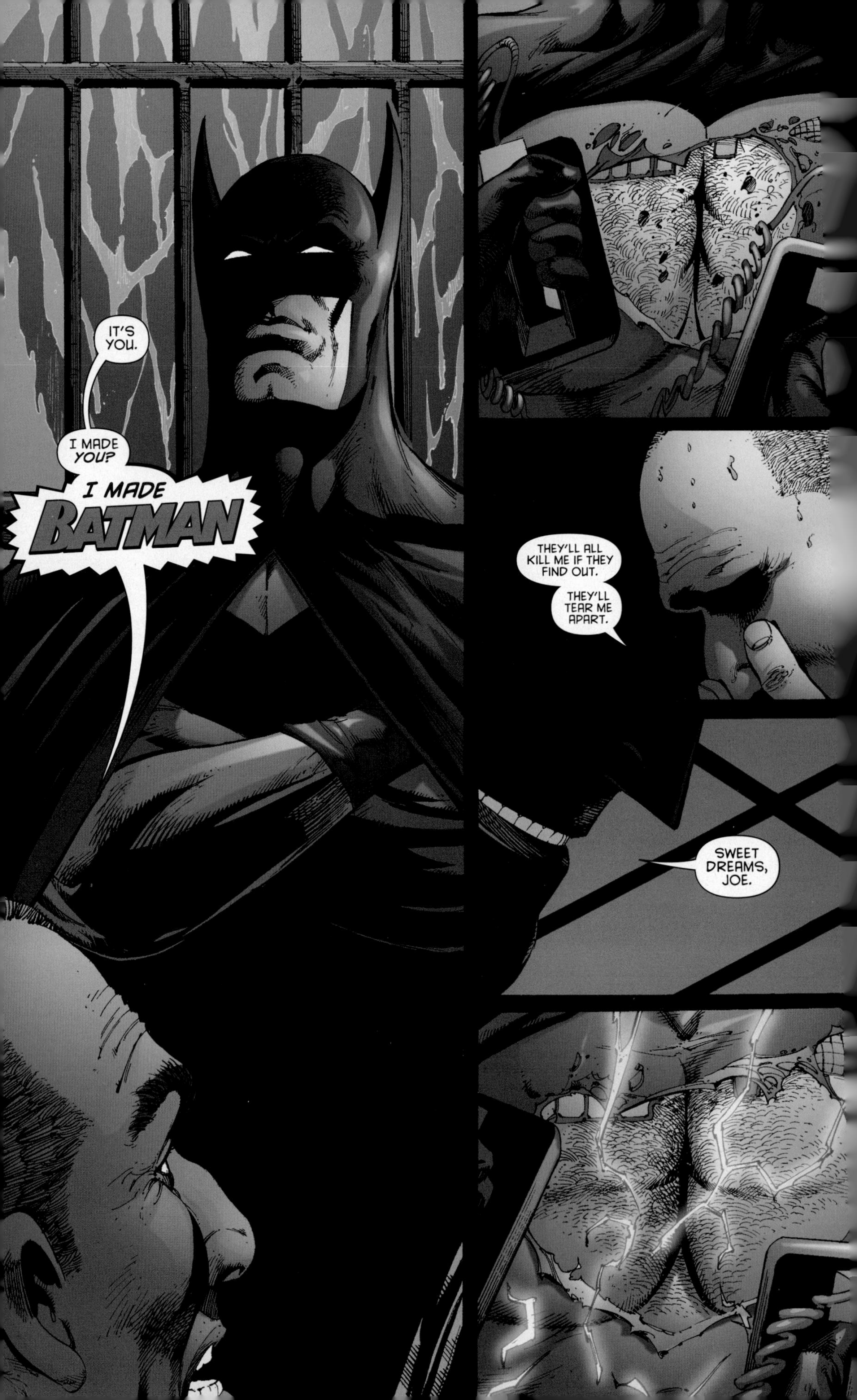
IT'S YOU.
I MADE YOU?
I MADE BATMAN
THEY'LL ALL KILL ME IF THEY FIND OUT.
THEY'LL TEAR ME APART.
SWEET DREAMS, JOE.

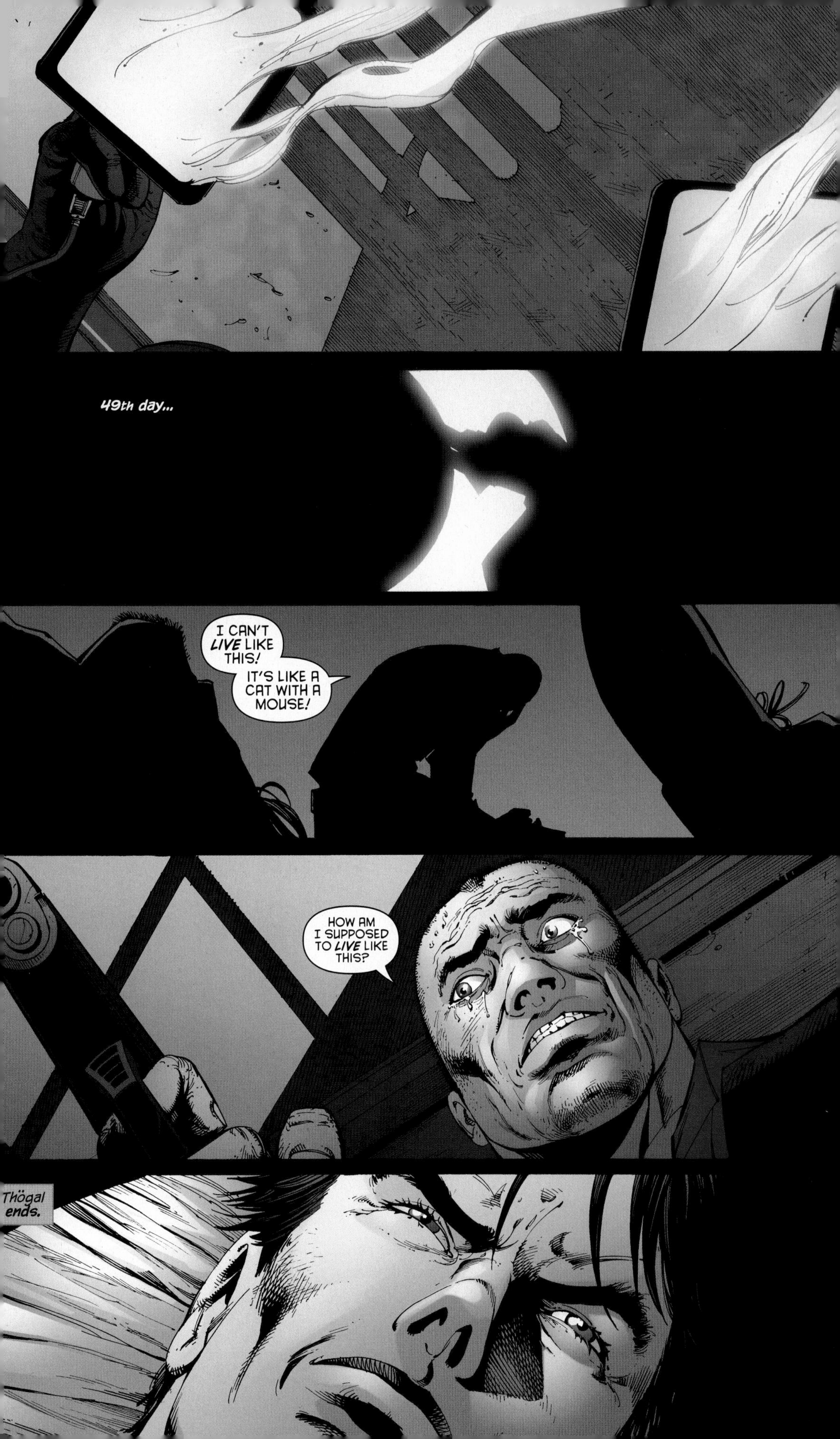
49th day...
I CAN'T *LIVE* LIKE THIS!
IT'S LIKE A CAT WITH A MOUSE!
HOW AM I SUPPOSED TO *LIVE* LIKE THIS?
Thögal ends.

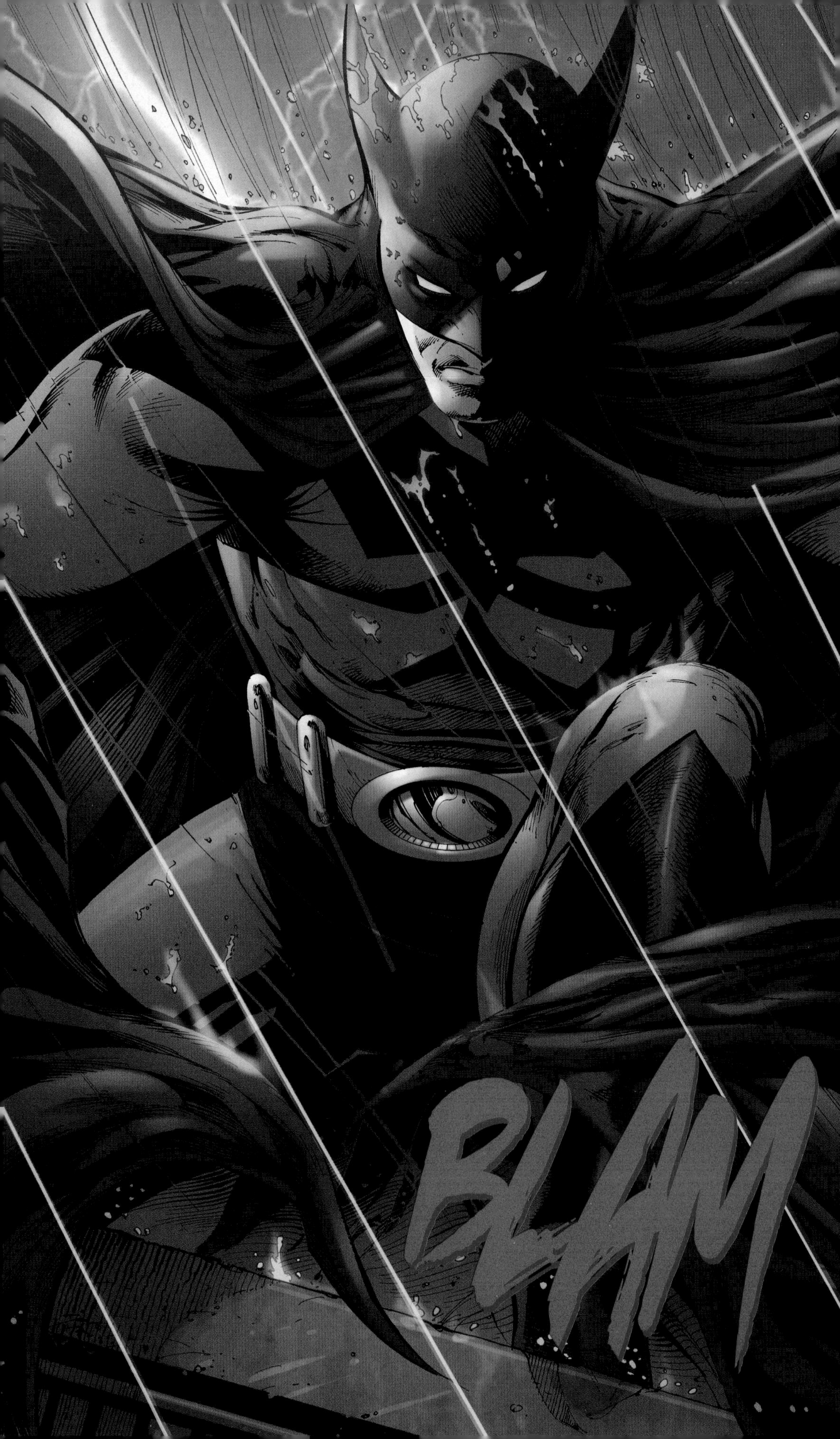
BLAM

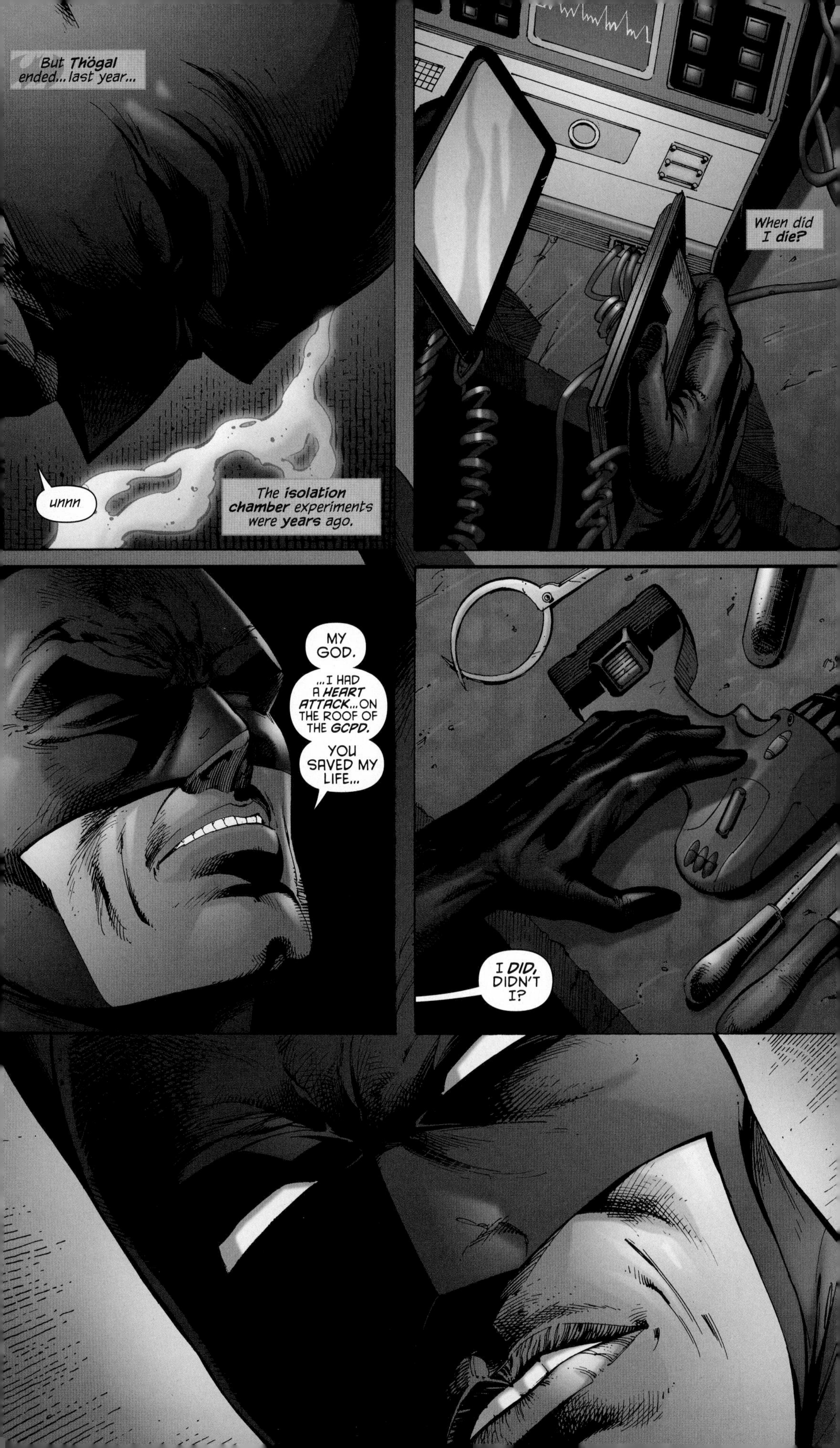
But Thögal ended... last year...
unnn
The isolation chamber experiments were years ago.
When did I die?
MY GOD.
...I HAD A HEART ATTACK...ON THE ROOF OF THE GCPD.
YOU SAVED MY LIFE...
I DID, DIDN'T I?

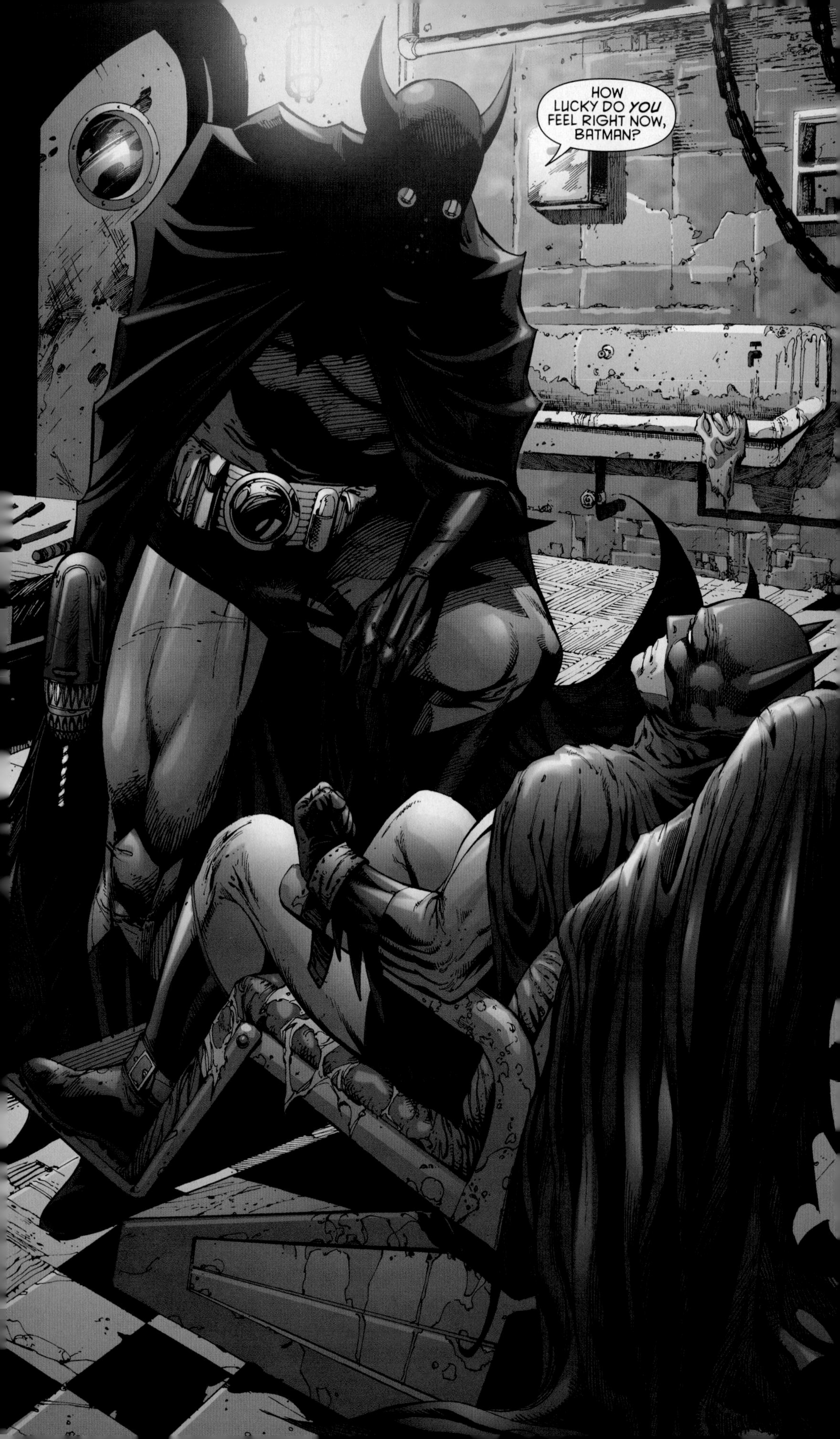
HOW LUCKY DO *YOU* FEEL RIGHT NOW, BATMAN?

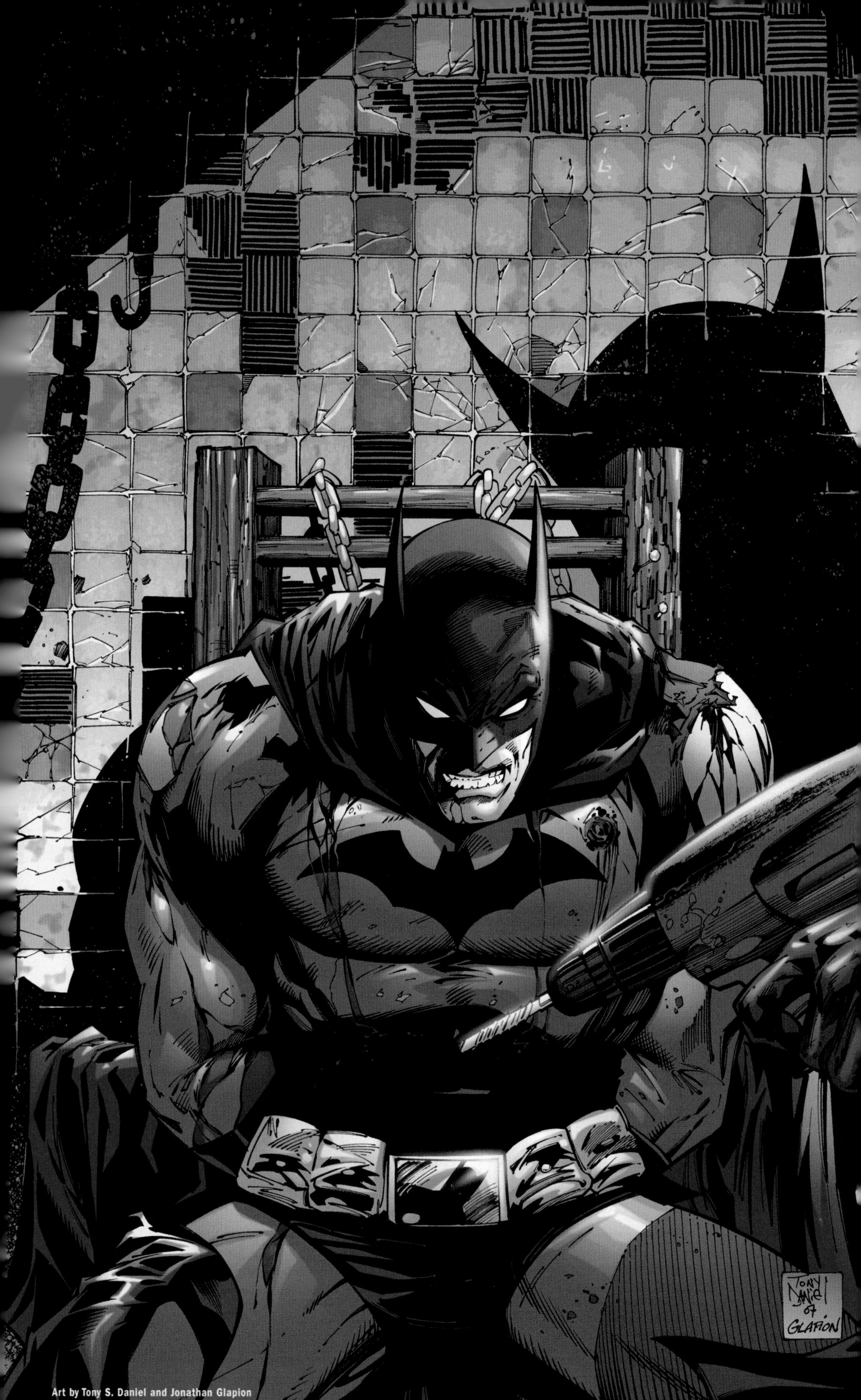
TONY DANIEL 07
GLAPION

Art by Tony S. Daniel and Jonathan Glapion

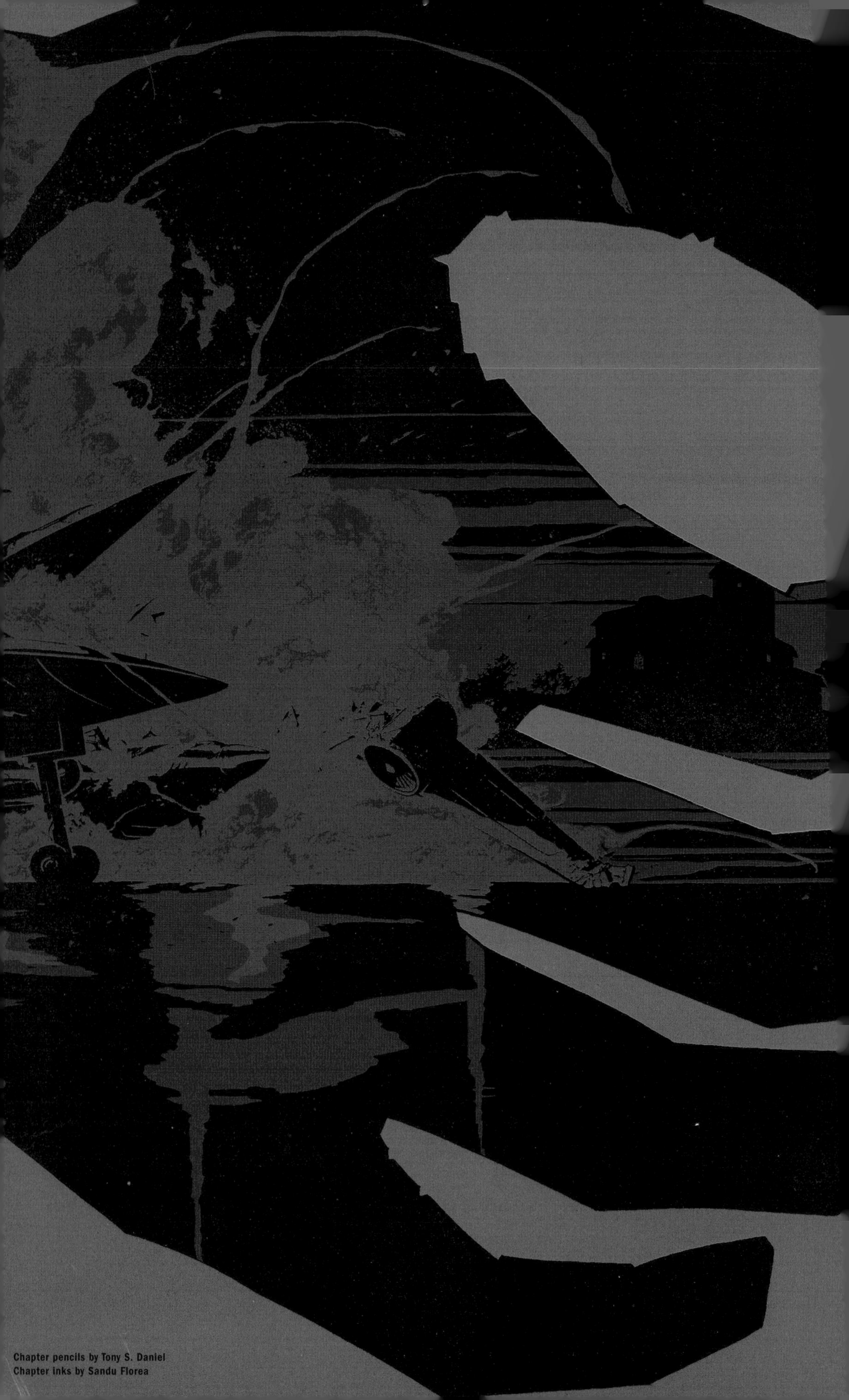

Chapter pencils by Tony S. Daniel
Chapter inks by Sandu Florea

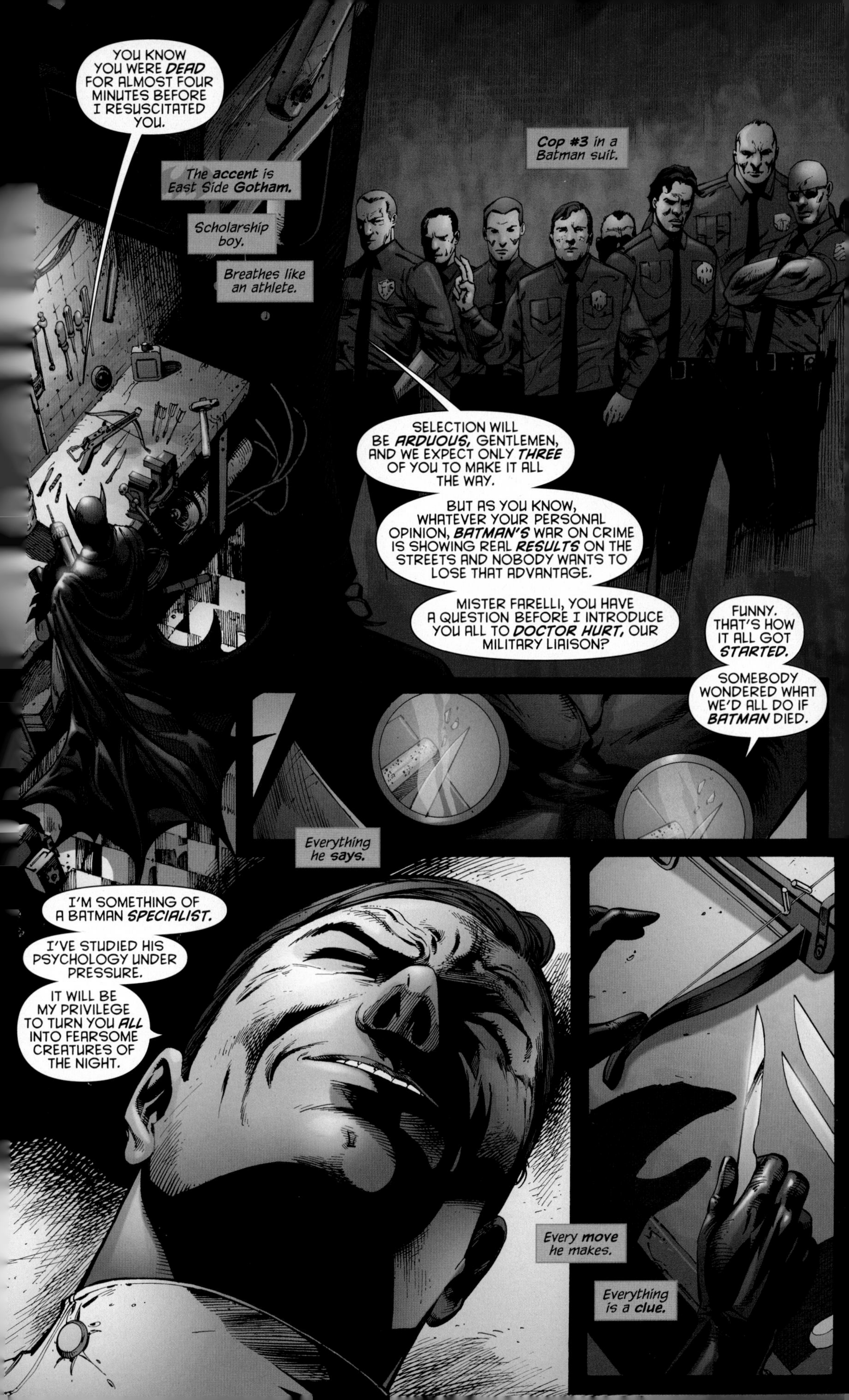
YOU KNOW YOU WERE DEAD FOR ALMOST FOUR MINUTES BEFORE I RESUSCITATED YOU.
The accent is East Side Gotham.
Scholarship boy.
Breathes like an athlete.
Cop #3 in a Batman suit.
SELECTION WILL BE ARDUOUS, GENTLEMEN, AND WE EXPECT ONLY THREE OF YOU TO MAKE IT ALL THE WAY.
BUT AS YOU KNOW, WHATEVER YOUR PERSONAL OPINION, BATMAN'S WAR ON CRIME IS SHOWING REAL RESULTS ON THE STREETS AND NOBODY WANTS TO LOSE THAT ADVANTAGE.
MISTER FARELLI, YOU HAVE A QUESTION BEFORE I INTRODUCE YOU ALL TO DOCTOR HURT, OUR MILITARY LIAISON?
FUNNY. THAT'S HOW IT ALL GOT STARTED.
SOMEBODY WONDERED WHAT WE'D ALL DO IF BATMAN DIED.
Everything he says.
I'M SOMETHING OF A BATMAN SPECIALIST.
I'VE STUDIED HIS PSYCHOLOGY UNDER PRESSURE.
IT WILL BE MY PRIVILEGE TO TURN YOU ALL INTO FEARSOME CREATURES OF THE NIGHT.
Every move he makes.
Everything is a clue.

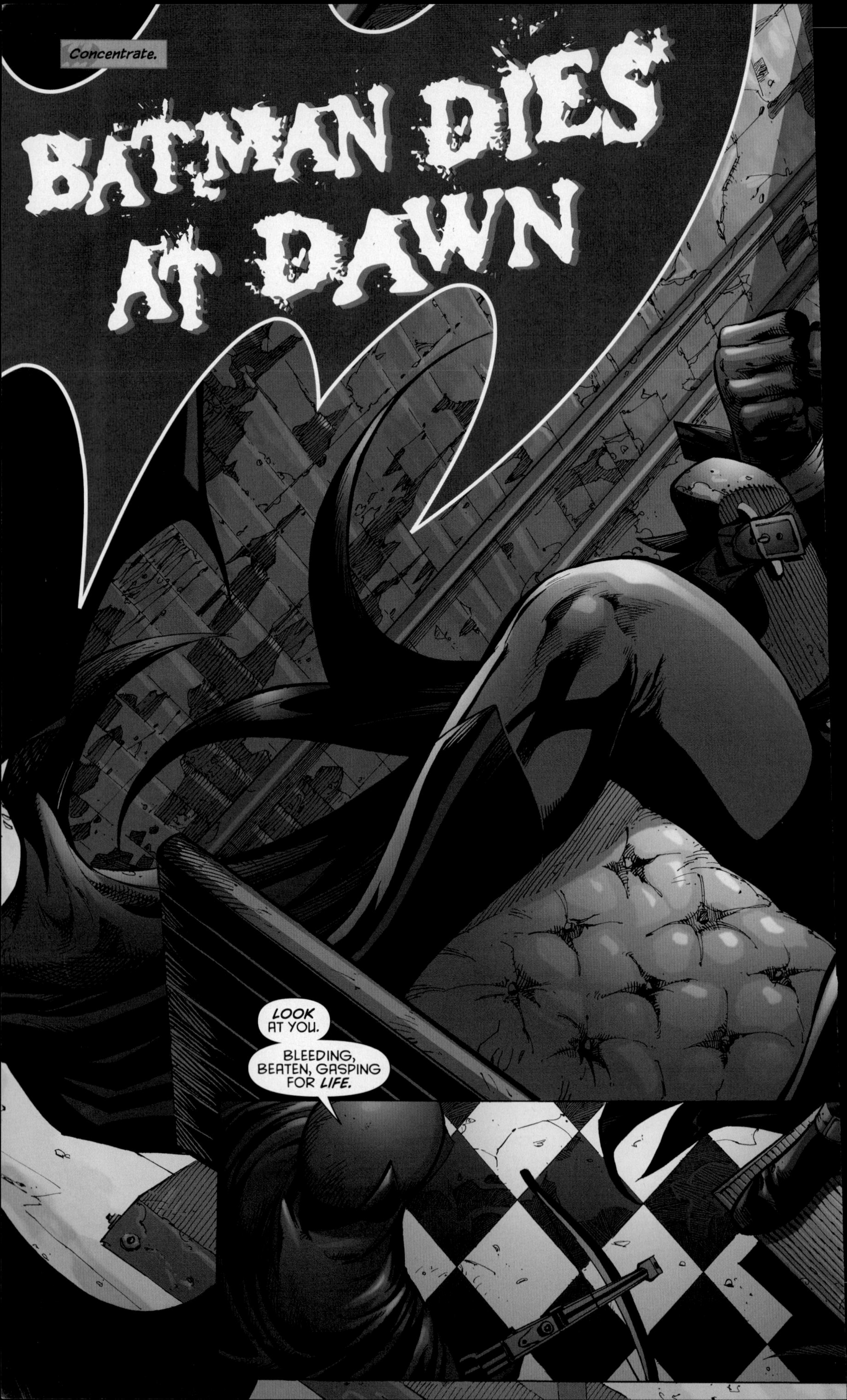
Concentrate.
BATMAN DIES AT DAWN
LOOK AT YOU.
BLEEDING, BEATEN, GASPING FOR LIFE.

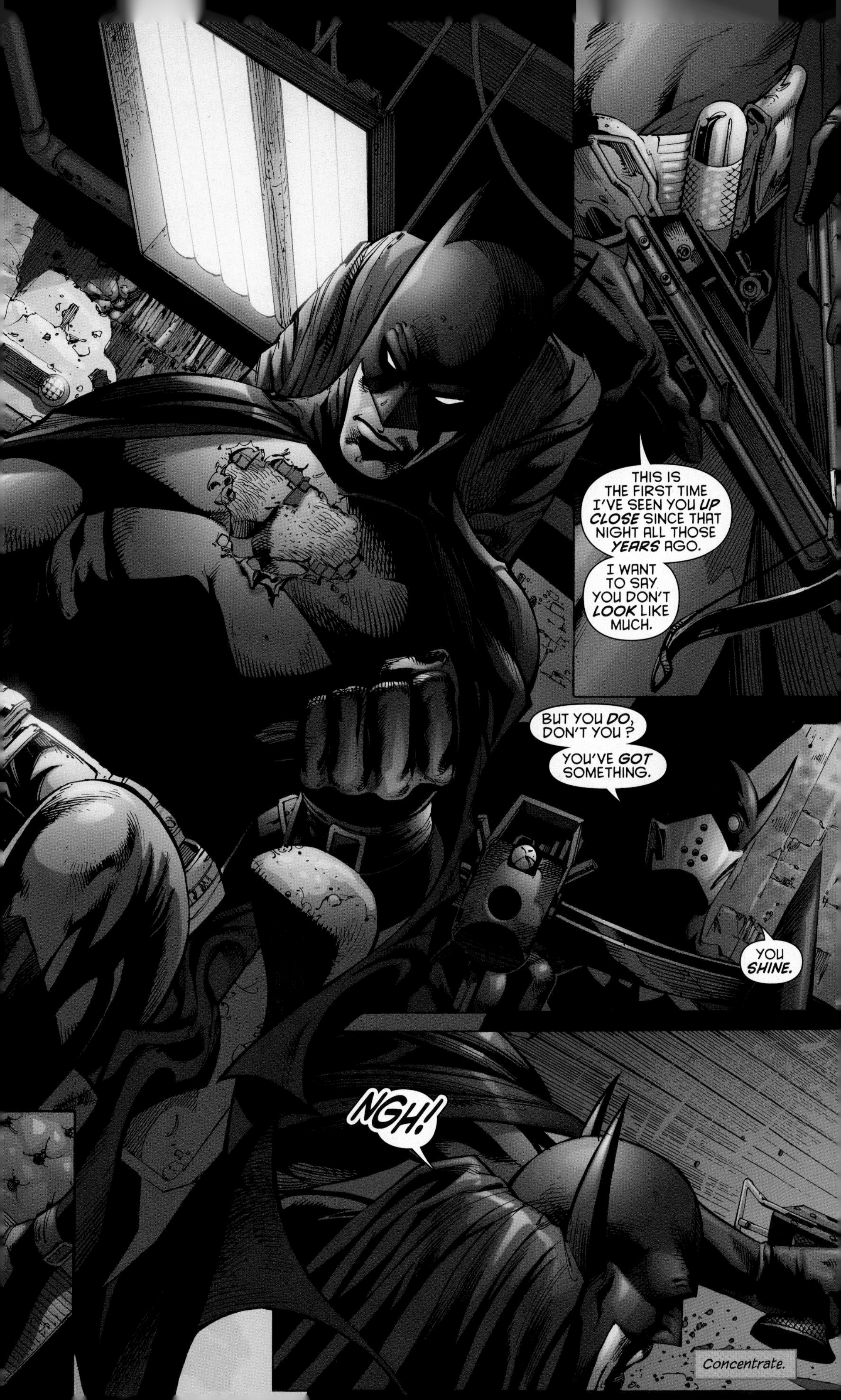
THIS IS THE FIRST TIME I'VE SEEN YOU *UP CLOSE* SINCE THAT NIGHT ALL THOSE *YEARS* AGO.
I WANT TO SAY YOU DON'T *LOOK* LIKE MUCH.
BUT YOU *DO*, DON'T YOU ?
YOU'VE *GOT* SOMETHING.
YOU *SHINE.*
NGH!
Concentrate.

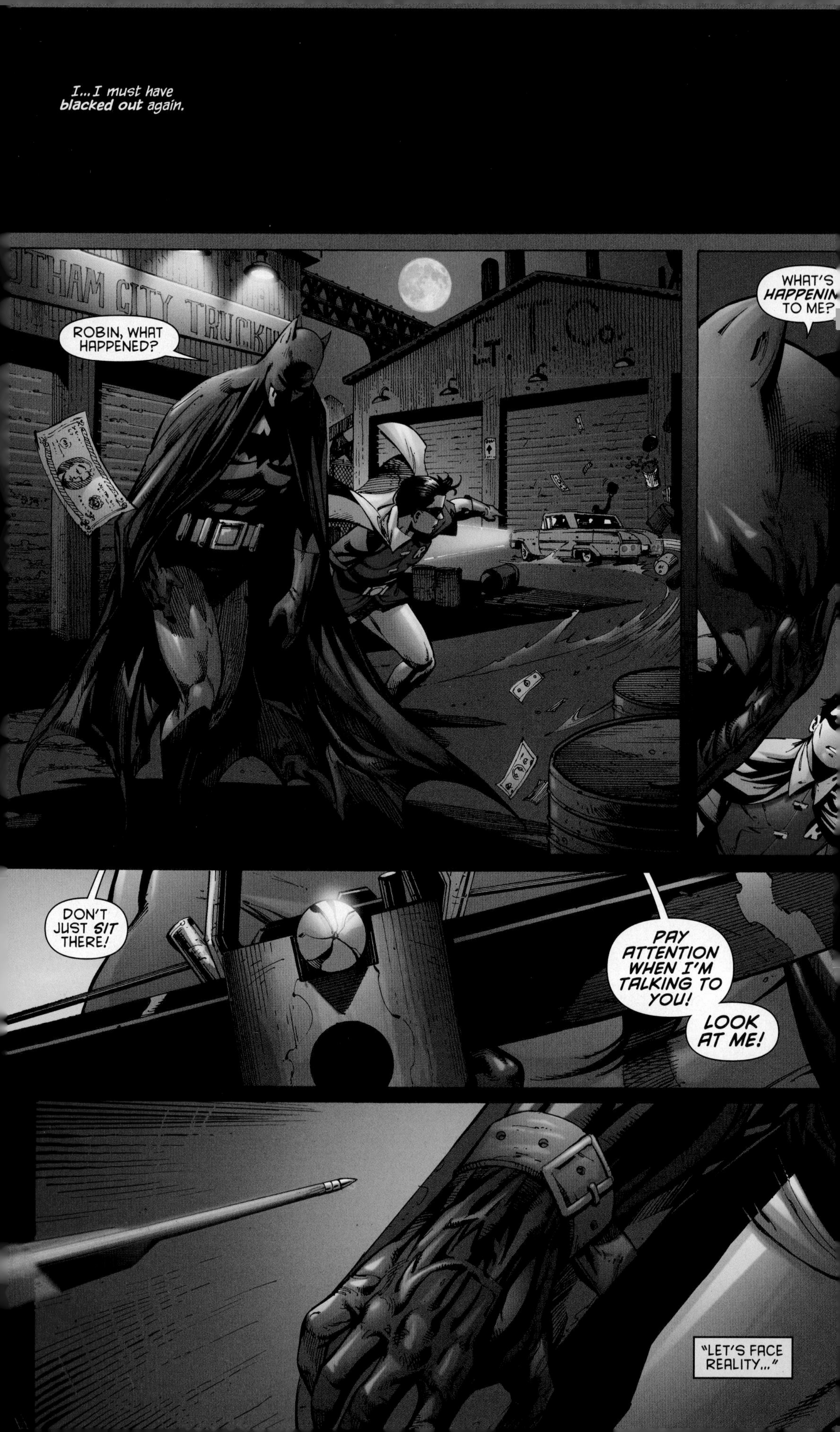
I... I must have blacked out again.
ROBIN, WHAT HAPPENED?
UTHAM CITY TRUCK
WHAT'S HAPPENIN TO ME?
DON'T JUST SIT THERE!
PAY ATTENTION WHEN I'M TALKING TO YOU!
LOOK AT ME!
"LET'S FACE REALITY..."

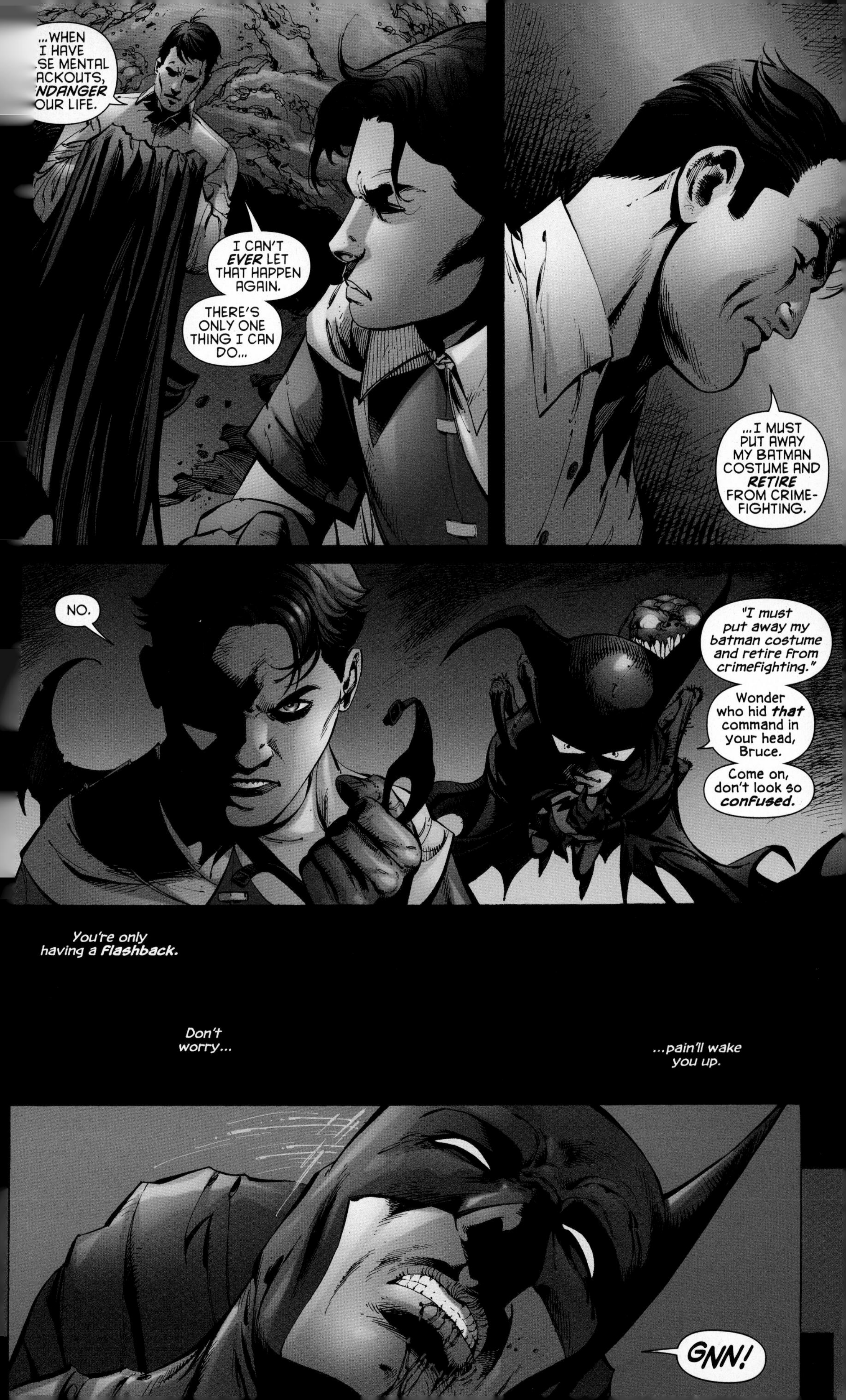
...WHEN I HAVE SE MENTAL ACKOUTS, NDANGER OUR LIFE.
I CAN'T EVER LET THAT HAPPEN AGAIN.
THERE'S ONLY ONE THING I CAN DO...
...I MUST PUT AWAY MY BATMAN COSTUME AND RETIRE FROM CRIME-FIGHTING.
NO.
"I must put away my batman costume and retire from crimefighting."
Wonder who hid that command in your head, Bruce.
Come on, don't look so confused.
You're only having a flashback.
Don't worry...
...pain'll wake you up.
GNN!

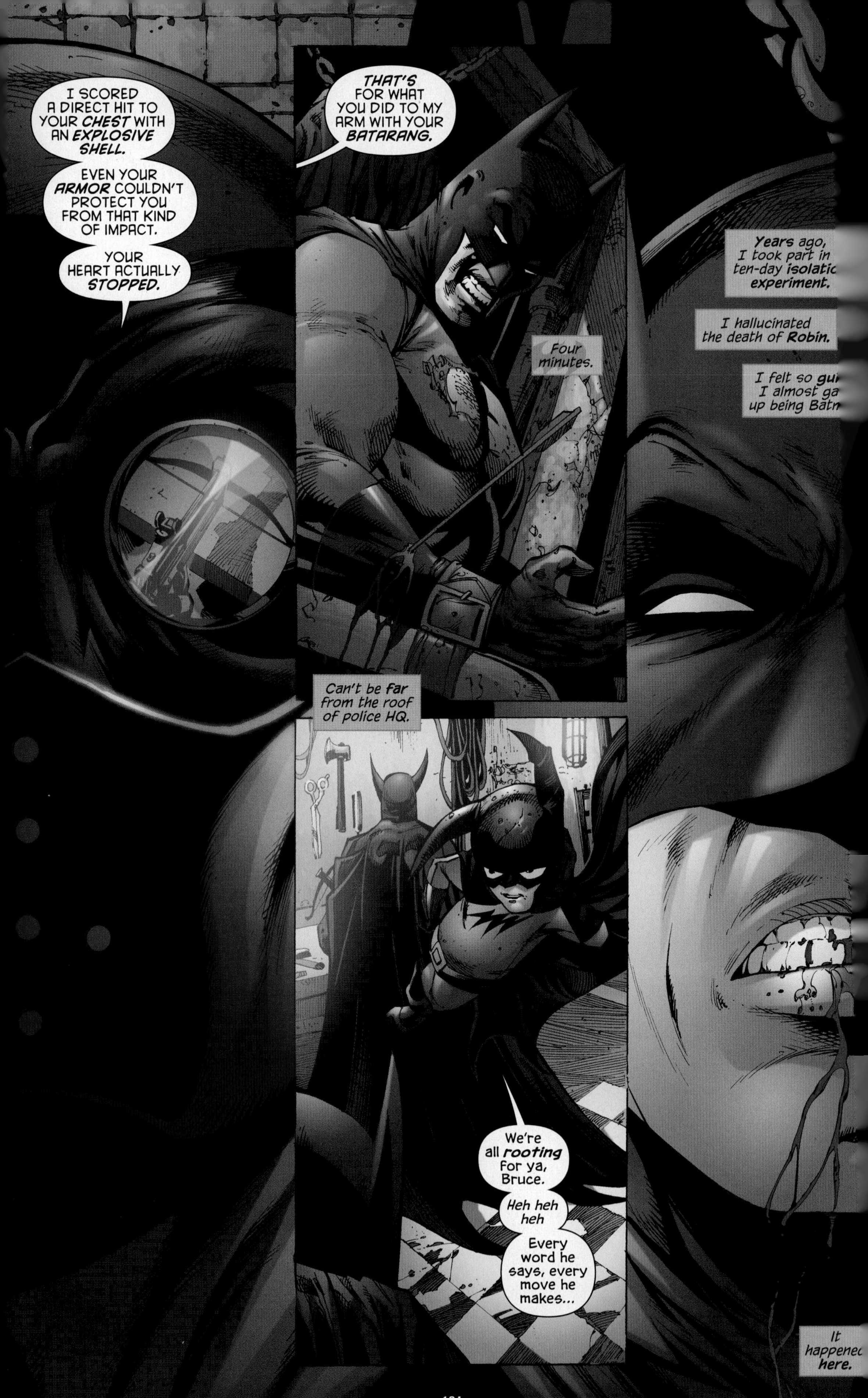

I SCORED A DIRECT HIT TO YOUR **CHEST** WITH AN **EXPLOSIVE SHELL.**
EVEN YOUR **ARMOR** COULDN'T PROTECT YOU FROM THAT KIND OF IMPACT.
YOUR HEART ACTUALLY **STOPPED.**
THAT'S FOR WHAT YOU DID TO MY ARM WITH YOUR **BATARANG.**
Four minutes.
Years ago, I took part in ten-day **isolati** **experiment.**
I hallucinated the death of **Robin.**
I felt so **gu** I almost ga up being Batm
Can't be **far** from the roof of police HQ.
We're all **rooting** for ya, Bruce.
Heh heh heh
Every word he says, every move he makes...
It happene **here.**

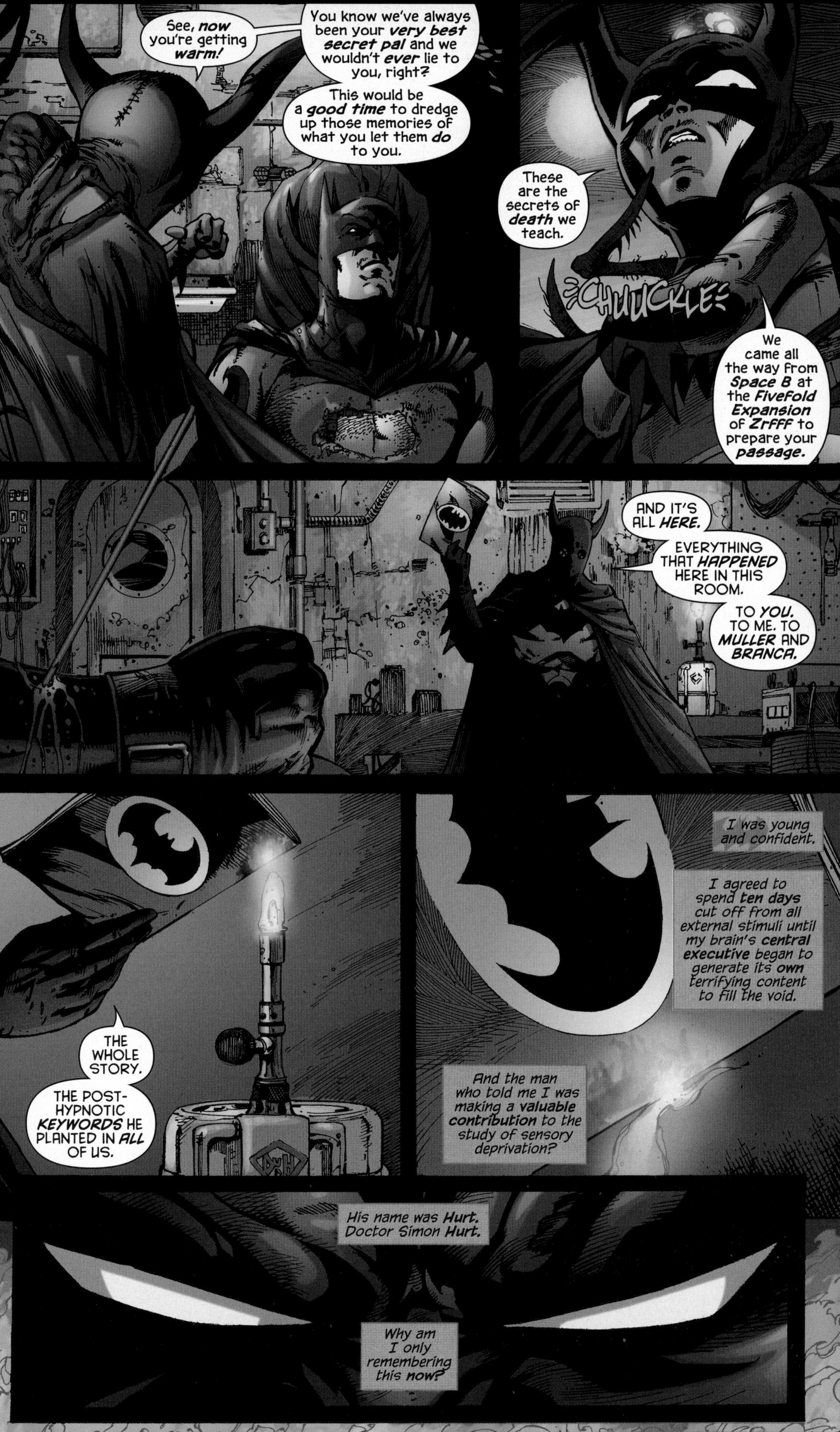
See, now you're getting warm!
You know we've always been your very best secret pal and we wouldn't ever lie to you, right?
This would be a good time to dredge up those memories of what you let them do to you.
These are the secrets of death we teach.
CHUUCKLE
We came all the way from Space B at the Fivefold Expansion of Zrfff to prepare your passage.
AND IT'S ALL HERE.
EVERYTHING THAT HAPPENED HERE IN THIS ROOM.
TO YOU. TO ME. TO MULLER AND BRANCA.
THE WHOLE STORY.
THE POST-HYPNOTIC KEYWORDS HE PLANTED IN ALL OF US.
I was young and confident.
I agreed to spend ten days cut off from all external stimuli until my brain's central executive began to generate its own terrifying content to fill the void.
And the man who told me I was making a valuable contribution to the study of sensory deprivation?
His name was Hurt. Doctor Simon Hurt.
Why am I only remembering this now?

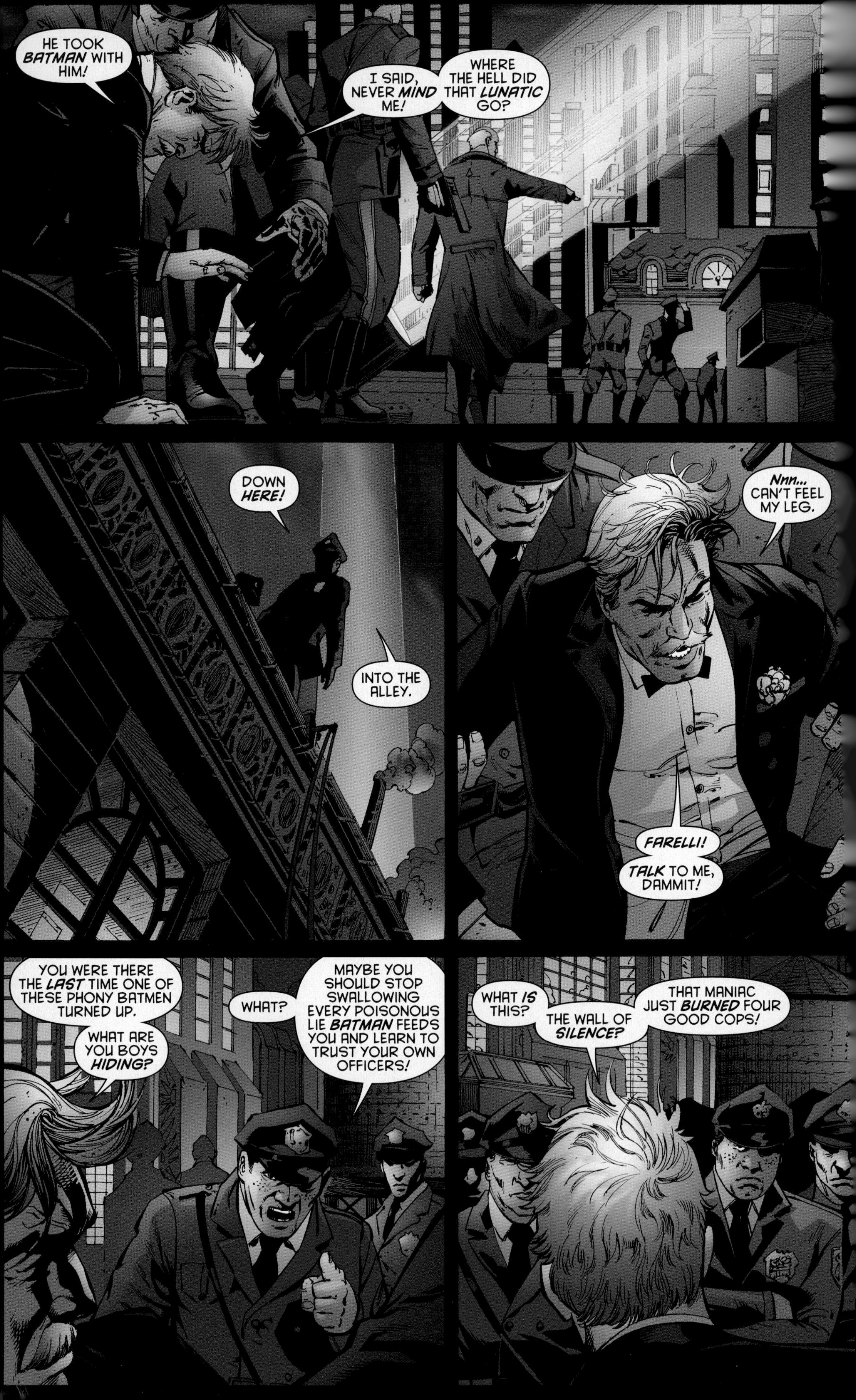
HE TOOK BATMAN WITH HIM!
I SAID, NEVER MIND ME!
WHERE THE HELL DID THAT LUNATIC GO?
DOWN HERE!
INTO THE ALLEY.
Nnn... CAN'T FEEL MY LEG.
FARELLI!
TALK TO ME, DAMMIT!
YOU WERE THERE THE LAST TIME ONE OF THESE PHONY BATMEN TURNED UP.
WHAT ARE YOU BOYS HIDING?
WHAT?
MAYBE YOU SHOULD STOP SWALLOWING EVERY POISONOUS LIE BATMAN FEEDS YOU AND LEARN TO TRUST YOUR OWN OFFICERS!
WHAT IS THIS?
THE WALL OF SILENCE?
THAT MANIAC JUST BURNED FOUR GOOD COPS!

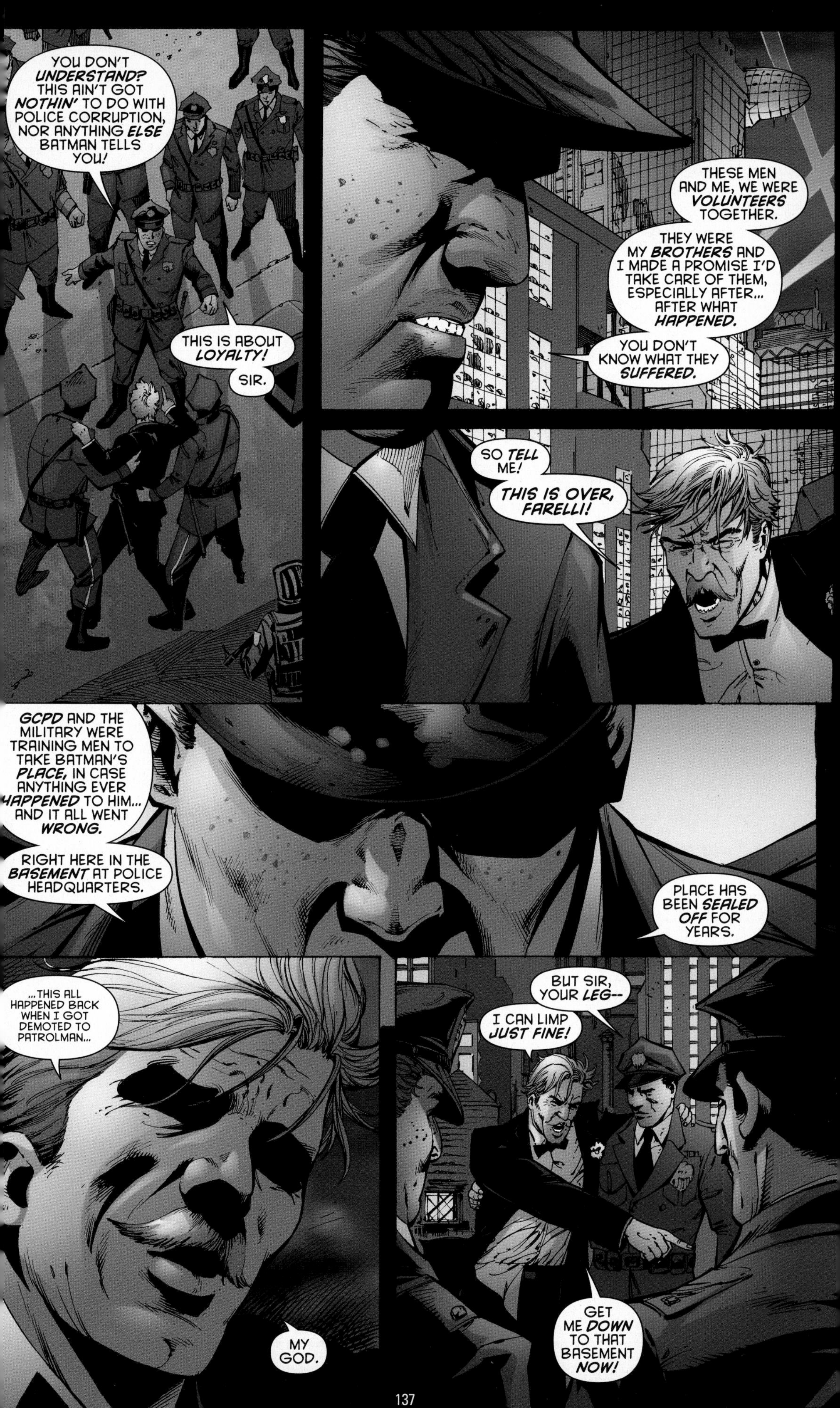
YOU DON'T UNDERSTAND? THIS AIN'T GOT NOTHIN' TO DO WITH POLICE CORRUPTION, NOR ANYTHING ELSE BATMAN TELLS YOU!
THIS IS ABOUT LOYALTY!
SIR.
THESE MEN AND ME, WE WERE VOLUNTEERS TOGETHER.
THEY WERE MY BROTHERS AND I MADE A PROMISE I'D TAKE CARE OF THEM, ESPECIALLY AFTER... AFTER WHAT HAPPENED.
YOU DON'T KNOW WHAT THEY SUFFERED.
SO TELL ME!
THIS IS OVER, FARELLI!
GCPD AND THE MILITARY WERE TRAINING MEN TO TAKE BATMAN'S PLACE, IN CASE ANYTHING EVER HAPPENED TO HIM... AND IT ALL WENT WRONG.
RIGHT HERE IN THE BASEMENT AT POLICE HEADQUARTERS.
PLACE HAS BEEN SEALED OFF FOR YEARS.
...THIS ALL HAPPENED BACK WHEN I GOT DEMOTED TO PATROLMAN...
MY GOD.
BUT SIR, YOUR LEG--
I CAN LIMP JUST FINE!
GET ME DOWN TO THAT BASEMENT NOW!

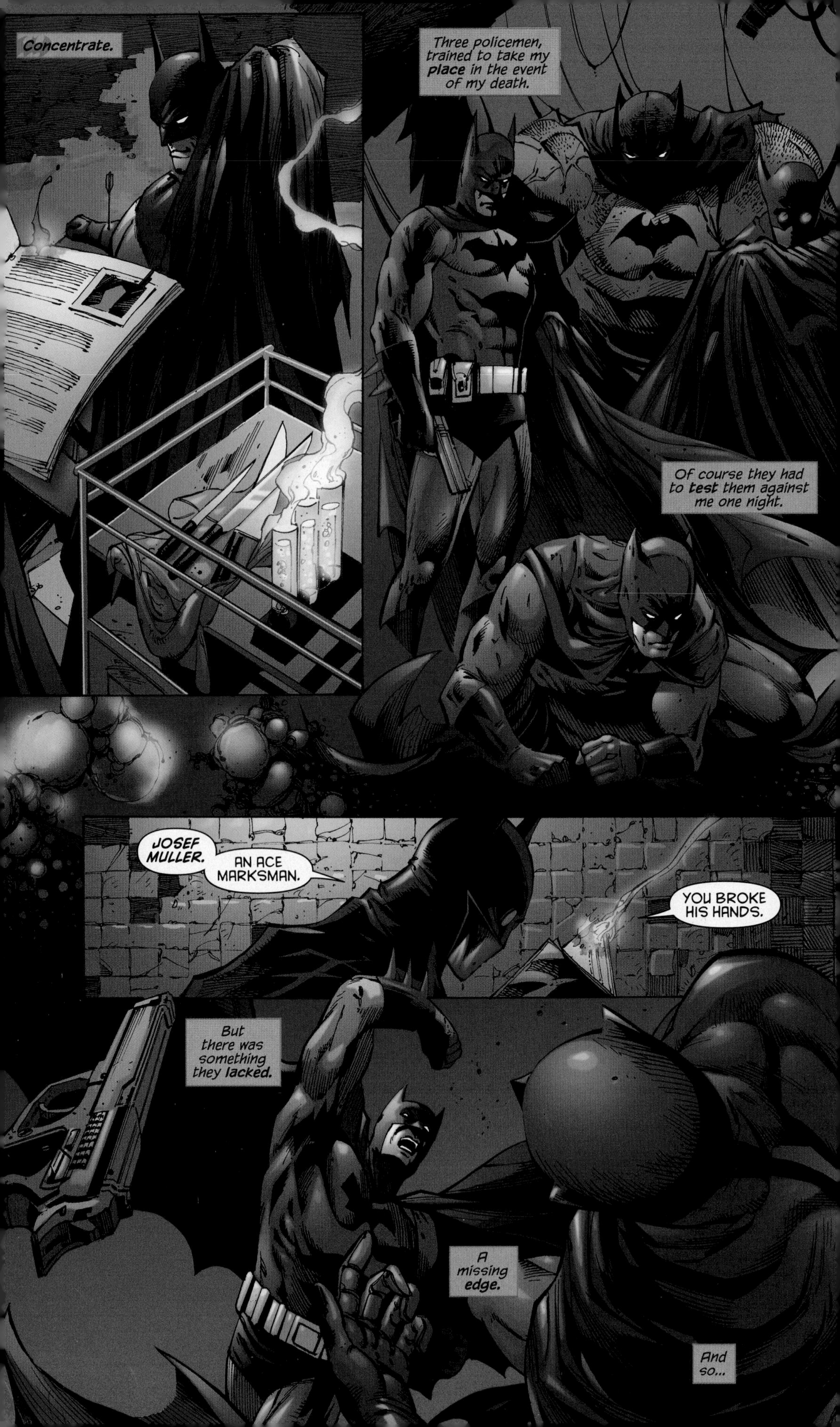
Concentrate.
Three policemen, trained to take my place in the event of my death.
Of course they had to test them against me one night.
JOSEF MULLER.
AN ACE MARKSMAN.
YOU BROKE HIS HANDS.
But there was something they lacked.
A missing edge.
And so...

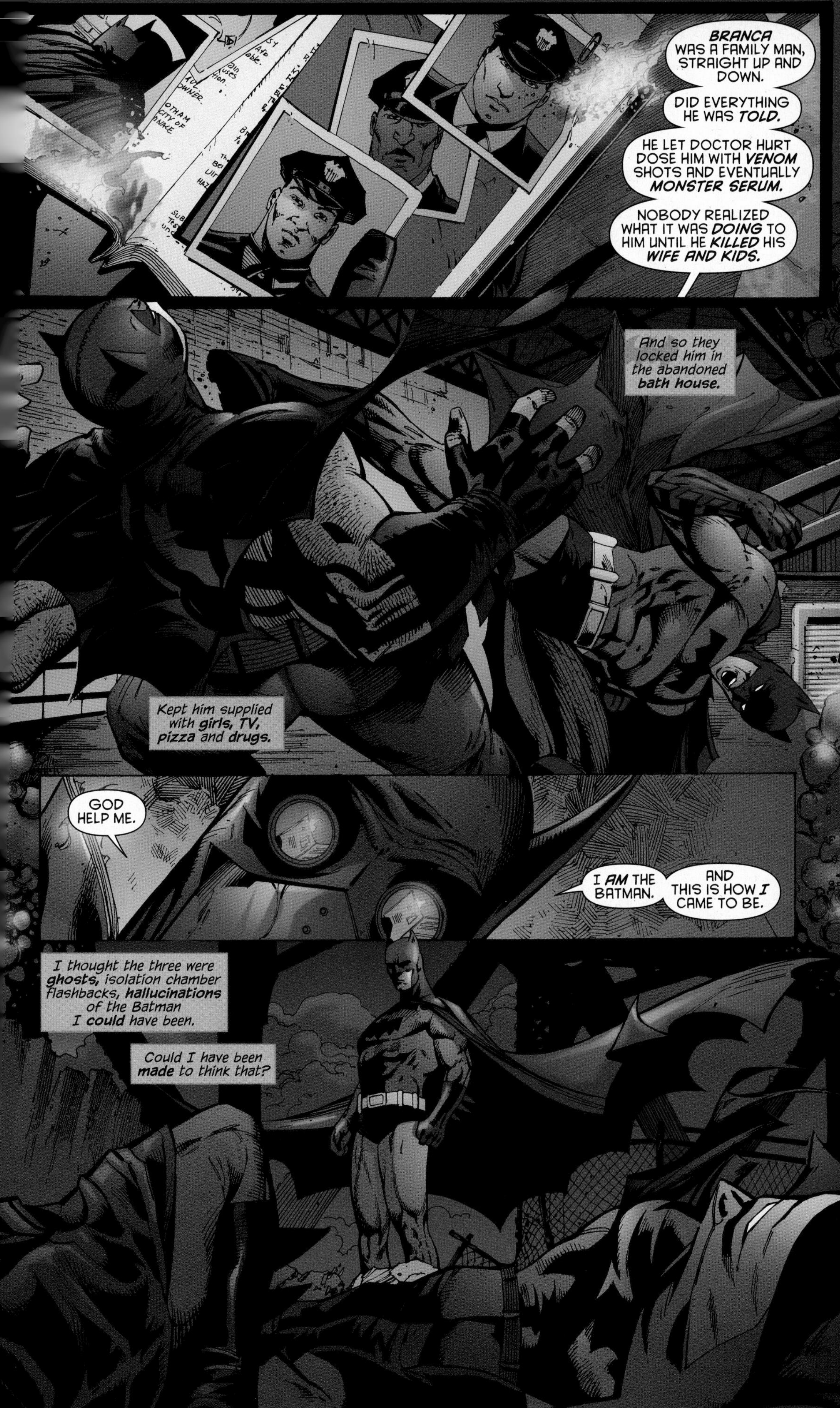
BRANCA WAS A FAMILY MAN, STRAIGHT UP AND DOWN.
DID EVERYTHING HE WAS TOLD.
HE LET DOCTOR HURT DOSE HIM WITH VENOM SHOTS AND EVENTUALLY MONSTER SERUM.
NOBODY REALIZED WHAT IT WAS DOING TO HIM UNTIL HE KILLED HIS WIFE AND KIDS.
And so they locked him in the abandoned bath house.
Kept him supplied with girls, TV, pizza and drugs.
GOD HELP ME.
I AM THE BATMAN.
AND THIS IS HOW I CAME TO BE.
I thought the three were ghosts, isolation chamber flashbacks, hallucinations of the Batman I could have been.
Could I have been made to think that?

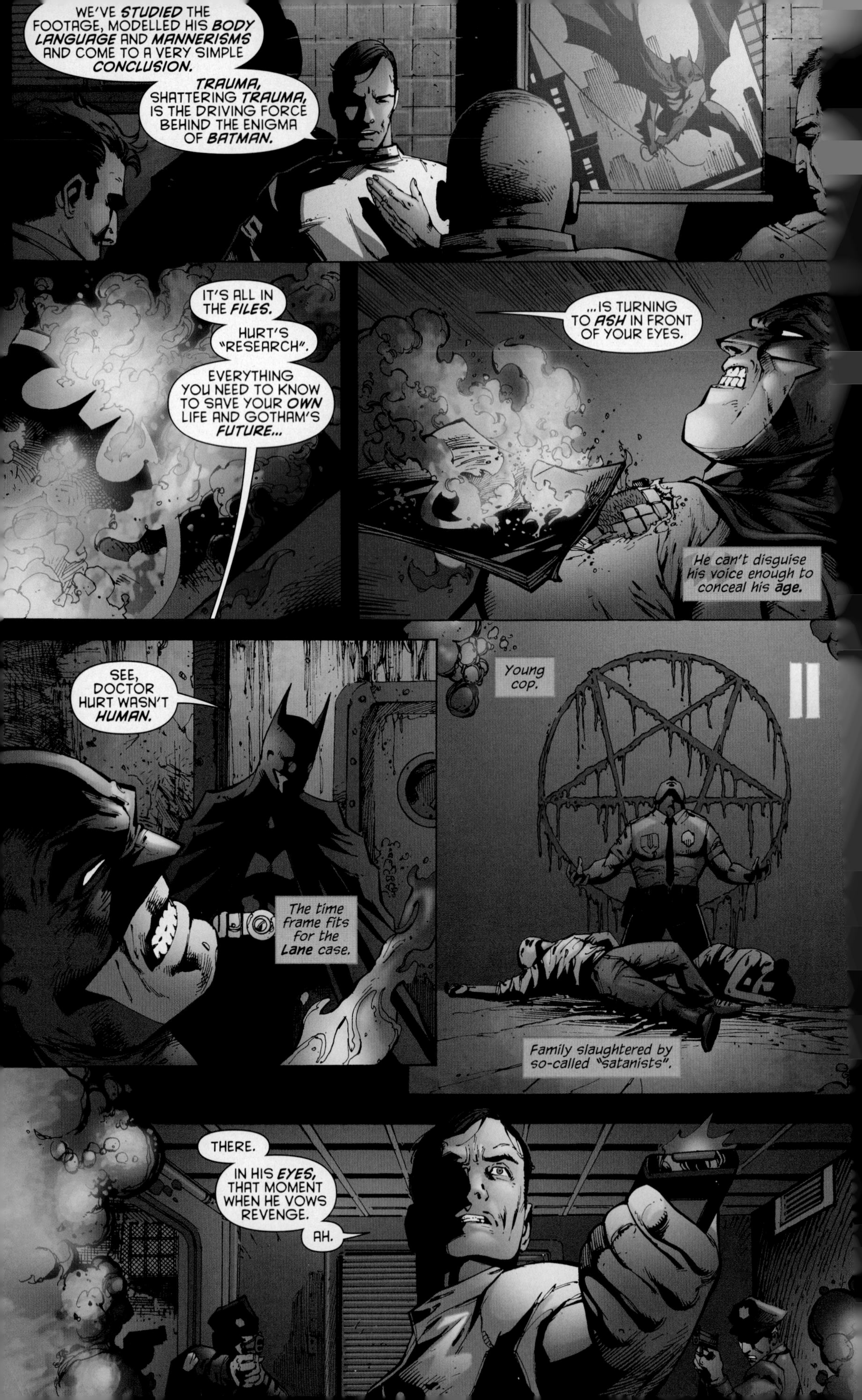

WE'VE STUDIED THE FOOTAGE, MODELLED HIS BODY LANGUAGE AND MANNERISMS AND COME TO A VERY SIMPLE CONCLUSION.
TRAUMA, SHATTERING TRAUMA, IS THE DRIVING FORCE BEHIND THE ENIGMA OF BATMAN.
IT'S ALL IN THE FILES.
HURT'S "RESEARCH".
EVERYTHING YOU NEED TO KNOW TO SAVE YOUR OWN LIFE AND GOTHAM'S FUTURE...
...IS TURNING TO ASH IN FRONT OF YOUR EYES.
He can't disguise his voice enough to conceal his age.
SEE, DOCTOR HURT WASN'T HUMAN.
The time frame fits for the Lane case.
Young cop.
Family slaughtered by so-called "satanists".
THERE.
IN HIS EYES, THAT MOMENT WHEN HE VOWS REVENGE.
AH.

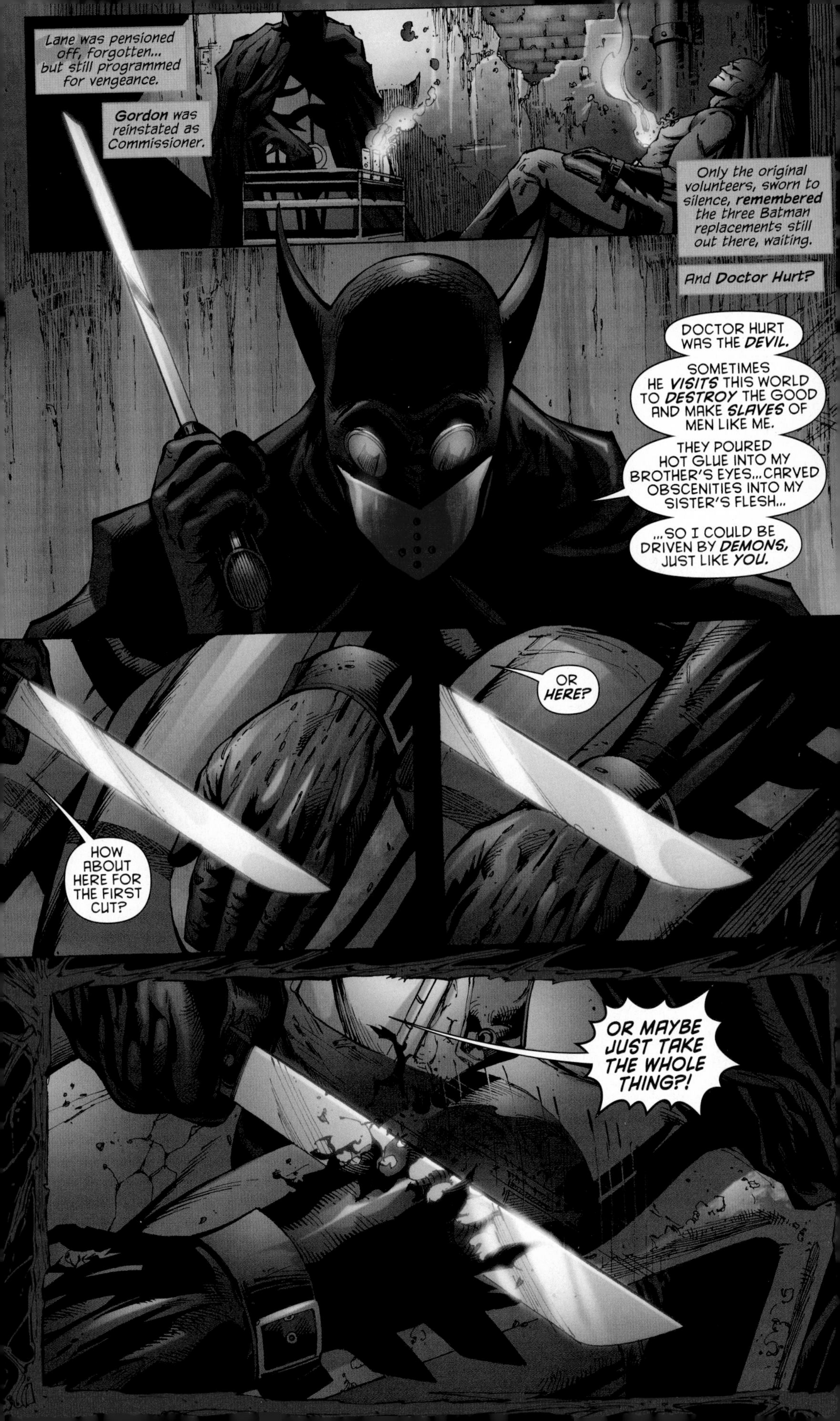

Lane was pensioned off, forgotten... but still programmed for vengeance.
Gordon was reinstated as Commissioner.
Only the original volunteers, sworn to silence, remembered the three Batman replacements still out there, waiting.
And Doctor Hurt?
DOCTOR HURT WAS THE DEVIL.
SOMETIMES HE VISITS THIS WORLD TO DESTROY THE GOOD AND MAKE SLAVES OF MEN LIKE ME.
THEY POURED HOT GLUE INTO MY BROTHER'S EYES...CARVED OBSCENITIES INTO MY SISTER'S FLESH...
...SO I COULD BE DRIVEN BY DEMONS, JUST LIKE YOU.
HOW ABOUT HERE FOR THE FIRST CUT?
OR HERE?
OR MAYBE JUST TAKE THE WHOLE THING?!

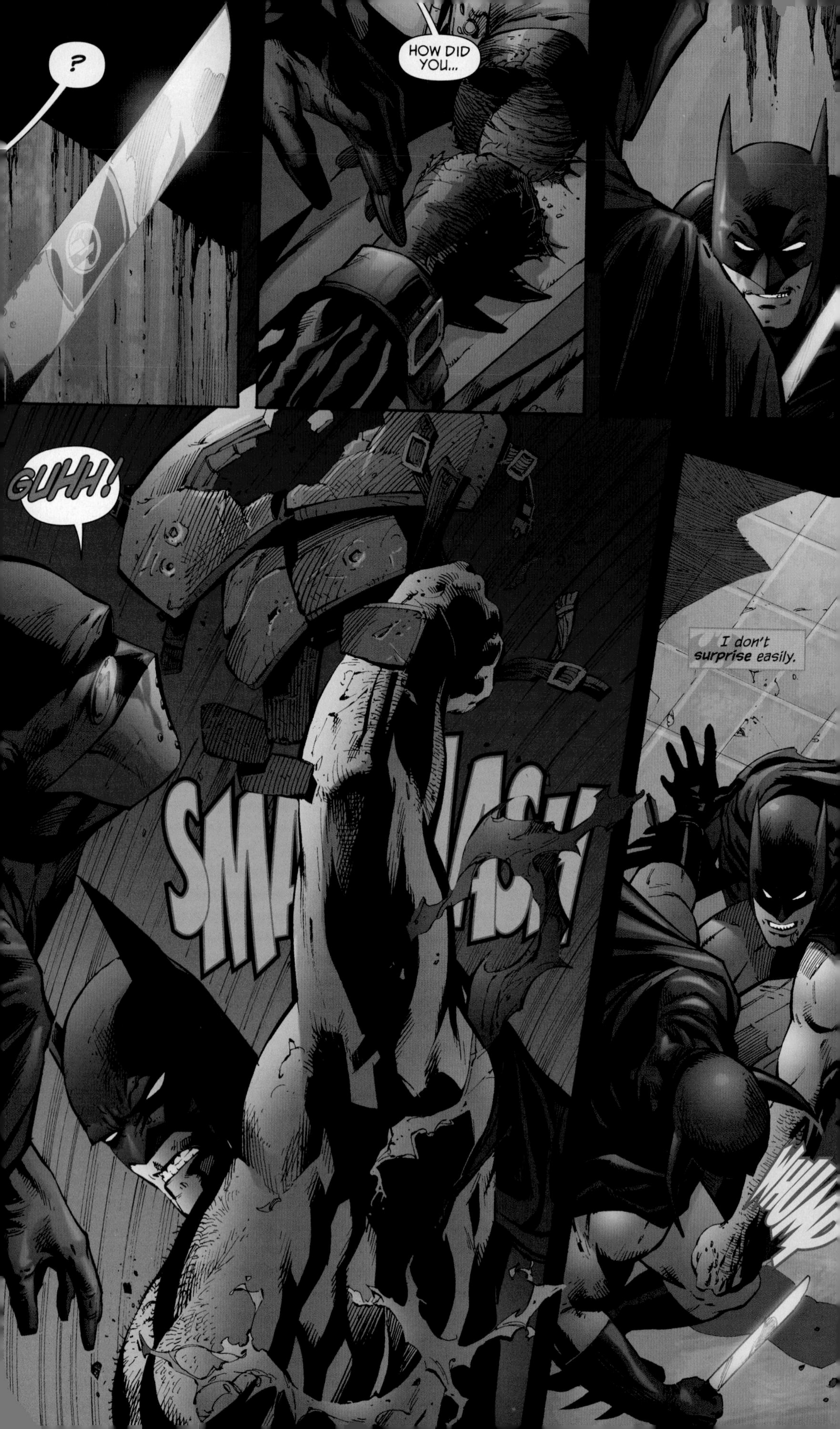
?
HOW DID YOU...
GUHH!
I don't surprise easily.

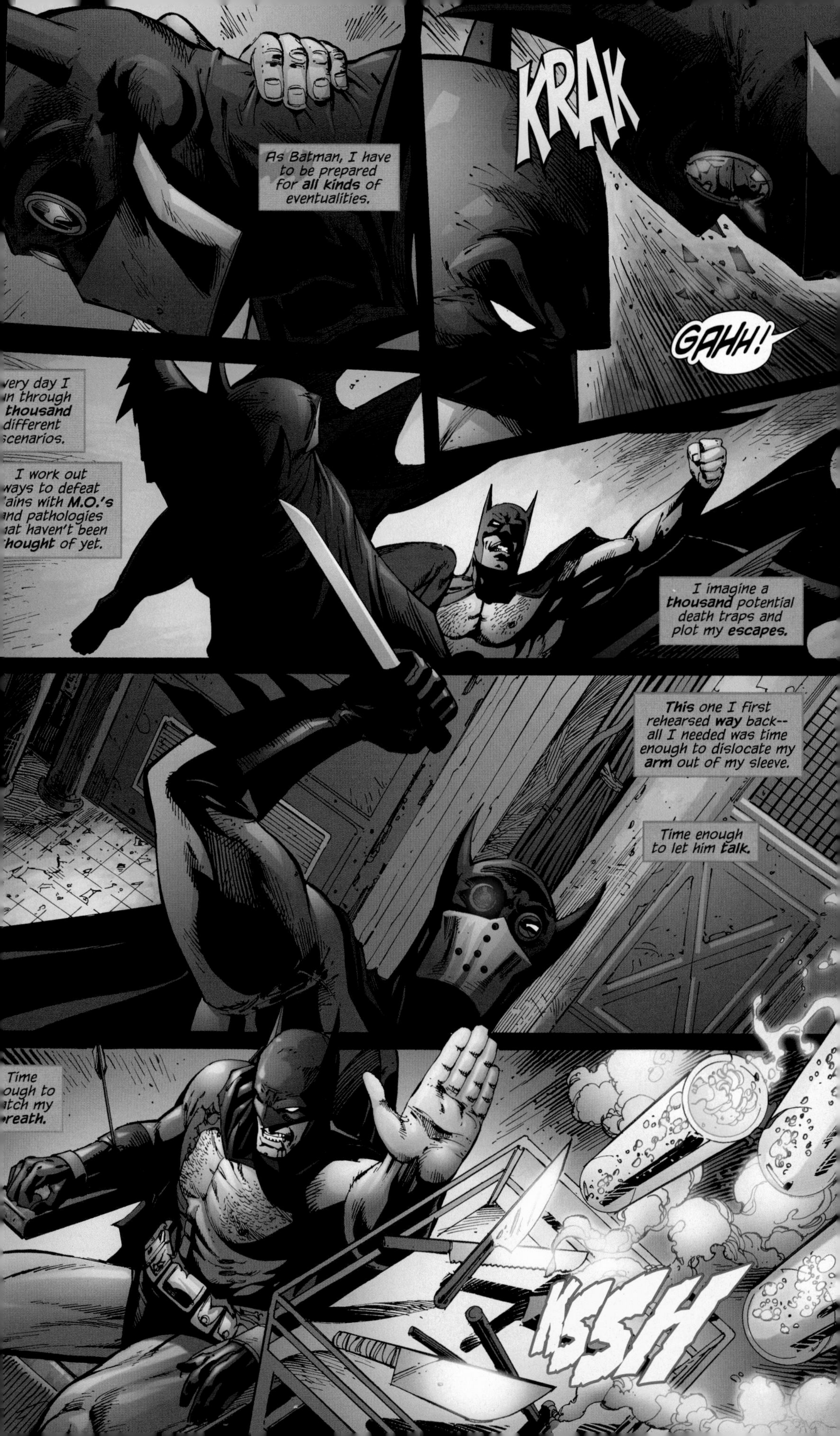

KRAK
As Batman, I have to be prepared for **all kinds** of eventualities.
GAHH!
very day I
n through
thousand
different
scenarios.
I work out
ways to defeat
/ains with **M.O.'s**
and pathologies
hat haven't been
thought of yet.
I imagine a **thousand** potential death traps and plot my **escapes.**
This one I first rehearsed **way** back-- all I needed was time enough to dislocate my **arm** out of my sleeve.
Time enough to let him **talk.**
Time
ough to
atch my
reath.
KSSH

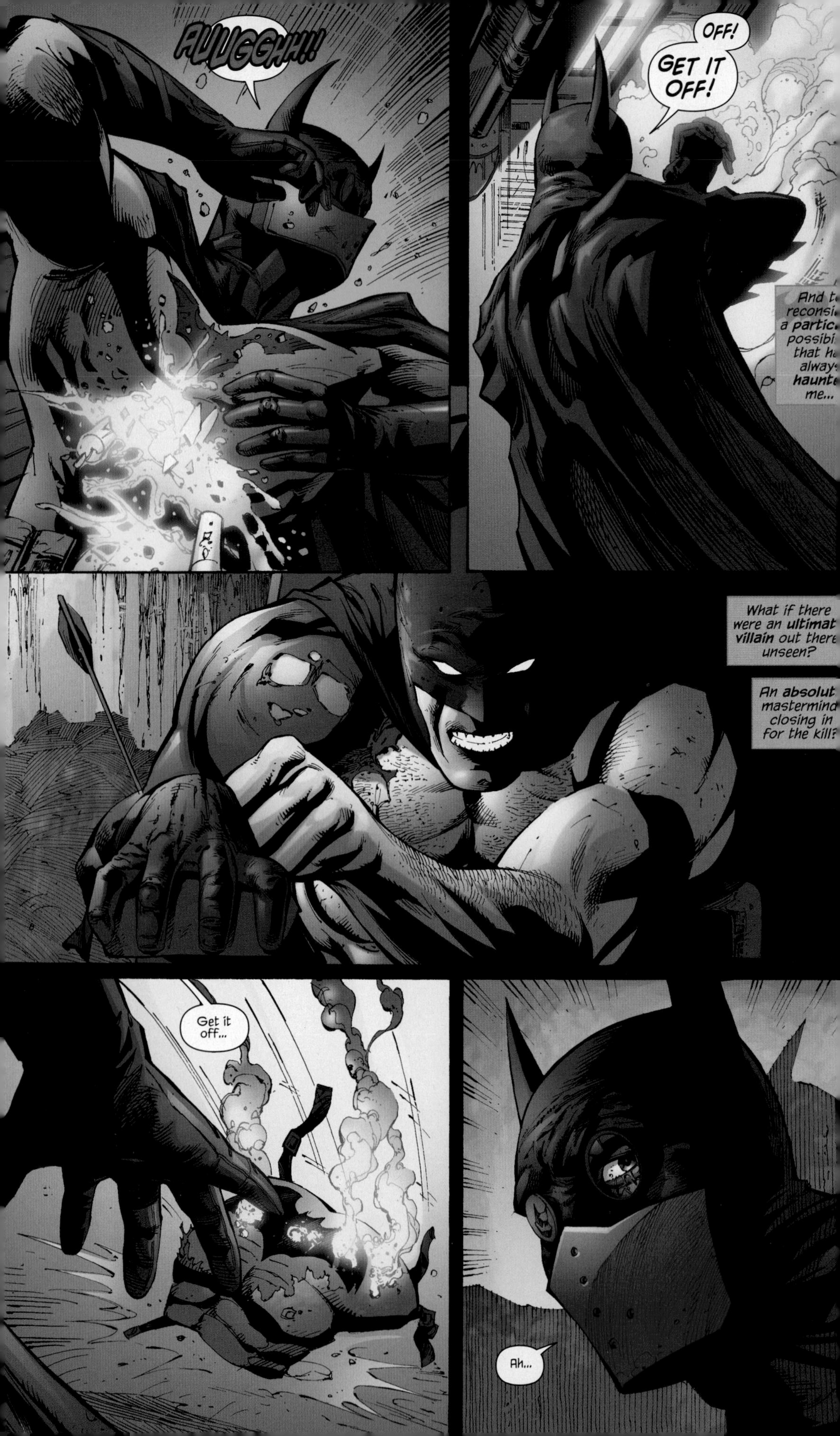

AUUGGHH!!
OFF!
GET IT OFF!
And t reconsi a partic possibi that h always haunte me...
What if there were an ultimat villain out there unseen?
An absolut mastermind closing in for the kill?
Get it off...
Ah...

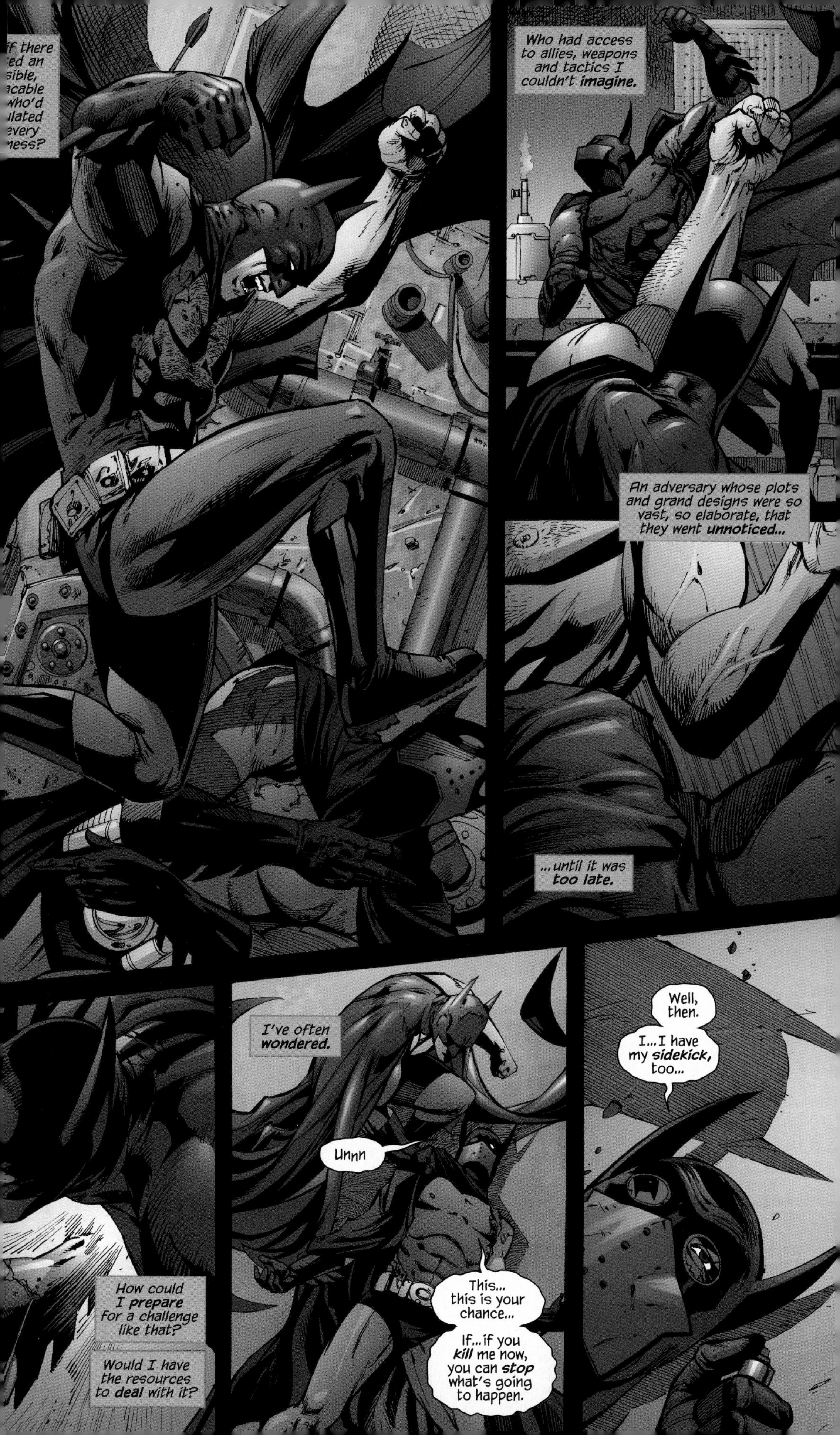

f there
ed an
sible,
acable
who'd
ulated
every
ness?
Who had access to allies, weapons and tactics I couldn't *imagine.*
An adversary whose plots and grand designs were so vast, so elaborate, that they went *unnoticed...*
...until it was *too late.*
How could I *prepare* for a challenge like that?
Would I have the resources to *deal* with it?
I've often *wondered.*
Unnn
This... this is your chance...
If... if you *kill* me now, you can *stop* what's going to happen.
Well, then.
I... I have my *sidekick,* too...

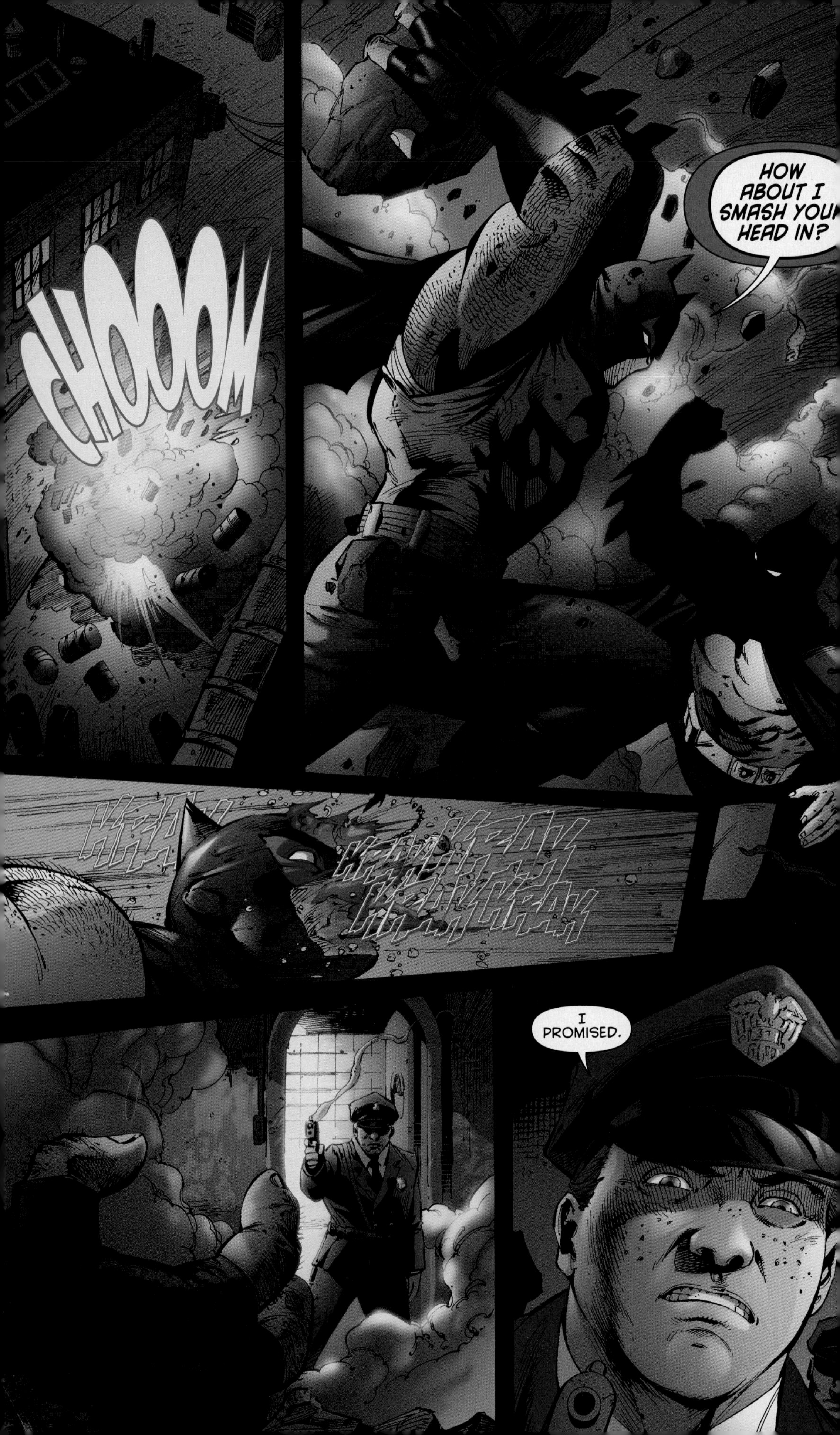
CHOOOM
HOW ABOUT I SMASH YOU HEAD IN?
I PROMISED.

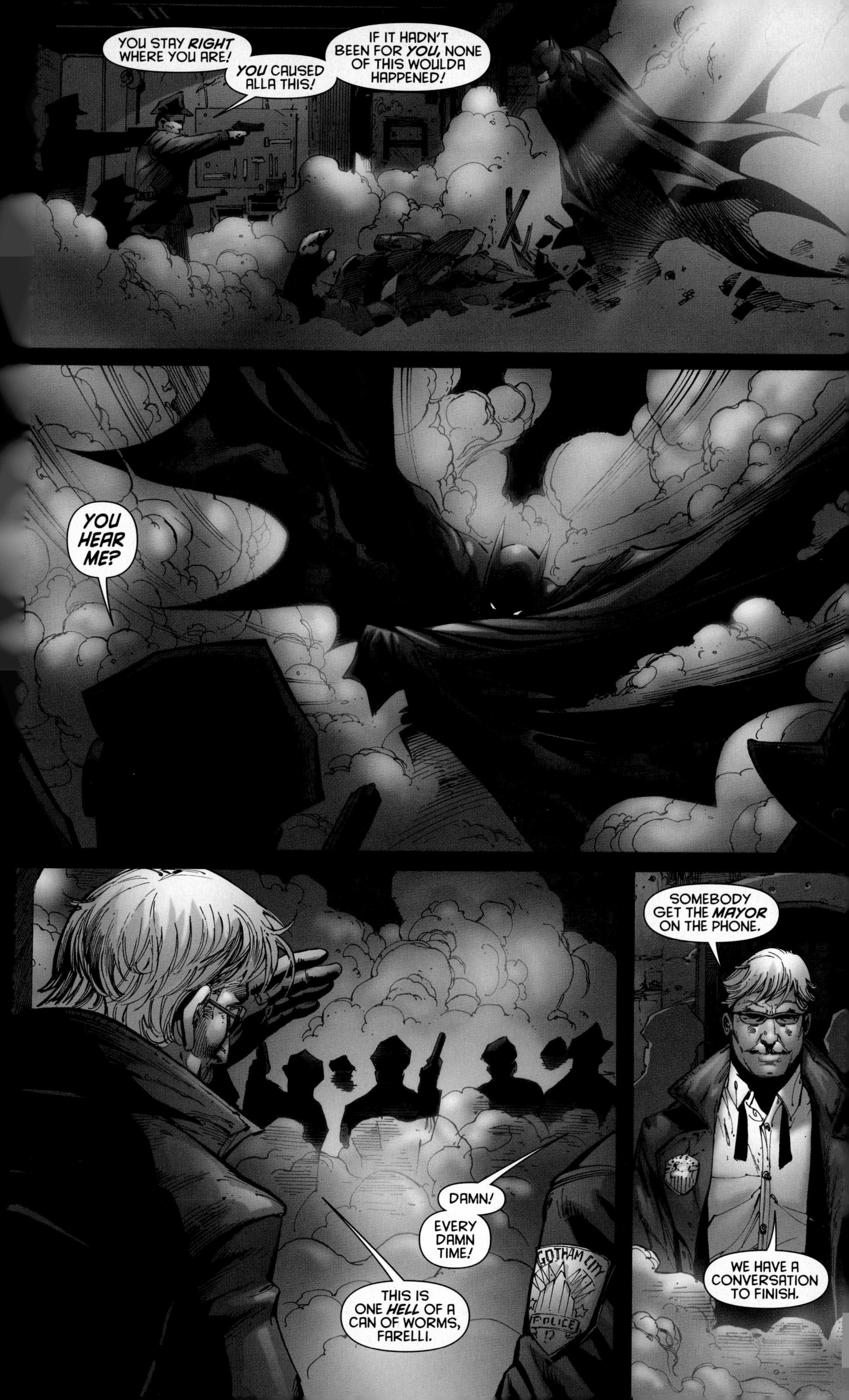
YOU STAY RIGHT WHERE YOU ARE!
YOU CAUSED ALLA THIS!
IF IT HADN'T BEEN FOR YOU, NONE OF THIS WOULDA HAPPENED!
YOU HEAR ME?
DAMN!
EVERY DAMN TIME!
THIS IS ONE HELL OF A CAN OF WORMS, FARELLI.
GOTHAM CITY POLICE
SOMEBODY GET THE MAYOR ON THE PHONE.
WE HAVE A CONVERSATION TO FINISH.

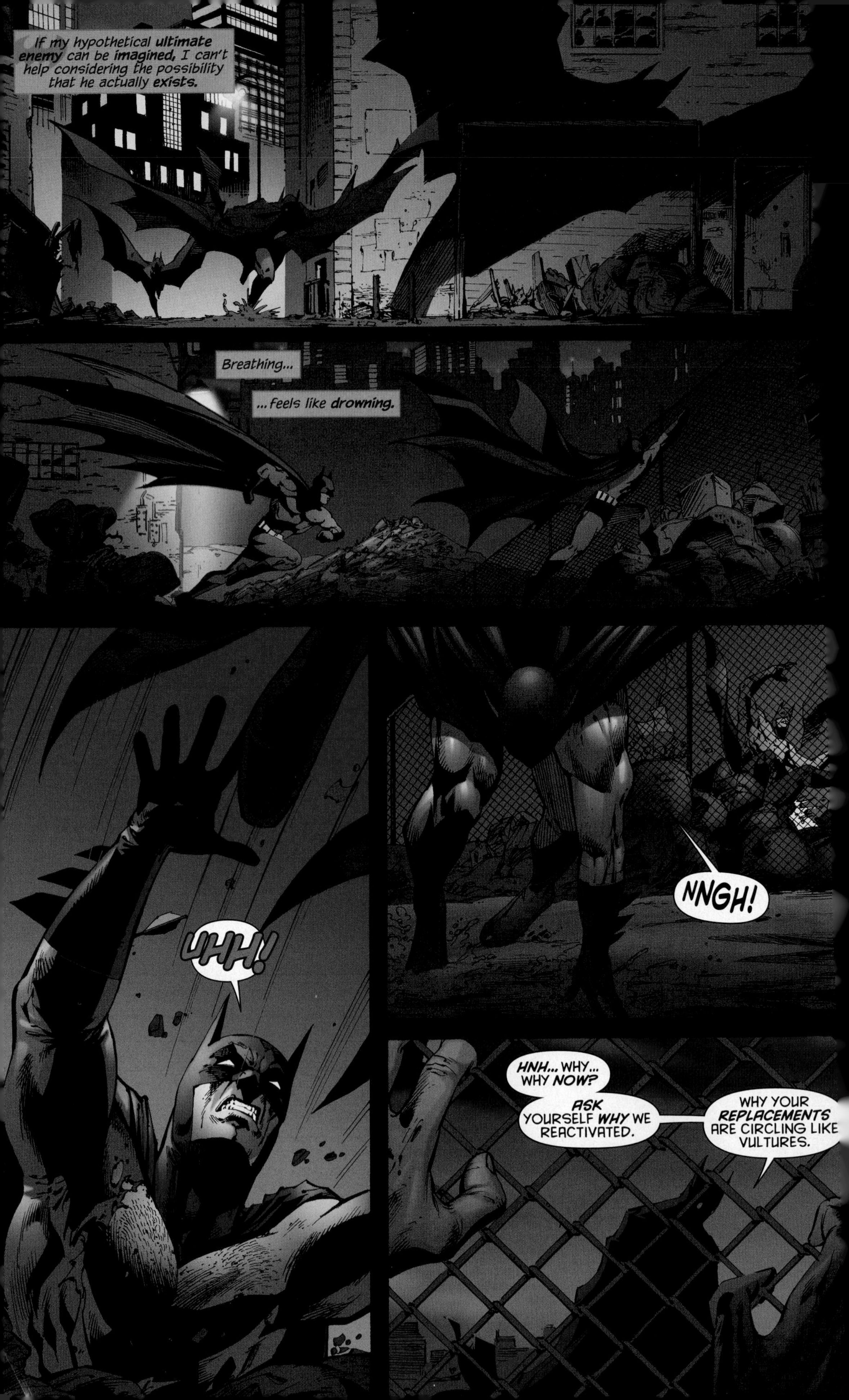

If my hypothetical ultimate enemy can be imagined, I can't help considering the possibility that he actually exists.
Breathing...
...feels like drowning.
UHH!
NNGH!
HNH... WHY... WHY NOW?
ASK YOURSELF WHY WE REACTIVATED.
WHY YOUR REPLACEMENTS ARE CIRCLING LIKE VULTURES.

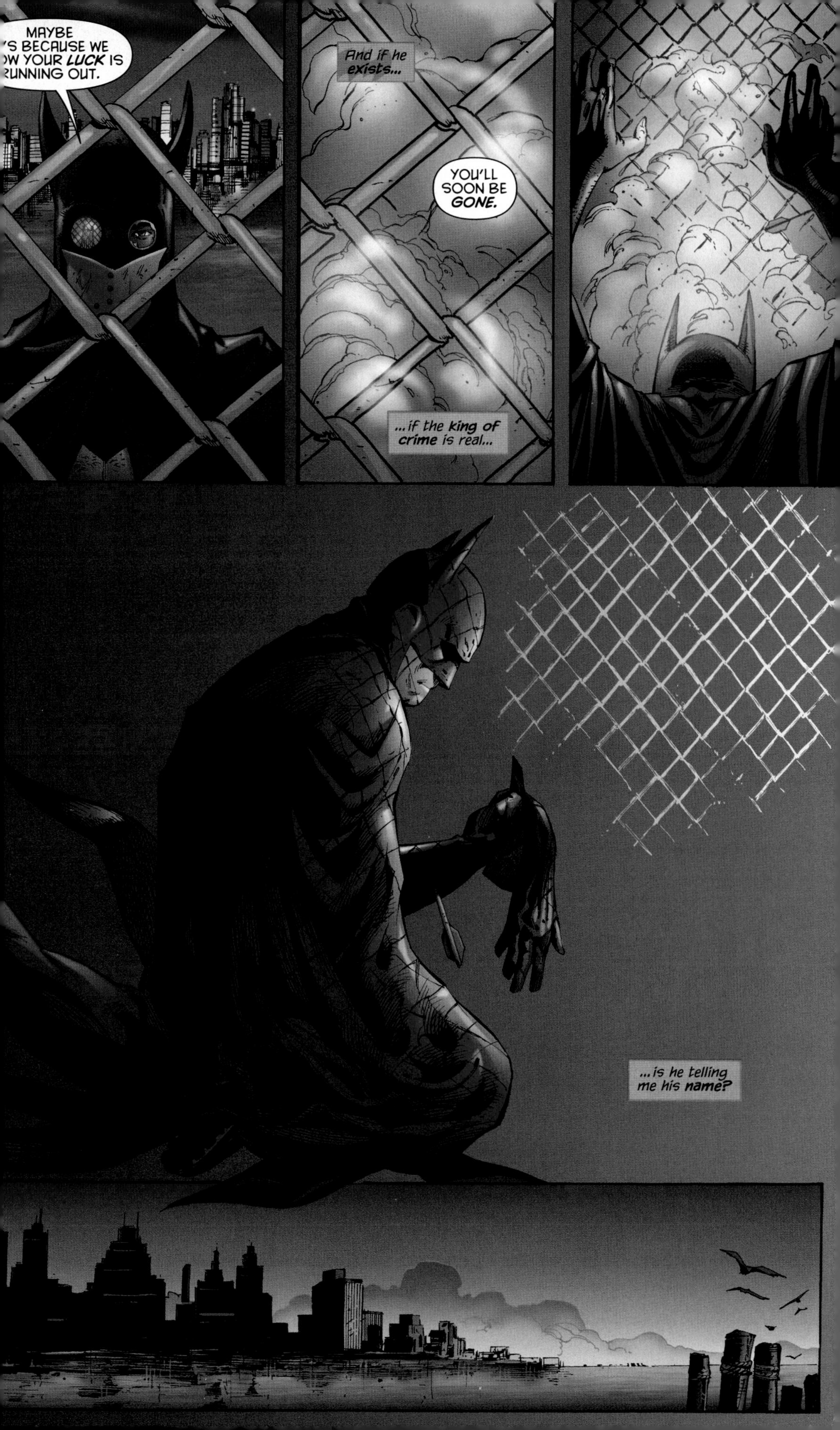
MAYBE
'S BECAUSE WE
OW YOUR LUCK IS
RUNNING OUT.
And if he exists...
YOU'LL SOON BE GONE.
...if the king of crime is real...
...is he telling me his name?

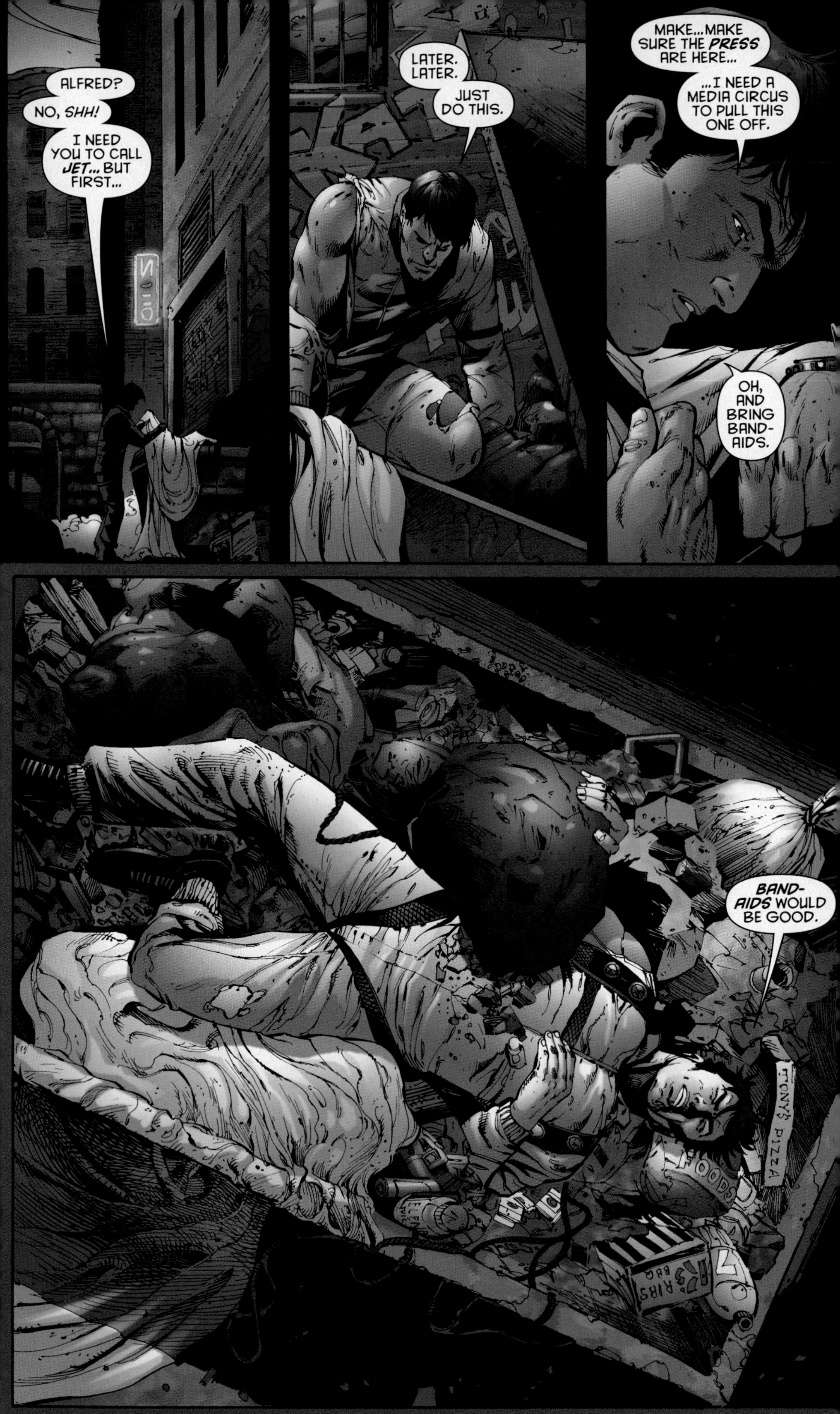

ALFRED?
NO, *SHH!*
I NEED YOU TO CALL ***JET***... BUT FIRST...
LATER. LATER.
JUST DO THIS.
MAKE... MAKE SURE THE ***PRESS*** ARE HERE...
...I NEED A MEDIA CIRCUS TO PULL THIS ONE OFF.
OH, AND BRING BAND-AIDS.
BAND-AIDS WOULD BE GOOD.
TONY'S PIZZA

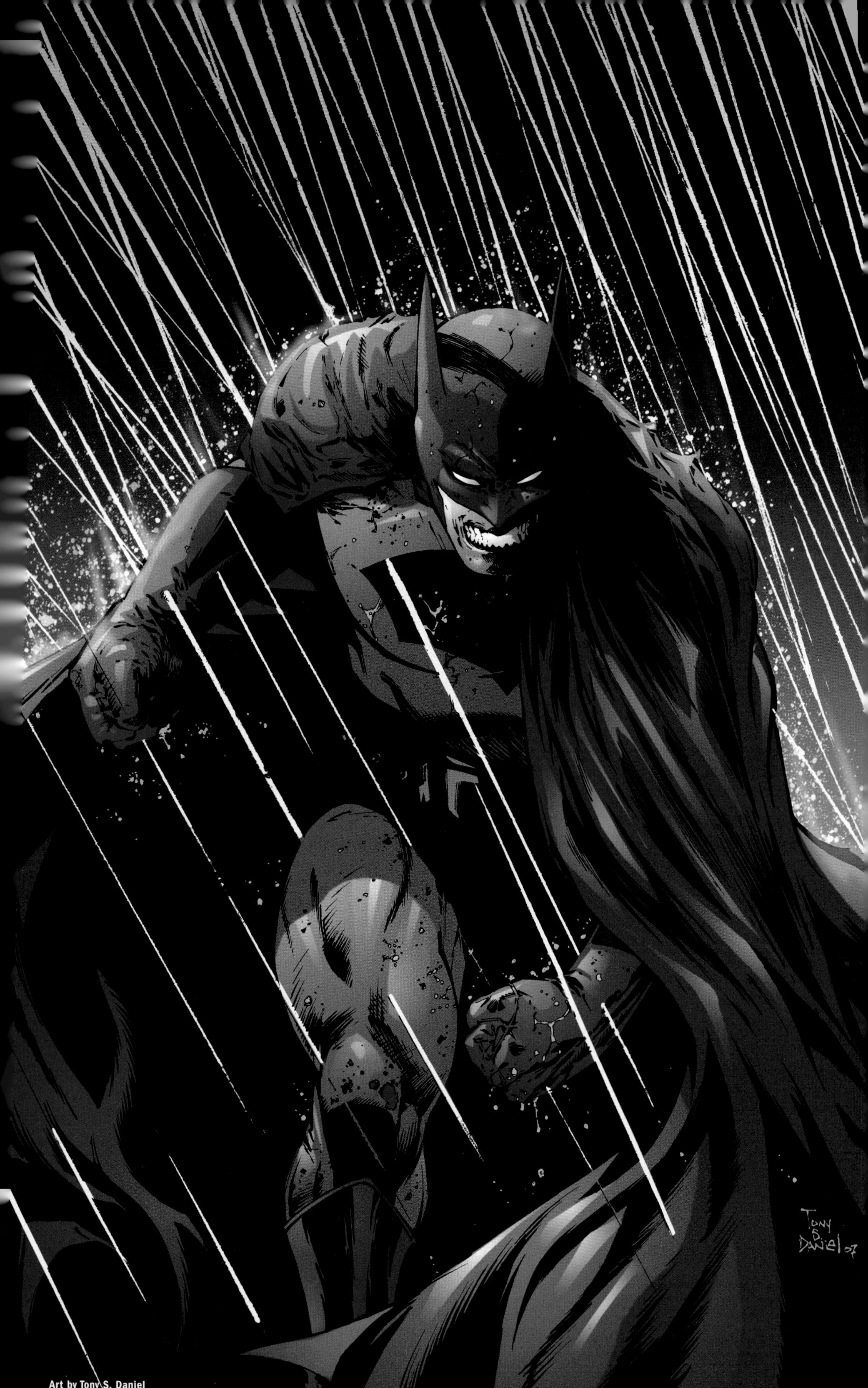

Art by Tony S. Daniel

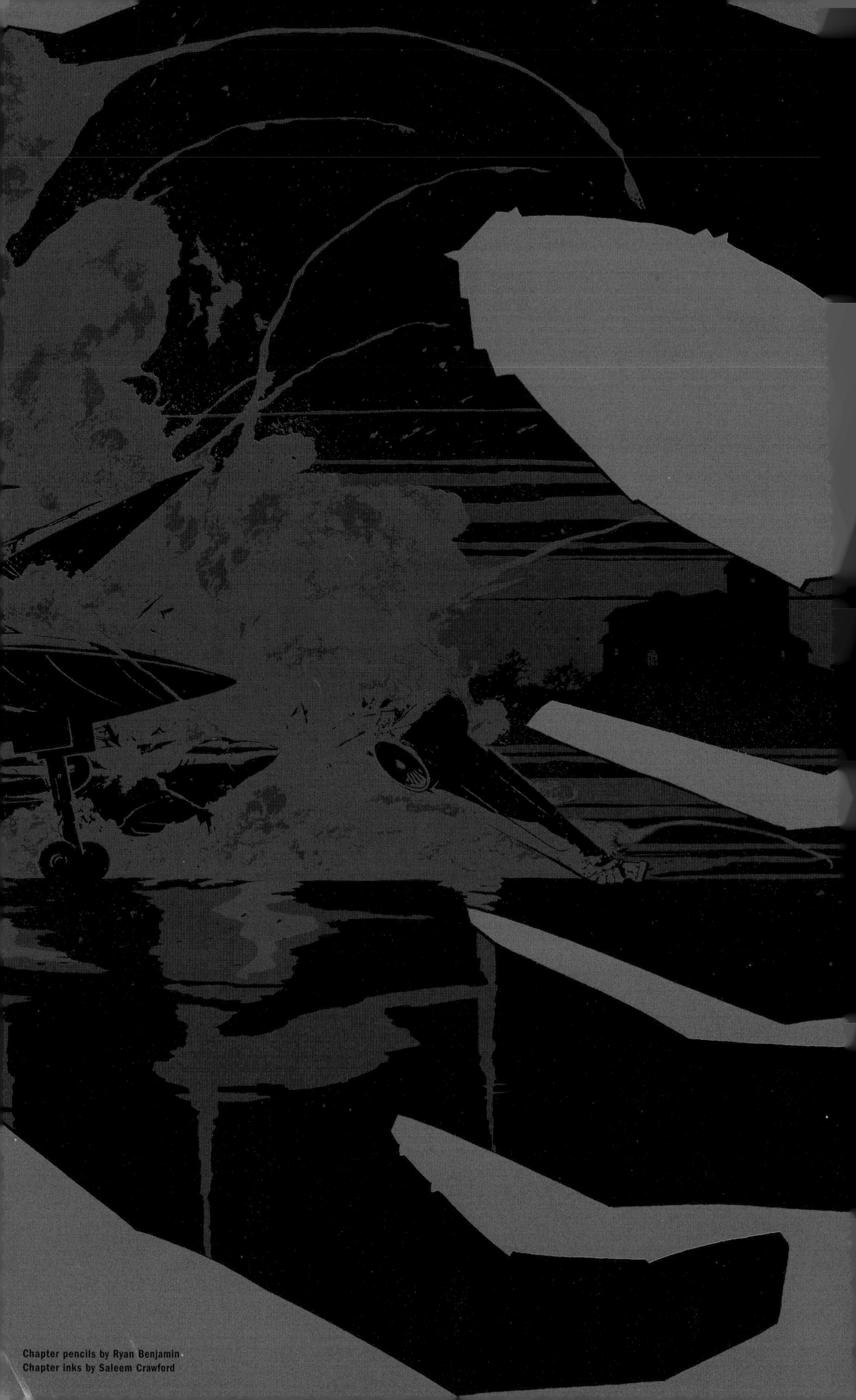

Chapter pencils by Ryan Benjamin
Chapter inks by Saleem Crawford

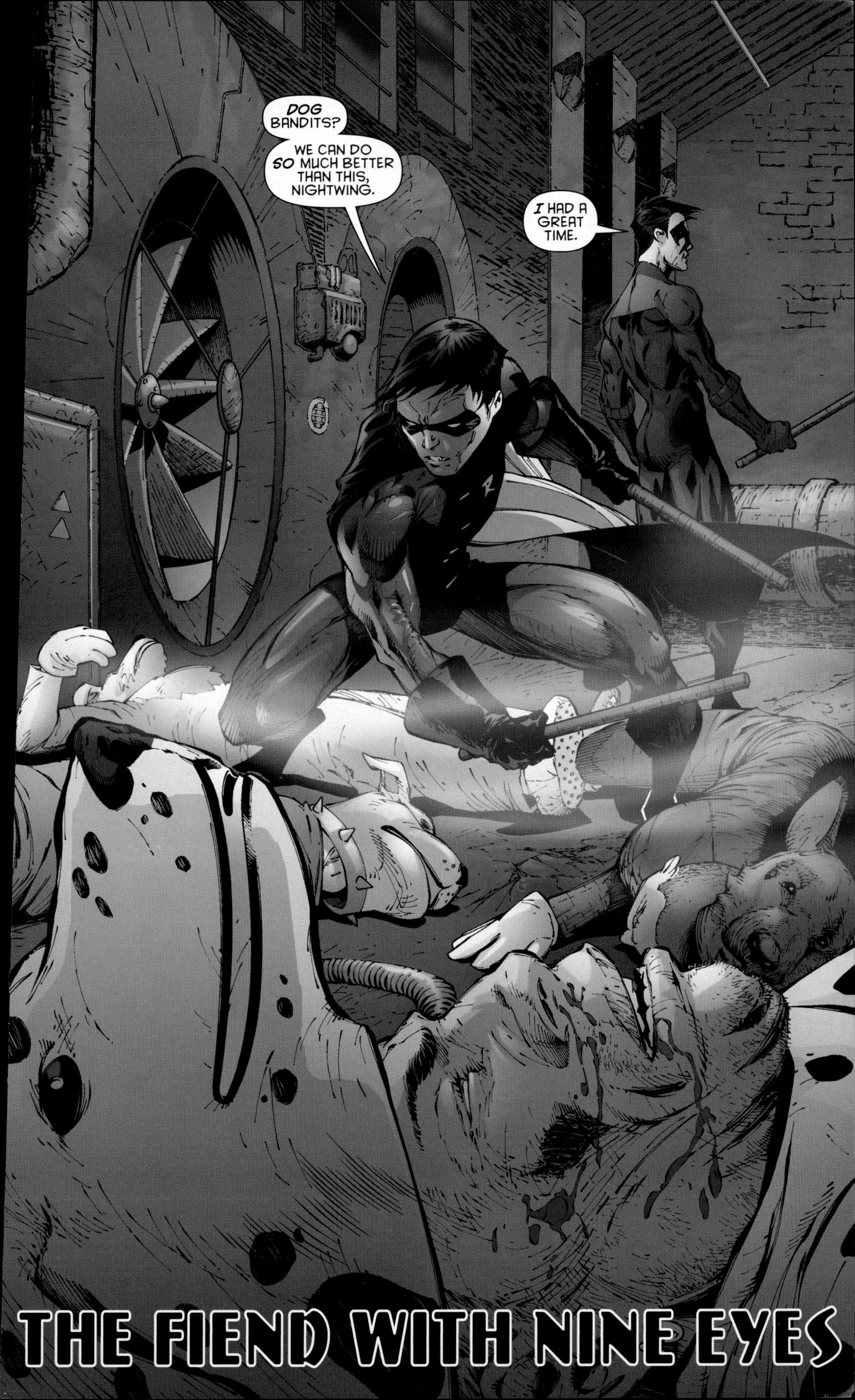
DOG BANDITS?
WE CAN DO SO MUCH BETTER THAN THIS, NIGHTWING.
I HAD A GREAT TIME.
THE FIEND WITH NINE EYES

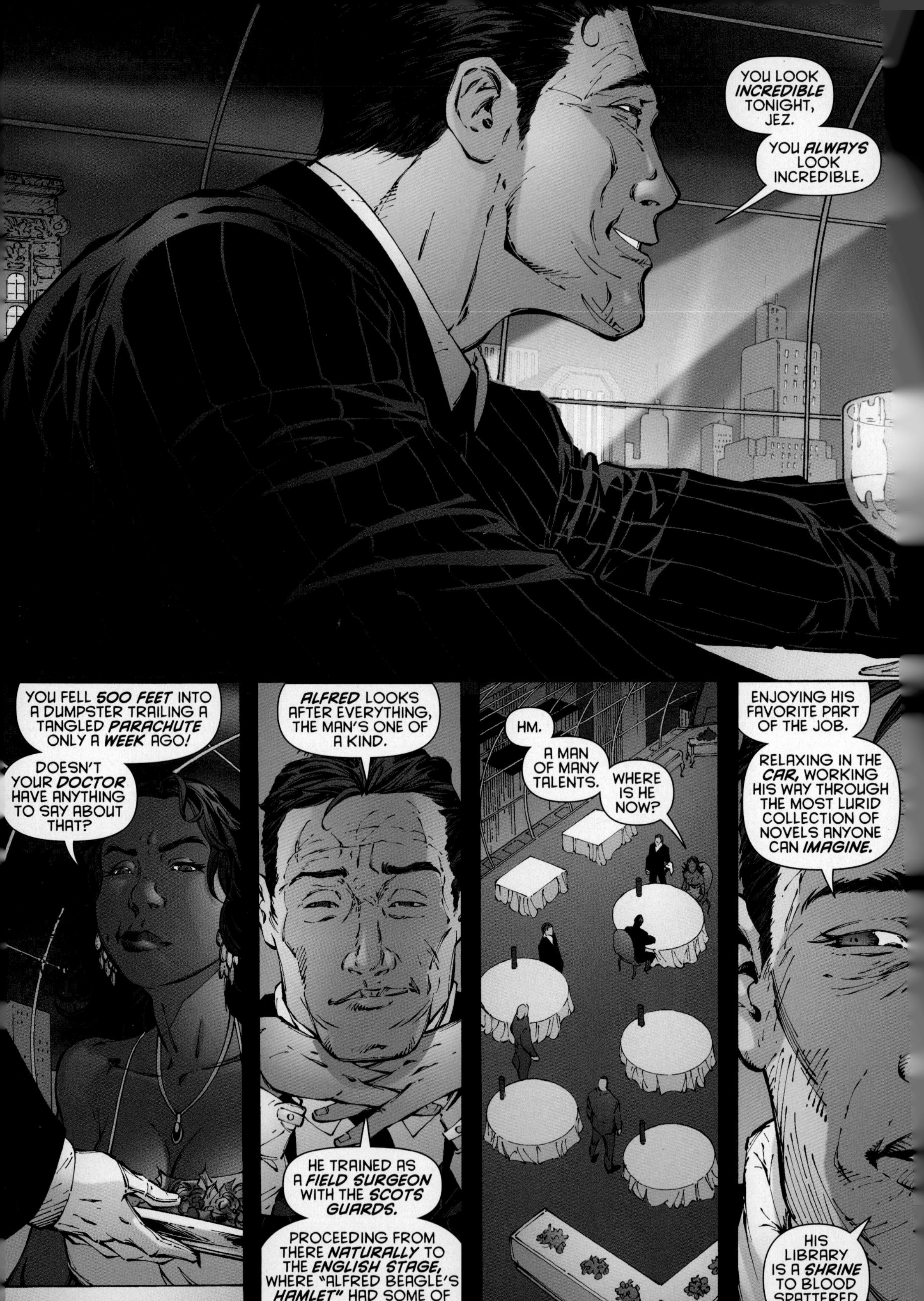
YOU LOOK INCREDIBLE TONIGHT, JEZ.
YOU ALWAYS LOOK INCREDIBLE.
YOU FELL 500 FEET INTO A DUMPSTER TRAILING A TANGLED PARACHUTE ONLY A WEEK AGO!
DOESN'T YOUR DOCTOR HAVE ANYTHING TO SAY ABOUT THAT?
ALFRED LOOKS AFTER EVERYTHING, THE MAN'S ONE OF A KIND.
HE TRAINED AS A FIELD SURGEON WITH THE SCOTS GUARDS.
PROCEEDING FROM THERE NATURALLY TO THE ENGLISH STAGE, WHERE "ALFRED BEAGLE'S HAMLET" HAD SOME OF THE CRUELEST REVIEWS IN THE HISTORY OF THE PERFORMING ARTS.
HM.
A MAN OF MANY TALENTS.
WHERE IS HE NOW?
ENJOYING HIS FAVORITE PART OF THE JOB.
RELAXING IN THE CAR, WORKING HIS WAY THROUGH THE MOST LURID COLLECTION OF NOVELS ANYONE CAN IMAGINE.
HIS LIBRARY IS A SHRINE TO BLOOD SPATTERED PROSE.

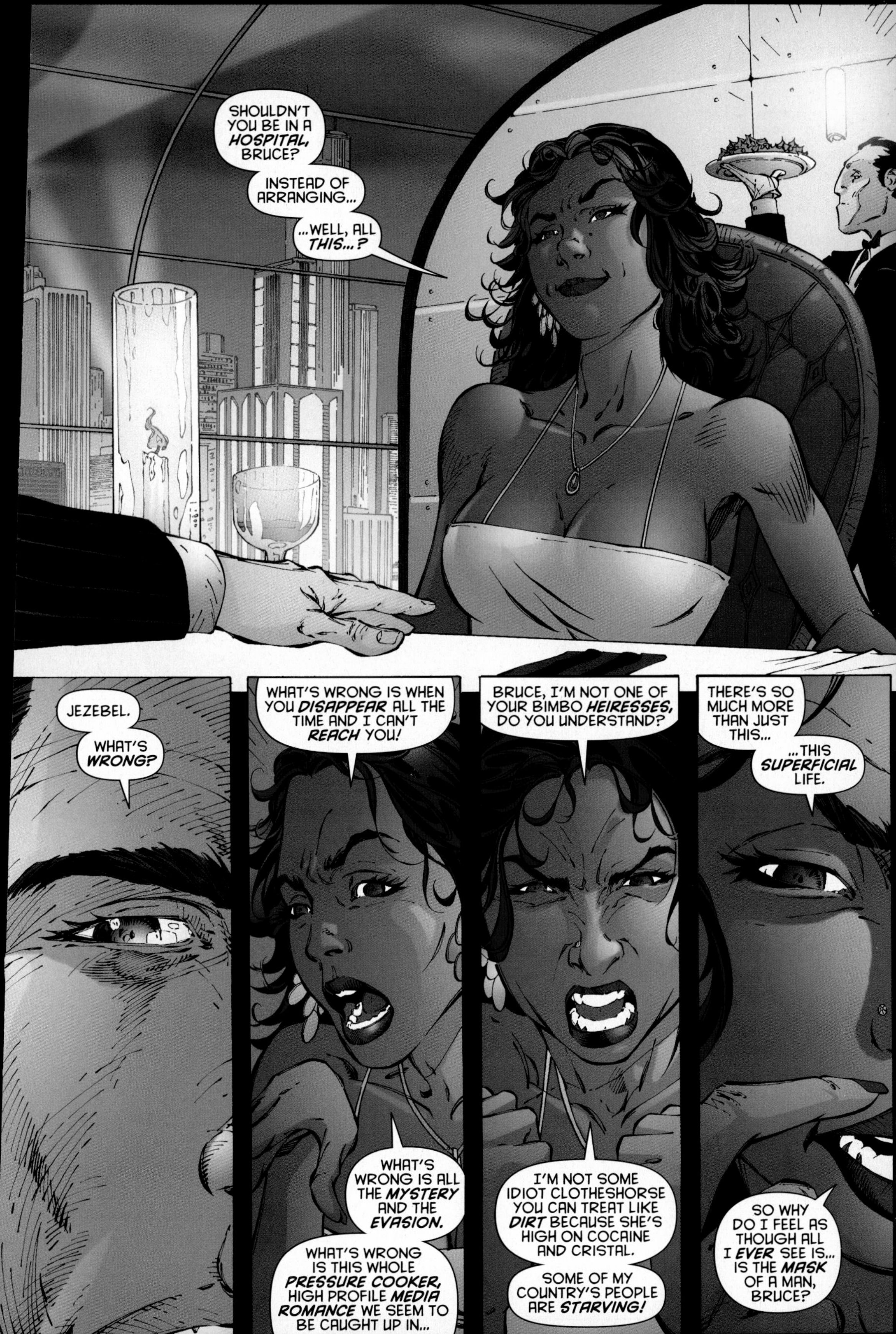
SHOULDN'T YOU BE IN A HOSPITAL, BRUCE?
INSTEAD OF ARRANGING...
...WELL, ALL THIS...?
JEZEBEL.
WHAT'S WRONG?
WHAT'S WRONG IS WHEN YOU DISAPPEAR ALL THE TIME AND I CAN'T REACH YOU!
WHAT'S WRONG IS ALL THE MYSTERY AND THE EVASION.
WHAT'S WRONG IS THIS WHOLE PRESSURE COOKER, HIGH PROFILE MEDIA ROMANCE WE SEEM TO BE CAUGHT UP IN...
BRUCE, I'M NOT ONE OF YOUR BIMBO HEIRESSES, DO YOU UNDERSTAND?
I'M NOT SOME IDIOT CLOTHESHORSE YOU CAN TREAT LIKE DIRT BECAUSE SHE'S HIGH ON COCAINE AND CRISTAL.
SOME OF MY COUNTRY'S PEOPLE ARE STARVING!
THERE'S SO MUCH MORE THAN JUST THIS...
...THIS SUPERFICIAL LIFE.
SO WHY DO I FEEL AS THOUGH ALL I EVER SEE IS... IS THE MASK OF A MAN, BRUCE?

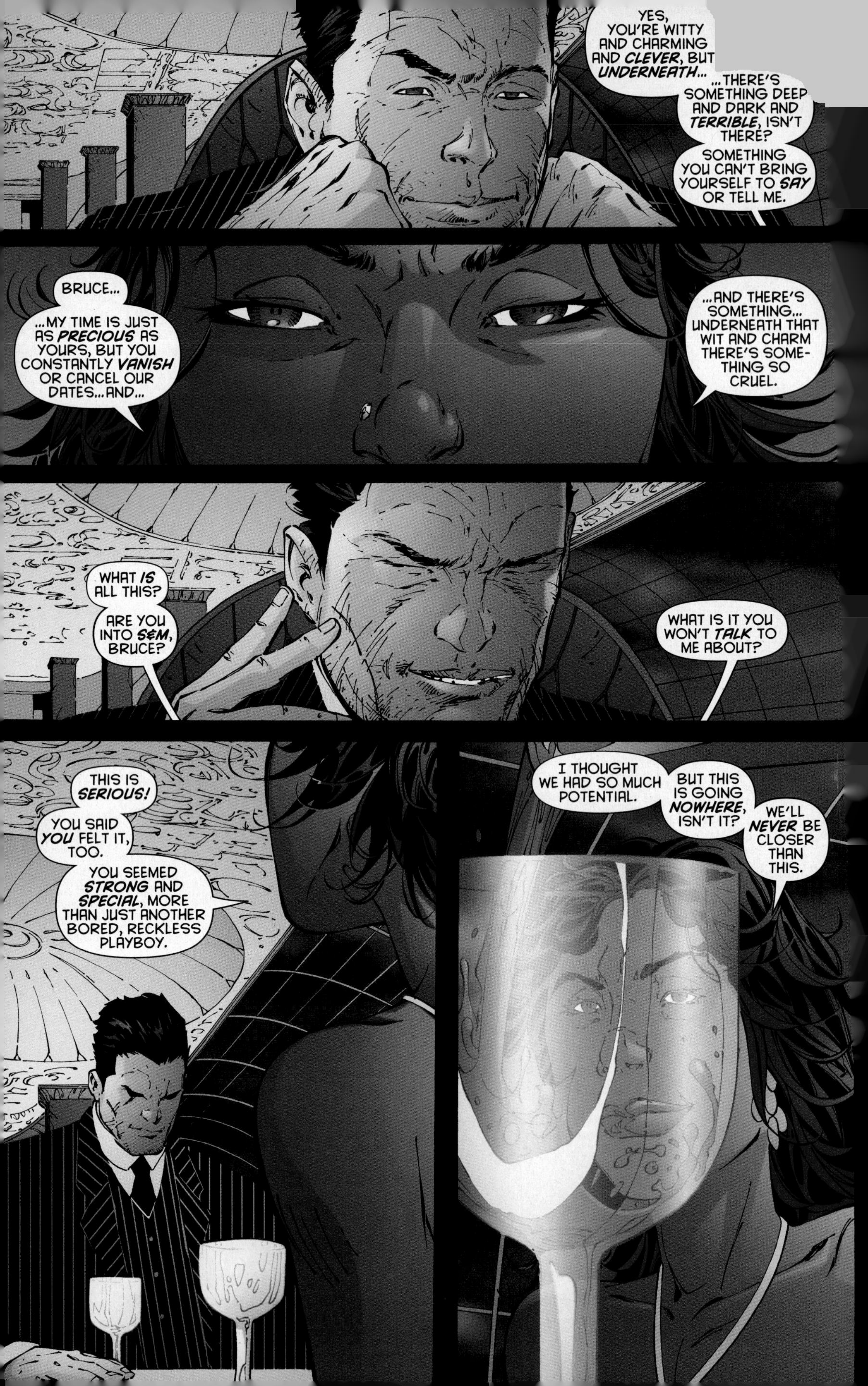
YES, YOU'RE WITTY AND CHARMING AND CLEVER, BUT UNDERNEATH...
...THERE'S SOMETHING DEEP AND DARK AND TERRIBLE, ISN'T THERE?
SOMETHING YOU CAN'T BRING YOURSELF TO SAY OR TELL ME.
BRUCE...
...MY TIME IS JUST AS PRECIOUS AS YOURS, BUT YOU CONSTANTLY VANISH OR CANCEL OUR DATES...AND...
...AND THERE'S SOMETHING... UNDERNEATH THAT WIT AND CHARM THERE'S SOMETHING SO CRUEL.
WHAT IS ALL THIS?
ARE YOU INTO S&M, BRUCE?
WHAT IS IT YOU WON'T TALK TO ME ABOUT?
THIS IS SERIOUS!
YOU SAID YOU FELT IT, TOO.
YOU SEEMED STRONG AND SPECIAL, MORE THAN JUST ANOTHER BORED, RECKLESS PLAYBOY.
I THOUGHT WE HAD SO MUCH POTENTIAL.
BUT THIS IS GOING NOWHERE, ISN'T IT?
WE'LL NEVER BE CLOSER THAN THIS.

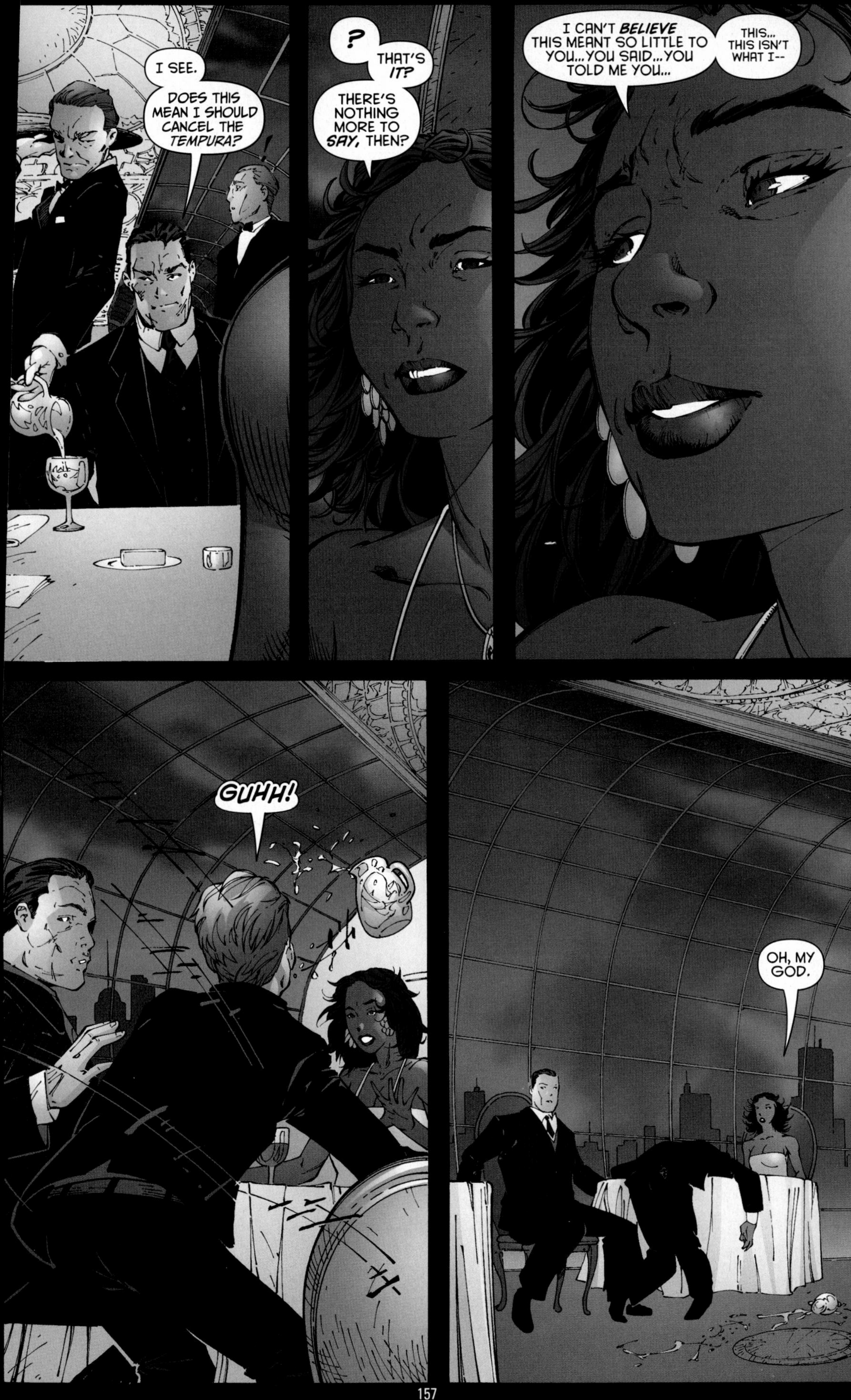

I SEE.
DOES THIS MEAN I SHOULD CANCEL THE *TEMPURA?*
?
THAT'S *IT?*
THERE'S NOTHING MORE TO *SAY,* THEN?
I CAN'T ***BELIEVE*** THIS MEANT SO LITTLE TO YOU...YOU SAID...YOU TOLD ME YOU...
THIS... THIS ISN'T WHAT I--
GUHH!
OH, MY GOD.

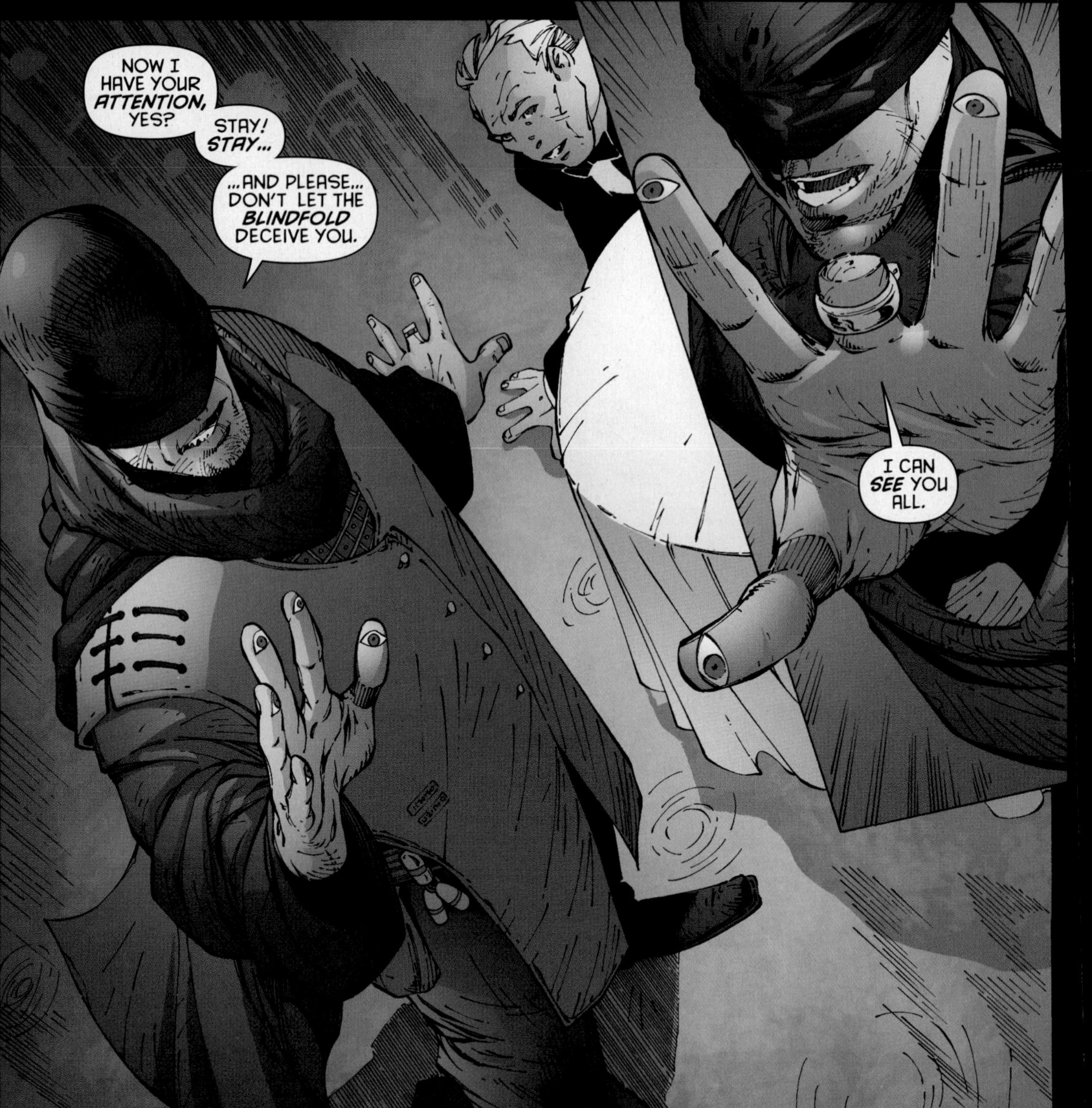
NOW I HAVE YOUR ATTENTION, YES?
STAY! STAY...
...AND PLEASE... DON'T LET THE BLINDFOLD DECEIVE YOU.
I CAN SEE YOU ALL.

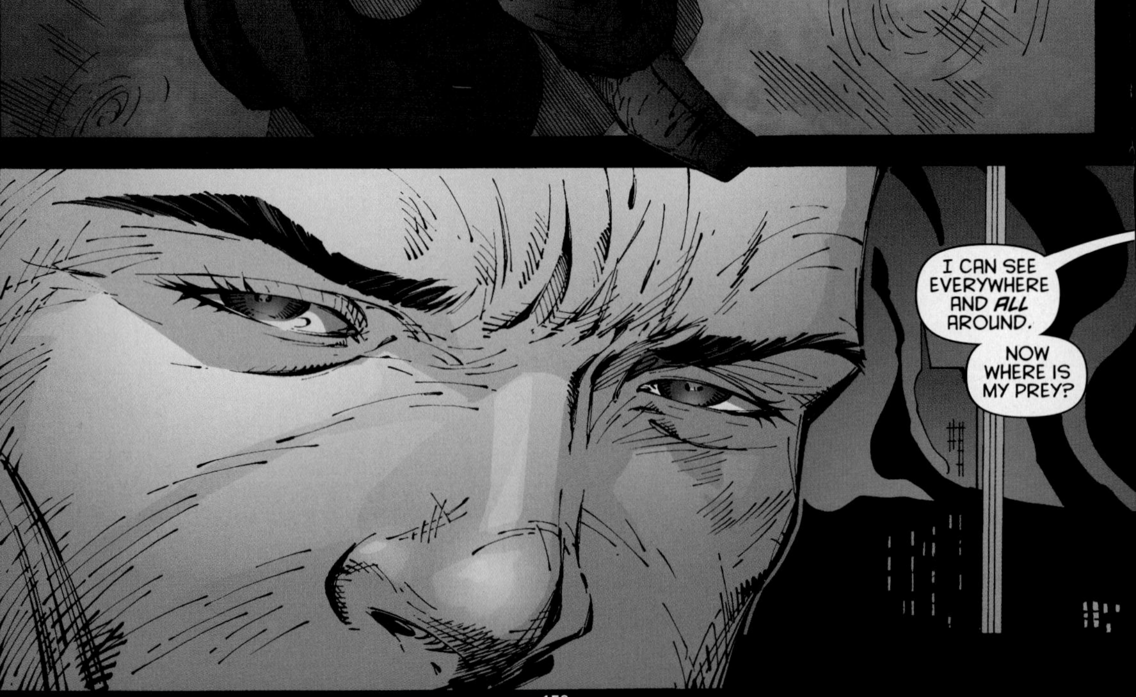
I CAN SEE EVERYWHERE AND ALL AROUND.
NOW WHERE IS MY PREY?

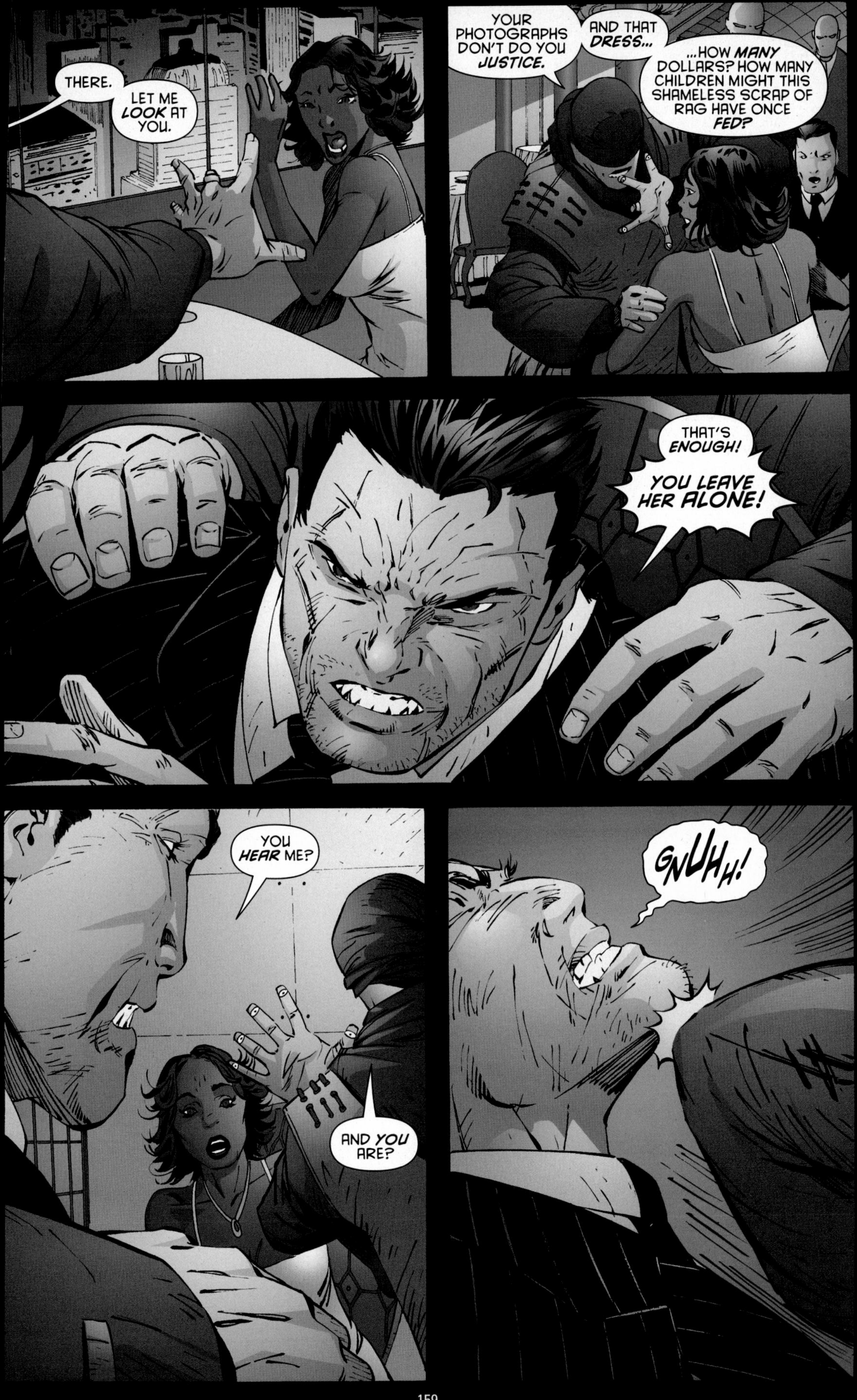
THERE.
LET ME LOOK AT YOU.
YOUR PHOTOGRAPHS DON'T DO YOU JUSTICE.
AND THAT DRESS...
...HOW MANY DOLLARS? HOW MANY CHILDREN MIGHT THIS SHAMELESS SCRAP OF RAG HAVE ONCE FED?
THAT'S ENOUGH!
YOU LEAVE HER ALONE!
YOU HEAR ME?
AND YOU ARE?
GNUHH!

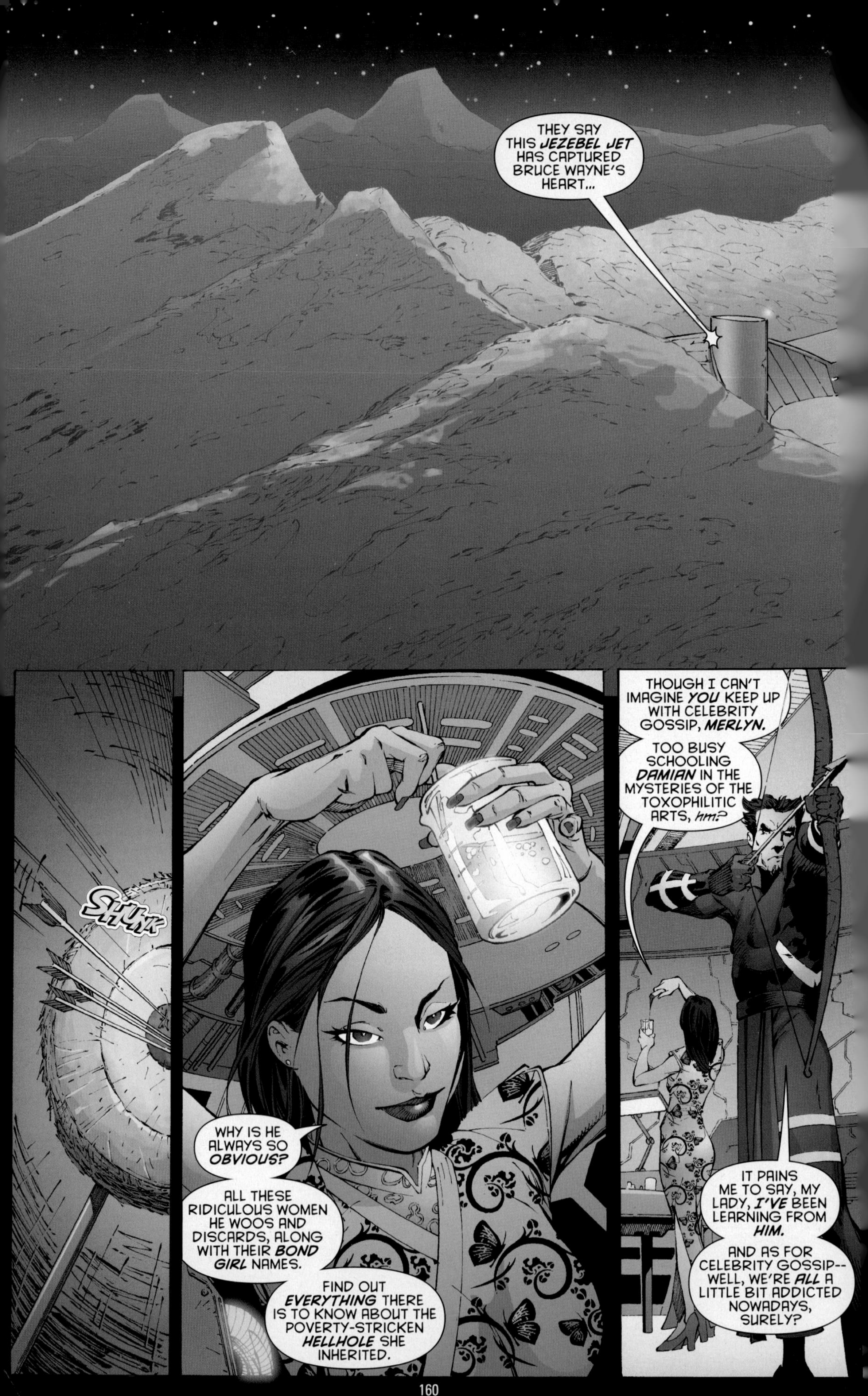
THEY SAY THIS JEZEBEL JET HAS CAPTURED BRUCE WAYNE'S HEART...
SHUNK
WHY IS HE ALWAYS SO OBVIOUS?
ALL THESE RIDICULOUS WOMEN HE WOOS AND DISCARDS, ALONG WITH THEIR BOND GIRL NAMES.
FIND OUT EVERYTHING THERE IS TO KNOW ABOUT THE POVERTY-STRICKEN HELLHOLE SHE INHERITED.
THOUGH I CAN'T IMAGINE YOU KEEP UP WITH CELEBRITY GOSSIP, MERLYN.
TOO BUSY SCHOOLING DAMIAN IN THE MYSTERIES OF THE TOXOPHILITIC ARTS, hm?
IT PAINS ME TO SAY, MY LADY, I'VE BEEN LEARNING FROM HIM.
AND AS FOR CELEBRITY GOSSIP-- WELL, WE'RE ALL A LITTLE BIT ADDICTED NOWADAYS, SURELY?

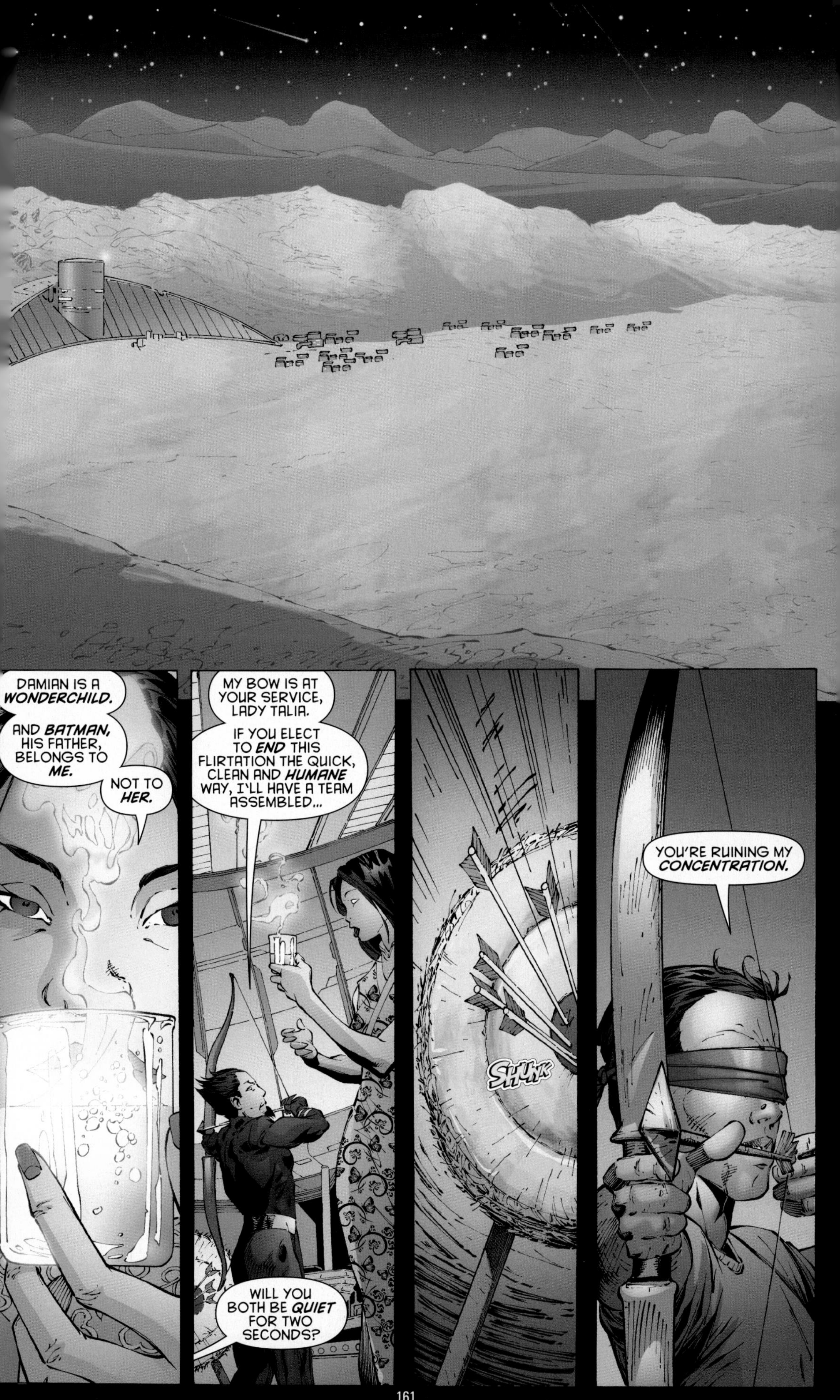
DAMIAN IS A WONDERCHILD.
AND BATMAN, HIS FATHER, BELONGS TO ME.
NOT TO HER.
MY BOW IS AT YOUR SERVICE, LADY TALIA.
IF YOU ELECT TO END THIS FLIRTATION THE QUICK, CLEAN AND HUMANE WAY, I'LL HAVE A TEAM ASSEMBLED...
WILL YOU BOTH BE QUIET FOR TWO SECONDS?
SHUNK
YOU'RE RUINING MY CONCENTRATION.

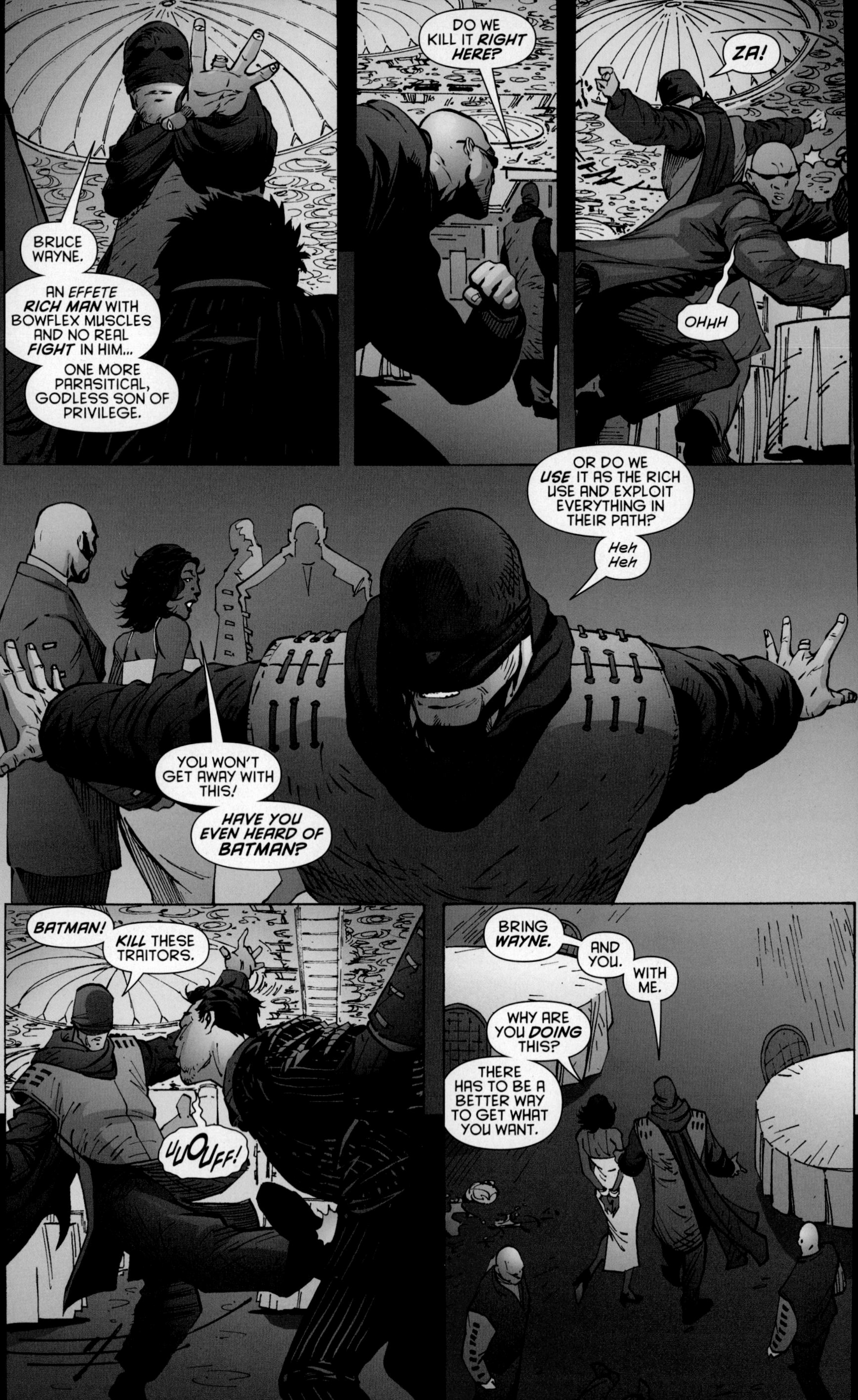
BRUCE WAYNE.
AN *EFFETE RICH MAN* WITH BOWFLEX MUSCLES AND NO REAL *FIGHT* IN HIM...
ONE MORE PARASITICAL, GODLESS SON OF PRIVILEGE.
DO WE KILL IT *RIGHT HERE?*
ZA!
OHHH
OR DO WE *USE* IT AS THE RICH USE AND EXPLOIT EVERYTHING IN THEIR PATH?
Heh Heh
YOU WON'T GET AWAY WITH THIS!
HAVE YOU EVEN HEARD OF BATMAN?
BATMAN!
KILL THESE TRAITORS.
UUOUFF!
BRING *WAYNE.*
AND YOU.
WITH ME.
WHY ARE YOU *DOING* THIS?
THERE HAS TO BE A BETTER WAY TO GET WHAT YOU WANT.

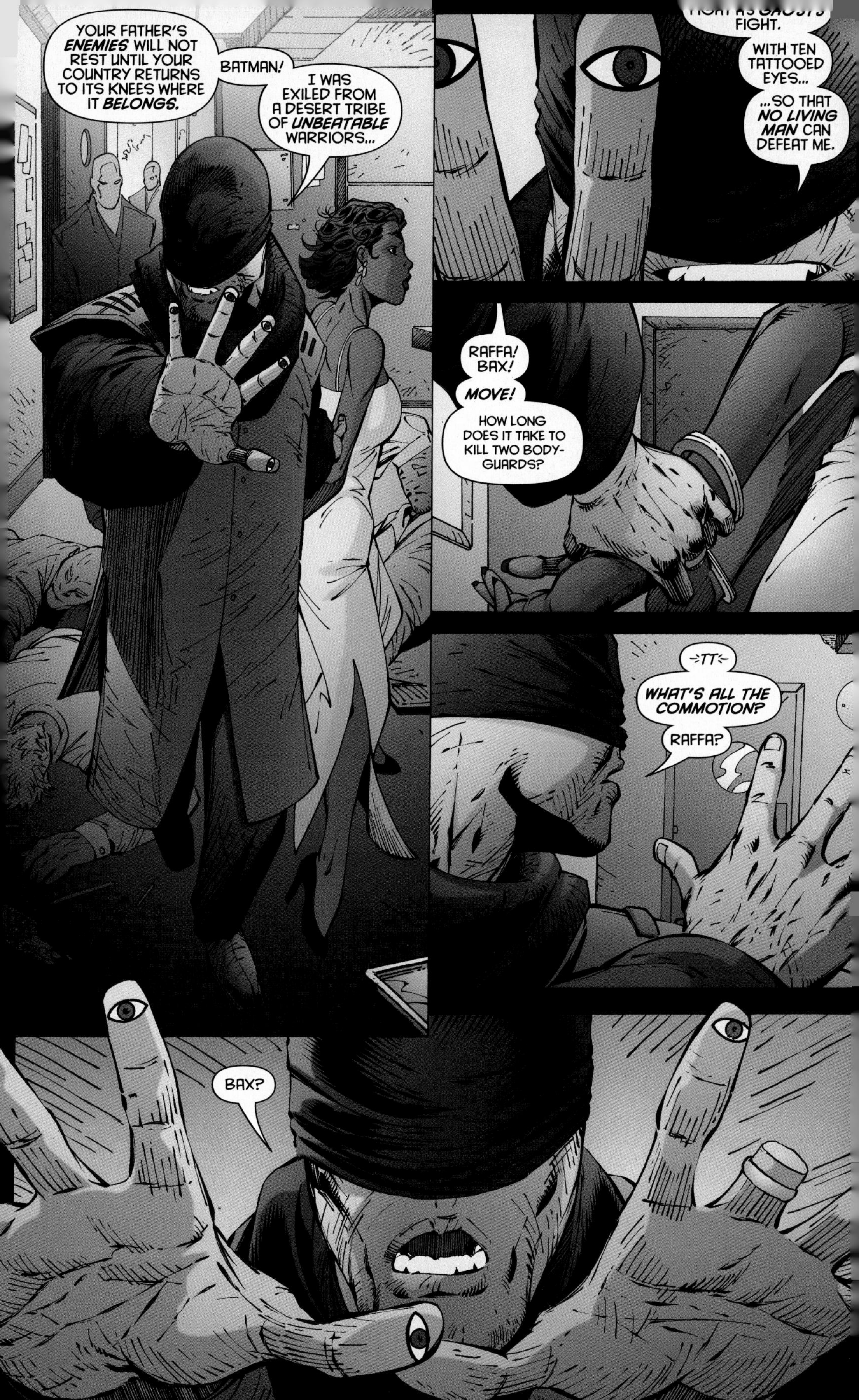

YOUR FATHER'S *ENEMIES* WILL NOT REST UNTIL YOUR COUNTRY RETURNS TO ITS KNEES WHERE IT *BELONGS.*
BATMAN!
I WAS EXILED FROM A DESERT TRIBE OF *UNBEATABLE* WARRIORS...
FIGHT.
WITH TEN TATTOOED EYES...
...SO THAT *NO LIVING MAN* CAN DEFEAT ME.
RAFFA! BAX!
MOVE!
HOW LONG DOES IT TAKE TO KILL TWO BODY-GUARDS?
TT
WHAT'S ALL THE COMMOTION?
RAFFA?
BAX?

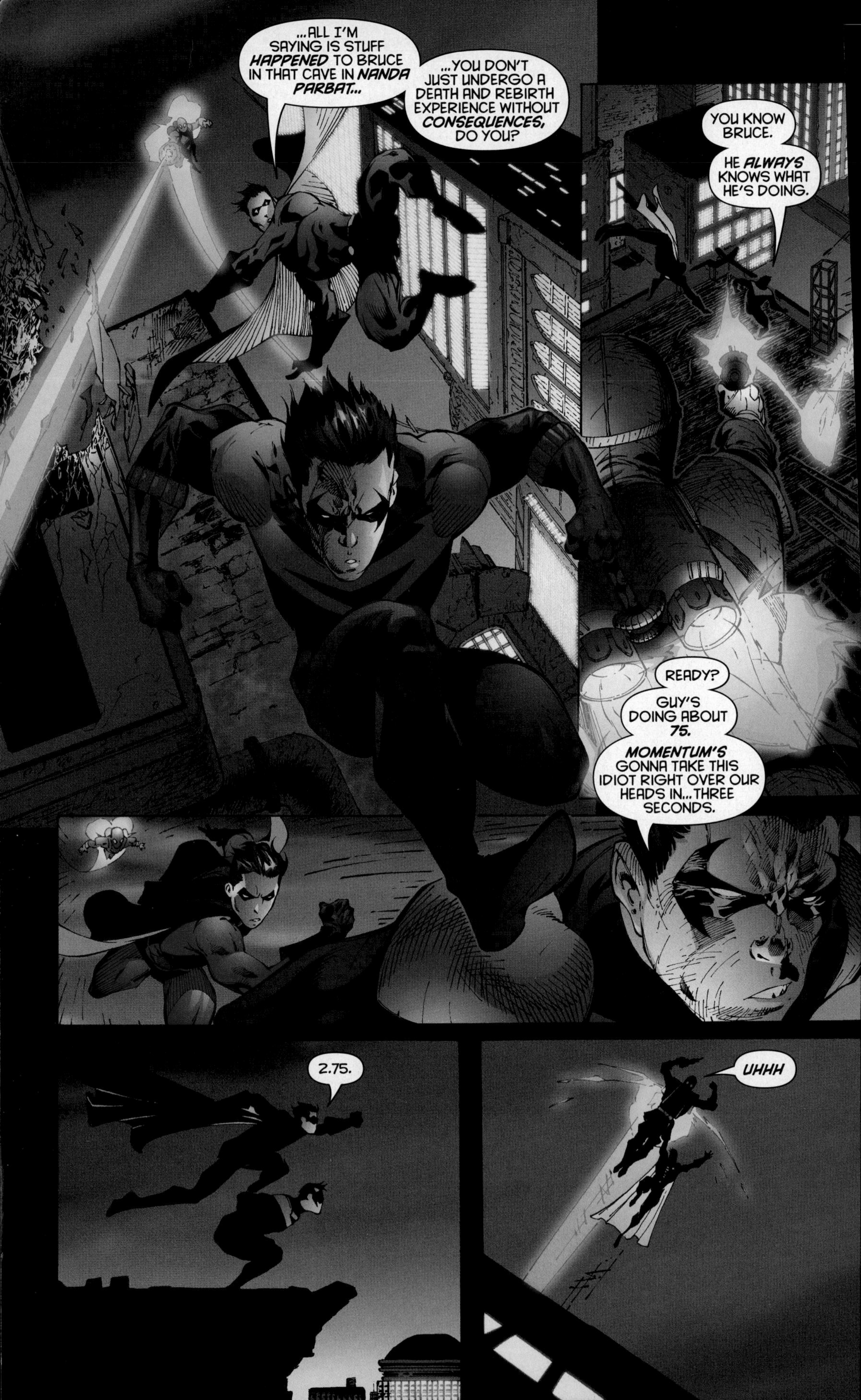
...ALL I'M SAYING IS STUFF *HAPPENED* TO BRUCE IN THAT CAVE IN *NANDA PARBAT*...
...YOU DON'T JUST UNDERGO A DEATH AND REBIRTH EXPERIENCE WITHOUT *CONSEQUENCES*, DO YOU?
YOU KNOW BRUCE.
HE *ALWAYS* KNOWS WHAT HE'S DOING.
READY?
GUY'S DOING ABOUT *75.*
MOMENTUM'S GONNA TAKE THIS IDIOT RIGHT OVER OUR HEADS IN...THREE SECONDS.
2.75.
UHHH

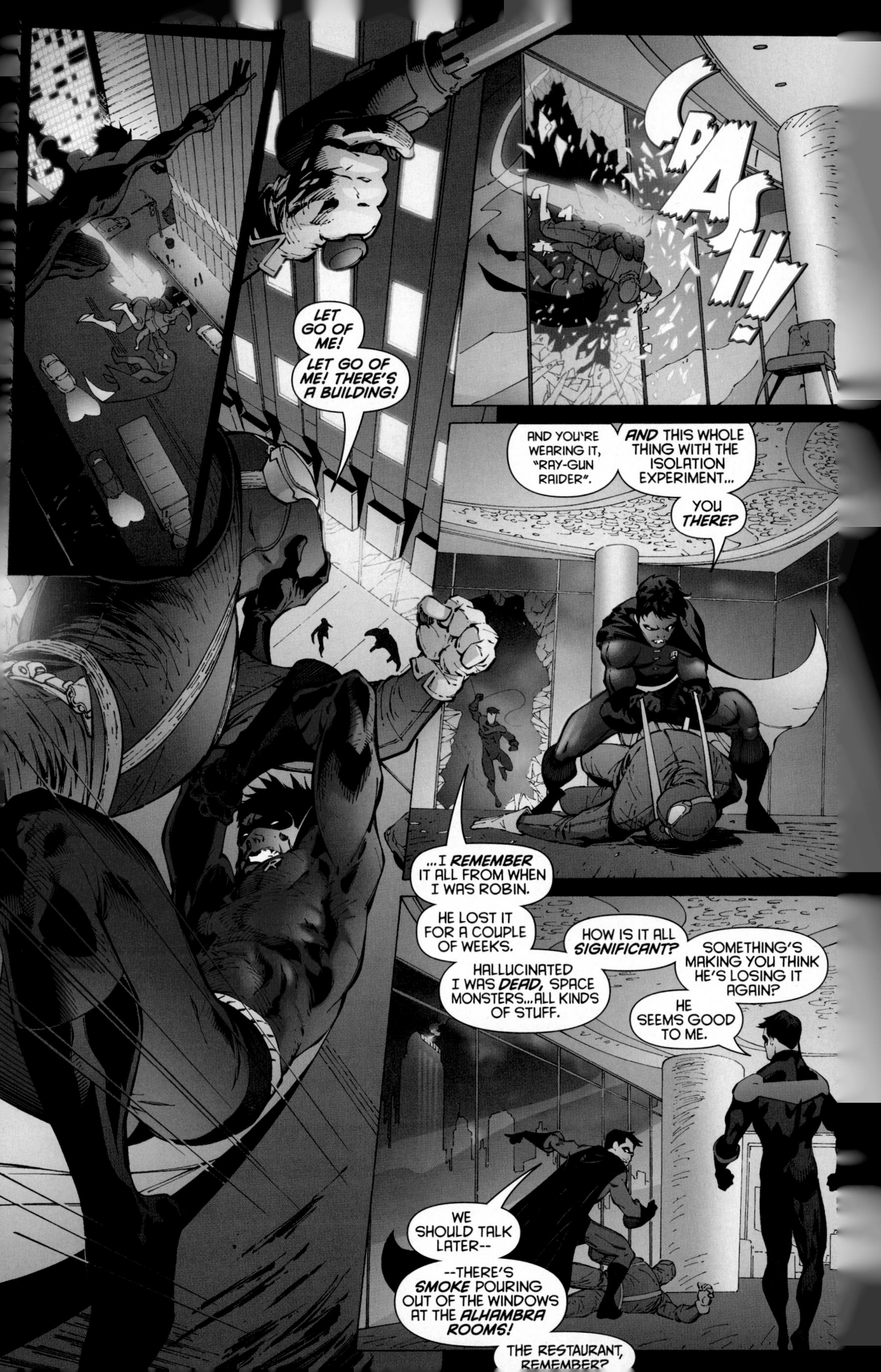

LET GO OF ME! LET GO OF ME! THERE'S A BUILDING!
CRASH!
AND YOU'RE WEARING IT, "RAY-GUN RAIDER".
AND THIS WHOLE THING WITH THE ISOLATION EXPERIMENT...
YOU THERE?
...I REMEMBER IT ALL FROM WHEN I WAS ROBIN.
HE LOST IT FOR A COUPLE OF WEEKS.
HALLUCINATED I WAS DEAD, SPACE MONSTERS...ALL KINDS OF STUFF.
HOW IS IT ALL SIGNIFICANT?
SOMETHING'S MAKING YOU THINK HE'S LOSING IT AGAIN?
HE SEEMS GOOD TO ME.
WE SHOULD TALK LATER--
--THERE'S SMOKE POURING OUT OF THE WINDOWS AT THE ALHAMBRA ROOMS!
THE RESTAURANT, REMEMBER?

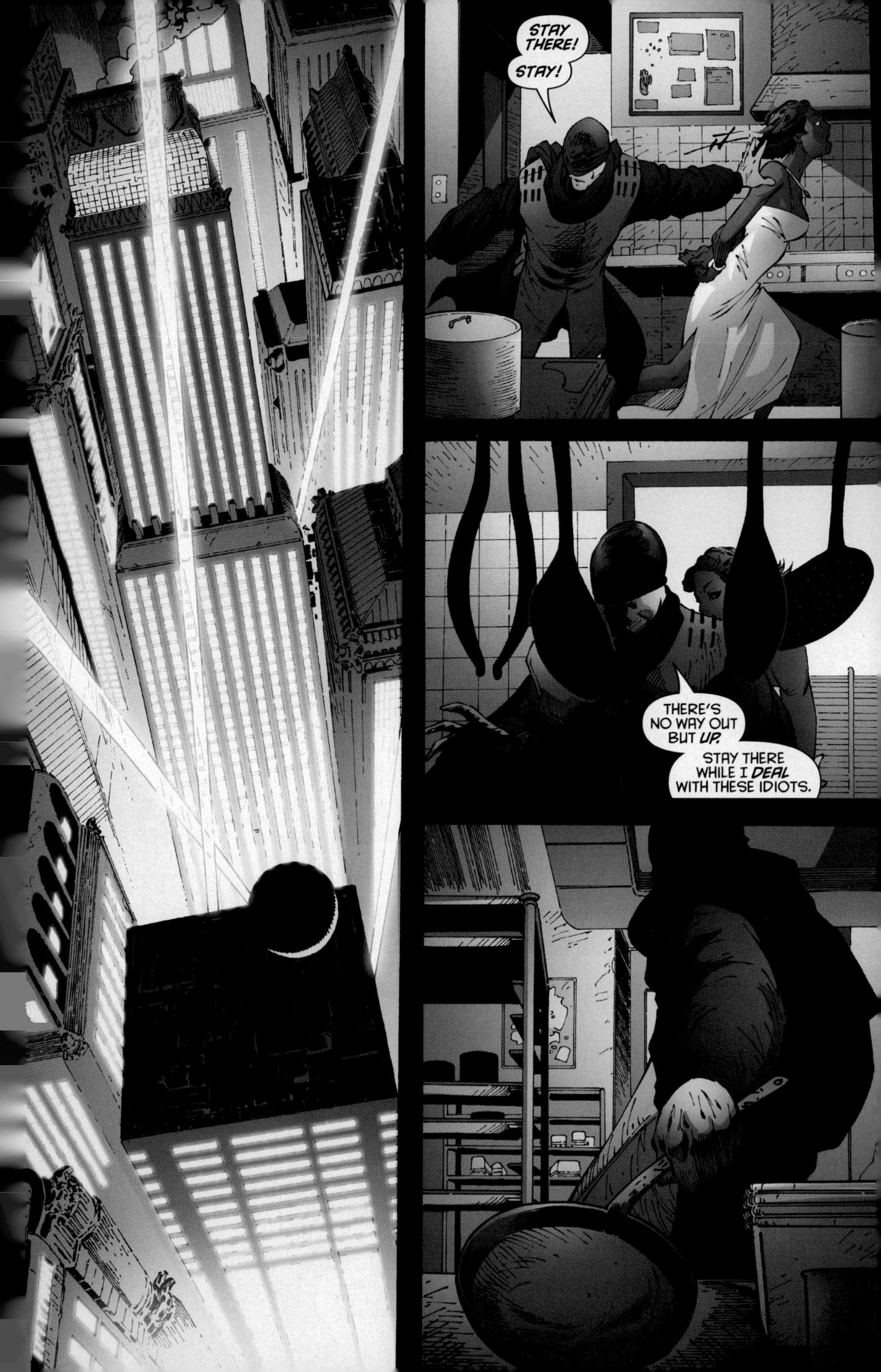
STAY THERE!
STAY!
THERE'S NO WAY OUT BUT *UP*.
STAY THERE WHILE I *DEAL* WITH THESE IDIOTS.

UH?
DDAH!
I'LL KILL YOU ALL!
WHO'S THERE?
FINGERS STILL ADJUSTING TO THE DARK?
HEH HEH HEH HEH
WHO'S THERE?

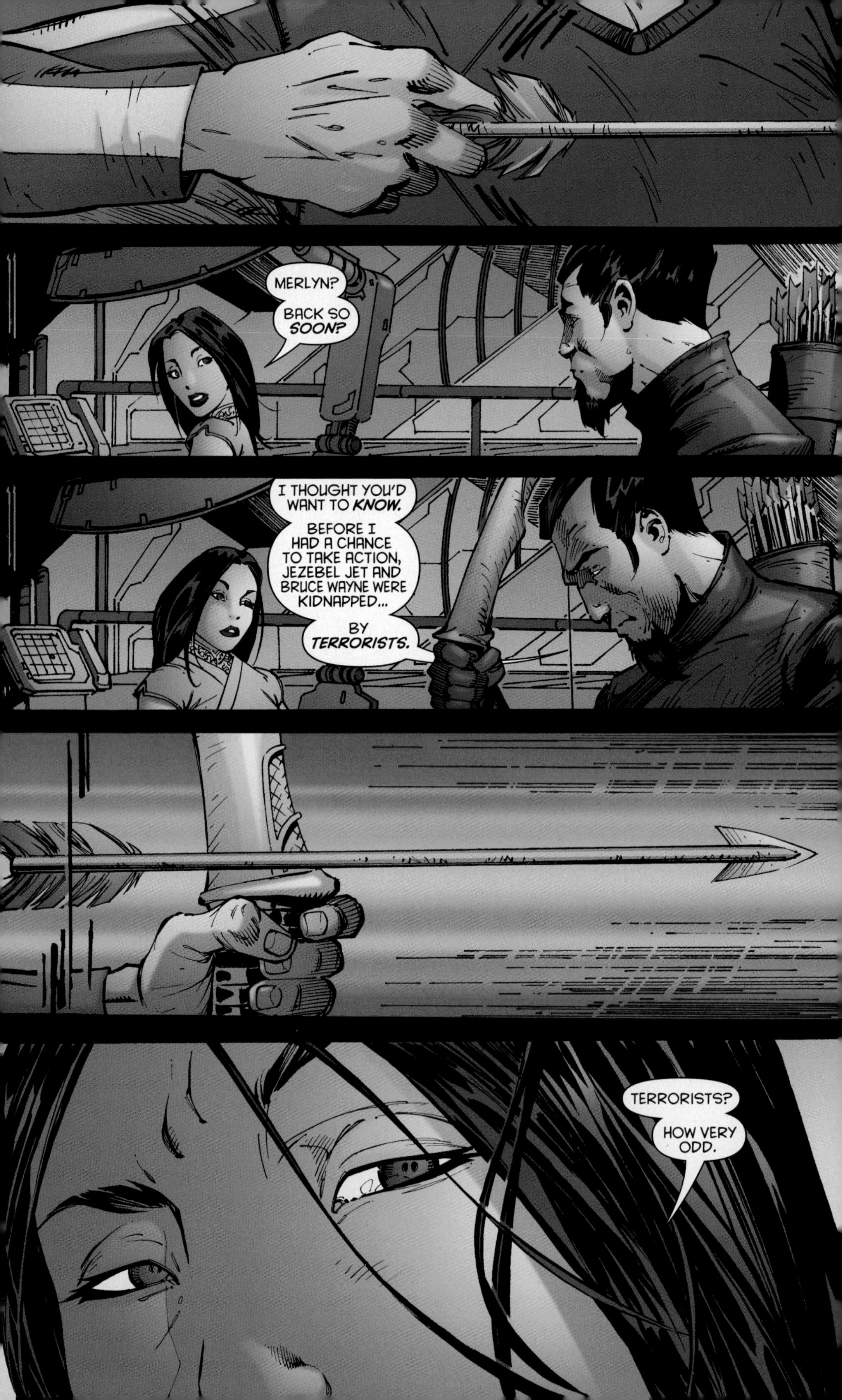
MERLYN?
BACK SO *SOON?*
I THOUGHT YOU'D WANT TO *KNOW.*
BEFORE I HAD A CHANCE TO TAKE ACTION, JEZEBEL JET AND BRUCE WAYNE WERE KIDNAPPED...
BY *TERRORISTS.*
TERRORISTS?
HOW VERY ODD.

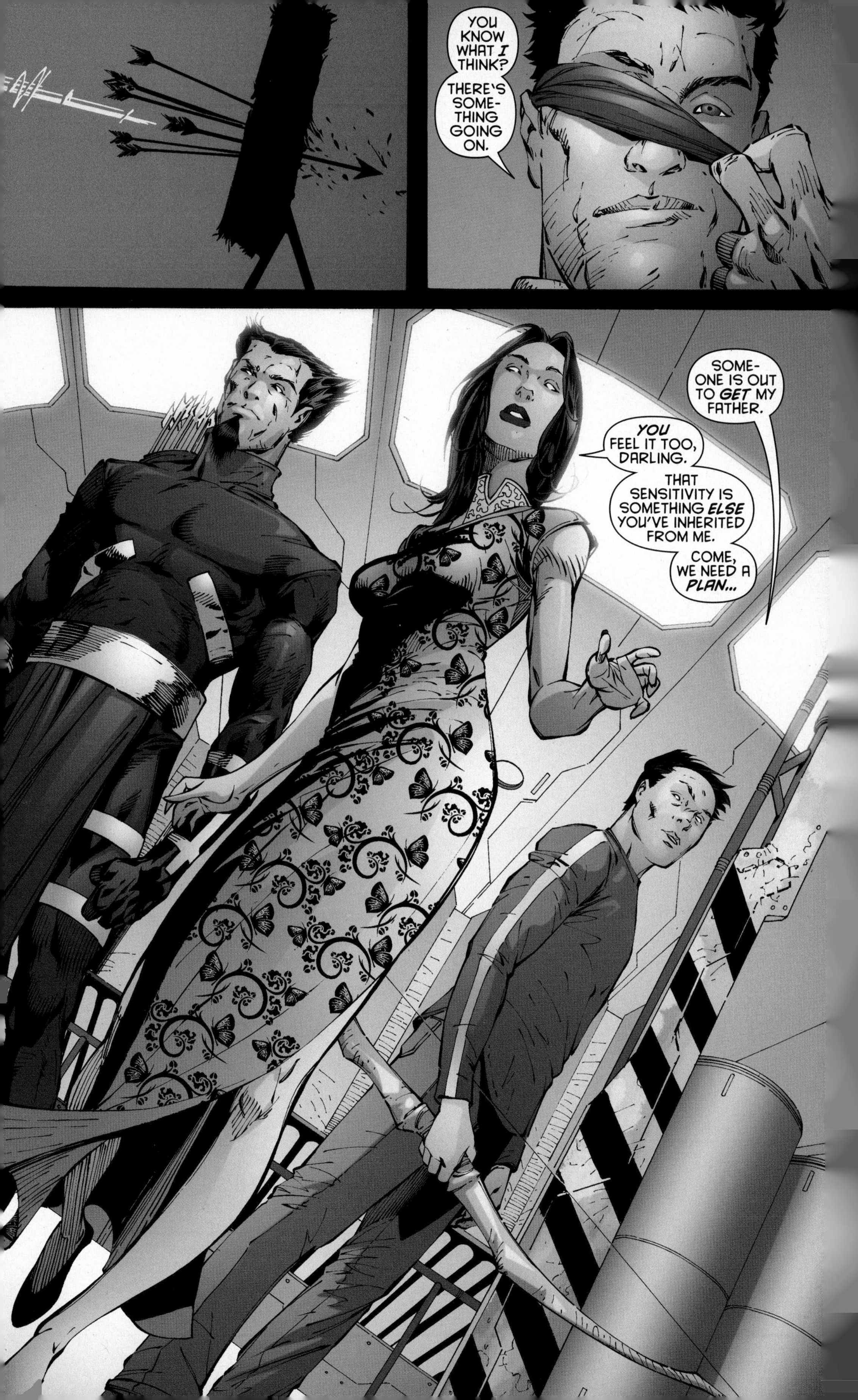
YOU KNOW WHAT *I* THINK?
THERE'S SOME-THING GOING ON.
SOME-ONE IS OUT TO ***GET*** MY FATHER.
YOU FEEL IT TOO, DARLING.
THAT SENSITIVITY IS SOMETHING ***ELSE*** YOU'VE INHERITED FROM ME.
COME, WE NEED A ***PLAN...***

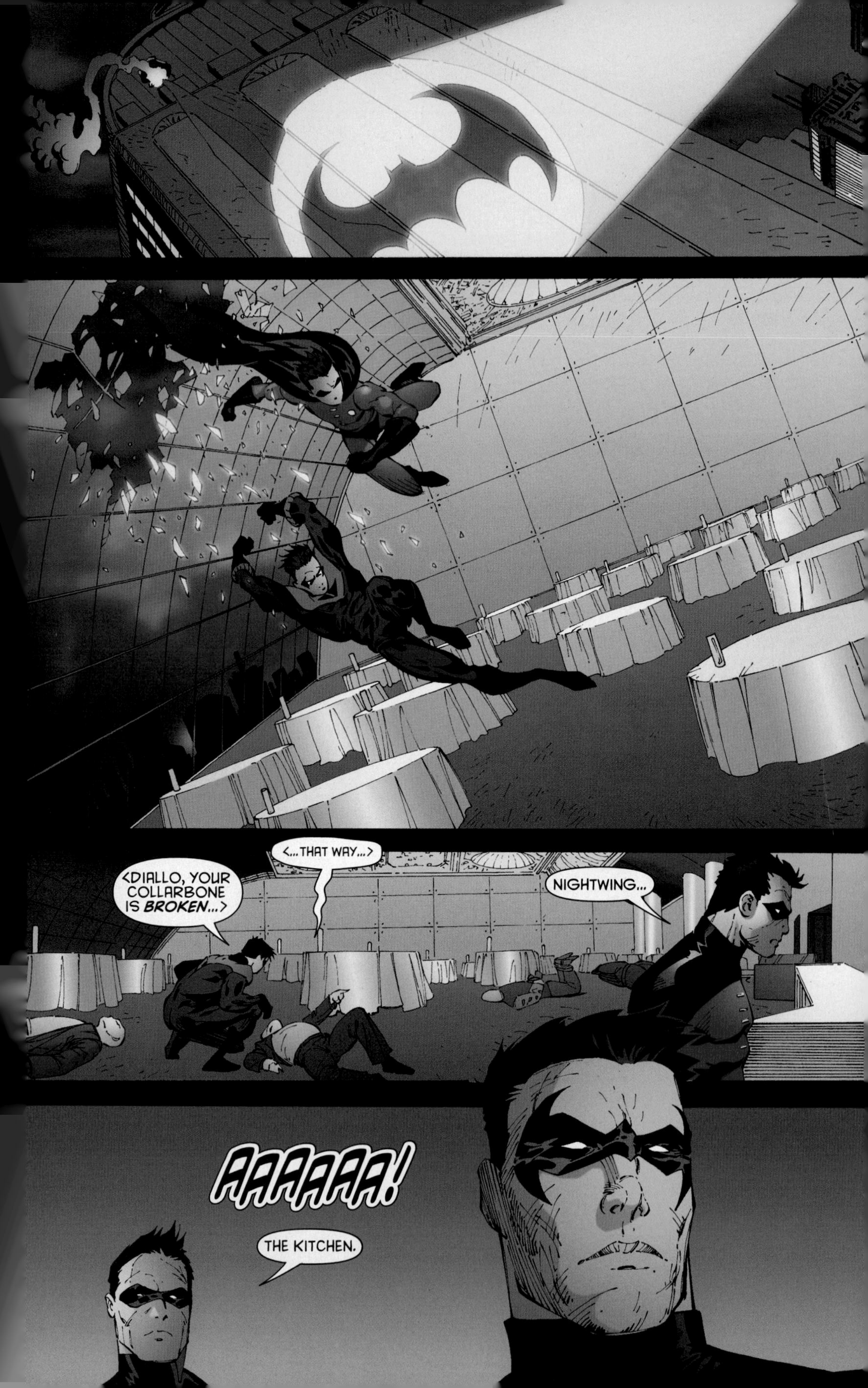
<DIALLO, YOUR COLLARBONE IS BROKEN...>
<...THAT WAY...>
NIGHTWING...
AAAAAA!
THE KITCHEN.

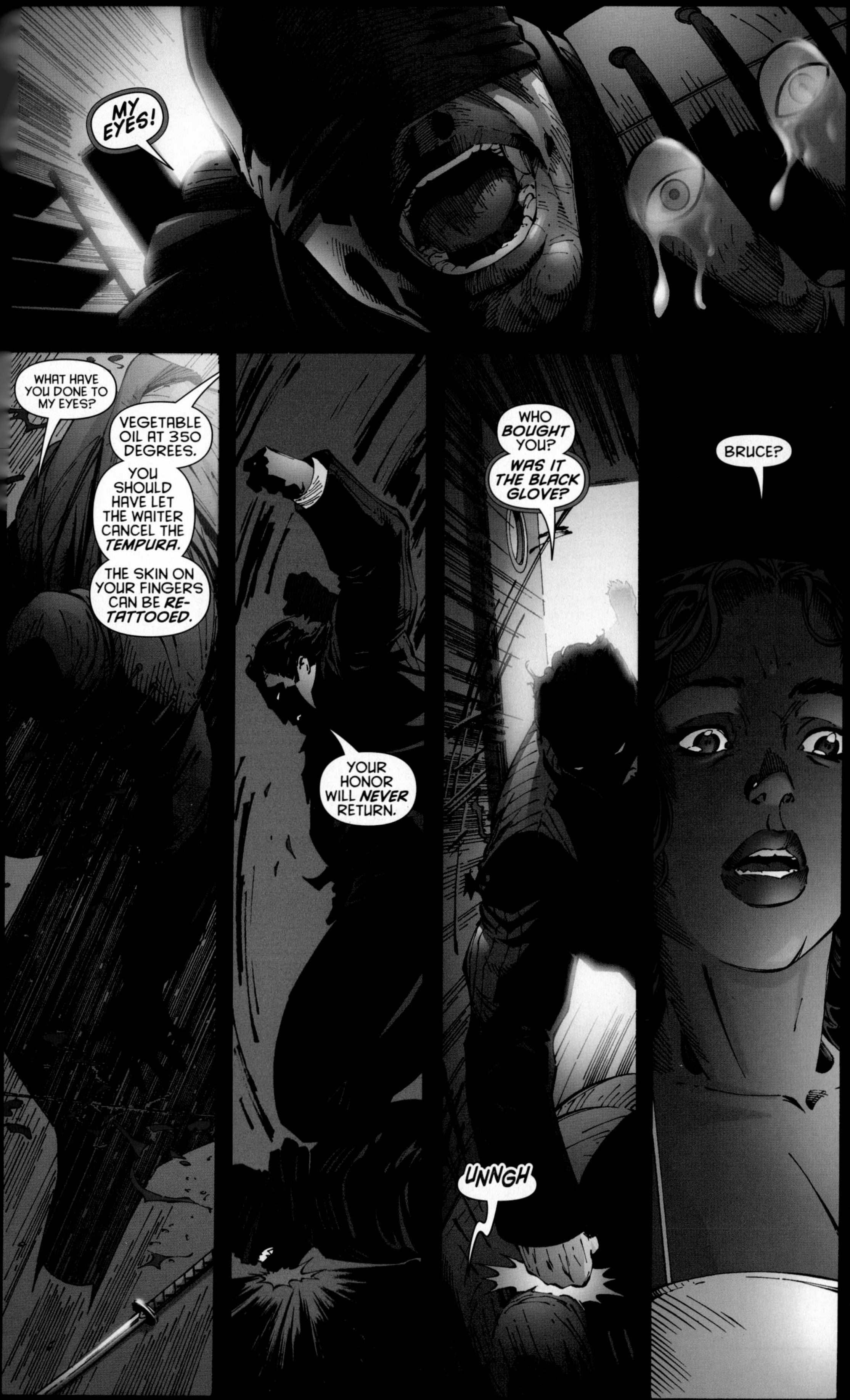
MY EYES!
WHAT HAVE YOU DONE TO MY EYES?
VEGETABLE OIL AT 350 DEGREES.
YOU SHOULD HAVE LET THE WAITER CANCEL THE *TEMPURA*.
THE SKIN ON YOUR FINGERS CAN BE *RE-TATTOOED*.
YOUR HONOR WILL *NEVER* RETURN.
WHO *BOUGHT* YOU?
WAS IT THE BLACK GLOVE?
UNNGH
BRUCE?

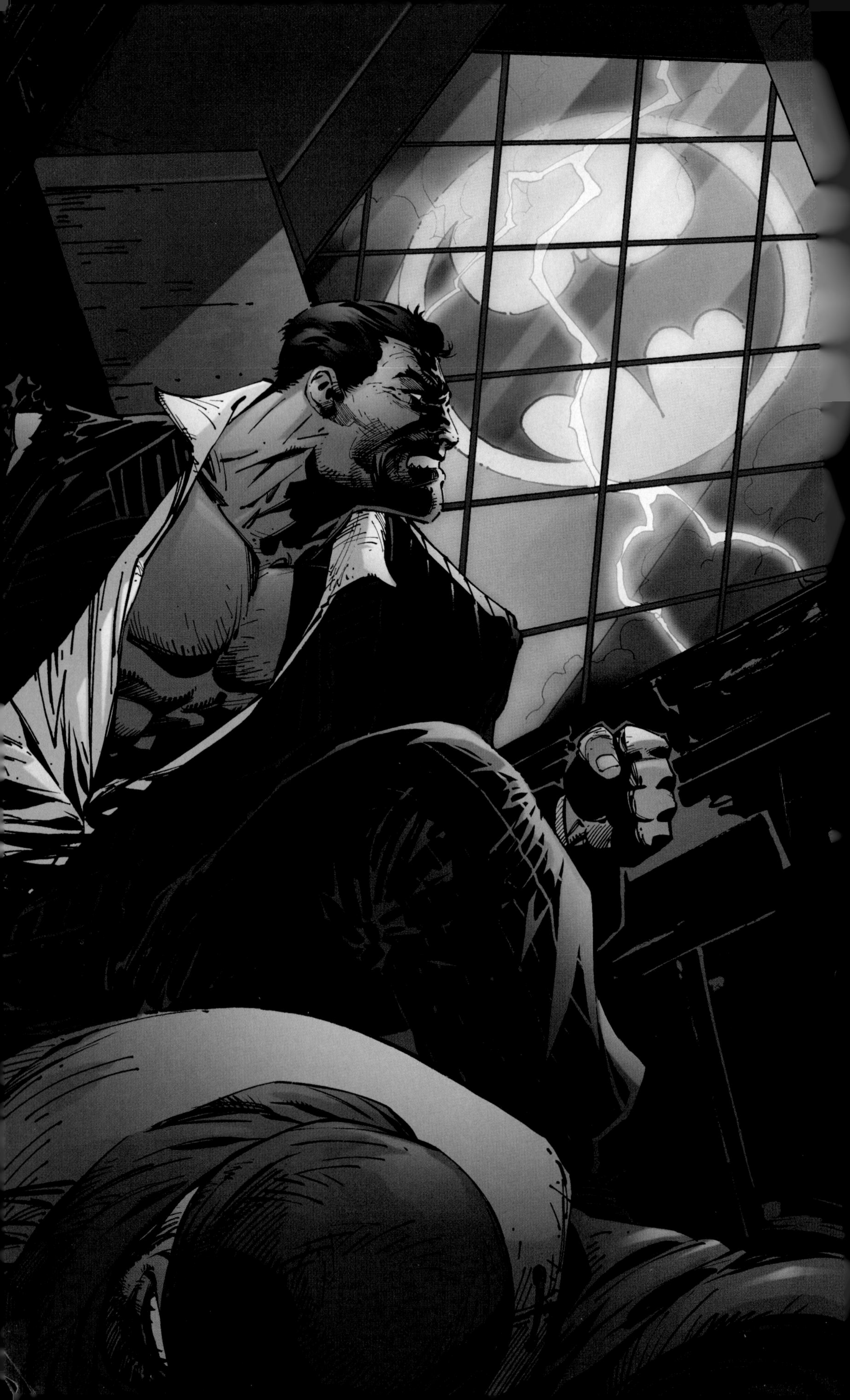

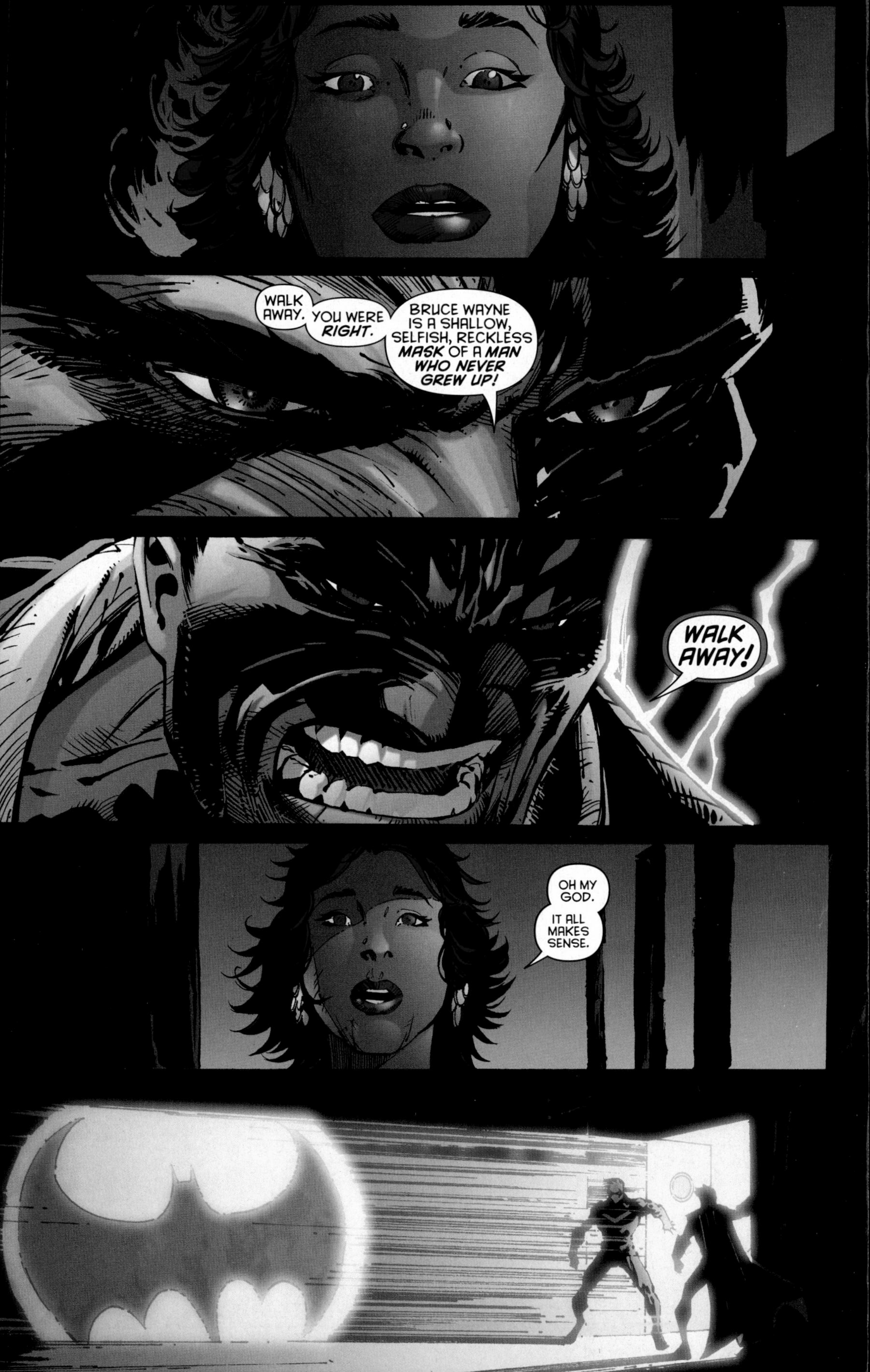

WALK AWAY.
YOU WERE *RIGHT.*
BRUCE WAYNE IS A SHALLOW, SELFISH, RECKLESS *MASK* OF A *MAN WHO NEVER GREW UP!*
WALK AWAY!
OH MY GOD.
IT ALL MAKES SENSE.

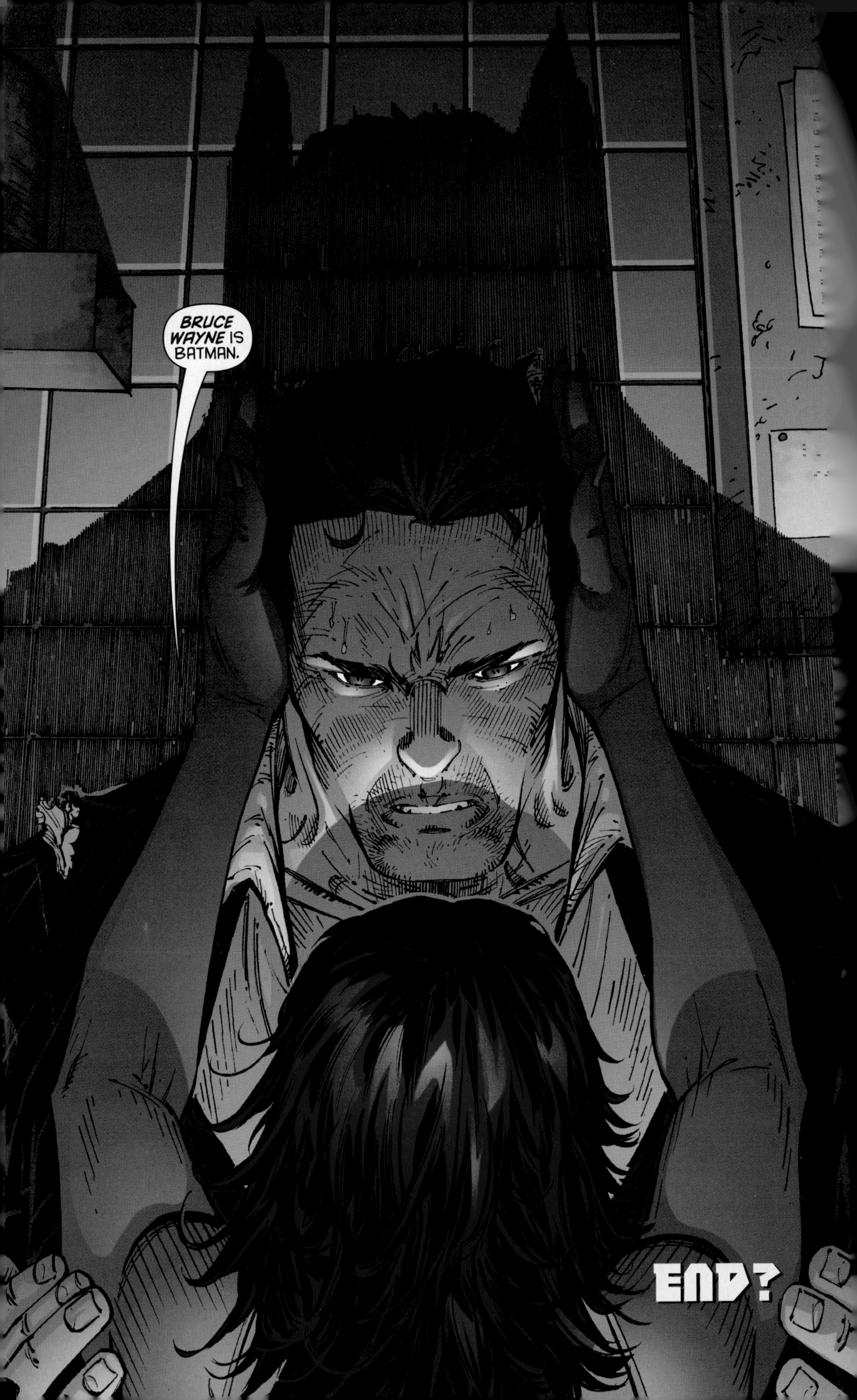
BRUCE WAYNE IS BATMAN.
END?

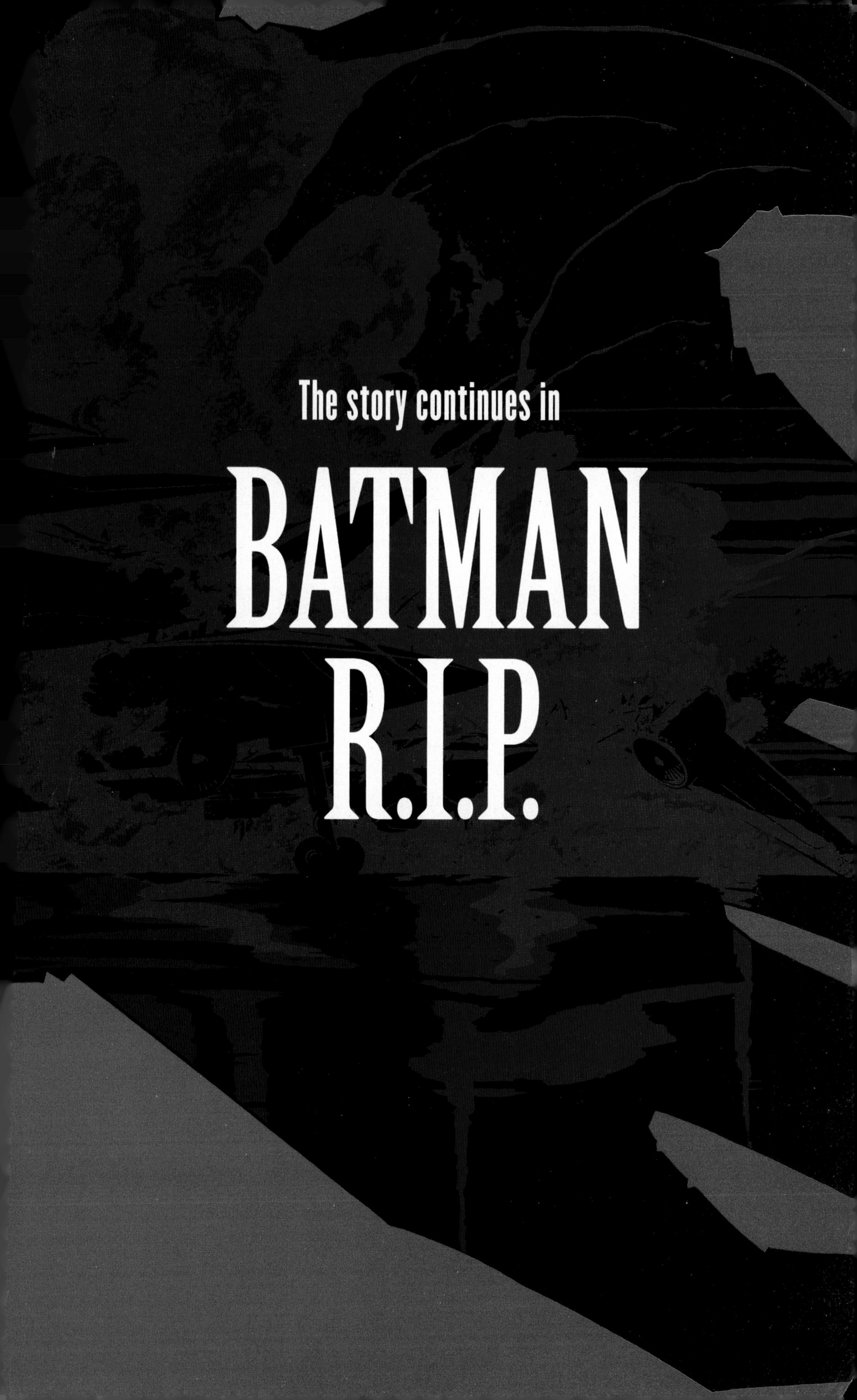
The story continues in
BATMAN
R.I.P.